Mapping Messianic Jewish Theology

'This is a seminal study of Messianic Jewish theology and required reading for anyone who seeks to understand the history and influence of Messianic Judaism.'

Dan Cohn-Sherbok, *Rabbi and Professor of Judaism, University of Wales*

'Richard Harvey's book fills a gap by not only explaining and analyzing the broad spectrum of theological views within the Messianic Jewish movement but doing so fairly. No seminary or study program focusing on Messianic Judaism should be without it.'

David Stern, *translator of* The Jewish New Testament *and* The Complete Jewish Bible; *and author of* The Jewish New Testament Commentary

'I think that Richard Harvey's important and eminently fair book is the most accurate description of the theological views and practical philosophical underpinnings put forth by leaders of the Messianic Jewish movement. This is the right book to read to gain a broad understanding of the issues.'

Daniel Juster, *Director of Tikkun International and Professor at the Messianic Jewish Bible Institute, The King's Seminary, Los Angeles*

'In this pioneering study Richard Harvey provides a lucid, accurate, and comprehensive survey of Messianic Jewish thought at the beginning of the 21st Century. His work will be of enormous value for those outside the movement who seek an orientation to its theological development, and also for those within who look for guidance in charting a path for the future.'

Mark Kinzer, *President of Messianic Jewish Theological Institute, based in Los Angeles and author of* Postmissionary Messianic Judaism

'Richard Harvey richly repays the promise of his many years of research in this field with a long-awaited book that does exactly what it says – providing a map of the complex territory of Messianic Jewish theology. The clarity and detail of Harvey's masterly analysis of the breadth of views on the most significant issues is enlightening and dispels simplistic stereotypes. This is a landmark survey of the movement's theology that builds a platform for its own ongoing theological development, and also provides a richly informative resource for those of us who, as Gentile believers, seek a scripturally critical engagement in the bonds of fellowship with our Jewish sisters and brothers in the Messiah.'

Christopher J. H. Wright, *International Director, Langham Partership International*

'To know and appreciate the game, you need to know the rules the players play by, the players and their tendencies. *Mapping Messianic Judaism* is such a theological scorecard. It reflects the history of discussion about the messianic movement, showing its diversity and vibrancy. It is a superb introduction into an often neglected sphere of the body of Christ. Well done and highly recommended!'

Darrell Bock, *Research Professor of NT Studies, Dallas Theological Seminary, USA*

Mapping Messianic Jewish Theology

A Constructive Approach

Richard Harvey

Paternoster:
thinking faith

MILTON KEYNES ● COLORADO SPRINGS ● HYDERABAD

First published 2009 by Authentic Media
9 Holdom Avenue, Bletchley, Milton Keynes, Bucks, MK1 1QR, UK
1820 Jet Stream Drive, Colorado Springs, CO 80921, USA
OM Authentic Media, Medchal Road, Jeedimetla Village,
Secunderabad 500 055, A.P., India
www.authenticmedia.co.uk

Authentic Media is a division of IBS-STL U.K., limited by guarantee,
with its Registered Office at Kingstown Broadway, Carlisle,
Cumbria CA3 0HA. Registered in England & Wales No. 1216232.
Registered charity 270162

British Library Cataloguing in Publication Data

A catalogue record for this book is available from the
British Library

BR
158
HAR

ISBN-13: 978-1-84227-644-0

Cover design by Paul Airy, Four-Nine-Zero Design
(www.fourninezerodesign.co.uk)
Print Management by Adare
Printed and bound in the UK by J F Print Ltd., Sparkford, Somerset

Contents

Studies in Messianic Jewish Theology Series Preface

Series Editor: Richard Harvey

Messianic Judaism is both a very ancient movement and a very modern movement. The earliest followers of Yeshua (Jesus) were Jewish and they did not consider their faith in Yeshua as a replacement of one religion (Judaism) with another (Christianity). For them faith in Jesus as the Messiah of Israel was a very *Jewish* way of being. But as time went on, and as believers from the nations became the majority group within the churches, the ways of Judaism and of the Jesus-Community began to separate, and both began to define themselves, in part, over against the other. Thus a Jew that became a believer in Jesus ceased to be a Jew – in the eyes of the Synagogue and of the Church – and became a Christian.

The late nineteenth and the twentieth centuries saw big changes in the self-consciousness of Jewish believers in Jesus. From the 1960s onwards a new wave of Jewish Yeshua-believers began and from it sprang modern Messianic Judaism. This diverse movement is composed of Jewish people who, like the first followers of Yeshua, view their acceptance of Jesus as Messiah to be fully compatible with their Judaism. As such Messianic Judaism presents a challenge to the self-understanding of both the Church and the Synagogue.

However, as a recent movement that lacks a historically continuous doxological and theological tradition of its own, Messianic Judaism is in the early stages of theological maturity. As a bridge between the worlds of Judaism and Christianity it needs to find ways of negotiating its self-identity, its practices, and its theologies by drawing on both Christian and Jewish traditions. And as a new movement it lacks practitioners who have been theologically trained in either tradition and who are able to undertake the task of theological reflection. But that is beginning to change as a growing number of participants are doing academic work for the benefit of the Messianic movement.

Studies in Messianic Jewish Theology is a series which seeks to provide explorative, academically informed reflections on Messianic Jewish theology and praxis. It is hoped that the studies in the series will be of benefit not merely to Jewish believers in Yeshua, but also to Christians and Jews in general seeking to understand what is a controversial but significant movement.

Acknowledgements

A book on the subject of Messianic Jewish Theology would not be possible without the help and support of many in the Messianic movement. My gratitude to those involved in Messianic Judaism in the USA, Israel and UK is heartfelt. Whilst it is not possible to mention by name all who have helped, my particular thanks go to those who have shaped my thinking, and contributed actively to my research. They include David Brickner, Arnold Fruchtenbaum, Peter Hocken, Daniel Juster, Mark Kinzer, Kai Kjær-Hansen, Lisa Loden, Baruch Maoz, Gershon Nerel, Rich Nichol, Susan Perlman, Jorge Quiñónez, Rich Robinson, Moishe Rosen, David Rudolph, Tsvi Sadan, Bodil Skjøtt and many others. Members of the Lausanne Consultation on Jewish Evangelism and the Messianic Jewish–Roman Catholic Dialogue Group have fed my thinking throughout.

The practical support of friends and colleagues and students at All Nations Christian College has been invaluable. Kate Wiseman in the library and Paul Davies have been my constant encouragers. William Ford, Pete C, Jonathan Norgate and Richard Briggs gave their vital expertise and encouragement in the closing stages. My thanks are also due to Robin Parry, the Editorial Director at Paternoster.

My doctoral supervisor Rabbi Professor Dan Cohn-Sherbok has given his time, wisdom and encouragement throughout. His interest in the subject and example of scholarship has been of great value, as have been his constructive criticisms throughout.

Finally, my family have been the making of my character and faith, of which this book is the product. My grandmother, Elaine Falk, who would have loved to see the completion of this project, has often been my inspiration. My parents have supported me in my choices throughout my life and have always been there for me. My wife Monica and children Rebekah and Joshua have encouraged me to persevere, and have understood at close hand the challenges of completing the part-time PhD upon which this book is based. To my wife I owe more than words can express, but in the words of Proverbs 31:29, 'Many daughters have done well, but you excel them all.' Thank you.

Abbreviations and Acronyms

BCE	Before Common Era
BMJA	British Messianic Jewish Alliance
CE	Common Era
CMJ	Church's Ministry among Jewish People.
FMC	Fellowship of Messianic Congregations
HB	Hebrew Bible
HC	Hebrew Christian
HCA	Hebrew Christian Alliance
HCAA	Hebrew Christian Alliance of America
HCAGB	Hebrew Christian Alliance of Great Britain
HFOI	Hamilton Friends of Israel
IAMCS	International Alliance of Messianic Congregations and Synagogues
IHCA	International Hebrew Christian Alliance
IMJA	International Messianic Jewish Alliance
JBY	Jewish Believer in Yeshua
JFJ	Jews for Jesus
JNT	*Jewish New Testament*
JNTC	*Jewish New Testament Commentary*
JUBU	Jewish Buddhist
LCJE	Lausanne Consultation on Jewish Evangelism
MJ	Messianic Jew
MJAA	Messianic Jewish Alliance of America
MJC	Messianic Jewish Congregation
MJM	Messianic Jewish Movement
MJRC	Messianic Jewish Rabbinical Council
MJT	Messianic Jewish Theology
MJTI	Messianic Jewish Theological Institute
MJRC	Messianic Jewish Rabbinical Council
NCHA	New Covenant Halakhic Approach
NEHC	New England Halakhic Council
PMJ	*Postmissionary Messianic Judaism*
Shab.	Tractate Shabbat, Babylonian Talmud
UCCI	United Christian Council in Israel
UMJC	Union of Messianic Jewish Congregations

Chapter 1

Introduction: Approaching Messianic Jewish Theology

The Question of Messianic Jewish Theology

Messianic Judaism is the religion of Jewish people who believe in Jesus (Yeshua[1]) as the promised Messiah.[2] It is a Jewish form of Christianity and a Christian form of Judaism, challenging the boundaries and beliefs of both.[3] The Messianic Jewish Movement[4] refers to the contemporary movement, a renewed expression of the Jewish Christianity of the early church. Messianic

---

[1] 'Yeshua', alternatively spelt 'Y'shua', is the preferred Messianic Jewish way of referring to Jesus, and will be used interchangeably with 'Jesus' throughout. See Moishe Rosen, *Y'shua: The Jewish Way to Say Jesus* (Chicago: Moody Press, 1995).

[2] A distinction is made here between Messianic Judaism (belief in Yeshua as Messiah) and other expressions of Jewish Messianism. *Pace* Eugene Fisher, 'Divided Peoples of the Covenant: Book Review of *After the Evil: Christianity and Judaism in the shadow of the Holocaust* by Richard Harries,' The *Tablet*, 23rd August 2003, 16. 'All branches of rabbinic Judaism, of course, are "messianic", so one wonders at the usage of the term in this title. Likewise, why the insistence on claiming to be a form of "Judaism"? Does being ethnically Jewish give these Jewish Christians (or Christian Jews), the right, once they have accepted Christ as their saviour, to redefine for other Jews what forms of "Judaism" are valid? Somehow the name, for me, breaches both common sense and common courtesy.' See also Michael Wyschogrod, *The Body of Faith* 2nd ed. (Northvale, NJ: Jason Aronson, 1996), 254–55. 'Authentic Judaism must be Messianic Judaism. Messianic Judaism is Judaism that takes seriously the belief that Jewish history, in spite of everything that has happened, is prelude to an extraordinary act of God by which history will come to its climax.' Cf. Aviezer Ravitzky, *Messianism, Zionism and Jewish Religious Radicalism* (Chicago: University of Chicago Press, 1996) for discussion of Messianic expectation in religious Zionism.

[3] This challenge is raised by David Rudolph, 'Messianic Jews and Christian Theology: Restoring an Historical Voice to the Contemporary Discussion.' *Pro Ecclesia* 14, no. 1. (March 2005): 65–86.

[4] Frequently shortened to 'Messianic movement' or MJM. See the list of acronyms and abbreviations for use of other terms.

Jews construct a new social and religious identity that they express communally in Messianic Jewish Congregations and Synagogues, and in their individual beliefs and practices. Since the early 1970s the significant numbers of Jewish people coming to believe in Jesus and the phenomenon of Messianic Judaism have raised several questions concerning Jewish and Christian identity and theology.

There are some 150,000 Jewish believers in Jesus worldwide, according to conservative estimates.[5] More than 100,000 are in the USA, approximately 5,000 in Israel, the remainder being found throughout the approximately 13 million world Jewish population.[6] There are over 200 Messianic groups in the USA, over 80 in Israel and many others around the world. Whilst they are not uniform in their beliefs and expression, the majority adhere to orthodox Christian beliefs on the uniqueness and deity of Christ, the Trinity and the authority of scripture. They express these beliefs in a Jewish cultural and religious context whilst affirming the continuing election of Israel (the Jewish people) with which they identify.

There have always been Jewish believers in Jesus, from the time of the early Church.[7] These 'followers of the way' or Nazarenes were known and

---

[5] Tuvya Zaretsky, ed., *Jewish Evangelism: A Call to the Church*, Lausanne Occasional Paper No. 60 (Thailand: Lausanne Committee for World Evangelisation, 2005), 5–11; Kai Kjær-Hansen and Bodil F. Skjøtt, 'Facts and Myths about the Messianic Congregations in Israel', *Mishkan* Double Issue 30–31 (Jerusalem: United Christian Council in Israel/Caspari Centre for Biblical and Jewish Studies, 1999), 71.

[6] Sergio DellaPergola, *World Jewish Population 2000*, vol. 100 (New York: Division of Jewish Demography and Statistics, American Jewish Year Book, 2000). 'We define as the core Jewish population all those who, when asked, identify themselves as Jews; or, if the respondent is a different person in the same household, are identified by him/her as Jews. This is an intentionally comprehensive and pragmatic approach. Such definition of a person as a Jew, reflecting subjective feelings, broadly overlaps but does not necessarily coincide with Halakhah [rabbinic law] or other normatively binding definitions. It does not depend on any measure of that person's Jewish commitment or behaviour – in terms of religiosity, beliefs, knowledge, communal affiliation, or otherwise. The core Jewish population includes all those who converted to Judaism by any procedure, or joined the Jewish group informally, and declare themselves to be Jewish. It excludes those of Jewish descent who formally adopted another religion, as well as other individuals who did not convert out but currently refuse to acknowledge their Jewish identification.' Whilst DellaPergola's definition excludes some Messianic Jews, who are considered to have 'formally adopted another religion', the estimate of the World Jewish Population is more reliable than others. For the purpose of the present study a child of Jewish parents or a convert to Judaism is considered Jewish, following Reform Judaism, and the majority of the Messianic movement.

[7] For this brief survey of the history of Jewish Christianity see Hugh J. Schonfield, *The*

accepted by the Church fathers (Jerome, Justin Martyr, Epiphanius) but as Judaism and Christianity emerged as separate ways in the 4th century it became increasingly unacceptable to ecclesiastical and rabbinic authorities to allow the legitimacy of Jewish expressions of faith in Christ.[8] Excluded from the Synagogue for their belief in the Trinity and divinity of Christ, and anathematised by the Church for continued practice of Jewish customs, they were known as Ebionites ('the poor ones') and suspected of legalism and an adoptionist Christology.

Small groups of Jewish Christians continued in the East, and Jewish converts to Christianity were afforded protection in the midst of an anti-semitic European church by institutions such as the *Domus Conversorum* (House of Converts) which was maintained by royal patronage. But it was not until the modern missionary movement and an interest in mission to the Jewish people that a community of testimony of Jewish Christians re-appeared.

In 1809 Joseph Samuel Christian Frey, son of a rabbi from Posen, Hungary, encouraged the formation of the London Society for the Promotion of Christianity Among the Jews, which became the Church's Ministry Among the Jewish People (CMJ).[9] Encouraged by CMJ and other Jewish missions the growing number of 'Hebrew Christians', as they called themselves, formed their own Prayer Union (1866), British (1888) and International Alliances (1925), and developed their own liturgies and Hebrew Christian Churches in Europe, Palestine and the USA. By the end of the 19th century it was estimated on the basis of baptismal statistics that over a million Jewish people had become Christians, many for reasons of assimilation and emancipation from the Ghettos into European society with access to commerce, education and secular society.[10] Nevertheless a recognisable number, such as Alfred Edersheim, Adolph Saphir, Augustus Neander and Bishop Samuel Schereschewsky wished to retain aspects of their Jewish

---

History of Jewish Christianity: From the First to the Twentieth Century (London: Duckworth, 1936; reprint, Ashford, Kent: Manna Books, 1995); Daniel Boyarin, *Borderlines: The Partitioning of Judaeo-Christianity* (Philadelphia: University of Pennsylvania Press, 2004); Dan Cohn-Sherbok, *Messianic Judaism* (London: Continuum, 2000).

[8] Becker, Adam H. and Annette Yoshiko Reed, eds., *The Ways That Never Parted: Jews and Christians in Late Antiquity and the Early Middle Ages* (Minneapolis: Fortress Press, 2007), vii.

[9] William Thomas Gidney, *The History of the London Society For Promoting Christianity Amongst the Jews: From 1809–1908* (London: London Society for Promoting Christianity Amongst the Jews, 1908).

[10] Figures frequently referred to are those of baptismal statistics compiled by Johan F.A. de Le Roi, *Geschichte der evangelischen Judenmission seit Entstehung des neueren Judentums* (Leipzig: Hinrichs, 1899). Other figures are apocryphal but the subject of frequent speculation.

identity alongside faith in Christ and were both a blessing to the Church and a testimony to their people.[11]

After the Second World War, the Holocaust and the establishment of the State of Israel, Jewish believers in Jesus from a new generation were concerned to rediscover their ethnic roots and express their faith from a Jewish perspective. In the wake of the Jesus movement of the 1970s 'Jews for Jesus' moved from being a slogan used on the streets of San Francisco to an organisation of Jewish missionaries to their people. At the same time, the Messianic Jewish Alliance of America encouraged the establishment of Messianic Congregations and Synagogues. In Israel a new generation of native-born Israelis ('*sabras*') were acknowledging Jesus as the Messiah, and starting Hebrew-speaking congregations. At the beginning of the twenty-first century an international network of Messianic groups exists, expressing denominational, theological and cultural diversity, but united in belief in Yeshua.

To varying degrees Messianic Jews observe the Sabbath, keep the kosher food laws, circumcise their sons and celebrate the Jewish festivals. They celebrate Passover showing how Yeshua came as the Passover Lamb, and practise baptism, linking it to the Jewish *mikveh*. They worship with their own liturgies, based on the Synagogue service, reading from the Torah and the New Testament. Their hermeneutic of scripture repudiates the tradition of Christian Anti-Judaism according to which 'the Jews killed Christ'[12] and the metanarrative of supersessionism that the Church replaces Israel as the 'new Israel'.[13] They argue for the continuing relevance of Torah observance, identifying themselves as Jewish members of the Church, and as a believing 'remnant' in the midst of Israel.

Messianic Jewish Theology (MJT) has developed in the light of its Protestant Evangelical background and its engagement with Jewish concerns. The doctrinal statements of Messianic Jewish organisations are uniformly orthodox, but are often expressed in Jewish rather than Hellenistic thought forms, and are more closely linked to Jewish concepts and readings of scripture. The Charismatic movement influences many Messianic Jews, although an increasing number opt for more formal styles of worship using the resources of the Jewish prayer book. They incorporate standard liturgical features such as the wearing of the *tallit* and the use of Torah scrolls. Most Messianic Jews are Premilliennial (but not necessarily Dispensationalists) in their eschatology, seeing God's purposes for Israel being played out with various degrees of linkage to the present political events in the Middle

---

[11] Cf. Louis Meyer, *Eminent Hebrew Christians of the Nineteenth Century: Brief Biographical Sketches*, ed. David A. Rausch (Texts and Studies in Religion) (Lewinston: Edwin Mellen Press, 1983).

[12] Rosemary Ruether, *Faith and Fratricide* (New York: Search Press, 1974).

[13] R. Kendall Soulen, *The God of Israel and Christian Theology* (Minneapolis, USA: Fortress Press, 1996).

East. Many advocate *aliyah* for Messianic Jews, although the majority of Messianic Jews live in the Diaspora. A growing number are concerned for reconciliation ministry with their Arab Christian neighbours.

MJT is both the process and product of theological reflection that articulates and explains the beliefs and practices found within the Messianic movement. It addresses its own adherents and the Jewish, Christian and wider communities to which it relates, presenting itself as both an authentic form of Jewish discourse and as an expression of faith in Jesus as Messiah. *What I aim to do in this book is to explain the nature of MJT, identifying its sources, norms, methods, content and results.* I will describe and evaluate the theology of its key practitioners and outline proposals for its future development.

The Methodology of 'Mapping Messianic Jewish Theology'

No previous study of Messianic Judaism has focused on the *theology* of the movement, or assessed it *theologically*.[14] Previous studies have employed anthropological, psychological and historical approaches in order to understand the *phenomenon* of Messianic Judaism, but the present study addresses its *theology*. My method is to employ both a *descriptive approach* – providing an account of the nature of MJT, describing its sources, methods, content and results – and a *constructive approach* – making recommendations for its future development. This methodology is a more adequate means of exploring the structure, shape and content of MJT than potentially reductionist approaches from other disciplines.

General discussion of theological method is beyond the scope of the present study, but the methods and criteria of both Jewish and Christian theology are relevant for MJT, as it develops its own theological integrity in interaction with both Jewish and Christian thought.[15] Byron Sherwin, who opposes the 'views of those who deign to claim there is no such thing as Jewish theology', has examined Jewish theological method.[16] He proposes that:

---

[14] See chapter 3 below.

[15] Cf. John Webster, 'Theological Theology' in *Confessing God: Essays in Christian Dogmatics II* (Edinburgh: Continuum International Publishing Group/T.&T. Clark, 2005), 11–32.

[16] Byron L. Sherwin, *Toward a Jewish Theology: Methods, Problems and Possibilities* (Lewiston: Edwin Mellen Press, 1991), 1. Cf. 'An Incessantly Gushing Fountain: The Nature of Jewish Theology' in Elliot N. Dorff and Louis E. Newman (eds.), *Contemporary Jewish Theology: A Reader* (Oxford/New York: OUP, 1999), ch.1, 7–22, 7. See also Gershom Scholem, 'Reflections on Jewish Theology' in *On Jews and Judaism in Crisis* (New York: Schocken, 1976), 261–97; Louis Jacobs, *A Jewish Theology*

The task of Jewish theology is to establish the nature and parameters of Jewish religious thought, to articulate coherently the authentic views of Judaism, and to demonstrate how the wisdom of the Jewish religious teachings of the past can address the perplexities of contemporary Jewish existence in a manner that is compatible with the thought and life of the Jewish faith community at a given juncture in time and space.[17]

Sherwin offers a methodology for 'doing' Jewish theology,[18] based on four criteria that 'characterise a valid Jewish theology' and are 'identical to those of any valid theology': *authenticity, coherence, contemporaneity* and *communal acceptance.*[19]

Authenticity depends on the nature and use of sources consulted, and the faith commitment of the individual consulting them. Coherence relates to the cohesion, clarity and communicability of a formulated theological perspective. Contemporaneity pertains to the successful application of past traditions to present situations. Communal acceptance refers to the ratification of a theological posture by committed members of a specific faith-community.[20]

The faith commitment of the Jewish theologian is vital to the task, as theology is not an 'intellectual parlour game but the articulation of a prior commitment'. Sherwin draws a sharp distinction between the 'objectivity' of the outsider, and the faith perspective of the insider.

The theologian cannot be a passive voyeur, a casual tourist surveying the landscape of a tradition. The scientist, the philosopher or the historian of religion can stand outside the arena of his or her inquiry as a disinterested observer. For the theologian, however, commitment precedes inquiry. Experience of the life of faith and participation in a faith-community anticipates theological investigation. Only the well-springs of individual religious commitment can generate a viable theology. Only from the passion of faith can theology emanate. Theology is passionate faith seeking understanding.[21]

(London: DLT, 1973); Eugene B. Borowitz, 'The Way to a Postmodern Jewish Theology' in *Judaism After Modernity: Papers from a Decade of Fruition* (Lanham: University Press of America, 1999), 125–54 and *Renewing the Covenant: A Theology for the Postmodern Jew* (Philadelphia: JPSA, 1991); Arthur A. Cohen, 'Theology' in *Contemporary Jewish Religious Thought*, edited by Arthur A. Cohen and Paul Mendes-Flohr (New York: The Free Press/Macmillan, 1988), 971–81.

[17] Sherwin, *Towards a Jewish Theology*, 9.
[18] Ibid., 3.
[19] Ibid., 9.
[20] Ibid.
[21] Ibid., 11.

Within Jewish theology a methodological pluralism exists, reflecting the concerns and emphases of various practitioners, as they articulate universal and general aims in particular historical, philosophical, cultural and religious contexts. MJT would affirm the need for the same criteria, with appropriate modifications as to the range and nature of sources consulted, and with the faith community referring specifically to the Messianic Jewish community within the larger Jewish community of which it claims to form a part.

The interaction between the general aims of theology and the particular tasks and concerns generated by different contexts lead to a methodological pluralism in Christian theology also.

> For most of the twentieth century, shared method – a common perspective on the proper task and form of theology – had been, in fact, a key point of agreement around which major 'schools of theology' formed ... If we had chosen this formal, conceptual route, the options before us would have been dazzling: We could have been liberals, postliberals or liberationists; feminists, Neo-orthodox dogmaticians, or process thinkers; historicists, pragmatists, cultural theorists, or postmodernists of either the Derridean or Marxist variety; and so on.[22]

As already mentioned, the present study employs a *descriptive* and *constructive* methodology. The organising metaphor behind *constructive theology* is that of 'theological geography'. Its task is the 'doctrinal mapping' of the 'territory' occupied by theology.[23] The content of MJT, the ontology of its subject matter, dictates its epistemology. MJT draws its methodology from

---

[22] Serene Jones and Paul Lakeland, eds., *Constructive Theology: A Contemporary Approach to Classical Themes* (Minneapolis: Fortress Press, 2005), 5.

[23] R.G. Gruenler, 'Constructive Theology' in *Evangelical Dictionary of Theology*, ed. Walter A. Elwell (Basingstoke: Marshall Pickering, 1985): 269–71. Constructive Theology emerged as a methodology in the 1970s. Its approach focused on three phases of enquiry: a historical survey and summary of key doctrines; an analysis of the questions addressed by contemporary concerns that challenge or critique the traditional formulations; and constructive proposals for how a contemporary theology may address and respond to these questions. Gordon Kaufman and the 'Workgroup on Constructive Christian Theology' exemplified the approach. For works produced by the 'Workgroup on Constructive Christian Theology' see Peter Hodgson and Robert King, eds., *Christian Theology: An Introduction to its Traditions and Tasks* (Minneapolis: Fortress Press, 1982/London: SPCK, 1983) and Jones and Lakeland, *Constructive Theology*. Its roots may be traced back to Karl Barth, and it has been employed by both conservative, critical liberal and postliberal theologians. It continues to impact on contemporary systematic theology and contemporary Jewish theologians such as Allen Gillman and Bruce Sherwin show similarities to this approach.

various sub-disciplines within theology, using the resources and results of biblical, historical, systematic and practical theology. It uses a variety of materials such as history, scripture, creeds and dogmas, contemporary contexts, prayerful reflection, commonsense experience, and insights from the social sciences.[24] It is apologetic and programmatic in its orientation. It proceeds on the basis of its own faith commitment and leads to its own theological proposals. Serene Jones expresses this faith-based and normative approach in the introduction to *Constructive Theology*: 'Like any good mapmaker, we do not do this just for the descriptive pleasure of charting; we do it in the hope that our maps might help individuals and communities make informed, reflective judgments about the shape of faithful ... living. In this regard we are mapmakers with a normative and pragmatic commitment, namely, the goal of enabling responsible faith.'[25]

The present study employs such a constructive theological method, both as the methodology of the study itself, and as a contribution to the construction of MJT. Combining the *construction* of MJT alongside its *study* illuminates both content and process. It not only provides a description and analysis of the content of MJT from a theological perspective but also makes proposals for the development of MJT by an engaged, reflective practitioner.

The use of the metaphor of 'mapping' fits in with the constructive theological method, as the 'map-maker' is both a traveller, observer, participant in and guide to the theological landscape in which they situate themselves. To what extent this method achieves its results with elegance, simplicity and coherence will be assessed in the conclusion.

Defining Messianic Judaism

A definition of Messianic Judaism is required to identify the boundaries of its theology. The terms 'Messianic Jew', 'Messianic Jewish' and 'Messianic Judaism' have been under negotiation since their introduction, and the subject of considerable and inconclusive discussion.[26]

> Finding agreement on definitions in the Messianic Jewish movement is problematic because of the decentralised and fluid nature of the movement. There are, at present, no agreed upon definitions, although some have attempted to suggest specific taxonomies.[27]

---

[24] Jones and Lakeland, *Constructive Theology*, 9.

[25] Ibid., 9.

[26] Richard Harvey, 'Who Is A Messianic Jew?' (Paper presented at the IHCA Theological Commission, Ramsgate, 1983).

[27] Cf. Bruce Stokes, 'Messianic Judaism,' 7, for the taxonomies of Juster, Stern and Schiffman. The situation in Israel, with the need for translation or invention of Hebrew terms, is similarly problematic. Cf. Rausch, *Messianic Judaism*, 87–111; Stokes, *Messianic Judaism*, 7–8; 36–37.

> After a quarter century of existence, one might have hoped that Messianic Judaism would have progressed beyond matters of fundamental self-definition. Unfortunately, such is not the case. Our movement still struggles with basic identity questions.[28]

It is not the purpose of this study to present a new definition of 'Messianic Jew' or 'Messianic Judaism' but to work with those currently in use. Therefore a brief survey of the history of the terms is given, and some contemporary understandings. The terminology has considerable theological significance, and a review of related terms describing Jewish believers in Jesus is also given.

In the 1970s the newer term 'Messianic Judaism' was adopted to express the vision and ideology of those forming Messianic Congregations and Synagogues, in preference to the current terms 'Jewish Christianity,' and 'Hebrew Christianity'. 'Jewish Christianity' was already in use to describe the first century Jewish believers in Jesus,[29] although there is no scholarly consensus as to how broadly or narrowly the term applies.[30] 'Jewish Christianity' variously represents: the Judaeo-Christianity of the early Church;[31] a heterodox form of Christianity;[32] a sub-group within the nascent church;[33] and a sect within Judaism. There is no consensus on how to demarcate the boundaries between 'Jewish Christianity' and 'Gentile Christianity' on the one hand, and 'Jewish Christianity' and other 'Judaisms' of the first century on the other.[34] For contemporary Messianic Jews the term was unacceptable. The label 'Christian', with its jarring overtones to Jewish people of Christians as 'other', and the legacy of Christian anti-Semitism and anti-Judaism, excluded them from the Jewish community. It also emphasised 'Christian' as the noun with 'Jewish' as the qualifying adjective, emphasising 'Christian' as *genus* with 'Jewish' as *species*.

---

[28] Mark Kinzer, *The Nature of Messianic Judaism*, 1.

[29] As were 'Judaeo-Christianity', 'Judaistic Christianity', etc.

[30] David C. Sim, *The Gospel of Matthew and Christian Judaism: The History and Social Setting of the Matthew Community*, Studies of the New Testament and Its World (Edinburgh: Continuum/T.&T. Clark, 1998): 24–27. Sim overviews the literature and methodological issues in defining 'Jewish Christianity'.

[31] Richard N. Longenecker, *The Christology of Early Jewish Christianity*, rev. ed. (Vancouver: Regent College Pub., 2001).

[32] Jean Daniélou, *The Theology of Jewish Christianity* (London: Darton, Longman and Todd, 1964), 55ff.

[33] James D.G. Dunn, *Unity and Diversity in the New Testament* (London, SCM Press, 1977), 25.

[34] Martin Goodman, Adam H. Becker and Peter Schafer, eds., *The Ways That Never Parted: Jews and Christians in Late Antiquity and the Early Middle Ages* (Minneapolis: Fortress, 2007).

David Daube, W.D. Davies and David Sim employ the term 'Christian Judaism' to situate the first century Jewish followers of Jesus within both Jewish and Christian communities and worldviews.[35] Recognising the inadequacy of previous boundary lines drawn between Judaism and Christianity, and between 'Jewish Christianity' and 'Gentile Christianity', they use the term to explore the theological and identity issues of the presumed Matthean and Johannine communities. However, for contemporary Messianic Jews, the term 'Christian Judaism' suffered from the same problems as 'Jewish Christian'.

The term 'Hebrew Christian' became current in the late 19th and early 20th centuries,[36] and was adopted in the formation of the Hebrew Christian Alliance (1867) and Hebrew Christian Prayer Union (1882).[37] It expressed a radical indigenising approach to Jewish evangelism that allowed Jews who 'converted' to Christianity to retain some measure of Jewish (Hebraic) culture and identity, although this did not mean subscribing to the 'Jewish religion'. Some Hebrew Christians advocated the setting up of Hebrew Christian Churches, with their own liturgies and polity, the equivalent of contemporary Messianic Jewish Congregations.[38]

The term 'Messianic Jew' was introduced at the beginning of the 20th century and became prominent in the 1970s as the preferred self-designation of those Jewish believers in Jesus who not only asserted their Jewish identity but also actively engaged in the formation of Messianic Fellowships, Congregations and Synagogues. 'Messianic Judaism' and 'Hebrew Christianity' became the focus of contention over theological, missiological and identity issues within the Hebrew Christian Alliance of America (HCAA), resulting in the change of name to the Messianic Jewish Alliance of America (MJAA) in 1974.[39]

> Though the existence of Messianic Jews dates back to the early Church – when Jewish believers in Jesus retained their distinctive Jewish lifestyle for several centuries – the specific term 'Messianic' experienced a surge in popularity in the 1970s when it was used to describe a moving of Jewish people to faith in Y'shua (Jesus) in the context of Jewish culture. While the term 'Messianic' was never

---

[35] Sim, *Christian Judaism*, 24. See also William Horbury, *Jews and Christians: In Contact and Controversy* (Edinburgh: T.&T. Clark, 1998), 11, 73–77.

[36] Hugh J. Schonfield, *The History of Jewish Christianity: From the First to the Twentieth Century* (London: Duckworth, 1936; reprint, Ashford, Kent: Manna Books, 1995). The Roman Catholic 'Association of Hebrew Catholics' founded by Fr. Elias Freedman has adopted the term 'Hebrew Catholic' (Kjær-Hansen, *Myths and Facts*, 289).

[37] Schonfield, *History of Jewish Christianity*, 115. Several terms were employed: *Benei Abraham*, Christian Israelite, Israelites of the New Covenant, etc.

[38] Ibid.

[39] Rausch, *Messianic Judaism*, 76.

formally defined, it was broadly used to describe someone who was both Jewish and a believer in Jesus. Today the term 'Messianic' has been adopted – and sometimes co-opted – by numerous groups and theologies.[40]

The term 'Messianic Judaism' has undergone further clarification and redefinition, with considerable variation in how it is to be understood. Mark Kinzer and Daniel Juster understand Messianic Judaism as a congregational movement. Their definition, adopted by the UMJC, states: 'Messianic Judaism is a movement of Jewish congregations and congregation-like groupings committed to Yeshua the Messiah that embrace the covenantal responsibility of Jewish life and identity rooted in Torah, expressed in tradition, renewed and applied in the context of the New Covenant.'[41] The statement is expanded by a short commentary, which explains how 'Messianic Jewish groupings' (groups that aim to become a full congregation) must be 'fully part of the Jewish people, and also united with the "Gentile Christian Church", which is the assembly of the faithful from the nations who are joined to Israel through the Messiah'. 'Together Messianic Judaism and the Gentile Church constitute the one Body of Messiah, a community of Jews and Gentiles who in their ongoing distinction and mutual blessing anticipate the shalom of the world to come.'[42]

Kinzer and Juster treat Messianic Judaism as a corporate, communal identity. A Messianic Jew must be part of a Messianic Jewish congregation or 'congregation-like grouping' with a commitment to 'Torah observance'. A Hebrew Christian who attended a mainstream Christian denomination would be excluded under this definition.

What is still under discussion is the extent to which Hebrew Christianity and Messianic Judaism overlap, can be distinguished, or are mutually exclusive.[43] Observers and practitioners reflect a variety of perspectives. For the present study, an inclusive definition of Messianic Judaism is used which does not exclude those who call themselves 'Jewish Christians' or 'Hebrew Christians', in order to survey the full range of theological reflection in the Messianic movement.

---

[40] Robinson, *The Messianic Movement*, 1.

[41] Russ Resnick, 'Defining Messianic Judaism (statement affirmed by the Delegates to the 23rd Annual UMJC Conference on July 31, 2002),' under 'Defining Messianic Judaism. UMJC Theology Committee, Summer 2002, Commentary', http://www.umjc.org/main/faq/definition/ResnickCommentary (accessed June 28, 2007).

[42] Ibid.

[43] See the discussion in Arnold Fruchtenbaum, *Israelology: The Missing Link in Systematic Theology* (Tustin, CA: Ariel Ministry Press): 746–48, where he argues for the interchangeable use of the terms 'Hebrew Christian' and 'Messianic Jew', rejecting attempts by some Messianic Jews to differentiate the terms as a 'totally false distinction,' (746).

A more generic and less theologically loaded term is 'Jewish Believer in Yeshua' (JBY),[44] which refers to all believers in Jesus who are Jewish, and links the Jewish believers in Jesus of New Testament times with the contemporary movement.[45] It is also reflects the Israeli perspective, where the semantic connotations of 'Messianic Jew' and 'Hebrew Christian' and the theological issues they raise do not easily translate into Hebrew or fit the Israeli context.

Structure of the Study

To set the scene for the theological study that forms the heart of this book, chapters 2 and 3 will overview a wide range of previous studies of Messianic Judaism. These studies shed much light on the movement and set the scene for the theological investigations that follow. What this overview also reveals is the pressing need for a far clearer theological mapping of the terrain of MJT than has been done hitherto, in order both for observers to better understand it, and for practitioners of Messianic Judaism to take the project of MJT forward in fruitful directions.

In this book I adopt the traditional subject divisions found in Jewish theology, of 'God, Torah and Israel'.[46] Within those categories, the doctrine of God, the person of the Messiah, the theory and practice of the Torah and the future of Israel are discussed in separate chapters. There is general agreement by outside observers and practitioners that these are the key theological issues that the Messianic movement must address.[47] They result from the 'irreconcilable differences' that have arisen between Judaism and

---

[44] Frequently shortened to 'Jewish Believer'.

[45] See Gershon Nerel, 'Modern Assemblies of Jewish Yeshua-Believers Between Church and Synagogue' in *How Jewish Is Christianity: Two Views on the Messianic Movement*, edited by Stanley N. Gundry and Louis Goldberg (Grand Rapids, MI: Zondervan, 2003): 92–107, 93. The orthographic distinction between the more commonly found spelling 'Yeshua' in contrast to 'Y'shua' (adopted by the organisation Jews for Jesus) is not important here.

[46] Cf. Louis Jacobs, *God, Torah, Israel: Traditionalism Without Fundamentalism* (Cincinnati: Hebrew Union College Press, 1990), ii–iv. The conceptual scheme is used in Louis Jacobs, *A Jewish Theology* (London: Darton, Longman and Todd, 1973). Eliot N. Dorff and Louis E. Newman, eds., *Contemporary Jewish Theology: A Reader* (Oxford: OUP, 1999) use a similar *schema*.

[47] Kjær-Hansen and Skjøtt's survey questions (*Facts and Myths*, 31) focus on these issues also. Their survey questions are: 'Is it clearly said that Jesus is born of a virgin and that he is divine? Is baptism mentioned explicitly? Is Israel mentioned explicitly, the State of Israel? Is there a specific eschatology? What is said about a continued keeping of the Law for believers?'

Christianity over the centuries.[48] Other theological topics are identified in the course of the discussion. I do not claim to provide a systematic exposition of all the elements needed for a comprehensive MJT, but simply to offer a preliminary mapping out of the theological territory in the most needed areas as presently covered by its leading thinkers. In my concluding chapter, theological issues yet to be addressed will be identified as a result of these findings.

Chapter 4 explores the Messianic Jewish understanding of God, tracing the substantial agreement between Jewish, Christian and Messianic Jewish theology on the existence, attributes and activities of God. Divergent understandings arise on the Trinitarian and Christological aspects, and these form the focus of Chapter 5, which examines the person and role of Yeshua, and identifies five different Christologies that have emerged within the movement. Chapter 6 introduces theoretical understandings of Torah within the movement, looking at the spectrum of views on revelation, biblical and rabbinic law and the development of Messianic Jewish *Halacha*.

Chapter 7 applies these understandings to the practical outworking of Torah, taking as examples the observance of Sabbath, Kashrut and Passover. Chapter 8 outlines the different eschatological ideas found concerning the future of Israel. The practical and political implications of the different systems are noted, and an assessment of eschatology within MJT is given. The concluding Chapter 9 summarises and evaluates the findings of previous chapters and reflects on the present state of the discipline of MJT. It proposes a typology for understanding its diversity, makes proposals for its future development and suggests questions for further research.

---

[48] See for example David F. Sandmel, Rosann M. Catalono, Christopher M. Leighton, eds., *Irreconcilable Differences? A Learning Resource for Jews and Christians* (Westview Press: Oxford, 2001); Trude Weiss-Rosmarin, *Judaism and Christianity: The Differences* (New York: Jonathan David, 1943).

Chapter 2

Previous Studies:
Anthropology, Social Psychology
and Historical Theology

Previous Studies

More than twenty significant studies of Messianic Judaism have appeared
since the 1970s, but none have focused primarily on its theology, nor
assessed it from a theological perspective. Anthropological, social psychological, historical and religious studies have addressed the nature,
development and organisation of Messianic Judaism, particularly in the
United States. The following select review assesses the strengths and
weaknesses of previous research, noting the methods, epistemological
assumptions and ontological presuppositions employed, and assessing
the implications of such work for the study of MJT from a theological perspective. Previous anthropological, social psychological, historical and
theological studies offer a cross-disciplinary understanding of Messianic
Judaism. Their contribution to the understanding of the theology of
Messianic Judaism is evaluated below.

Anthropological Approaches

A Marginalised Fundamentalist Sect

B.Z. Sobel's study of an earlier Hebrew Christian[1] group, the 'Messengers of
the New Covenant', describes a 'marginal group' arising from the Protestant
missionary movement.[2] Hebrew Christians are fundamentalists[3] who 'tend

---

[1] The issues involved in defining 'Hebrew Christianity' and 'Messianic Judaism' and
distinguishing between them are discussed in the previous chapter, pp.8–12.

[2] B. Zvi Sobel, *Hebrew Christianity: The Thirteenth Tribe* (New York: John Wiley and
Sons, 1974). Sobel was Professor of Sociology in the University of Haifa.

[3] No definition is given of 'Fundamentalism' and a pejorative meaning is intended.

to view all phenomena in monistic terms'[4] with the essential truths of the Bible as the only resource necessary for interpreting reality. They 'construct a universe of discourse' enabling them to form immediate relationships with a 'degree of intensity and familiarity' that would normally take months of intimate association.[5] The Hebrew Christian 'rejects the academic world' and prefers an 'anti-intellectual crusading zeal' to the complexity of living with uncertain theological answers (such as other Jewish people have towards the Holocaust). In their response to marginality the 'Messengers of the New Covenant' espouse a simple fundamentalist form of Christianity overlaid with Dispensationalism, combining this with their identification with the first Jewish Christians of the early church.[6]

Sobel's interest in the theology of the Hebrew Christian movement is peripheral, and is limited to a few pages of his book-length study.[7] The doctrinal statements of some Hebrew Christian groups are included[8] but there is no extensive description of Hebrew Christian theology. Sobel concentrates on sociological issues such as Hebrew Christianity's marginal nature and institutional forms. The movement is likely to fail due to the 'inability of Hebrew Christianity to clarify for itself its reason for being and to lay out a course of action expressing a commonly affirmed ethos'.[9] According to Sobel it lacked direction and the strength to continue into the next generation. This was an infelicitous judgment in the light of the burgeoning of the Messianic movement that, unknown to Sobel, was happening at the time of his study. Nevertheless Sobel provides an interesting snapshot of the movement just before the influx of a new, younger generation of Jewish Christians in the 1970s. His study should now be seen in the light of more recent developments in the MJM, and as an account affected by the unconcealed negative predispositions of the researcher towards the subject matter in hand.

Ethnic Judaism on the Church-Sect Continuum

According to Rachael Kohn, Messianic Judaism constructs an *ethnic Judaism* with new religious values, which redefines Jewish identity 'in conformity with the tradition and trends of the dominant culture'.[10] Kohn highlights the success of Messianic Judaism, reflecting her own anxiety over assimilation

---

[4] Ibid., 44.

[5] Ibid., 11.

[6] Ibid., 112–13.

[7] Ibid., 44–45; 111–12.

[8] Ibid., 111–12.

[9] Ibid., 311.

[10] Rachael L.E. Kohn, 'Hebrew Christianity and Messianic Judaism on the Church-Sect Continuum' (PhD diss., McMaster University, 1985); 'Ethnic Judaism and the Messianic Movement,' *Journal of Jewish Studies* 29 no. 2 (December 1987): 85–96, 92.

and concern for Jewish continuity. In contrast to its predecessor, Hebrew Christianity (and the Jewish community in general), Messianic Judaism is effective in retaining the next generation by its emphasis on Jewish religious and cultural traditions. Kohn's understanding of Judaism as an 'ethnicity' permits 'alternative sources of religious inspiration and new religious doctrines' to be added to it.[11] Messianic Judaism thus teaches the wider Jewish community, afflicted with 'religious complacency', a painful but necessary lesson about its need to involve the next generation. With such concerns and assumptions her study proceeds.

Kohn locates both Hebrew Christianity and Messianic Judaism on the newly developed Stark-Bainbridge *church-sect continuum* model.[12] Kohn assesses the degree of tension between a sect and its environment. She identifies the older group, Hebrew Christianity, as a *para-church* midway between denomination and sect. Hebrew Christianity is established within the Christian context, but unrelated to Judaism, and thus at a low degree of tension with its environment. The newer group, Messianic Judaism, is seen to be in a relationship of 'high tension' with its environment, at the sect end of the continuum. Individual organisations within the Messianic movement vary widely in their relationships to the environment, occupying multiple positions on the church-sect continuum. To explain this variation Kohn considers 'social movement propositions'. These explain how and under what conditions these changes occur. An analysis of the Canadian Hebrew Christian group, the 'Hamilton Friends of Israel' (HFOI) shows how a single organisation can occupy two different points on the church-sect continuum simultaneously. Kohn explains this with reference to the skilful use of leadership functions, buttressed by the symbolic value of a Jewish leader. The HFOI reflects the larger trends in the Hebrew Christian and Messianic Jewish movements in general, and the different 'agendas' of the Jewish and non-Jewish followers in particular.[13]

Kohn summarises the shared theology of Hebrew Christianity and Messianic Judaism in order to locate them on the church-sect continuum, and a brief section is included on the doctrinal foundations of Messianic Judaism.[14] However, Kohn does not examine MJT beyond showing its origins in Hebrew Christianity and the Jewish missions movement. MJT serves as an ideological rationale for individual and group identity, but such theology is assumed to be a modified form of 'Protestant Fundamentalism' with particular context-generated emphases. Kohn's approach to the

---

[11] Ibid., 93.

[12] Rodney Stark and William Sims Bainbridge, 'Of Churches, Sects, and Cults: Preliminary Concepts for a Theory of Religious Movements,' *Journal for the Scientific Study of Religion* 18, no. 2 (June 1979): 117–133.

[13] Kohn, 'Hebrew Christianity and Messianic Judaism,' iii–iv.

[14] Ibid., 115–19.

theology of the movement is peripheral to her interest in the link between ethnicity, identity and revitalisation, and the situating of Messianic Judaism on the Stark-Bainbridge continuum.

Revitalisation through Mazeway Resynthesis

Messianic Judaism recreates a first-century Judaism, according to social anthropologist and Baptist minister Bruce Stokes.[15] Stokes understands Messianic Judaism as the revitalisation of ethnicity through the *mazeway resynthesis* of tradition, using the model proposed by cognitive anthropologist Anthony Wallace.[16] The maze is 'the mental image of society and culture'.[17] Revitalisation movements challenge existing understandings of social reality, allowing the creation of new realities as the maze is manipulated to reduce stress. Mazeway psychological processes form individual and group identity in response to changing social contexts. This results in the creation of Messianic Congregations, which reinforce the psychological reality of their participants and construct new social realities. Stokes applies Wallace's methodology and epistemology to the modern Messianic movement, tracing its development through five stages.[18]

The first stage, the *steady state*, sees no revitalisation, as Judaism and Christianity are mutually exclusive from the fourth century to the Reformation. The second and third stages, *individual stress* and *cultural distortion*, overlap from the Reformation to the mid-twentieth century. During this period the Hebrew Christian movement emerges as a resynthesis of identity in the light of the personal freedoms of the Reformation and the Enlightenment, the Jewish missions, the growth of Zionism and the rediscovery of ethnicity.

The fourth of Wallace's stages, *revitalisation*, involves five steps, beginning with *mazeway reformulation*. Joseph Rabinowitz initiated this in the 1880s by linking Torah-based Judaism to belief in Jesus.[19] The second step of

---

[15] Bruce H. Stokes, 'Messianic Judaism: Ethnicity in Revitalization' (PhD diss., University of California, Riverside, 1994).

[16] Anthony F.C. Wallace, 'Revitalization Movements,' *American Anthropologist* 58 (1956): 264–81.

[17] Roy G. D'Andrade, *The Development of Cognitive Anthropology* (Cambridge: Cambridge University Press, 1995), 17.

[18] Stokes, 'Messianic Judaism,' 162–67.

[19] Stokes interpretation of Rabinowitz echoes that of contemporary 'Torah-observant' Messianic Jews, who see him as a forerunner. However, Kai Kjær-Hansen's study, *Joseph Rabinowitz and the Messianic Movement*, translated by Birger Petterson (Edinburgh: Handsel Press, 1995) shows that he was opposed to rabbinic tradition. 'The Mishna and Talmud are not to be used for establishing any doctrines, but regarded only as an everlasting memento of the spirit of deep slumber which God

communication publicised this new way through the representative writings of Paul Lieberman, David Stern and Daniel Juster, pioneers of Messianic Judaism in the 1970s.[20] The third stage of *organisation* into denominational structures (the IAMCS, UMJC and FMC)[21] transformed Messianic Judaism from Weberian 'charismatic' to 'bureaucratic' power structures. The fourth stage of *adaptation to resistance*[22] modified Messianic Judaism in the light of the responses of traditional Judaism and historic Christianity. Stokes postpones the discussion of the last phase, *cultural transformation and routinisation*, for further study.

Stokes distinguishes two types of Messianic Judaism. Hebrew Christianity[23] denies that its link with ethnic Judaism requires Torah observance and favours a stronger connection with historical Christianity. The second type of Messianic Judaism has a 'stronger attachment to the Jewish peoplehood component and also is unwilling to abandon much of the religious ritual and symbolism based on Torah and found in Judaism'.[24] This second type revitalises Judaism and Jewish identity by 'appealing to a first-century form of Judaism that is consistent with the acceptance of Jesus as the Messiah' which preceded the 'historic and Gentile-dominated Christian Church'. This type sees itself as a revitalised form of Judaism, not Christianity. Stokes does not illuminate further the theological content or significance of this re-invention of tradition.

Stokes projects three possible outcomes for the movement's future. Gentiles or Hebrew Christians will dominate, and absorb the movement into Christianity as an ethnic or denominational substructure.[25] Alternatively, the increase of Torah observance will draw Messianic Jews and Gentiles into mainstream Judaism, without the need to maintain belief in Jesus as a requirement. The third possibility, which Stokes advocates, is that

---

has permitted to fall upon us' (Article 7, 'Articles of Faith of the New People of Israel – Sons of the New Covenant,' in Kjær-Hansen, *Joseph Rabinowitz*, 104).

[20] Paul Lieberman, *The Fig Tree Blossoms: Messianic Judaism Emerges* (Indianola, Iowa: Fountain Press, 1976, 3rd ed. 1980); David Stern, *Messianic Jewish Manifesto* (Jerusalem: Jewish New Testament Publications, 1988); Daniel C. Juster, *Jewish Roots: A Foundation of Biblical Theology for Messianic Judaism* (Rockville: Davar Publishing, 1986).

[21] International Alliance of Messianic Congregations and Synagogues, Messianic Jewish Alliance of America and Union of Messianic Jewish Congregations.

[22] Stokes, 'Messianic Judaism,' 166.

[23] Stokes' use of the term 'Messianic Judaism' to include both 'Hebrew Christianity' and 'Torah-observant Messianic Judaism' demonstrates the confusion that is found in both academic studies and the writings of Messianic Jews as they try to define and distinguish the two without adequate and agreed criteria. See above, pp. 8–12.

[24] Ibid., 175.

[25] Ibid., 179.

Messianic Judaism becomes a religion in its own right, distinct from Judaism and Christianity, 'condemning the movement to a period of heavy opposition and then a limited degree of acceptance, followed by a full acceptance of its existence, although not its validity'.[26] Stokes recognises that a theological rationale can be given for Messianic Judaism as an 'act of God' which cannot be examined by social science, but he does not speculate on this, focusing rather on the processes of psychological identity and social group formation to describe the movement.

Theological Amalgam for a Hybridised Identity

Jewish Christians form a hybridised but independent religious identity, building a tradition that is both Jewish and Christian. Bulent Senay[27] explores this interplay between social context, identity-formation and the 'theology'[28] of the new movement. Jewish Christianity challenges existing boundaries, proposing a new internal worldview that confuses and disrupts previous understandings of the relationship between Jewish Christians and the Jewish community.[29] Such confusion of patterns and communication is due to the very nature of Jewish Christian identity, which is a 'hybridity creating a doubleness that both brings together, and fuses, but … also maintains separation, and a process of systematic "bricolage" that is merged and fused into a new worldview and theological amalgamation.'[30] Jewish Christian identity is thus in the 'twixt of displacement and re-invention' and is 'under surveillance' by both Jewish and Christian traditions.

In response to such suspicion, the 'imagined community' of Jewish Christianity constructs its own self-conception, by means of its 'theology'. Its understanding of the early church is the controlling metaphor that unites Jewish and Christian symbols, creating a sense of historical continuity and a new form of tradition. Contemporary Jewish Christianity is an ethno-religious movement that rescues, rediscovers and restores the tradition of the first century Jewish believers in Jesus that continued for at least four centuries afterwards. After the intervening centuries contemporary Jewish

---

[26] Ibid., 180.

[27] Bulent Senay, 'The Making of Jewish Christianity in Britain: Hybridity, Identity and Tradition' (PhD diss., University of Lancaster, 2000).

[28] Senay uses quotation marks throughout in referring to the 'theology' of Messianic Judaism, without explanation. The use of 'scare quotes' alerts the reader to an ironic or self-distancing position on the part of the researcher.

[29] For Senay the terms 'Jewish Christianity' and 'Messianic Judaism' are interchangeable. The British Messianic movement in which Senay did his research did not have the same problems of integration of the younger 'Messianic Jews' with the older generation of 'Hebrew Christians'.

[30] Ibid., i.

Christianity then emerged from being a 'missionary tool' of the 1890s to become a 'tradition-making' movement.

Senay sees Jewish Christianity with its 'dislocated "theology"' as an example of religious hybridisation within postmodern globalisation. Jewish Christianity is a unique religious movement with its own distinctive 'theology' providing a '*Weltanschauung*, a world-view, a perspective on life, which unites those who believe and divides them from those who do not share their faith'. This provides a 'context, a direction and a meaning; it provides a language, a means of communication and interpretation; and it provides a reason for performing what is required by this set of meanings'. Therefore it is valid to call Jewish Christianity a 'theology', with its own Christology and interpretation of history, adherence to which is necessary for its members to stay within the movement.[31]

This 'theology' is one of the most important resources of the Jewish Christian movement. Not all accept all its doctrines and only a few have a sophisticated understanding of them, but seeing how their 'theology' relates to life is needed to understand Jewish Christianity. 'Theology' plays two roles in recruiting new members. Workshops and other activities are organised around lectures or speeches about Jewish Christian beliefs and life-style. Also, the members present themselves as the sort of people they are because they live according to Jewish Christian beliefs. Jewish Christians tell their 'guests' that it is knowledge of this 'belief', which gives them happiness and a purpose that makes them 'different'. Their 'theology' is also a source of much of the antagonisms engendered by the movement.[32] Those who strongly hold to Judaism and Christianity consider it a heresy. Four key topics of Jewish Christian 'theology' are examined: Yeshua – the Jewish Messiah; the Tri-unity of God from a Messianic Jewish perspective; the second coming of the Messiah and Zionism; and Chosenness and the State of Israel.[33] Without discussing their nature and content in depth, their significance for identity construction is emphasised.

For both Senay and Stokes, the internal coherence of the group's belief system is important. For Stokes, the attempt to reconstitute the Jewish Christianity of the early church has inherent appeal for his own religious position as a Baptist minister seeking to restore Christianity to a 'pure' biblical form. For Senay, the fascination of seeing a non-Western expression of Christianity re-emerge has significance to him as a secular sociologist of religion within present-day Turkey. His own sympathy with the formation of such a 'theology' of Jewish Christianity gives him an organising framework for comparison with other religious systems outside the main religious traditions. For both the 'mazeway resynthesis' of the group's members in

---

[31] Ibid., 234–35.
[32] Ibid., 236.
[33] Ibid., 261ff.

forming the rationale for their activities is important, and they describe what they see as the distinctive beliefs of the movement, but without subjecting these to theological analysis or critique.

Construction of the Messianic Jewish Self

Carol Harris-Shapiro uses ethnography to study the construction of identity within the Messianic Jewish movement.[34] The research work was based on participant-observation in the late 1980s in one of the largest Messianic Congregations, Beth Yeshua in Philadelphia. Harris-Shapiro answers the question 'What is Messianic Judaism?' by situating the construction of the 'Messianic Jewish self' in the contexts of Hebrew Christianity, 'Spirit-filled Christianity' and American Judaism.[35] As a Reconstructionist Rabbi and anthropologist she recognises the tension between anthropological meaning and religious truth. Rather than describe or evaluate Messianic Judaism in theological terms, she explores its basis for construction of self and community. The ethnographic work, based on participant-observation, personal interviews and case studies, includes consideration of the coherence of Messianic Judaism as a belief-system that gives meaning to its adherents.

Harris-Shapiro reviews the ideological and institutional history of the movement, tracing its origins to Hebrew Christian missions to the Jews in the nineteenth and twentieth centuries.[36] The beliefs of Messianic Jews are shaped and coloured by these developments. Whilst the Jewish origins of Christianity provide one of the major legitimating factors, Protestant missions provided the structure and language of the 'Messianic Jewish approach'. The Counterculture of the 1960s supplied the 'people, methods and ethos that revitalised the movement'.[37] An overview of the development of Messianic Judaism falls into four sections, the first and briefest being the founding of Christianity. Then follows the indigenising approach of the missions movement that produced Hebrew Christian congregations.[38] A third section considers the influence of the Counterculture on the nascent Messianic Judaism of the 1960s and 1970s. The final section traces the development, role and authority of the modern Messianic Congregation.

---

[34] Carol A. Harris-Shapiro, 'Syncretism or Struggle: The Case of Messianic Judaism' (PhD diss., Temple University, 1992), published as *Messianic Judaism: A Rabbi's Journey through Religious Change in America* (Boston: Beacon Press, 1999). References are to the 1992 edition.

[35] Ibid., 25ff.

[36] Ibid.

[37] Ibid., 26.

[38] Ibid., 26–33.

Despite having sympathy with Messianic Judaism, and some personal links with the movement since childhood, Harris-Shapiro refrains from direct evaluation of the theology of Messianic Judaism, preferring to let its existence challenge the wider Jewish community to an appropriate response.

Identity Formation and Boundary Negotiation

Shoshanah Feher's anthropological study of a Messianic Congregation in Southern California focuses on identity construction and boundary negotiation.[39] The members separate the 'pagan trappings' of mainstream Christianity from its true theology, which is found in the 'strongly conservative doctrines' of Christian Fundamentalism, linked to personal forms of worship and the promise of salvation.[40] A survey of the background, birth and growth of the movement identifies the appeal of the movement to the baby-boomer generation, offering both stability and flexibility of identity, combining religion and ethnicity in a novel way.[41]

The Messianic movement gives new meanings to symbols drawn from both Judaism and Christianity, allowing the construction of new identities through participation in the congregation and performance of actions that confirm these newly forged religio-ethnic identities.[42] Messianic Judaism is a 'collective community of texts', the texts inherited through the history of the movement, and the texts of the lives of individuals and families. The 'collective story gives free rein in constructing a working definition of Messianic Judaism as it applies to their daily and personal lives'.[43] For Feher, the processes of identity formation and group membership are the key to the construction of beliefs and dogmas, but theological issues are not discussed outside of their relevance to boundary and identity issues.

Ethnographic Self-Understanding

Leigh Berger's autoethnography combines field research in a Sephardi Messianic Jewish Congregation in South Florida with her own search for

---

[39] Shoshanah Feher, *Passing Over Easter: Constructing the Boundaries of Messianic Judaism* (Walnut Creek: Alta Mira Press, 1998); 'Challenges to Messianic Judaism,' in *Voices of Messianic Judaism: Confronting Critical Issues Facing a Maturing Movement*, ed. Dan Cohn-Sherbok (Baltimore: Lederer Books, 2001), 221–28. This updates her research after a 10 year break.

[40] Ibid., 91, 137.

[41] Ibid., 43–60.

[42] Ibid., 143.

[43] Ibid., 141.

personal, Jewish and academic identity.[44] Berger sees herself on a parallel journey of self-definition as she explores the ambivalence and perplexities of Messianic Jewish identity.[45] Defining themselves as Jewish and believing in salvation through Yeshua places Messianic Jews in an undefined border-land rejected by the mainstream Jewish community and misunderstood by mainstream Christians.[46] Berger explores the nature of Messianic Jewish life and spirituality through personal interviews, participation in congregational life and her own reflections, but does not focus on Messianic Jewish beliefs. Messianic Jewish identity is transformational,[47] creating and occupying an in between space, re-inventing tradition and fostering nostalgia for a past that appeals to the postmodern social construction of self-hood, with its capacity for heteroglossia, and the living out of two seemingly contradictory identities.[48]

Devra Jaffe sees Messianic Judaism resulting from the social forces of Protestant missions, the counterculture of the 1960s and the resurgence of Jewish ethnic identity.[49] Her ethnography explores the construction of culture and identity created between the boundaries separating Jewish and Christian communities. The Messianic Jewish community and its culture blur the boundaries of both Jewish and Christian identity. Messianic Jews infuse Christian meaning into Jewish symbol and ritual. They invent tradition and re-interpret history to validate this new construct.

Jaffe conducted fieldwork in Messianic Congregations in Philadelphia and Houston, examining personal stories, congregational worship, dancing, *kashrut*, circumcision, Sabbath and other ritual expressions. The author is aware of her own perspective as both an anthropologist and a Conservative Jew, and follows closely the approach and conclusions of Harris-Shapiro. 'So, are they Jewish or Christian? On which side of the boundary do Messianic Jews belong? ... Perhaps the Jewish or Christian question is just the wrong question to ask.'[50]

---

[44] Leigh Paula Berger, 'Messianic Judaism: Searching the Spirit' (PhD diss., University of South Florida, 2000). Berger's methodology is reviewed in Carolyn Ellis, *The Ethnographic I: A Methodological Novel about Autoethnography*, Ethnographic Alternatives Book Series 13 (Lanham, MD: Rowman and Littlefield, 2004).

[45] Ibid., 38.

[46] Ibid., iv.

[47] Ibid., 265.

[48] Ibid., 251. Mikhail Bakhtin uses *Heteroglossia* to describe distinctive varieties of speech within the same linguistic code. Homi K. Bhabha applies his theories to the discourse of hybridised identities in *The Location of Culture* (New York: Routledge, 1994), 142–44.

[49] Devra Gillet Jaffe, 'Straddling the Boundary: Messianic Judaism and the Construction of Culture' (MA thesis, Rice University, Houston, 2000).

[50] Ibid., 67–68.

Conceptual Space on the Continuum

The Messianic movement 'occupies a space between Orthodox Judaism and Christianity', with its own special features, characteristics and aims, according to Esther Foreman.[51] As an anthropological study, combining questionnaires, participant observation and interviews, it focuses on identity negotiation and construction within individuals, groups, and society.

Foreman compares two Messianic Congregations in London, showing how individuals and groups negotiate their boundaries of practice and identity within the Movement.[52] Messianic Judaism occupies a self-created space on a 'continuum' between Judaism and Christianity. Within this 'conceptual space' Christians, Messianic Believers[53] and Messianic Jews can formulate their identity, influenced by the number and proportion of Christians and Jews within that group as well as its history and leadership. Foreman's work is similar to that of Feher and Harris-Shapiro, and is of interest as it focuses on the Messianic movement in the UK, which according to Foreman is 'at least twenty years behind North American Messianic Judaism in terms of its organisation, structure, support and community'.[54] Her discussion of the theology of the movement is limited to a brief summary of the main historical stages of the development of Messianic Judaism from the Jewish Christianity of the early church to the Hebrew Christian movement of the nineteenth and twentieth centuries.

Minor Studies

Barry Abramson described varieties of Messianic Jewish belief and expression in Israel and the USA, using an ethnographic approach to describe the different manifestations of the Messianic movement, but does not provide a system or model for interpreting and classifying them.[55] Jacques Gutwirth

---

[51] Ester Foreman, 'Messianic Judaism in London: A Study of a Continuum Between Judaism and Christianity' (MA thesis, King's College, London, 2002).

[52] *Beit Yeshua*, Finchley, led by John Fieldsend and *B'nai Maccabim*, Hendon (in Borehamwood since 2001) led by Ruth Fleischer-Snow.

[53] Foreman uses this term to describe those who are not Jewish but are attracted to Messianic Jewish Congregations. Others use the term only referring to Jewish believers in Jesus.

[54] Ibid., 4.

[55] Barry Abramson, *The Differences between Israeli and American Messianic Jewish Believers and the Implications for the Future* (MA thesis, All Nations Christian College, Ware, UK, 2005). Abramson described the varieties of Messianic Jewish belief and expression in Israel and the USA, using an auto-ethnographic approach to describe the different manifestations of the Messianic movement, but does not provide a system or model for interpretation and classification.

produced a phenomenological study of *Ahavat Zion*, a Messianic Jewish Congregation in Los Angeles, looking at the history of the Messianic Movement, aspects of the life of individuals and the nature of the congregation.[56] Messianic Judaism is, he suggests, a revitalisation of tradition within Judaism, based on an evangelical Christian ideology. Whilst lifestyle, liturgy and life-events are observed and described perceptively and at length, there is no theological reflection or evaluation.

Francine Samuelson reviewed the history of Messianic Judaism in the USA, exploring the theology and social institutions of the movement, focusing on the UMJC. She sets Messianic Judaism in the Stark-Bainbridge church-sect-cult taxonomy, reflects on its controversial nature for both Christians and Jews, and characterises its theology through the works of Daniel Juster and David Stern.[57]

Reflection on Anthropological Studies

Using contemporary cultural theory about social space, hybridity and heteroglossia, Harris-Shapiro, Feher, Berger and Foreman all engage in a more sympathetic interaction with the Messianic movement through participant-observation and ethnographic method. Their interest in the ideological basis for the movement adds to their understanding of the social forces that make up Messianic Jewish identity, and explains how the Jewish and Christian communities respond. Whilst they listen carefully to the texts and stories of the group members, they do not engage with the belief system in a critical way in terms of religious or theological issues, preferring rather to allow the group's belief system to challenge their own identity-construction and beliefs.[58]

---

[56] Jacque Gutwirth, *Les Judéo-Chrétiens d'aujourd'hui* (Paris: Les Éditions du Cerf, 1987). *Ahavat Zion,* one of the first Messianic Congregations in the USA, is now under the leadership of Stuart Dauermann of the *Hashivenu* group.

[57] Francine K. Samuelson, 'Messianic Judaism: Church, Denomination, Sect, or Cult?' *Journal of Ecumenical Studies* 37, no. 2 (2000): 161–86.

[58] Two further anthropological studies, based on research among Israeli Messianic Congregations, appeared after the present study, but confirm our observations. Evert W. van de Poll, *Sacred Times For Chosen People: Development of the Messianic Jewish Movement and its Holiday Practice* (Boekencentrum, Zoetermeer, 2008) and Keri Zelson Warshawsky, *Returning To Their Own Borders: A Social Anthropological Study of Contemporary Messianic Jewish Identity in Israel* (PhD Dissertation, Hebrew University of Jerusalem, 2008).

Social Psychological Approaches

Brother or Other? Messianic Jews and JUBUs

Elliot Cohen's social psychological study of the 'controversial Messianic group' Jews for Jesus includes his own perspective as a Jewish Buddhist on issues of power, identity and ideology within Judaism.[59] He discusses the Jewishness of Jesus, the history of Christian anti-Semitism, and 'questions relating to the parameters of modern Jewish identity (religious to ethno-cultural)'. He then examines the 'perceived *otherness*' of the Jews for Jesus group. 'This otherness concerns the way the group is silenced and invalidated through being related to via the discourse of the cult, including issues and allegations of brainwashing or mind control, to be located within the grand narratives of Psychiatry and Psychology.'[60]

For Cohen the 'receiving and rendering of their faith as ideology, their speech as mere rhetoric, the use or usurpation of Jewish terms and symbols' is addressed within a 'discourse and semiotic framework of analysis'. Cohen presents an alternative model for understanding the conflict between Jews for Jesus and the Jewish community by counterbalancing the 'voice of the individual' with the 'voice of the community'. By way of contrast and in order to reflect on his own presuppositions he concludes with a discussion of his own JUBU (Jewish Buddhist) identity noting the positive or inconclusive responses he encounters. Cohen's interest in the theology of the movement is limited to how it functions as ideology and as discourse, without reference to the contents or construction of such theology.

> Simultaneously being both a Jewish and a Christian Sect, Messianic Judaism is seen as a relatively novel yet legitimate form of Christianity, i.e. a Christian sect. It accepts all the tenets of fundamentalist Christianity pertaining to the person of Christ, the Trinity, and the Immaculate Conception [*sic*] etc. However it is not accepted as being part of the Jewish tradition in any way, shape or form.[61]

---

[59] Cf. Julienne Lipson, *Jews for Jesus: an Anthropological Study* (New York: AMS Press, 1990); Ruth Tucker, *Not Ashamed: The Story of Jews for Jesus* (Colorado Springs: Multnomah, 2000).

[60] Eliot Marc Cohen, 'Brother or Other: Jews for Jesus' (PhD diss., Manchester Metropolitan University, 2004). Whilst not all in the Messianic movement accept the organisation 'Jews for Jesus' as part of it, the study by Cohen is applicable to Messianic Jewish identity in its broader sense. Other studies of 'Jews for Jesus' do not always distinguish between the generic term for JBYs and the missionary organisation founded by Moishe Rosen in the 1970s.

[61] Ibid., 203–4.

As a social psychologist Cohen is interested in the reception of Messianic Judaism within the Jewish community.

> Currently Judaism cannot, and will not allow itself to even begin to consider recognizing the legitimacy of Messianic Judaism as this could be construed as accepting the possibility that Jesus was the Messiah. Due to its [Judaism's] doctrinal position it can therefore only relate through opposition ... As there can be no legitimate 'Messianic Jewish' identity, the identity that is left is often construed to be that of a deceiver, a liar and cult member and recruiter, 'a wolf in sheep's clothing', a 'sheep stealer' and psychologically troubled individual. [62]

As a Jewish Buddhist and an admirer of Jesus his own perspective is brought into the study: 'My parents permitted me to admire him (JESUS), but warned me never to worship him, since that day I always have and I never will.'[63]

Cohen is interested in the discourse of Messianic Jews. He writes that '[t]he Messianic-Jewish religious discourse may be understood as a hybrid discourse that negotiates between the ethno-cultural Jewish identity and the new Christian faith. It appears that the various free floating components of Jewish identity (termed their Jewishness) now have a centre of gravity and orbits around their discovery of Jesus as the Jewish Messiah.'[64] He also explores the role of theology as ideology. Following John Thompson, ideology is 'meaning in the service of power'.[65]

> In this way meaning is seen as something that is attributed to something by someone in a position of power; meanings are given, not made. If one has the power to give meaning then one is able to take meaning, to consign the meaning of one's enemy to the realms of the meaningless, nonsense. As themes of truth are tightly bound with themes of meaning, ideology becomes a truly awesome power, and a potentially devastating weapon. [66]

Ideology functions as 'social cement', an 'inert collection of beliefs the purpose of which may simply be to create or facilitate a "sense of belonging"'. MJT, like other ideologies, rationalises, universalises and puts into narrative the view of reality of the group. Cohen's research does not bear directly on the study of MJT. Yet his insights are valuable, especially as he sees the construction of Messianic Jewish identity from an ideological

---

[62] Ibid., 204.

[63] Ibid., 401.

[64] Ibid., 354.

[65] John B. Thompson, *Ideology and Modern Culture* (Oxford: Blackwell, 1990).

[66] Cohen, 'Brother or Other,' 303.

perspective, and understands the role of theology in this process. As a Buddhist himself, Cohen is noncommittal in his evaluation of the beliefs of Messianic Judaism.

Minor Studies

Natalia Yangarber-Hicks focuses on the identity of Messianic Jews by setting questions of ethnic identity construction and personal identity in the light of the historical and theological background of modern Messianic Judaism.[67] She shows how the background of the movement influences and affects the personal experience of its members.

Pauline Kollontai's two articles explore why a sample of British Messianic Jews have chosen this 'system of belief rather than stay within traditional Judaism or become Christian'.[68] Through interviews she concludes that Messianic Jews 'are critical of their religious upbringing as Jews', although 'traditional aspects of Judaism remain important and relevant to their Messianic belief.'[69] They choose 'not to become Christian' because of the Church's previous and present anti-Judaism. In recent years Messianic Judaism has grown considerably worldwide and has caused much concern within the contemporary Jewish community. Kollontai explores identity issues in the light of the questions the Jewish community itself asks about Jewish identity, 'given that the various branches of contemporary Judaism are deeply divided over central tenets of faith and practice'.[70] Belief in Jesus as the Messiah is considered in the light of traditional Jewish views.

Historico-Theological Approaches

Whilst the above approaches are not without theological concerns, historical studies have paid more attention to the theology of the movement in order to explain its emergence, development and present state. However, few explore the breadth found in the movement and easily assume it has a monolithic theology. The governing interpretive paradigm of such studies is the emergence of Messianic Judaism in reaction to its parent Hebrew Christianity whilst still under the influence of Protestant Fundamentalism.

---

[67] Natalia Yangarber-Hicks, 'Messianic believers: reflections on identity of a largely misunderstood group,' *Journal of Psychology and Theology* 33, no. 2 (2005): 127–39.

[68] Pauline Kollontai, 'Messianic Jews and Jewish Identity,' *Journal of Modern Jewish Studies* 3, vol. 2 (July 2004): 195–205; 'Between Judaism and Christianity: The Case of Messianic Jews,' *Journal of Religion and Society* (2006): 1–9.

[69] Kollontai, 'Between Judaism and Christianity,' 1.

[70] Kollontai, 'Messianic Jews,' 195.

New Religious Movement

David Rausch, in a pioneering study of the modern movement, assessed the emergence of contemporary Messianic Judaism in the late 1970s.[71] His chapter on the 'Theology of Messianic Judaism' describes its key beliefs.[72] The three emphases of Messianic Judaism that define it according to Rausch are separation from Hebrew Christianity,[73] congregational expression and Torah-based community life.[74] The Jewishness of Jesus, the early church and the scriptures are the basis for a Messianic Jewish lifestyle.[75] Messianic Judaism's hermeneutics, views of inspiration, and eschatology have little to distinguish it from Fundamentalism and Dispensationalism.[76] Nevertheless traditional Jewish motifs such as the *Shema* affirm the nature of God.[77] Rausch's final section on 'traditional Messianic Judaism' describes those Messianic Jews who come from a more 'traditional' Jewish background, and find Messianic Congregations too 'liberal' in their lack of observance of orthodox rabbinic *Halacha*.[78] Rausch recognises a 'spectrum of views' on these issues, and that a 'doctrine' of rabbinical tradition is needed.[79]

Rausch had previously studied American Fundamentalism and was 'immediately drawn to the correlations between both theologies'. After 'many hundreds' of interviews with Messianic Jews he concludes that 'their theology is that of the Fundamentalist/Evangelical movement in which Hebrew Christian theology is rooted.'[80] The characterisation of Messianic Judaism as a Jewish-flavoured variant of North American Fundamentalism is the main explanatory model.[81]

Rausch accurately describes Messianic Judaism in the late 1970s and early 1980s, many of whose features have been maintained up to the present. The

---

[71] David A. Rausch, *Messianic Judaism: Its History, Theology and Polity* (Lewiston, NY: Edwin Mellen Press, 1982).

[72] Ibid., ch. 7, 117–44.

[73] Ibid., 118.

[74] Ibid., 119. What 'Torah-based community life' consisted of in the late 1970s and early 1980s was not clearly defined. 'Torah observance' is discussed below in chapters 6 and 7.

[75] Ibid., 119–24.

[76] Ibid., 124–31.

[77] Ibid., 125.

[78] Ibid., 135–42.

[79] Ibid., 134. Rausch anticipates the current debate within the movement on the meaning and place of Torah, which will be discussed in chapter 6 and 7.

[80] Ibid., 144, footnote 24.

[81] Rausch's section on 'Gentile Influence on Jewish Christianity' (ch.4, 51–70) discusses the proposal of John Toland (1670–1722) for a Nazarene form of Christianity where Jews who believe in Jesus are still 'for ever bound to the law of Moses' (52).

study was well received within the movement itself, bringing it publicity and legitimation. Here was an academic, not involved in the movement, giving it its first public airing. Reviews were critical, however, of the way Rausch included a romantic interest in the possibility of Jewish orthodoxy within the Messianic movement, his identification of Messianic Jewish thought with Fundamentalism, and his oversimplification of the Hebrew Christian/Messianic Jew antithesis.[82]

Neglected Element in Jewish-Christian Relations

Walter Riggans sets the theology of Messianic Judaism in the context of Jewish-Christian relations and religious identity.[83] Key practitioners 'speak for themselves, and at some length' on Christology, ecclesiology, hermeneutics, Jewish identity, relationship to Judaism, and the role of the Messianic movement within Jewish-Christian relations.[84] Riggans uses the writings of James Hutchens, Arnold Fruchtenbaum and Daniel Juster – pioneers of Messianic Congregations in the USA – to express Messianic thought on these issues, clarifying misconceptions that had 'clouded previous studies of the movement'. He identifies the theological roots of the key thinkers within North American Conservative Evangelicalism, and associates their particular distinctives within the movement. Hutchens's work is informed by the contextualising theology of the Fuller School of World Mission. Fruchtenbaum uses the system of Dallas Dispensationalism.[85] Juster, according to Riggans, is 'least comfortable with the label' of Conservative Evangelicalism, and is the least amenable to being associated with a Protestant theological grid, but works within the covenantal theology of Wheaton Theological College, the missiological framework of Lutheran evangelicalism,[86] and a self-imposed restriction of his thought in using only Jewish terminology.[87]

---

[82]　Mitch Glaser, 'Review of David Rausch's *Messianic Judaism: Its History, Theology and Polity*' in *LCJE Bulletin* (August 1983), 6.

[83]　Walter Riggans, *Messianic Judaism and Jewish-Christian Relations: A Case Study in the Field of Religious Identity* (PhD diss., University of Birmingham, 1991).

[84]　Ibid., i.

[85]　Ibid., 7.

[86]　Juster himself does not see much significance in his brief association with Lutheranism. 'Riggans says I was influenced by Lutheran evangelism. I do not know why he would say this, though I was a member of a Lutheran Church for two years. If I were to point to any stream it would be mainstream American Evangelicalism as represented by Wheaton and Trinity Evangelical Divinity School' (email correspondence, 14th September 2003).

[87]　Ibid., 8.

Riggans summarises their contributions as 'well able to represent the range of theological skills, parameters and views which are to be found today'.[88] Whilst reporting these in detail, he does not evaluate the theological methods or assumptions with which they operate. His study is primarily descriptive, with the apologetic aim of situating the movement positively within orthodox Christianity on topics such as Christology. He discusses the acceptance of Messianic Jews within the Jewish community, and the validation of Messianic Jewish identity. There is no critical engagement with how MJT develops. It is accepted as a *fait accompli*.

A brief discussion on exegetical method occupies the 'hermeneutics and methods of interpretation' section. Here Riggans clearly identifies the methods of conservative evangelicalism in the hermeneutics of Hutchens, Fruchtenbaum and Juster. He concludes that

> It is of course disappointing that the writers exhibit no real rigorous discipline in setting out for us their hermeneutical principles and contexts, though Juster is more considerate here than the others. But what is not in doubt is that they are all more at home in the world of Reformation Christian hermeneutics than that of Jewish midrashic hermeneutics. The thirteen Middoth of R. Ishmael are conspicuous by their absence.[89]

Riggans himself, in his own writing, advocates a more appropriate theological method, combining Jewish and Christian theological approaches.[90]

A Tool for Mission

Yacov Ariel devotes a major section of his study of Jewish missions in America to the rise of Messianic Judaism.[91] The ideology and practices of Messianic Judaism emerge, he says, from the nineteenth century pietism and evangelicalism of the Jewish missions.[92] These were Premilliennial, chose to use Jewish rather than Christian symbols, and tried to establish congregations and Hebrew Christian brotherhoods. Whilst the self-perception of being simultaneously Jewish and Christian could be found in the 19th and early 20th century Jewish missions, the novelty of the Messianic movement in the 1970s was that a '[s]et of notions and aspirations that had previously been expressed only sporadically, partially and hesitantly found a stronger

---

[88]   Ibid.

[89]   Ibid., 211.

[90]   E.g. Walter Riggans, *Yeshua Ben David* (Crowborough: MARC/Olive Press, 1995).

[91]   Yacov Ariel, *Evangelising the Chosen People: Missions to the Jews in America 1880–2000* (Chapel Hill, NC: University of North Carolina Press, 2000), 'The Rise of Messianic Judaism', 220–50.

[92]   Ibid., 220.

and more assertive voice and became a more acceptable option for Jewish converts to Christianity.'[93]

The rise of Messianic Judaism was 'in many ways the logical outcome of the ideology and rhetoric of the movement to evangelise the Jews'.[94] According to Ariel, Jewish Christians then acted independently of the Jewish missions in pioneering the first MJCs.[95] They shaped the self-perception of the movement as autonomous, and encouraged it to be more assertive and outgoing in its Jewish expression.[96]

Ariel identifies the main features of Messianic Judaism – its historical development, representative congregations, typical practices and key reactions to it from Christian leaders. As for the theology of Messianic Judaism: 'Having built a unique subculture within the larger evangelical camp, Messianic Jewish thinkers have produced a series of theological and apologetic tracts that have come to define and defend the movement's path. In accordance with the relatively pluralistic nature of Messianic Judaism, their work has not been unified or uniform and has given voice to a large spectrum of opinions.'[97]

Theologically Messianic Judaism is 'far from united or uniform and has, in fact, many subdivisions and groups, colours and shades'.[98] This diversity is expressed in the charismatic/non-charismatic divide, and attitudes toward Jewish tradition.[99] But the majority of Messianic Jews 'have found a middle road between the more traditionalist and the more moderate Hebrew Christian approach'.[100] Ariel focuses on the 'better-known theologians' – John Fischer, Arnold Fruchtenbaum, Dan Juster and David Stern[101] –

---

[93] Ibid., 221.

[94] Ibid., 223.

[95] Such an account of the independence of the first Messianic Congregations accepts uncritically the historiography of the Postmissionary school that argues an original independence of the forerunners of the modern movement from the start. Whilst this is an important aspect of the self-understanding of the Messianic movement, it can scarcely be maintained in the light of an examination of the influences and support that the early congregational leaders received from Christian missionary organisations and individuals. Joseph Rabinowitz, the archetypal forerunner of the modern Messianic movement, received much support from Pastor Faltin, an agent of CMJ. Cf. Kai Kjær-Hansen, *Joseph Rabinowitz and the Messianic Movement* (Edinburgh: Handsel Press, 1995), 53–56.

[96] Ariel, *Evangelising the Chosen People*, 222.

[97] Ibid., 248.

[98] Ibid., 240.

[99] Ibid., 241.

[100] Ibid., 245.

[101] The work of others is also discussed in the chapter, including James Hutchens, Michael Schiffman and Louis Goldberg.

giving their biographies and main contributions. Fruchtenbaum's thought reflects his dispensational premillenialism. Stern, influenced by the missiology of Fuller Seminary, maintains the priority of evangelism. Juster's more 'traditional' and less charismatic approach reflects his Presbyterian background and emphasises the primary purpose of Messianic Jewish Congregations in 'fostering the goals of Jewish outreach and evangelism'. Ariel concludes

> Whereas the different theologians vary in their vision of Messianic Jewish life and practices, they all agree on some major points, among them the centrality of evangelism to Jewish Christian congregations and the fact that such communities do not separate Jews from the church but rather allow them, on an optional basis, their own space and a connection to their roots and ethnicity. The writers also emphasise the high priority Messianic Jews should give to evangelism and the duty of non-Jews to support them in their efforts.[102]

As Ariel's focus is on evangelism and missions, it is not surprising that he highlights this concern. However, as shall be observed below, this oversimplifies a complex debate within the movement on the need and nature of such activity, and neglects the emergence of the 'new paradigm' of *PMJ* described below. Ariel's prediction of a continuing evangelistic emphasis in the movement has yet to be demonstrated.

Seventh Branch of Judaism

Dan Cohn-Sherbok calls for the acceptance of Messianic Judaism within the plurality of contemporary 'Judaisms'.[103] Early Jewish Christianity, the emergence of Hebrew Christianity in the nineteenth century, the growth of the Hebrew Christian Alliance of America and Jewish missions in the early twentieth century form the historical background. The modern movement's history, belief, practices, calendar, lifecycle, liturgy and observance are detailed. In the third section on the 'Authenticity of Messianic Judaism' Cohn-Sherbok summarises briefly the theology of the movement on Jesus the Messiah, the importance of Messianic Congregations, the authority of scripture, the Triune nature of God and eschatology.[104]

Cohn-Sherbok considers the findings of recent court cases, examining the status of Messianic Jews in *Halacha* and under Israel's 'Law of Return'. In his final chapter, 'Models of Messianic Judaism' he makes his own case for Messianic Judaism's acceptance within the Jewish community.[105] Advocates

---

[102] Ibid., 249.

[103] Dan Cohn-Sherbok, *Messianic Judaism* (London: Continuum 2000).

[104] Ibid., 169–72.

[105] Ibid., 203–13.

of Jewish pluralism, as opposed to orthodox and non-orthodox exclusivism, should have no problem in recognising Messianic Judaism as one of seven valid forms of Judaism, and see this as the 'only reasonable starting point for inter-community relations in the twenty-first century'.[106] Such an overture was warmly welcomed within the Messianic movement, but Cohn-Sherbok's pluralist agenda raises significant soteriological questions about the movement's relationship to other 'Judaisms'.[107]

---

[106] Ibid., 213. The seven forms are Hasidic, Orthodox, Conservative, Reform, Reconstructionist, Humanist and Messianic Judaism. Secular Zionism and Feminism are not mentioned.

[107] A further collection of essays edited by Dan Cohn-Sherbok presents differing views within the movement on a range of theological and practical issues. Dan Cohn-Sherbok, ed., *Voices of Messianic Judaism: Confronting Critical Issues Facing a Maturing Movement* (Baltimore: Lederer Books, 2001).

Chapter 3

Previous Studies:
Theological Studies by Practitioners

Advocates and Practitioners

Whilst the boundary between observers and practitioners is not always clear, the following section reviews studies by practitioners and advocates of Messianic Judaism, who employ both supportive and critical perspectives, and demonstrate their own engagement in the construction of MJT.

Contextualisation and Rediscovery

Arthur Glasser, Dean of Fuller Seminary's 'School of World Mission', encouraged Messianic Judaism as an example of contextualisation.[1] James Hutchens and Philip Goble pioneered Messianic Congregations in the 1970s under his influence.[2] Messianic Judaism is a contextual Christian theology, a rediscovery of the Jewish Christianity of the early church in the setting of contemporary Jewish life. A 'dynamic equivalent' of the Christian faith in Jewish terms is needed, restoring Christianity's 'original Jewishness' and allowing the gospel to be replanted in its original seedbed.

---

[1] See Hanne Kircheiner, 'Arthur Glasser and Jewish Evangelism' (MA diss., All Nations Christian College, 2006).

[2] Hutchens, James, 'Messianic Judaism: A Progress Report,' *Missiology* 5 no. 3 (July 1977): 279; 'A Case for Messianic Judaism' (PhD diss., Fuller Theological Seminary, 1974). There is considerable discussion in missiology (theology of mission) on the construction of indigenous theologies, which is beyond the focus of this study. The methodological issues raised are important for a consideration of Messianic Judaism and Messianic Jewish thought, and reference can be made to the construction of 'local' (Schreiter), 'vernacular' (Dyrness), 'contextual' (Bevans) and 'ethno-theologies' (Conn) that are found in the current literature. Cf. Harvie Conn, 'Ethnotheologies' in *Evangelical Dictionary of World Missions*, ed. A. Scott Moreau (Grand Rapids: Baker, 2000): 328–30.

Hutchens' doctoral dissertation and Goble's practical manuals have been influential since the 1970s. Glasser, as a missiologist with great sympathy for the movement, has remained an active participant-observer in the development of Messianic Judaism.[3] His concern with the development of MJT is clear in his section 'Messianic Jewish Theologizing – Should we expect Messianic theology to develop?'

> Within the world of missiological investigation, it has become virtually axiomatic to affirm that when a separate people begin to move Christ-ward, three phenomena begin to surface that reflect its validity: 1) They develop their own musical forms for worship; 2) They organize themselves in surprisingly distinct ways to carry out their evangelistic obedience; and, 3) They start to theologize concerning the dominant truths that characterize their reflection on scripture. Some even have observed that in their theologizing these new believers come up with ideas that give a measure of concern to the traditional guardians of the Church's faith![4]

Glasser notes that 'we are only beginning to see this reality emerge.' Reviewing recent papers on MJT given at Lausanne Consultation on Jewish Evangelism meetings, he notes the development of 'new insights that are not found in traditional theology'.[5] These are a Holocaust theology 'on the basis of the Deuteronomist[ic] philosophy of history'; a theology of the State of Israel 'in relation to a fresh word from God (Isaiah 2:3), hence the importance of a Messianic Jewish presence confronting the Jewish nation there'; the determination of Jewish believers 'to imitate Yeshua in the Gospels when it comes to relating themselves to Jewish history and tradition'. Christology is the most important theological question. 'Possibly most significant of all, some Messianic Jewish people are probing the Christological texts and lengthy record of the Christological debates of the Church Fathers as few others in our day are doing. They are earnestly seeking a truly accurate and complete knowledge of the full humanity and eternal deity of the Lord Himself.'[6] Glasser notes a further topic.

---

[3] Arthur F. Glasser, 'Thoughts from a Longtime Friend' in *Voices of Messianic Judaism,* ed. Dan Cohn-Sherbok (Baltimore: Lederer, 2001), 229–34.

[4] Arthur F. Glasser, 'More Issues in Jewish Evangelization ['LCJE Gatherings in North America (1985–1997) – Part 2']', *Missionary Monthly* (March 1998): 20–21, 20.

[5] The Lausanne Consultation on Jewish Evangelism (LCJE) is a major networking group of Evangelicals involved in Jewish Evangelism, which has an active interest in the development of Messianic Judaism. Cf. David Harley, ed., *Christian Witness to the Jewish People,* Lausanne Occasional Paper no. 7 (1980).

[6] Ibid. Glasser overstates the case here and does not refer to the wealth of contemporary theological work on the Trinity, or scholars such as Bauckham and Hurtado who specifically investigate the Jewish background of Christian Trinitarian claims.

Beyond the contribution of these papers, the one of possibly greatest significance to Messianic Jews explored in depth [in the papers] is the manner in which the Oral Torah, the philosophical theologies of the Middle Ages, and the modern period of the Enlightenment shaped the Jewish understanding of Tanakh [the Jewish Bible], in contrast to the way in which Messianic Jews understand it today.[7]

The Development of Messianic Jewish Theology

Harald Hegstad, a Norwegian Lutheran, notes the theological significance of Messianic Judaism for Christian and Jewish self-understanding.

> The present challenge is to give a theological interpretation of the reality the Messianic Jewish movement represents. This includes the burning question of an adequate self-understanding for the Messianic Jews, but also what this means for the self-understanding of the church. In my opinion these two fundamental challenges should not be treated as two different and separate challenges, but as two aspects of one basic challenge, common for Messianic Jews and for gentile Christians. I am inclined to believe that David Stern is right when he states that 'without Messianic Judaism … both the Jewish people and the church will fail to achieve their proper and glorious goals'.[8]

Hegstad surveys questions involved in the construction of MJT, but does not propose solutions.

Realised Eschatology

Robert Winer and Ruth Fleischer-Snow, activists within the Messianic Jewish Alliance of America (MJAA), understand Messianic Judaism as an eschatological revival of Jewish people coming to know Israel's Messiah.[9] Their historical surveys of the movement are coloured by their commitment to the aims of Messianic Judaism and their experience of the emergence of Messianic Judaism in reaction and response to Hebrew Christianity in the 1970s. The restoration of Israel takes place through 'spiritual' and 'political' Zionism, as Messianic Judaism is a 'Zionism of the Spirit'. Messianic Judaism is a provisional structure for the End Times. It needs some

---

[7] Glasser, 'More Issues in Jewish Evangelization,' 21.

[8] Harald Hegstad, 'The Development of a Messianic Jewish Theology – Affirmations and Questions,' *Mishkan* 25 (1996): 60.

[9] Robert I. Winer, *The Calling: The History of the Messianic Alliance of America 1915–1990* (Philadelphia: MJAA, 1990). Ruth Fleischer-Snow, 'The Emergence of a Distinctively Jewish Faith in Jesus 1925–1993' (PhD diss., Kings College, London, 1993), privately published as *So Great a Cloud of Witnesses* (1996).

organisational development and the mobilising of people and resources, but not institutions or theological systems. Whilst their historical approaches incorporate the theological distinctives of the movement – such as the Jewishness of belief in Jesus, the need for Messianic Jewish congregations and lifestyle, and the eschatological significance of return to the land of Israel – these positions are stated without further theological investigation.

Two Types of Messianic Judaism

Gabriela Reason compares theological trends within the two main organisations of Messianic Congregations in the USA.[10] The Messianic Jewish Alliance of America (MJAA) and Union of Messianic Jewish Congregations (UMJC) positions on Torah observance, Jewish practices, Gentiles, evangelicalism and relationships with the Jewish community are contrasted, from the perspective of an evangelical concerned with theological drift. The UMJC identifies closely with the Jewish community and seeks acceptance within it, whilst the IMJA[11], with its revivalist and Fundamentalist leanings, remains within evangelical sub-culture. Reason's concern is the proximity of the MJAA and the UMJC to Evangelicalism. She discusses how theologies of Torah observance, mission and conversion affect the movement, which she wishes to remain on an evangelical basis. 'I am here concerned with presenting a general Messianic Jewish understanding of this theology, not a precise presentation of the theology itself.'[12]

The Messianic Judaism of the MJAA, influenced by Charismatic and Fundamentalist Christianity, maintains the 'saved' versus 'unsaved' distinction, maintains unity with the Church whilst preserving 'physical distinctions'. The UMJC, on the other hand, challenges the 'saved' versus 'unsaved' dichotomy, associating more strongly with the Jewish community through its Torah observance. Reason tracks the post-formative developments of the 1990s, particularly the innovations of the Hashivenu movement within the UMJC. This welcomes the conversion of Gentiles to Messianic Judaism and formulates *Halacha* in a systematic fashion. However, there is no investigation of the underlying theological roots.

Field Guide to the Messianic Movement

Rich Robinson's 'Field Guide' introduces evangelical Christians to the diversity of Messianic Judaism, describing the features and the contours

---

[10] Gabriela Reason (née Karabelnik), 'Competing Trends in Messianic Judaism: The Debate Over Evangelicalism' (Senior thesis, Department of Religious Studies, Yale University, 2002).

[11] International Messianic Jewish Alliance, the international parent body of the MJAA.

[12] Ibid., 22 (footnote 55).

of the movement.[13] Working with the mission agency Jews for Jesus he employs a conservative evangelical perspective, criticising those who compromise on the need for direct evangelism as the price of acceptance within the Jewish community.

> There have always been two somewhat competing positions in the Messianic movement concerning how Jewish believers in Jesus are to relate to the Jewish community at large. Some have been eager for the Jewish community to recognize the legitimacy of Jewish believers in Jesus. Much of the impetus for developing the Messianic congregational movement has been to 'show' the Jewish community that we are 'real' Jews; hence the trend to naming assemblies 'Synagogues,' calling the leaders 'rabbis,' etc.[14]

Robinson describes several streams within the Messianic movement and adjacent to it including *Hashivenu*, the emergent 'Torah observant' group.[15] The group's desire for acceptance and its re-definition of evangelism have, according to Robinson, serious implications for ecclesiology and soteriology. He critiques such positions, making his own theological position clear. His normative approach proposes standards for 'healthy' Messianic Jewish congregations. They should stay focused on the gospel and the uniqueness of the Messiah as the way of salvation. Increased Torah observance distracts from the gospel. Whilst pinpointing theological weaknesses from the critical standpoint of North American evangelicalism, Robinson does not explore the theological evolution of the movement and the subgroups within it.[16]

Strengths and Weaknesses of Previous Studies

Previous studies argue that the theology of Messianic Judaism, like its predecessor Hebrew Christianity, is transposed from the Protestant Evangelicalism of the Jewish Missions and American Fundamentalist Christianity. Whilst this paradigm provides one possible entry point into

---

[13] Rich Robinson, ed., *The Messianic Movement: A Field Guide for Evangelical Christians from Jews for Jesus* (San Francisco: Purple Pomegranate Productions, 2005).

[14] Ibid., 132–33.

[15] Ibid., 131–50.

[16] Minor studies include Deborah Pardo-Kaplan, 'Jacob vs. Jacob: JBYs quarrel over both style and substance,' *Christianity Today* 49, no. 2 (February 2005), http://www.ctlibrary.com/34339 (accessed June 26, 2007); John Fieldsend, *Messianic Jews: Challenging Church and Synagogue* (Tunbridge Wells: Monarch Publications, 1993). Fieldsend's study combines the autobiographical accounts of members of the London Messianic Congregation in the 1980s with several theological essays by the author, on a variety of topics relevant to Messianic Judaism.

the field, emphasising the turbulent beginnings of the Messianic movement in the 1970s, it makes certain assumptions about the nature of the belief-system being described, risking a reductionist assessment limited by the theoretical framework of the observer. Consideration and explanation of the diversity and innovative nature of the theology is limited. The present book not only describes such theological diversity, but also proposes a typology for its understanding.

The refusal by most Jewish observers to see Messianic Judaism as a valid form of Judaism is also problematic, as the apologetic purposes of both observer and observed clash in this area. If Messianic Judaism is a 'marginal group' its theology cannot be accepted as a valid 'Jewish' theology. Yet its theology, as we shall see, makes this very claim. It would appear that the agenda behind some studies of Messianic Judaism is to deny any possible theological validity or legitimacy to the claims made by Messianic Jews. This hardly allows for a detailed discussion of the theology of Messianic Judaism. As such it is not in the interest of such studies to assess the heterogeneous nature of the movement or its theology, but rather to see it as a monolith.

Theological Approaches

Engaged Messianic Jewish practitioners contribute a fifth group of studies – attempts to offer serious, Messianic Jewish, overtly theological reflections. Their aim is the development of MJT. Whether programmatic, speculative or systematically constructive, they employ their own faith-perspectives in identifying and addressing key issues in both description and development of the discipline, and their studies contribute to the growing theology of the movement.[17]

Proposals for Messianic Jewish Theology

In 1978 David Stern's *Messianic Jewish Manifesto* gave a rationale for Messianic Judaism. Stern proposed several theological options for Messianic Jews.[18] His categories reflect the emergence of Messianic Judaism from Hebrew Christianity in the 1970s. The two main options are those of

---

[17] Daniel Juster, 'Towards a Messianic Jewish Theology' in *Jewish Identity and Faith in Jesus*, ed. Kai Kjær-Hansen (Jerusalem: Caspari Centre for Biblical and Jewish Studies, 1996), 57–62. An important study by a Roman Catholic theologian sympathetic to the Messianic movement appeared after the present study. Peter Hocken, *The Challenges of the Pentecostal, Charismatic and Messianic Jewish Movements: The Tensions of the Spirit: New Critical Thinking in Religion, Theology and Biblical Studies* (Ashgate: Oxford, 2009).

[18] David Stern, *Messianic Jewish Manifesto*, 234–38.

'Ultimate Messianic Jew (UMJ)' (as 'Messianic' as possible) and 'Ultimate Hebrew Christian (UHC)' (as 'Hebrew Christian' as possible). Within these are the sub-categories; 'Ultimately Jewish but Limited Messianic possibilities (UJLM)'; 'Ultimate Hebrew Christianity of Today (UHCT)'; 'Present Limit of Hebrew Christianity (PLHC)'; 'Present Limit of Messianic Judaism (PLMJ)'. Stern argues that Jewish believers in Jesus should become 'fully Jewish' and 'fully Messianic' as much as possible, but does not specify what this entails.

Stern's discussion is unsatisfactory, limited as it was by the then incipient nature of the Messianic Movement, its lack of theological development and congregational expression, and its assumption of an antithetical relationship with Hebrew Christianity, the parent movement within which it emerged and from which its leaders in the 1970s and 1980s were at pains to distance themselves. In a 2003 review of the progress of Messianic Judaism Stern summarised developments over thirty years: 'Messianic Jewish congregations have expended a great deal of energy into developing and refining theological, ceremonial and practical ways to express Jewishness.'[19] Yet MJT is still in its infancy. 'I expect continued progress in developing Messianic Jewish theology, and not only in the areas of ecclesiology and Torah. We will express with increasing clarity our theology of what Christians mean when we talk about the "Trinity" and the "deity of Jesus".'[20]

Stern calls for 'a systematic theology book in Hebrew (preferably a Messianic Jewish one, but *any* will do)', acknowledging that hopes expressed in his 1987 work had yet to be realised. There he recognised the need for a 'Messianic Jewish systematic theology'.

> Christian theology tends to underplay or misrepresent Jewish phenomena. Jewish theology largely ignores the New Testament. Since any genuine reconciliation of the Church and the Jewish people must conform to biblical truth, what is needed before any program of action can be designed is a thought framework that can do justice to both the Messianic and the Jewish elements of any theological topic. The name for such a thought framework is Messianic Jewish systematic theology.[21]

Stern does not develop such a framework, but limits himself to 'pointing out topics which need theological treatment and hinting at ways to go about it'. He even questions whether such a theology is possible: 'However, in this book I do not offer finished theology – if there is such a thing.'[22]

---

[19] David Stern, 'Summary Essay: The Future of Messianic Judaism,' in *How Jewish is Christianity? Two Views on the Messianic Movement*, edited by Stanley N. Gundry and L. Goldberg (Grand Rapids: Zondervan, 2003), 182.

[20] Ibid., 191.

[21] David Stern, *Messianic Jewish Manifesto*, 85.

[22] Ibid.

MJT is a 'consumer-oriented theology,' addressing four different audiences.

> I define systematic theology as the presentation of biblical truth in an organised fashion, by subject matter, in a manner that will be understood by its intended audience. My emphasis on the audience is purposeful; I do not believe that theology should be merely whatever its author wishes to say, placed in the marketplace for whoever will buy. A producer-oriented theology is selfish; theologians ought to consider the consumer.[23]

Stern's concern that such theology should be relevant to the 'consumer' would strike chords with all theologians, although few would compromise the depth of their engagement with the subject matter of theology at the expense of a populist approach. It might even be argued that the superficiality and lack of depth that has characterised much that has gone under the name of MJT in the past thirty years of the Messianic movement results from an overemphasis on such a populist approach, keeping the discipline within the narrow confines of a North American evangelicalism heavily influenced by the streams of Dispensationalism in which Israel and the Jewish people occupy a significant but limited role. Few Messianic thinkers have addressed or broken free of such moorings, to the detriment of the theological development and health of the movement.

Stern identifies the four audiences to which a 'consumer-oriented theology' must address itself.

> Although this is a general principle applicable to any theology, it is an absolute must for Messianic Jewish theology, because we have not one audience but four. They are the four mutually exclusive categories of humanity mentioned in the preceding chapter: Messianic Jews, non-Messianic Jews, Gentile Christians and the rest of mankind. Confusion is created and damage done when theologians write about Messianic Jewish subjects without considering who will read what they have written.[24]

Understanding the different group interests helps Messianic Jews articulate their theology appropriately. For example, 'Christians who write against Messianic Judaism or against Jewish evangelism clarify the theological issues we must address to defend Messianic Judaism within the Church.'[25]

Non-Messianic Jews engaged in apologetics against the New Testament and Christian readings of the Old Testament 'show us areas needing clarification, especially areas where the Messianic Jewish position may need to be

---

[23] Ibid.

[24] Ibid.

[25] Ibid., 88.

distinguished from more traditional Christian views' that do not sufficiently acknowledge the Jewish background of the New Testament.
Similarly the approach of an unsympathetic Jewish observer of Hebrew
Christianity such as B.Z. Sobel helps 'by sharpening our perception of
Jewish attitudes against institutionalising Jewish belief in Yeshua as the
Messiah, and his work'. The contribution of those studying the Messianic
movement from anthropological and sociological perspectives (that are
often a mask for Jewish reactions to Jewish believers in Jesus) 'points out
directions for bettering our movement'.[26]

The Quest for Messianic Jewish Theology

Despite its title, Arnold Fruchtenbaum's book *Hebrew Christianity* addressed
several theological issues that concern Messianic Judaism, such as the role
of Messianic Jewish Congregations and the place of the Law.[27] The contemporary Messianic movement can learn lessons from the theological
developments of early Jewish Christianity and apply these in the construction of MJT.[28] Without offering specific proposals, he 'raises specific
questions with which the development of a Messianic theology must deal'.

The seven issues Fruchtenbaum raises, but does not address directly, are:
(1) the problem of definitions, not merely between 'Hebrew Christianity'
and 'Messianic Judaism', but also between 'Jewishness' and 'Judaism'; (2)
the relationship between 'biblical Judaism' (fulfilled in the New Testament)
and 'Rabbinic Judaism'; (3) whether Messianic Judaism should be seen as 'a
Jewish branch of the Church or part of the umbrella of Judaism'; (4) whether
it is accurate to say that Jews and Christians worship the same God, when
the Triune God of the scriptures is 'exactly the type of God that Judaism
claims not to believe in'; (5) the role of the Mosaic Law in the life of the Jewish

---

[26] Ibid., 89.

[27] Arnold G. Fruchtenbaum, *Hebrew Christianity: Its Theology, History and Philosophy*
(Tustin, CA: Ariel Ministries Press, 1983). Fruchtenbaum's position has changed
over the years, as has the recognition that whilst he was originally in the 'Hebrew
Christian' camp he is now an advocate (and founder) of Messianic Congregations.
Cf. Fruchtenbaum, *Hebrew Christianity*, 51: 'Some extreme elements are hotly advocating dropping terms such as "Christ" or "Christian" on the flimsy ground that
these terms are Greek rather than Hebrew. Others wish to claim that they are representing a Messianic movement "within Judaism," which in no way can really be
true.' This should be contrasted with his statement of support for Messianic Jewish
congregations in 'Messianic Congregations May Exist Within the Body of Messiah'
in Stanley N. Gundry and Louis Goldberg, eds., *How Jewish is Christianity? Two
Views on the Messianic Movement* (Grand Rapids: Zondervan, 2003), 109–28.

[28] Arnold G. Fruchtenbaum, 'The Quest for a Messianic Theology,' *Mishkan* 2 (Winter
1985): 1–17.

believer; (6) the nature of the authority of the New Testament; (7) the proper terminology for Messianic congregations, whether they should be known as 'Church', 'assembly' or 'synagogue;' and what style of worship should be adopted.[29] These represent only a sample of the key issues, but 'failure to deal with these questions and issues in a satisfactory manner could easily lead to another Nazarene-Ebionite split that would certainly weaken the movement, if not destroy it once again as it did in the fourth century. Because loyalty to Jewishness sometimes supercedes loyalty to the scriptures in the Messianic movement, this could occur very easily.'

Fruchtenbaum sees no practical difference between 'Hebrew Christian' and 'Messianic' theology.

> For most of the Jewish-Christian history in this [20th] century, the terms Hebrew / Jewish Christian and Messianic Jew were used interchangeably and without any real distinction. Only in the 1970s did various factions develop in the Jewish-Christian movement so that one may now distinguish between Hebrew /Jewish Christians and Messianic Jews, though there is no agreement as to just where that line should be drawn.[30]

Using the terms interchangeably, Fruchtenbaum argues that the purpose of both 'Gentile theology' and 'Messianic theology' is '[t]o develop a proper systematic theology based on the exegesis of scripture from the grammatical-historical hermeneutical principles in order to get to the actual meaning intended by the original writers, and in our case, particularly the New Testament writers.'[31] Previous Christian theology forced Jewish Christianity to become 'gentilized' so a 'Messianic theology' is needed that is

> [f]irst and foremost an attempt to develop a systematic theology deduced from the fact that the writers of the New Testament were Jews, and that the New Testament was written against a backdrop of first century Judaism, Jewish culture and a Jewish frame of reference.
>
> Secondly, Messianic theology is an attempt to maintain and to accommodate Jewishness in the face of a Gentile majority.
>
> Thirdly, since Messianic theology must be biblical theology, it can also correct Gentile theology by separating that which is biblical from that which is merely Gentile.[32]

---

[29] Ibid., 15.

[30] Ibid., 16. Fruchtenbaum assumes the distinction between the Nazarenes, who are taken by the Church Fathers to be orthodox, and the Ebionites, who are seen as heretical. It is not clear to later historians how easily this distinction can be made, as the same group may have been viewed variously by Church Fathers (and Church historians).

[31] Ibid., 6.

[32] Ibid.

A survey of the theology of early Jewish Christianity and recent Hebrew Christianity generates the 'basic questions and issues ahead of us in the development of a Messianic theology'. Fruchtenbaum's underlying presuppositions reflect a particular evangelical approach, based on the theological grid of Revised Dispensationalism, with an emphasis on a 'Jewish' rather than 'Gentile' approach to scripture, which is, however, neither defined nor explained.[33]

Shaping Postmissionary Messianic Jewish Theology

Mark Kinzer advocates a Torah-observant 'Postmissionary' form of Messianic Judaism. Messianic Judaism is a species of Judaism rather than a contextualised Christianity.[34] It has yet to be fully identified, differentiated and described. Its distinctives are unclear, and its theology embryonic. When we ask, 'What is Messianic Judaism?' we really mean 'What should Messianic Judaism be?' This is a 'theological question' about the divine purpose of Messianic Judaism and its relationship to the Church and the Jewish community. Kinzer expands the question, setting an agenda for further theological exploration.

> The question we are now asking ... requires sophisticated biblical exegesis, and much more. How do we understand certain biblical texts, whose meanings are at times ambiguous, and which reflect a social reality drastically different from our own, and then apply them to our world? How do we then relate to Jewish history after the destruction of the temple, and to the form of Judaism that crystallised around the *Mishnah* and the *Talmuds*? How do we think about the churches and their chequered history, especially in their dealings with Judaism and the Jewish people? These questions, and many others like them, are implicit in the deceptively simple question, 'What is Messianic Judaism?' To answer them, we must do far more than cite biblical proof-texts. We must engage in the disciplined intellectual activity that we call theology.[35]

Although Kinzer has yet to produce a systematic theology, his lecture course at the Messianic Jewish Theological Institute (MJTI) gives a 'working definition' of MJT:

---

[33] Arnold Fruchtenbaum's interpretation of Dispensationalism is best identified as Revised Dispensationalism, following the distinctions made between Classical, Revised and Progressive Dispensationalism adopted by Craig A. Blaising and Darrell L. Bock, *Progressive Dispensationalism* (Grand Rapids: Baker, 1993), 9–56, 'The Extent and Varieties of Dispensationalism'.

[34] Mark Kinzer, *The Nature of Messianic Judaism: Judaism as Genus, Messianic as Species* (West Hartford, CT: Hashivenu Archives, 2000), 1.

[35] Ibid., 2.

Messianic Jewish theology is disciplined reflection about God's character, will, and works, and about God's relationship to Israel, the Nations, and all creation, in the light of God's irrevocable election of Israel to be a kingdom of priests and a holy nation, and God's creative, revelatory, and redemptive work in Messiah Yeshua. Messianic Jewish theology is rooted in divine revelation (Torah), pursued in the context of Jewish communal life and tradition and in respectful conversation with the entire Christian theological tradition, and informed by prayer, by experience of the world, and by all available sources of human knowledge and understanding.[36]

Theology is 'a framework for integrating our understanding of God and our relationship to Him in a way that is true to Biblical Revelation, coherent with our knowledge of the world, and rooted in the life and tradition of the community of faith'.[37] Such a definition is framed to fit the 'substance of our own particular tradition' rather than a variety of religious traditions. The content of Messianic Jewish beliefs 'shape the mode in which we explore their meanings and implications'.[38]

Disciplined reflection involves *coherence, integration* and *dialectic*. Coherence is necessary as all theology attempts to 'rationally reconcile apparent contradictions internal to the sphere of Revelation'. Just as aggadic[39] literature deals with the reconciliation of discrepancies in conflicting texts of scripture, and the theology of the Church fathers recognises the 'need to grapple with the Oneness and Threeness of G-d, and the Divine and Human natures of Messiah,' so MJT must address the obvious tensions between 'our Jewish and Messianic commitments'.[40] Integration of MJT involves 'taking diverse elements and not only rendering them coherent, but also fashioning them into a whole, with a particular *shape*'.[41] 'The shape of a theology is in fact one of its most important features: how the various pieces are put together, what is at the centre and receives greatest stress, what is more peripheral and seen in relation to that centre.'[42]

Mark Kinzer shapes MJT by adopting the basic framework of traditional Judaism, but then interpreting it 'in a way that thoroughly integrates our Messianic faith, building it right into the infrastructure without replacing the existing materials'.[43]

---

[36] Mark Kinzer, 'The Shape of Messianic Jewish Theology (Session 1): What Is Messianic Jewish Theology?' (MJTI Lecture, Fuller Theological Seminary, 2005), 1.

[37] Ibid., 22.

[38] Ibid., 1.

[39] The Aggadah is the story component of Jewish literature, dealing with legends, interpretations of narrative portions of scripture.

[40] Ibid.

[41] Ibid.

[42] Ibid.

[43] Ibid., 8.

Much that goes under the name of MJT is derivative.

> It is common in Messianic Judaism to draw our basic theological framework from some existing system of Christian theology (Dispensational/Pentecostal-Charismatic/Baptist/etc.), dress it up in tallit and kippah (i.e., use Hebrew terminology), and then add or expand material addressing specific issues of importance to Messianic Jews (the land and state of Israel, the role of the Jewish people in the end times, the Rabbis and Torah observance, the place of Messianic Jews in the body of Messiah).[44]

Kinzer emphasises the significance of Yeshua interpreted in the light of the Tanakh and Jewish tradition. However, this can lead to the imbalance of 'those who revere Rabbinic tradition, and draw their theological framework from traditional Orthodoxy (or ultra-Orthodoxy), adding an occasional reference to Yeshua'.[45] Kinzer expresses his own Conservative Jewish roots here, in reaction to an unreconstructed Orthodoxy.

Dialectic avoids the risk that 'in seeking to bring coherence and integration to the data of Revelation we would iron out ambiguities and tensions which are essential to maintain'.[46] Theology, like reality in general, is beset with paradox, antinomy and irresolvable tension. The theological task confronts us with our human finitude and the limits of rationality. Both biblical and rabbinic thought is 'often highly dialectical'. The balance is maintained '[n]ot by formulating a position that is precisely nuanced and qualified, but instead by asserting absolutely and without qualification two extreme and apparently incompatible positions.'[47] For Kinzer 'Israel's enduring covenantal vocation and Yeshua's pivotal role in the divine plan are central *presuppositions* of Messianic Jewish theology, not the products of its reflective process. They function as criteria in assessing the truth-value of other beliefs. Thus, these are beliefs that provide the basic shape of Messianic Jewish theology.'[48] Without these two 'twin convictions' at the centre, the theology in question 'is no longer *Messianic Jewish* theology'. They must be a 'central presupposition *for* all theological reflection' rather than derived '*through* theological reflection'.

All theology is 'pursued in a particular context'. MJT's primary context is that of 'Jewish communal life and tradition' but in 'respectful conversation with the entire Christian theological tradition'. Thus the conceptual tools, structural framework and 'programmatic priorities' of any theology are 'largely determined by its social and historical context'.[49] MJT cannot claim

---

[44] Ibid.
[45] Ibid.
[46] Ibid., 2.
[47] Ibid.
[48] Ibid.
[49] Ibid., 5.

to be 'one definite, final and universal theology' as it is the theology of one particular faith community amongst many. It will adapt and change as its context changes. MJT does not replace other Christian or Jewish theologies, but informs and influences them. Whilst Messianic Jews 'would like to see all Jews become Messianic Jews,' current distinctives will remain. 'Thus, we are also not trying to replace Orthodox, Conservative and Reform Jewish theology!'[50] 'Even within Messianic Judaism, there can never be a single, definitive, and unchanging Messianic Jewish theology ... there will always be diversity within our movement, as in the Jewish world as a whole; we will also need to adapt to new circumstances.'[51]

Kinzer has given serious consideration to the development of MJT, and employs his methodology in his major study *Postmissionary Messianic Judaism* (PMJ).[52] Here he reviews the history of Hebrew Christianity and Messianic Judaism in the light of his requirements for 'Postmissionary Messianic Judaism'. In calling for a 'bilateral ecclesiology in solidarity with Israel that affirms Israel's covenant, Torah, and religious tradition' Kinzer applies his own tests to the theology of previous Hebrew Christianity and 'Missionary Messianic Judaism', finding them wanting.[53] However, his own proposals have yet to be formulated into a theological system.

This review of previous studies demonstrates the need for further work on the nature of MJT from the theological perspective of a reflective practitioner. Our goal in the chapters that follow is to survey the theological views of key practitioners of Messianic Judaism as they speak on issues vital to the development of its theology. This mapping task is a critical preliminary for the construction of MJT and necessary for the future growth of the Messianic movement and its theological maturity.

---

[50] Ibid., 6.

[51] Ibid.

[52] Mark Kinzer, *Postmissionary Messianic Judaism: Redefining Christian Engagement with the Jewish People* (Grand Rapids: Brazos, 2005), 263–302; 'From Missionary to Postmissionary Messianic Judaism'.

[53] Ibid., 299.

Chapter 4

The Doctrine of God in Messianic Jewish Theology

Introduction

No previous study has examined the question of God in Messianic Judaism. Yet this foundational topic is vital for an understanding of both the content and process of MJT. This chapter describes how Messianic Jews formulate their understanding of God, examining the method, resources and results of their discussion. It highlights issues of concern, and indicates where a Messianic Jewish understanding of God must explore new ground. However, before considering what Messianic Jews say about God, we must set the context within which their contribution is to be located.

God in Judaism, Christianity and Messianic Judaism

In both Judaism and Christianity the doctrine of God is central. 'There can be no disputing of the fact that the central idea of Judaism and its life purpose is the doctrine of the One Only and Holy God, whose kingdom of truth, justice and peace is to be universally established at the end of time.'[1] The *Shema* (Deut 6:4) declares the existence, identity, unity and authority of God, as do the first five of Maimonides' 13 Articles of Faith.[2] The Jewish understanding of God is seldom presented as systematic theology, but is addressed philosophically.[3] The being, activity and attributes of God form the outline for this discussion, which includes subcategories of God's unity and singularity, personhood, transcendence, immanence, eternal nature, omnipotence

---

[1] Kaufman Kohler, *Jewish Theology Systematically and Historically Considered* (New York: Macmillan, 1918), 15.

[2] Louis Jacobs, *Principles of the Jewish Faith: An Analytical Study* (New York: Basic Books, 1964), 14.

[3] Louis Jacobs, 'God' in *Contemporary Jewish Religious Thought*, ed. Arthur A. Cohen and Paul Mendes-Flohr (New York: Macmillan/Free Press, 1988), 290.

and omniscience. Jewish thought requires discussion of God's revelation, creation, providence and goodness in the light of biblical and traditional sources, and historic and contemporary philosophical questions.[4]

Christian theology pursues similar investigative pathways, with the doctrine of the Trinity lying at its heart. Discussion of theological method and the nature of revelation are the *prolegomena* to the systematic exposition of God's existence, personhood and perfections, in interaction with Christian tradition, Jewish thought and contemporary philosophy.[5] Both traditions affirm that the one God of Israel created the universe through his word, made humanity in his image, revealed himself to them and called them to know him and walk in his ways.[6] He has revealed his Torah to Israel, and will send the Messiah to redeem Israel and the nations in the last days. But Jewish tradition does not accept the revelation of God through his living Word and Incarnate Son. Jewish tradition sees the Trinitarian claim as unacceptably compromising the doctrine of the Unity of God.[7]

Messianic Jews have yet to develop a full 'Doctrine of God', for three reasons. First, Messianic Jews work without a developed theological and philosophical tradition, whereas 'mainstream' Judaism and Christianity have centuries' worth of systematic and philosophical reflection about 'God', worked out in diverse historical contexts, upon which they can draw. And whilst the recent 19th and 20th century forbears of the modern Messianic movement such as Joseph Rabinowitz, Paul Levertoff and Jacob Jocz were concerned with such issues, their works are not generally referred to by contemporary Messianic leaders.[8]

Secondly, Messianic Jews have focused on issues relevant to their own particular apologetic, pastoral and cultural needs. Where Messianic Jews

---

[4] Louis Jacobs, *A Jewish Theology* (London: DLT, 1973), 20.

[5] J.I. Packer, 'God' in *New Dictionary of Theology*, ed. Sinclair B. Ferguson, David F. Wright and J.I. Packer (Leicester: IVP, 1988), 274–77. Cf. Alistair McGrath, *Christian Theology: An Introduction*, 3rd ed. (Oxford: Blackwell, 2001), 265–317.

[6] For the sake of discussion, the traditional ascription of gender is made in describing God as 'he'. This follows the pattern of most Messianic Jewish Theology. The usage of the terms 'Man' and 'Mankind' is retained in quotations, but is otherwise resolved into more gender-inclusive language.

[7] Peter Ochs, 'The God of Jews and Christians' in *Christianity in Jewish Terms*, ed. Tikva Frymer-Kensky, David Novak, Peter Ochs, David Fox Sandmel and Michael A. Signer (Boulder: Westview Press, 2000), 60.

[8] Cf. Kai Kjær-Hansen, *Joseph Rabinowitz and the Messianic Movement* (Edinburgh: Handsel Press, 1995), 103. Cf. Dan Cohn-Sherbok, *Messianic Judaism* (London: Continuum, 2000), 21; Jorge Quiñónez. 'Paul Phillip Levertoff: Hebrew-Christian Scholar and Leader', *Mishkan* 37 (2002): 21–34; Jacob Jocz, *The Jewish People and Jesus Christ: A Study in the Controversy Between Church and Synagogue* (London: SPCK, 1949).

have discussed God, the emphasis has been on the Trinity and the Incarnation, and other aspects of the subject have followed the lines of Protestant Dogmatics.[9] Daniel Juster states that, 'There is little on [the general theology of God in MJT] since Messianic Jewish theology tends to focus on specific issues of concern, often in an apologetic context ... My section in *Jewish Roots* on God is limited.'[10]

Thirdly, the task of investigating both Jewish and Christian theological traditions, then synthesising them creatively and coherently into a new *theologoumenon* is a challenge. It is relatively easy to map the theological trajectories of Judaism and Christianity, demonstrating points of comparison, similarity, contrast and mutual influence or contra-distinction. But there have been few attempts to construct a doctrine of God that produces a coherent statement from a study of the two traditions.

Creedal Statements

The Creeds and Articles of Faith produced by Messianic Jewish organisations are uniformly orthodox from a Christian perspective. The first modern Messianic Jewish creed, composed by Joseph Rabinowitz for the 'Israelites of the New Covenant', affirms traditional aspects of God's nature. 'There is but one true and living God, not corporeal, without divisions, [unable to] be apprehended by the bodily senses, of great goodness, power and wisdom beyond comprehension, who creates, forms, makes and upholds everything by His Word and by His Holy Spirit. All things are from Him, all things in Him, and all things to Him.'[11]

Rabinowitz adopted the Hebrew translation of the Book of Common Prayer, omitting the phrase 'three Persons of one substance in the Godhead'.[12]

---

[9] Whilst half of Louis Jacobs' *A Jewish Theology* is given to discussing God (21–151) and Alistair McGrath's *Christian Theology: An Introduction* devotes some eighty pages (265–344), Messianic Jews give little space in their published works to this fundamental topic. David Stern devotes just two pages to the nature of God. Daniel Juster does not even have a section on God in his *Jewish Roots: A Foundation of Biblical Theology for Messianic Judaism*, although he devotes ten pages to the question 'Is the Messiah Divine?' The subjects of God, the Trinity or the nature of Messiah do not appear in *Voices of Messianic Judaism*, a collection of essays by Messianic Jewish thinkers 'confronting critical issues facing a maturing movement'. Similarly Dan Cohn-Sherbok, *The Jewish Faith* (London, SPCK: 1993), 29–71 and Kohler, *Jewish Theology*, 29–205.

[10] Dan Juster, e-mail message to author, March 26, 2005.

[11] Kai Kjær-Hansen, *Joseph Rabinowitz*, 103. Cf. Dan Cohn-Sherbok, *Messianic Judaism* (New York: Cassell, 2000), 21.

[12] Kjær-Hansen, *Joseph Rabinowitz*, 98.

He said that whilst Gentiles, who are accustomed to polytheism, need instruction that the three persons in the Holy scriptures are one, Jews find it very difficult to use the number three, even though they know from scripture that the One God is three Persons or 'personalities'. 'The believing Gentiles call the three persons in the Godhead: 'Father, Son and Holy Ghost'; we name them: 'One God, and His Word, and His Holy Spirit', which is the same. Why should the Christian Church burden Israel with doctrines, which were taught them from false conceptions of the Godhead?'[13]

Messianic Jewish organisations make similar statements. The MJAA basis of belief affirms: 'GOD – We believe that the Shema, "Hear O Israel, the Lord our God, the Lord is one" (Deut 6:4), teaches that God is *Echad*, as so declared: a united one, a composite unity, eternally existent in plural oneness.'[14] The UMJC similarly asserts, 'We believe that there is one G-d, eternally existent in three persons.'[15]

Detailed Presentations

Messianic Jewish contributions on the Doctrine of God reflect various approaches, methods and concerns.[16] Baruch Maoz begins with God's existence, essence and attributes.[17] The fatherhood of God, the divine and human natures of the Son, and the Person of the Holy Spirit follow. 'Important but wrong views' are refuted, as are heretical Christologies.[18] Maoz invites readers to adopt a 'Reformation approach' to scripture, as found in Calvin, the Puritans, and contemporary Reformed Dogmatics. The Westminster Confession is included.[19] Apart from translation of concepts into Hebrew there is little engagement with Jewish sources.

---

13 Ibid., 107–8.

14 MJAA, 'MJAA Doctrinal Basis, Article 2,' http://mjaa.org/StatementofFaith.html, (accessed August 8, 2005).

15 UMJC, 'UMJC Doctrinal Statement, Article 2,' http://www.umjc.org/main/documents/DoctrinalBasis.pdf (accessed August 8, 2005). The spelling 'G-d' is retained in Messianic Jewish materials where it occurs. It expresses concern that even in translation the name of God might not be profaned.

16 Many others were approached, but have not produced material on the topic.

17 Baruch Maoz, *Lessons on the Doctrine of God: A Tutorial on the Biblical Doctrine of God* (Rishon Le Tzion, Israel: Grace and Truth Congregation, 1997).

18 Eg. Atheism, Agnosticism, Polytheism, Dualism and Pantheism. The heretical Christologies are Docetism, Ebionism, Modalistic Monarchianism, Arianism, Nestorianism, Eutychianism and Appolinarianism.

19 'There is only one living and true God. He is infinite in his substance and perfection, a most pure spirit, invisible, without body, parts or passions, unchangeable, immense, eternal, incomprehensible, almighty, most wise, most holy, most free,

Arnold Fruchtenbaum expounds God as Father of the Son, of creation, heavenly beings, Israel and all believers.[20] He considers the love and revelation of God through the Son and the scriptures.[21] The Trinity is explained in the light of heresies.[22] Fruchtenbaum does not interact with Jewish philosophical tradition or Christian theological debate. His method is biblical exposition with little use of secondary sources.

David Stern finds that the traditional Christian and Jewish understandings of God are sufficient, up to the point where they are seen to divide. 'In theology proper, the study of the nature of God, one can begin with the elements common to Jewish and Christian understanding or 'Judeo-Christian tradition', – for example, the oneness, eternality, omnipotence and holiness of God. But soon one must deal with the two chief issues which divide, the divinity of the Messiah and the inner nature of God.'[23] For Stern, the historical interactions of Judaism and Christianity bring non-Messianic Judaism to the point of 'utterly denying the possibility of the incarnation and insisting on the absolute unity of God in a way that negates most Christian assertions about the [T]rinity.'[24] Yet Stern believes that there are 'hints within Judaism' that the opposition 'is not so monolithic'. Whilst Stern does not give a detailed presentation of the Doctrine of God, his views are found in comments on biblical passages in the *Jewish New Testament Commentary*.[25]

Louis Goldberg's chapter 'Specific observations on the Doctrine of God' engages with the classical sources of Judaism and Christianity.[26] First he

---

most absolute. He causes everything to work according to the determination of his unchangeable and most righteous will for his own glory. He and his will are most loving, gracious, merciful, long-suffering, abundant in goodness and truth. He forgives evil, rebellion and sin; the rewarder of those that diligently look for him, as well as most just and terrible in his judgments. He hates all sin and will by no means pronounce the guilty innocent.' Baruch Maoz, *Lessons on the Doctrine of God: A Tutorial on the Biblical Doctrine of God* (Rishon Le Tzion, Israel: Grace and Truth Congregation, 1997), 73.

[20] Arnold Fruchtenbaum, *God the Father* (Tustin: Ariel Ministries, 1985).

[21] Arnold Fruchtenbaum, *The Grace of God* (Tustin, Ariel Ministries, 1985); *The Bible and Divine Revelation* (Tustin: Ariel Ministries, 1983); *The Inspiration of the Scriptures* (Tustin: Ariel Ministries, 1983).

[22] Arnold Fruchtenbaum, *The Trinity* (Tustin: Ariel Ministries, 1985). The heresies are Arianism, Sabellianism, Socinianism, Unitarianism and Tritheism.

[23] David Stern, *Messianic Jewish Manifesto*, 93.

[24] Ibid.

[25] David Stern, *Jewish New Testament Commentary* (Jerusalem: Jewish New Testament Publications, 1992), *passim*.

[26] Louis Goldberg, 'A Messianic Jewish Theology' (manuscript held at Jews for Jesus Memorial Research Library, San Francisco, 2003), 24–195. To be published as *God, Torah, Messiah: The Messianic Theology of Dr Louis Goldberg*, ed. Richard A. Robinson (San Fransisco: Purple Pomegranate Productions, forthcoming).

formulates and explains propositions about God from the biblical material. Then problems are addressed, and the 'practical value' for the believer is emphasised. The material is well suited for discipleship and catechesis.

Mark Kinzer's unpublished lectures on 'God and the Messiah' incorporate classical and contemporary Jewish and Christian material, demonstrating a reflective approach to the construction of a doctrine of God.[27] Kinzer's published work does not address the question directly, but his recent *Postmissionary Messianic Judaism* has a section on the nature of Revelation.[28]

Revelation

Before considering the nature and being of God some discussion of revelation is necessary. Whilst no detailed doctrine of revelation has been proposed, and the topic has yet to be fully developed, some broad outlines to the subject may be discerned.

General and Special Revelation (Maoz)

For Baruch Maoz natural revelation has limitations, as the evidence of nature is not sufficient to give us full knowledge of God. It is useful for those who do not accept the authority of scripture as revelatory, 'although the knowledge it offers is very tenuous and very limited'. 'It can hint something about the existence of God and a very little bit about his nature.'[29]

Natural revelation does show us that belief in God is not 'some kind of otherworldly conviction' and 'reminds us of the value of everything to be found in this universe'. But a more reliable revelation is required. 'In order to know God securely we need more than a revelation, we need a revelation that is reliable, that can interpret itself.'[30] And the only authoritative revelation is found in the scriptures. 'The Bible is God's relation [*sic*] of himself to mankind ... the Bible meets one of mankind's greatest needs by telling about God, and by doing so in the most reliable and secure way possible: It is God speaking about himself in the Bible, using the clearest means that man can understand – words.'[31] Without the Bible we would not know the existence of God, his infinite nature, his role as creator and sustainer of the universe,

---

[27] Mark Kinzer, 'God and the Messiah: Course Outline, MJ518' (Messianic Jewish Theological Institute, Fuller School of Theology, 2004).

[28] Mark Kinzer, *Postmissionary Messianic Judaism: Redefining Christian Engagement with the Jewish People* (Grand Rapids: Brazos, 2005), 38–46: 'Theology and History: Divine Action in Human History'.

[29] Maoz, *Lessons on the Doctrine of God*, 21, 'Sources of Knowledge of God'.

[30] Ibid.

[31] Ibid., 21–22.

his will, wisdom and personhood. From scripture we learn of his sovereignty and purposefulness, his love and triune nature. In scripture we 'learn that God is indeed more than a person, he is a trinity of persons – an eternal society of love, wisdom, will and self-consciousness that does not depend in any way on the universe he has created.'[32]

Following the Reformation teaching on the perspicuity of scripture and the role of the Holy Spirit in making real the truths of scripture, Maoz affirms that knowledge of God is only possible through God's gracious act of self-revelation. Without the help of the Holy Spirit we are 'limited to a very painful degree in our ability to understand God, who is infinite'. We have an innate tendency to twist and distort what we do not understand.

> God the Holy Spirit expands our understanding, brings truths declared in Scripture to our attention, helps us to understand the relation of one truth to another and overcome our sinful tendency to distort the truth. But all his work in this relation has to do with our understanding what God has said about himself in the Bible. The Holy Spirit does not reveal to us truths about God that are not in the Bible.[33]

Maoz's approach is clear, consistent and programmatic, but with no recourse to Jewish tradition or theological method. And whilst acknowledging the value of Christian tradition, he believes that it is only helpful in giving a deeper understanding of the meaning of *scripture* – the Reformation principle of *sola scriptura* is uppermost in Maoz's thoughts.

The Supremacy of Special Revelation (Fruchtenbaum, Stern, Goldberg and Juster)

Arnold Fruchtenbaum also distinguishes between *general revelation* and *special revelation*.[34] God reveals himself through nature, providence, the preservation of nations and individuals, and conscience. But, in good Protestant fashion, he maintains that general revelation cannot offer salvation, only being able to bring condemnation.[35] Therefore special revelation is needed to correctly interpret the truths of general revelation, to 'furnish man with a revelation of salvation', and harmonise what appear as 'contradictory elements' in general revelation such as the goodness and severity of God. God's special revelation takes place through theophanies such as the 'Angel of Jehovah' and the presence of the *Shechinah* glory; through miracles, direct communication through audible voices, the casting of lots, dreams and

---

[32] Ibid., 22.

[33] Ibid., 18.

[34] Fruchtenbaum, *The Bible*, 1.

[35] Ibid., 5.

visions; and by means of angels, the incarnation, and the scriptures.[36] The scriptures contain a partial revelation of God, but this is sufficient to bring us to redemption and is all God has chosen to let us know 'for now'.'The Scriptures are the Word of God, the written revelation of God, by which one can rightfully interpret all the other forms of revelation.'[37]

Scripture itself is progressively revealed, as God chose not to give the 'entire Word at one time.' 'Step by step, the plan and purpose of God was unfolded. Each step was completely flawless and completely whole until the final revelation came. Man now has a complete revelation in the written Word of God, and there is no need to know that which is beyond the scriptures.'[38] Fruchtenbaum does not discuss the status of Jewish or Christian tradition as revelation, but affirms the Protestant doctrine of *sola scriptura*.

For David Stern, general revelation is sufficient for us to acknowledge that God exists: 'If you do not know God, it is not God's fault but yours. The characteristics of God that make his existence self-evident, **his eternal power and his divine nature,** are **known** to you, because God has made it plain to you.'[39] However, revelation by word is needed for any knowledge of God:

> In days gone by, when the *Tanach* was being written, God spoke: 'Thus saith the Lord!' Some people claim to believe in God but not that he 'spoke'. A moment's reflection will cast a shadow on the viability of this position. If God did not 'speak,' if he has not revealed anything specific, if there are none of his words extant which can guide a person toward true knowledge about God, humanity and the relationship between them, then God is unconnected with life, irrelevant.[40]

Louis Goldberg similarly affirms God's self-revelation in scripture, as its key affirmation is not the existence of God but the fact that he has spoken. 'Of course, if God has spoken, He must exist and His revelation may properly be used as an argument for this existence. But in the Bible the emphasis is always on The Revelation, not upon the rational uses to which it may be put.'[41]

Daniel Juster also considers scripture to be the supreme medium of revelation from which we know God as personal.

---

[36] Ibid., 7, 12.

[37] Ibid., 12.

[38] Ibid., 13.

[39] David Stern, *JNTC*, 331 (Romans 1:18–20). Words in bold refer to the biblical text on which the commentary is based.

[40] Ibid., 661 (Heb 1:1).

[41] Goldberg, *Messianic Jewish Theology*, 42.

The Scriptures tell us, 'In the beginning God created the heavens and the earth' (Genesis 1:1). The biblical description of God is a description of an infinite being of unlimited intelligence and moral perfection. Only Scripture gives the revelation of a personal, infinite God. To say God *is personal* means He has real attributes of self-consciousness, intelligence, will, and the ability to act, judge, and relate to other people in special ways. [42]

Juster refers to the traditional Jewish discussion of God's self-revelation of thirteen attributes (Ex. 34:6–7).[43] The picture is 'sharpened' as we progress through scripture. God 'identifies with the outcast and the dispossessed' in Exodus. He reveals his Law, showing that he is a God of the 'highest moral standards.' 'He is clearly committed to truth, marital fidelity, business honesty, honouring parents, caring for the orphan and widow, justice in the courts, charity for the needy and care for the alien (foreigner).'[44]

God's moral nature and holiness lead to his anger and judgement of our sin, but his mercy always precedes judgement, and it is only when Israel has refused God's mercy that judgement strikes. He is both a loving Father and a severe Judge, 'depending on where we stand with Him'. The history of Israel 'gives us an extensive revelation of God' but it is not the 'fullest revelation of God'. This is found in Yeshua, because the image of God in Man is marred by the fall. It is only in focusing on the Messiah that the true nature of God may be seen.

Revelation in Yeshua (Juster)

God reveals in part through the cosmos, human nature and direct speaking to his servants. Yet this can be 'distorted and inadequate', as can miracles, providence and the life and experience of his people. But the Torah and New Covenant are perfect in original form, and the Messiah is the 'complete, perfect and final form of God's revelation of Himself'.[45]

God's revelation in scripture does not contain all knowledge, but is sufficient and complete in itself for our need of a relationship with him.

> The epitomy of that revelation is the Messiah Himself, whereby in him all the fullness of deity dwells in bodily form (Col 2:9) … While the written Torah is held sacred and supreme, Yeshua the Messiah represents the highest revelation of

---

[42] Daniel C. Juster, *Growing to Maturity: A Messianic Jewish Discipleship Guide*, 2nd ed. (Rockville: Union of Messianic Jewish Congregations Press, 1985), 25–29. Sections B 'The Person of the Messiah' and C 'The Work of the Messiah' take up the bulk of the chapter (30–44).

[43] Juster, *Growing to Maturity*, 2.

[44] Ibid., 27.

[45] Ibid., 53.

God, and it is a reminder that He is the living Torah, or Word, and that in him 'are hidden all the treasures of wisdom and knowledge' (Col 2:3). We cannot afford to ignore him; he has much to teach us![46]

Canonical, Cumulative and Communal Revelation (Kinzer)

Mark Kinzer's treatment of revelation considers the place of tradition in the interpretation of scripture. His definition links event and interpretation.

> **Revelation:** a divine action imparting knowledge of God and God's will, exe-cuted through (a) historical events and prophetic encounters in the life of Israel; (b) communal reflection on those events and encounters in the light of Israel's tra-dition; (c) a canonical text that describes those events and encounters within the context of the community's reflection upon them; and (d) communal reflection on the canonical text in the light of God's ongoing historical engagement with Israel and the Nations.[47]

'Revelation' refers both to the 'foundational canonical text', and to the 'on-going process of reflecting upon it or its implications for daily life'. It is a 'divine action', God's act of self-disclosure. What God reveals is not detached facts or propositions, but his own will and person. The means of revelation are historical events, prophetic encounters, communal reflection and communal tradition which 'grows out of communal reflection on his-torical events and prophetic encounters, culminating in a canonical text'. 'Revelation is thus a complex act involving both God, and human beings in community, relating to one another in a sustained manner over a period of time. This is why a theology rooted in Revelation must be pursued within the context of a community and tradition which participates in the revela-tory event/process.'[48]

Revelation can be understood in four ways. As *existential challenge* it is the 'foundation of all biblically-based theological traditions', bringing the con-viction that God has '[e]ntered into our world, engaged human beings in a living dialogue, and has revealed and continues to reveal something of Himself, His will, His works, and His relationship to us in a way that human beings can understand.'[49]

Following Abraham Heschel, Kinzer states that revelation brings the responsibility to respond appropriately in obedience and faith to the 'per-sonal direction for how we must live our life' which is why '*halakhah* takes

---

[46] Ibid.

[47] Mark Kinzer, *The Shape of Messianic Jewish Theology: Session #1: What Is Messianic Jewish Theology?*, 3.

[48] Ibid.

[49] Ibid.

practical precedence over *agaddah'*. Theology is not a 'detached science', but a 'personal struggle to conform our minds to what G-d has revealed and continues to reveal about Himself, His will, His works, and His relationship to us, and what it means for us and our community in our present historical and social juncture.'[50]

As *story* revelation is a 'biblical mode of presenting truth' that is not primarily abstract and propositional but 'concrete, particularist, and narratival'. The series of stories in scripture constitute a 'grand Master-Story' which 'grounds our individual and corporate sense of who we are, what our lives mean, why we live, and what is our destiny'. It is a canonical narrative that focuses on the role of Israel, Yeshua and the Messianic Community.

Scriptural revelation should be heard as a *multi-vocal chorus*, with the 'real differences' acknowledged and respected. There should be no 'rush to harmonize' but 'we should first seek to hear each voice in its own distinct pitch', recognising how different theological traditions in Judaism and Christianity have emphasised different aspects of scripture to answer the needs of differing contexts. Revelation in scripture must be understood as 'multi-layered, with each unit having many possible levels of meaning'. 'Each Jew at Sinai hears something different; it is the sum total of what is heard that constitutes Revelation in its fullness. This is the traditional Jewish view, but not so common in either conservative evangelical thought (especially dispensationalism) or historical-grammatical exegesis.'[51]

Finally, revelation must be seen as a *contextualized message with universal implications*. Biblical revelation, as the set of stories describing the 'living encounter between God and a particular group of finite, historical human beings' is itself 'human and limited, while at the same time being a genuine message from Beyond'.

Scripture, like the 'enfleshed Word', is both human and divine. Its inspiration is corporate and developmental rather than merely individual, resulting from a 'divine-human partnership' rather than as a 'passive/mechanical' response. Whilst scripture is 'inspired, infallible, and a uniquely authoritative tradition', it is still a 'species' within the 'broader genus' of 'Tradition'. Therefore the authority and status of rabbinic and Church tradition is 'bound to one's participation in and identification with a community which respects that tradition'. 'If one believes that a particular community is G-d-ordained and G-d-preserved, then it is reasonable to see the overall development of that community's tradition as divinely superintended so that it might serve as a fit vehicle for the interpretation and application of Revelation.'[52]

---

[50] Ibid.

[51] Ibid., 4.

[52] Ibid., 5.

For Kinzer, the doctrine of Revelation calls for a sophisticated engage-ment with both Jewish and Christian tradition. As shall be observed in his discussion of the status of the oral law, this leaves tradition and community with significant authority in their mediation of the scriptures and their role as the interpretive medium through which the scriptures may be under-stood. [53]

The Existence of God

MJT, in line with much Jewish and Christian tradition, does not attempt to prove the existence of God, regarding it as a 'first truth' that is axiomatic for all further discussion. This truth is asserted by scripture and confirmed by philosophical arguments for the existence of God.

God's existence as a 'given'

Whilst there are some rational supports for the claim that 'God exists' these merely confirm and illustrate the fundamental given, that God *is*. For Baruch Maoz the 'assumption with which the Bible begins' is the existence of God. It is taken for granted as an 'obvious fact' on which everything that can be said about God is based. 'There may be discussion as to what kind of God exists, but atheism – the denial that God or gods of some kind exist – is a modern aberration that preceding generations never imagined. The scrip-tures not only assume that God exists, but that all mankind knows that he exists, even if such knowledge is unconsciously suppressed (Rom 1:19–32; 2:15).'[54]

For Maoz God's existence is evidenced by the cosmological, teleological and anthropological arguments he goes on to discuss, but these arguments are not conclusive, and must still be accepted on the basis of faith.[55] 'These are the basic arguments used to support belief in God as he is described in the Bible. It is important to remember that these supports are not conclusive proofs and that the existence of God cannot be proven, just as many other important things in life cannot be proven.'[56] Nevertheless Maoz is emphatic: 'God exists, period. Hallelujah!'[57]

Daniel Juster also finds the existence of God self-evident.[58] The scriptures do not seek to prove this, but assume it by the evidence of creation, and the

---

[53] Cf. Chapter 6 below.
[54] Maoz, *Lessons*, 15.
[55] Ibid., 18–20.
[56] Ibid., 20.
[57] Ibid., 25.
[58] Juster, *Jewish Roots*, 25–29.

miraculous history of Israel in the call and blessing of Abraham, and the exodus from Egypt.[59] Whilst 'the existence of an intelligent creator God is an obvious conclusion from the observation of the created order,' knowledge of God through creation and conscience is limited, and the 'fuller knowledge' of what God is like is only obtained through the Bible. Here God's character is revealed more comprehensively through his words and works.

For David Stern too the existence of God is axiomatic and does not need to be proved. 'Only "the fool has said in his heart 'there is no God'," (Psalms 14:1, 53:2[1]) – meaning not "no God exists" but "no God exists who actively concerns himself with people's thoughts and deeds and judges them." This is as close as the Bible comes to "proving the existence of God," for there is no reason why it *should* prove it.'[60]

Louis Goldberg also does not make proving the existence of God a primary concern. 'The question of whether God exists or does not will not be a major burden in this book.'[61] Nevertheless, Goldberg does ask two questions about God's existence, the first being whether there is a God. This question falls within the area of the philosophy of religion, and he thinks that how one answers it is dependent on one's choice of pre-suppositions. 'Hopefully, those engaged in the pursuit of whether God exists or not will choose the presuppositions that lead them to assert that He does.'[62] The second question, 'If He does exist, has He revealed Himself?' lies within the field of apologetics, and again, the choice of presuppositions about the possibility of revelation is critical: 'And, once again, the idea is to choose the set of presuppositions that will best answer the problems we face and will therefore assert He does exist and that He has revealed himself. In doing theology, however, a study of this subject does presuppose God exists and that He has revealed Himself.'[63]

For Goldberg it is significant that both Torah and New Covenant *begin with God*, rather than philosophical issues. 'Since man, who is a sinner, cannot wait for the settlement of all the intellectual problems of Theism, and since the Bible was written for sinful men, it brings the reader without delay into the presence of God – "**In the beginning God**" (Gen 1:1).'[64]

Without the existence of God, there is no *adequate* explanation for the origin and existence of the universe; the moral and intellectual nature of humanity; and the universal idea of God. The Bible, Yeshua and our own experience of God cannot be adequately accounted for. Yet whilst the Bible does present 'arguments' for the existence of God, they are direct appeals

---

[59] Ibid., 25.

[60] Stern, *JNTC*, 331 (Rom 1:18–20).

[61] Goldberg, *Messianic Jewish Theology*, 37.

[62] Ibid.

[63] Ibid.

[64] Ibid.

rather than logical arguments. Its primary method is 'direct and practical', appealing not to reason but to faith. Like a rose, whose beauty and fragrance are 'immediate channels of revelation' which are sufficient for those who are 'unspoilt by agnostic speculation, so also there are channels of revelation concerning God which are immediate. "God hath spoken" – concerning Himself, His nature, and His work – in ways which are more universally accessible and convincing than in the case of any other fact of human experience.'[65]

God's existence, whilst it cannot be proved, is a necessary premise from which to move forward, and the basis on which to discuss His nature, attributes and actions. But before we do that a word is in order about the *unique nature* of divine existence in MJT.

God's Self-Existence (Goldberg)

Goldberg affirms the 'self-existence of God', presenting biblical passages such as Ex. 3:14 for consideration. When Moses is asked the name of the God who sent him, his announcement of the Tetragrammaton signifies God's self-existence.

> What is noteworthy, this word is related to YHWH, the name for God, LORD, not pronounced today by all Jewish people, including Messianic Jews and read instead as: *Adonai*. The name is derived from *hayah*, or, 'to be', and therefore it forms the basis of speaking of God as ever continuing and so, inherent, therefore, from this verb, is the self-existence of His very being.[66]

Goldberg summarises the doctrine of God's self-existence: His existence lies 'wholly within Himself'. He is not dependant on anything external, and is an 'absolute existing being', whereas humans are 'contingent' beings. God has his existence 'in His very being.' That is to say that God's existence is not dependent upon anything outside of God's own being. Creation, on the other hand, humanity included, is 'dependent upon God for life itself'.

Goldberg comments on the *practical value* of this 'facet of truth'. It is a comfort and encouragement to the believer. Our lives are not 'streams to be cut off when we die' but are *united to the self-existent Father*. 'Because of Yeshua's promise that the dead in Him will one day hear his voice and that we shall live, that is, be raised from the dead with a glorified body, nevermore to be separated from Him, in a sense, we are tied to this God who is self-existent.'[67] This is a fruitful theological idea which warrants further reflection.

---

[65] Goldberg, *Messianic Jewish Theology*, 41.
[66] Ibid., 60.
[67] Ibid., 61.

The Nature of God

In exploring the nature of God, MJT adopts the categories of Jewish and Christian thought, focusing on the personhood, essence, characteristics and attributes of God. These headings organise the discussion.

The Personhood of God (Maoz and Goldberg)

Baruch Maoz argues for the personhood of God by analogy with the personhood of humanity. A person is a being that has self-consciousness, moral conscience, will and intelligence. Because humans are persons, Maoz argues that '[t]he being that caused the universe to exist and who gave it its purposefulness must be at the very least a person himself ... I say "must" because we have already concluded that this Being is the cause of everything else. I say "at least" for the simple the reason that the cause must be greater than what it has caused.'[68]

Louis Goldberg has problems with the notion of 'personality' (by which he means what we are calling 'personhood'): '[P]ersonality is perhaps the most important fact in the world as far as living beings are concerned, yet, in spite of its certainty and effects, no fact is more elusive as to its definition.'[69] He feels that older definitions of personhood, focused on knowledge, emotion and will, are inadequate in the light of recent scientific studies that claim that such features are found in non-human animals also. 'Modern definitions' dispute the separate existence or entity of the mind, or soul, or any other intangible entity, and reduce what theologians have traditionally understood as the soul to functions of the brain that can be measured by scientific means. Goldberg proposes a 'biblical definition' of personality as 'a name given to the nucleus of a definite group of functions or characteristics,' both of God and man.[70] For his purposes Goldberg considers aspects of the personhood of God under the headings of life, goodness, intelligence, purpose, agency, freedom, self-consciousness and emotional capacity.

Although not a feature of MJT writings to date, in Jewish and Christian tradition discussion of the personal nature of God must also take account of the issues of anthropomorphism and the apophatic language of the *via negativa*.[71] The God of Israel is the transcendent creator of all that is, and consequently cannot be contained by human language and concepts. All language about *this* God will therefore fall short of the reality to which it points. So God is personal but care must be taken in supposing that God is a

---

[68] Maoz, *Lessons*, 19–20.
[69] Goldberg, *Messianic Jewish Theology*, 23.
[70] Ibid.
[71] Cf. Jacobs, *Jewish Theology*, 'The *Via Negativa* and God as *Person*', 38–55; Kohler, *Jewish Theology*, 'The Essence of God', 72–81.

'person' *in the same way* that creatures can be persons. MJT needs to fully assimilate such thinking if it is to avoid falling into some elementary traps in its God-Talk.

The Essence of God (Maoz and Goldberg)

For Baruch Maoz a 'short but reliable' description of the essence of God is 'the self-existent, eternal and indivisibly one spirit who exists in a Trinity of Persons that are equal in essence and in attributes, although not in deeds.'[72]

Maoz separates the essential characteristics of God from the inessential when asking the question 'What kind of God exists?' He defines his terms: 'The two important terms we will be using in this lesson are 'essence' (*mahut*) and 'person' (*havaya*). The word essence refers to those characteristics of the nature of God without which God would not be God. Both kinds of attributes are included in the essence. The word 'person' refers to distinctions within the Godhead.'[73] The essence of God, for Maoz, cannot be reduced to one quality such as holiness, but depends on the combination of several incommunicable attributes. 'The Bible also tells us that God is all-knowing, almighty, sovereign, present everywhere, holy, wise, loving, good, true and righteous. All these characteristics are of the essence of Godhood. If any one of these characteristics was not true of God, God would not be God.'[74]

By contrast, Louis Goldberg believes the essence of God to be his holiness. 'In His essence, God is holy and one of his attributes is his righteousness.'[75] God's holiness is his defining quality. 'For example, He can never lie, or lead anyone to do likewise because that would go against his righteousness and underlying it all, His holiness, which is the essence of His very being.'[76]

Goldberg is aware of the discussion about the essence and attributes of God in Jewish and Christian theology. Some see Love as the essence of God because of the statement 'God is love' (1 Jn 4:9). But, he observes, 'most theologians insist that the essence of God is holiness because He is Holy. From what has been observed from the scripture already, holiness seems to be the dominant theme when speaking of God's very being, as in Isaiah 6:1–3; and 57:15; and other passages.'[77] The holiness of God is, for Goldberg, not merely an attribute, but 'His essence', as it describes 'who God is fundamentally'. 'From this centre flow all the attributes, and yet, while a person can

---

[72] Maoz, *Lessons*, 35.
[73] Ibid., 22.
[74] Ibid., 76.
[75] Goldberg, *Messianic Jewish Theology*, 27.
[76] Ibid., 30.
[77] Ibid., 79.

understand some of the aspects of holiness, it will be quite difficult to describe this essence from a positive stance.'[78]

Both Maoz and Goldberg here reflect and summarise the language of Jewish and Christian dogmatics, without pursuing any new lines of investigation.

The Attributes of God (Maoz)

Baruch Maoz defines divinity as the sum of the attributes of God. '*Divinity* (*elohut*) is that mass of attributes that make God what he is and distinguishes him from all and any other beings. By definition, divinity is indivisible and cannot be imparted, earned or taken because it includes the attribute of self-existence that neither began nor can end.'[79] Within the Divinity there are communicable and incommunicable attributes. Incommunicable attributes are those which are true of God alone, and distinguish him from his creatures.

> After all, the difference between us and our maker has to do with what he and we are. It is an absolute difference, not only a relative one. Communicable attributes are those, which, although true of God, are also true in a relative sense of man, who bears the image of God. All of God's attributes are those qualities without which God would not be God. They exist in God by necessity, simply because he is God.[80]

The characteristics of God are interrelated, flowing from his greatness and glory. They do not exist separately from him. 'It is important that we do not think as if these characteristics are parts of God or that they exist in any way apart from his person. God is one. There is but one God and all his wonderful characteristics are united into one in him. His goodness is almighty and his endless power is always good, and wise, and eternal.'[81] Maoz thus divides the attributes of God along the conventional lines of Christian and Jewish thought. The incommunicable attributes are those of omnipotence, omniscience and sovereignty. The communicable attributes are those of wisdom, love, holiness, truth and righteousness. Humanity only shares in the communicable characteristics, with finite knowledge, limited power, and little control of his life and circumstances.

---

[78] Ibid., 76.

[79] Baruch Maoz, 'Lectures on The Person of Christ – Part One – Introduction' (unpublished, 2003), 5.

[80] Maoz, *Lessons*, 22.

[81] Ibid., 37.

In spite of this, his abilities and characteristics are aspects of the image of God in man. God's communicable characteristics are also to be found in man, although to a much lower degree than they are found in God. Man can be relatively holy, wise, loving, good, true and righteous. These, too, are aspects of the image of God in man.[82]

Maoz's discussion of the attributes of God assumes, but does not directly refer to, the centuries of reflection on divine attributes in both Jewish and Christian traditions. Little has been said on this topic by other Messianic thinkers. The contributions of Maimonides and Aquinas, Barth and contemporary Jewish thinkers, are absent from the current discussion about divine attributes in MJT.

The Unity of God

MJT has keen interest in the unity of God, as it constructs its discourse between the two theological traditions of Judaism and Christianity. Louis Jacobs notes that 'Trinitarians deny that their belief is non-monotheistic but from the Jewish point of view the Christian doctrine offends against the pure monotheistic principle.'[83] The way in which MJT negotiates this antinomy is observed below. The manner of discussion is more apologetic than systematic.[84]

A Trinity of Persons (Maoz)

For Baruch Maoz God is indivisibly One: 'There is only one God. The Bible declares it, logic confirms it and the universe adds its confirmation of this truth. To say that there is one God is equal to saying that all the divine attributes are united in one God.'[85]

However, this One God exists as Trinity. Maoz stresses the difference between the Hebrew words *yachid* and *echad*, challenging (but without directly referring to) the Maimonidean use of the term in the 2nd Principle of Faith. For Maimonides God's Oneness is absolute in that it is *not composed of parts*. For Maoz, on the other hand, God's oneness is a *composite yet undivided unity* of Father, Son and Spirit.

---

[82] Ibid., 46.

[83] Louis Jacobs, *Principles of the Jewish Faith* (New York, Basic Books, 1964), 71.

[84] Cf. Burt Yellin, Rachmiel Frydland and Marvin Rosenthal, 'Studies Supporting The Triune Nature of G-d,' http://www.messianic-literary.com/trinity.htm (accessed June 2007).

[85] Maoz, *Lessons*, 28.

The Bible speaks of a solitary one with the Hebrew world *YACHID* (Gen. 22:2). But that is not the common biblical word used to describe God. The more common word is *ECHAD*. *ECHAD* means more than just 'one', it means a composite one. For example, we read that the evening and the morning combine to make the one day (Gen 2:24) ... That is a bit similar to what God is like. [86]

God's unity implies his omnipresence, the indivisibility of his attributes, and his lack of internal contradiction. His unity is still 'pure and simple' and in 'harmony with himself.' He is without inner contradictions, and his perfections of will and ability, wisdom and love, are in complete harmony. 'God is one. He is at one with himself. In other words, he is a perfect one – a characteristic in which he differs from everything else that exists.'[87] God's oneness also shows him to be set apart from his creation. 'God's oneness is within himself. We are not saying that he is one with the world because that would be equal to saying that God is the world and the world is God. Hinduism and other forms of eastern mysticism teach this, but the Bible tells us that God is distinct from the world. He made it. He works in it. But he is not part of it.'[88]

For Maoz the doctrine of the Trinity does not conflict with the unity of God. He exists as a Trinity of Persons – Father, Son and Spirit – which are his very essence.[89] Maoz admits this is 'something well beyond our understanding,' and whilst many attempts can be made to understand it, '[t]he Bible simply assumes the Trinity, just as it assumes that God exists. It never argues the point. We believe in the Trinity because the Bible teaches us to do so. Whatever human wisdom has to say about the matter, we know that the highest form of wisdom is to believe what God has revealed in his word.'[90] Whilst 'Trinity' is not a biblical *word*, the *concept* is biblical and so the term can be used – if handled with wisdom – to describe what the Bible teaches. 'If a term truly expresses what the Bible teaches, there is no reason on earth why we should not use it. "Trinity" is just such a term. It is shorthand, a summary of what the Bible teaches about God's mysterious and wonderful nature: the One God is a Trinity (essence) of Persons (*havayot*): Father, Son and Holy Spirit.'[91]

For Maoz the doctrine of the Trinity, like other truths about God, is 'beyond human discovery or proof'. Humanity can only know what God chooses to reveal. The 'plural' nature of God is demonstrated from the Hebrew scriptures, following the traditional pattern of Christian

---

[86] Ibid.
[87] Ibid.
[88] Ibid.
[89] Ibid., 30.
[90] Ibid.
[91] Ibid., 31.

apologetics. The plural term for God (*Elohim*), the occurrence of plural verbs (Gen 1:26, etc.), the Angel of the LORD, references to the coming Messianic figure as 'God', and the threefold invocation of the name of God in the *Shema* (Deut 6:4) all point to God's 'plural' nature, despite the attempts of some to give alternative interpretations. Maoz does not deal with alternative traditions of interpretation, or the hermeneutical and historico-critical issues that arise from such argumentation.

Maoz challenges the modalism that claims 'the one and uncomposite God appeared in human history in different forms, once as Father, once as Son and once as Spirit'. Not so! The three Persons are 'distinct' and not to be confused. And, whilst all three Persons are equally divine, there is an 'order' within the Godhead. 'So there is not only a glorious plurality in the Godhead, but an eternal order. The Father commands, the Son accomplishes and the Spirit applies. Everything that the Son does, he does according to the will of the Father, and everything that the Spirit does is done in order to glorify the Son.'[92] This 'eternal community of equally divine Persons' is the 'essence of the Godhead'. 'The doctrine of the Trinity makes sure that God is God, perfect and complete in himself, because it shows again how free God is from all he has made. The Father loves the Son and the Spirit, and each loves the other through all eternity in a divine joy that none of us can ever understand.'[93]

Maoz's doctrine of the unity of God is wholly orthodox from a Christian perspective, yet this is at the expense of any substantial engagement with Jewish thought or expression that goes beyond the biblical data. His matrix of interpretation leaves little room for new articulation of Trinitarian concepts.

Echad and Yachid (Fruchtenbaum)

Arnold Fruchtenbaum gives a definition of the unity of the Godhead that allows for Trinitarian thought.[94] 'Perhaps the best and simplest definition of the Trinity is that there is only one God, but in the unity of the Godhead there are three eternal and co-equal Persons; the same in substance or essence, but distinct in subsistence or existence.'[95]

Yet Maimonides' second Principle of Faith excludes the possibility of a plural unity. In declaring that God's unity was unlike that of any other, his choice of the word *yachid* rather than *echad* was deliberate. 'The Rambam [Rabbi Moses ben Maimon] was well versed in classical Hebrew and surely

---

[92] Ibid., 33.
[93] Ibid., 34.
[94] Arnold Fruchtenbaum, *Jewishness and the Trinity* (Tucson: Ariel Ministries, 1985); 'Creeds in Judaism' in *Mishkan* 34 (2001), 40–46.
[95] Fruchtenbaum, *The Trinity*, 1.

would have recognized that the word *echad* is ambiguous as to the nature of oneness and did not always carry the concept of an absolute oneness (Gen. 2:25).[96] The choice of *yachid* was deliberate, as the meaning of the word did not have primarily a 'numerical emphasis' but stressed uniqueness. Maimonides employed it to rule out the possibility of one being sharing in the divinity of another. 'Thus to eliminate the ambiguity or any possibility of a plurality or Trinity in the Godhead he chose to use *yachid* which conveys an absolute oneness.'[97]

Fruchtenbaum does not discuss the context of the Maimonidean project to harmonise Aristotelian thought with biblical revelation, but assumes the choice of *yachid* is an anti-Trinitarian move.

Biblical Trinitarianism (Stern)

David Stern, like Maoz, recognises that the term 'Trinity' is not scriptural. 'The word "Trinity" appears nowhere in the New Testament; it was developed later by theologians trying to express profundities which God has revealed about himself.'[98] Such profundities are the result of further illumination beyond what is revealed in scripture, although they are found there in outline. 'The New Testament does not teach tritheism, which is belief in three gods. It does not teach unitarianism, which denies the divinity of Yeshua the Son and of the Holy Spirit. It does not teach modalism, which says that God appears sometimes as the Father, sometimes as the Son, sometimes as the Holy Spirit, like an actor changing masks.'[99] The mystery of the 'plural' nature of God, and the reluctance of some Messianic Jews to be associated with Christian language and terminology, should not prevent them from accepting the truth of God's word. Some Messianic Jews prefer to use the term 'triunity' to avoid 'such a non-Jewish term with a traditionally Christian ring to it'. 'But the bottom line is that it is more important to believe God's word and to trust in him than to argue over particular doctrinal or verbal formulas used in attempting to describe the nature of God.'[100] Whilst Stern sees clearly the issues involved, he stops far short of addressing them.

Composite Unity (Goldberg)

Louis Goldberg acknowledges the problem Messianic Jews face in asserting the plural unity of God, and deals more directly with non-Trinitarian views. 'Some Messianic Jews have sought to ingratiate themselves with the Jewish

---

[96] Ibid.

[97] Fruchtenbaum, 'Creeds in Judaism', 43.

[98] Stern, *JNTC*, 86.

[99] Ibid.

[100] Ibid.

community and are speaking of God as simply a Unity. However, to this writer, this [move] accommodates too much to the Jewish position of how to understand God as interpreted by the rabbis and therefore gives away what the scriptures would assert.'[101] Goldberg asks: 'While Israel's Confession in Deuteronomy 6:4 is an affirmation that God is one, is there a possibility whereby the word, *'ehad*, suggests something other than an absolute one, or only one?'[102]

Whilst the *Tanak*, the Jewish Bible, is no 'happy hunting ground' within which to find evidence for the Trinity, there are clear indications of the 'plural' nature of God, which Goldberg expounds along the traditional lines of Jewish-Christian polemics. Nevertheless, he is cautious in arguing for the plural nature of God from his reading of Deut. 6:4.

> But does that enable one to confidently assert that in Israel's great confession: 'The Lord our God, the Lord is one' (Deut. 6:4), the word *'ehad* also represents some collective reference to the very being in God? This writer would hesitate to affirm such a statement based on the few usages of *'ehad*. This writer's *hasid* friend as well as the rabbis will insist, from their system of hermeneutics, the Confession proclaims that God is only one and that *'ehad* is just that![103]

However, the plural unity of God cannot be *ruled out* by such passages, and Goldberg cites Rashi on the *Metatron* for support in his reading of Ex. 23.20. 'Rashi suggests, "Our rabbis said that he (the angel) is Metatron … whose name is even as the name of His Master, for Metatron has the numerical value (314) of Shaddai, the Almighty" (Sanhedrin 38b), which is an astounding statement.'[104]

Goldberg reports the debate on Metatron, referring to the Talmudic and Karaite interpretations of the passage.[105] His argumentation, beloved of

---

[101] Louis Goldberg, 'Recontextualising the Doctrine of the Trinity as Formulated by the Council of Nicaea' (LCJE Regional Conference, Chicago, 1996), 26.

[102] Goldberg, 'A Messianic Jewish Theology', 9.

[103] Ibid., 11.

[104] M. Rosenbaum and A. M. Silbermann (trans.), *Pentateuch with Rashi's Commentary* (London: Shapiro, Vallentine, 1930), 126, cited in Goldberg, ibid.

[105] Goldberg refers to Gershom Scholem, 'Metatron' in *Encyclopedia Judaica* 11 (New York: MacMillan, 1971), 1443–46. 'Scholem provides a further discussion on this mysterious word, *Metatron*, indicating that various ideas appear in the Talmud and Karaite literature and a number of mysterious assertions are made of him. He is the only one who can sit in the presence of God; he is some kind of a heavenly scribe, recording the good deeds of Israel. But a further question remains as to why the special name, YHWH, is in him. In the Karaite literature, specifically by Kirkisani, he is regarded as the lesser YHWH, but this view has been rejected by Israel's teachers. The major traditional opinion against considering him deity in any way is that no one wanted to assert this mysterious person is another deity.' Ibid., 9.

missionary apologetics, uses Talmud, Midrashim and Kabbalah in support.[106] He is also aware of the need for a more systematic presentation. The New Testament writers were not writing a detailed philosophical or theological treatise.

> These writers were not inclined to enter into any rationalistic explanations of this mystery or provide a philosophic understanding of how God can be One and yet have three Persons in the One God. That became the work of the non-Jewish believers, who being trained in Greek philosophy, Plato and Aristotle, proceeded to outline their beliefs in their particular contextualization. [107]

Instead, they began with their own proclamation of the unity of God, which was transformed by their understanding of the significance of Yeshua, and gave their own 'simple statements' such as that of Peter: 'You are the Messiah, the Son of the Living God' (Matt. 16:16), which was an 'astounding statement indeed by a religious Jew'. [108]

Reviewing the New Testament evidence for the deity of each Person of the Trinity, Goldberg asserts: 'All of these statements are proclamations of the infinite mystery of who God is. The Jewish writers listened to what Yeshua had to say concerning himself and his relationship with the Father and also noted his deeds, and came to the conclusion that in a mystery God is more than mere one, the lone God of religious Judaism, and of Islam as well.'[109] Aware of the inconclusive nature of this discussion, Goldberg invites the reader to make their own decision.

> One might conclude with all the statements made by Yeshua and the Messianic Jewish writers, they were either 1) out of their minds, 2) completely misguided and gullible, or, 3) everyone of them spoke the truth. The third is the only obvious conclusion: Yeshua and the writers were rational beings; they were not incoherent with what they said or did and no one ever concluded they were void of their faculties ... And that leaves every last Jewish person with the challenge to examine carefully what are the claims concerning the nature of God: Is He Merely One, or, Is He One God, but in a mystery, three Persons who comprise the one Godhead? A person's future destiny is at stake, depending on what will be the final decision.[110]

---

[106] Robert Chazan, *Daggers of Faith* (California: University of California Press, 1989), 160; Richard Harvey, 'Raymundus Martini and the Pugio Fidei: A Survey of the Life and Works of a Medieval Controversialist' (MA Diss., University College, London, 1991), 56. Midrash was here employed in ways unintended or desired by the original authors, and against the grain of the underlying theological grid on which such interpretation was built.

[107] Goldberg, 'A Messianic Jewish Theology,' 9.

[108] Ibid., 19.

[109] Ibid.

[110] Ibid., 34.

Whilst leaving the discussion inconclusive, Goldberg has at least begun to address the issues that Jewish tradition poses to the understanding of the Unity of God as Tri-unity. However, little new ground has been covered, and further engagement with the theological and philosophical underpinnings of the doctrine is needed.

Differentiation within the Godhead (Kinzer)

Mark Kinzer focuses on differentiation within the Godhead, seeing it as the 'archetype of created differentiation' in creation and humanity.[111] Following R. Kendal Soulen, Kinzer argues that just as differentiation is a 'crucial feature of the created order', so this reflects the divine archetype of the creator's self-differentiation.[112] The relationship between husband and wife, which is the 'paradigm of male/female differentiation in scripture', corresponds to the God/Messiah relationship, where the two share a 'common nature, with one deriving from the other; one is ordered in relation to the other; the two are united.'[113]

Thus also the Father/Son imagery applied by the New Testament writers to God and Yeshua expresses the relationship between parents and children, especially as it was lived out in the first-century Mediterranean world between father and son, and corresponds to the God/Messiah relationship. Kinzer therefore suggests that '[t]he Divine Image is a corporate and not just an individual property, and that the elements of order, difference, and mutual dependence existing among human beings are a reflection of the life of the Godhead.'[114]

Transcendence, Immanence and Omnipresence

Messianic Jews accept traditional Jewish and Christian understandings of the transcendence and immanence of God. They are particularly concerned with the concept of the *Shekinah*, in the light of the Incarnation.

Presence and Immanence (Maoz)

Baruch Maoz asserts the transcendence and immanence of God along the lines of classical Christian theism, beginning with the nature of God as spirit

---

[111] Mark Kinzer, 'Session #9: Creation, Covenant, & Consummation: Part III: Differentiation & Blessing'.

[112] R. Kendal Soulen, *The God of Israel and Christian Theology* (Minneapolis: Fortress Press, 1997).

[113] Kinzer, *Creation, Covenant and Consummation*, 1.

[114] Ibid., 2.

and warning against the danger of anthropomorphism. God as spirit has 'no material existence'. His presence is not a 'physical one'. 'He is pure spirit (Jn. 4:24). Once again, all the biblical descriptions of his physical presence (such as Ex. 33:23) are anthropomorphisms. They are not literally true but are meant to convey a truth that no one should deny.'[115] Because God is spirit, he is not limited by a physical body or any kind of physical existence. He is everywhere at all times, throughout creation, including heaven and hell. Nowhere can exist without his sustaining presence.

> When we say that, we are not saying that part of God is one place and another part somewhere else. God cannot be cut up into parts and he has no physical existence. We can't say that 90% of him is in one place and only 10% somewhere else. He is present everywhere in the fullness of his deity, power, wisdom, love and holiness. That is why we do not have any 'holy places'. Nowhere is more holy than another.[116]

Nevertheless, God's 'special presence' is at times localised in particular places. This is a 'moral presence', not a physical one, an anthropomorphism indicating that God is 'more obviously at work' in speaking to man and 'teaching him in terms he can readily understand'. This does not imply pantheism, which speaks of God's presence 'everywhere at all times' but fails to distinguish between Creator and Creation. 'Such a theory robs God of his personality, denies his holiness and his love and makes the world and all that happens in it into a kind of blind fate or a blind process from which the only salvation possible is a loss of individuality, not a moral and spiritual transformation. In other words, an end to existence.'[117] It is only in the Incarnation that the transcendent became fully immanent and the presence of God was fully localised. There the 'eternal unchanging spirit took on real humanity'. The Incarnation of Jesus was a reality, 'not just a façade'. His birth, upbringing, human needs and emotions, friendships and physical sufferings, death and resurrection, testify to his deepest humanity. 'It is an interesting fact that the Gospel of John, which is so insistent about the deity of Christ, also takes care to emphasize his humanity.'[118]

Sh'kinah and Incarnation (Juster, Stern and Goldberg)

Daniel Juster sees the divinity of Yeshua as the clearest manifestation of the presence of God. 'Yeshua's divinity is not an idolatrous teaching at all as some non-believers claim. Rather his divinity simply teaches that he is God

---

[115] Maoz, *Lessons*, 30.

[116] Ibid., 44.

[117] Ibid., 45.

[118] Ibid., 60–61.

in manifestation. It is perfectly within God's power and prerogative to manifest Himself in this way. Since man is created in God's image we are led to the conclusion that a manifestation in human form is the clearest revelation of God.'[119]

David Stern also explores the divinity of the Messiah as part of the unity of God, under the topic of the *Sh'kinah*. Rabbinic understanding explains Heb 1:2 which speaks of the Son as 'radiance': 'literally, "the glory", best rendered Jewishly as the *Sh'kinah*, which the *Encyclopaedia Judaica* article on it defines as "the Divine Presence, the numinous immanence of God in the world … a revelation of the holy in the midst of the profane".'[120]

Stern asserts that Philo, the Talmud, Midrashim and Sa'adia Gaon all contribute to an understanding of the *Sh'kinah* which may be applied, somewhat anachronistically, to Yeshua. The *Sh'kinah*, God's 'manifest glorious presence', is the key to understanding how God's transcendence and immanence are localised. The *Sh'kinah* is associated with the 'light' of the glory of God. According to Sa'adia Gaon, the rabbinic concept is identical to the biblical 'glory of God', the 'splendour of light which acts as intermediary between God and man, and which sometimes takes on human form'. Stern acknowledges that the *Sh'kinah* is nevertheless a created being, just as Yeshua is both the firstborn of all creation and also co-eternal with the Father.

> The phrase 'firstborn of all creation' does not mean that Yeshua was the first created being but speaks of his eternal sonship. Yeshua's firstbornness does not merely antedate the creation of the material world but is an essential and eternal element of the inner nature of God. Timelessly and eternally the Word of God, who became flesh in Yeshua the Messiah (Yohanan 1:1, 14) is in the relationship of firstborn Son to the Father; this is a necessary part of the one God's description of himself.[121]

For Stern the 'defensive theological position' of Maimonides' third article of faith[122] is unfounded. 'Maimonides clearly did not mean to contradict the *Tanakh*'s own descriptions of God as having physical features such as a back, a face and an outstretched arm. He meant to exclude incarnation. In the light of the New Testament a Messianic Jew can simply pronounce him wrong.'[123]

Stern agrees that God's nature is not physical or material, but 'would insist that' the third article does not exclude the incarnation of the Word as

---

[119] Juster, *Jewish Roots*, 35.

[120] Stern, *JNTC*, 662.

[121] Stern, *JNTC*, 605 (Col. 1:16).

[122] 'I believe with perfect faith that the Creator, blessed be his name, is not a body, that he is free from all material properties, and that he has no form whatsoever'.

[123] Stern, JNTC, 156 (Jn. 1:1).

Yeshua 'if it is understood as an occasional, rather than essential, attribute of God, an event necessitated because sin occurred in human history.'[124]

Stern's explanation raises more questions than it answers. It does not fully address the underlying issues of the divine-human nature of the Messiah, but demonstrates the need for a deeper engagement with the theological and philosophical issues at stake. Without examining more closely Christian Trinitarian thought and the Jewish monotheistic tradition in depth, Stern merely points the way forward for MJT, if it is to develop a detailed and coherent understanding of the unity of God.

Louis Goldberg also examines the *Sh'kinah* in Jewish tradition. Quoting Alan Unterman's article in the *Encyclopaedia Judaica*, he comments:

> So sensitive were the rabbis within Israel as to the danger of equating the 'Spirit,' 'the Holy One,' 'the *Sh'kinah*,' with God, thereby creating a hypostasis, they became extremely sensitive to insist that any work by any three of these designations for God Himself 'must be viewed purely figurative and not as representing a separable aspect of God or as being in any sense a part of the Godhead. The latter notion is totally alien to the strict monotheism of rabbinic Judaism for which the unity of the divine Essence is a basic premise.'[125]

Whilst Stern and Goldberg follow up some of the rabbinic understanding of the *Sh'kinah* for their own purposes, they lack the nuance and theological depth required to put forward a truly creative synthesis of the two traditions. MJT will need to go further in its attempt to construct a theology of the *Sh'kinah* that engages with both traditions, but there are certainly grounds set for further exploration.

Omnipresence and Anthropomorphism (Goldberg and Stern)

According to Goldberg, God is immanent in the midst of His creation, everywhere present at the same time, but is not tied to any object in the universe. 'He is not corporeal, that is, locked in any object. He is free to be anywhere. God is also transcendent, above and beyond creation as well. The point is that in any theological system concerning His presence, one must always remember to start with God. The universe proceeded from Him when He spoke it into existence.'[126]

Despite problems with biblical anthropomorphisms such as 'the Lord came down to see the city and tower which the sons of men had built' (Gen. 11:15), or the prayer Yeshua taught his disciples to pray, beginning with, 'Our Father in heaven' (Matt. 6:9), this is merely the 'language of

---

[124] Ibid.

[125] Goldberg cites Alan Unterman, 'Shekinah' in *Encyclopaedia Judaica*, 14: 1350.

[126] Goldberg, *Messianic Jewish Theology*, 61.

appearance'. God can be in many places at once, even though this aspect of God – his being both immanent and transcendent – is 'somewhat mind-boggling'. 'Yet the fact of His being in both places at the same time is no problem for Him. We are the ones who have the problem visualising his omnipresence.'[127]

The practical value of this 'great truth of God' is a warning to the ungodly and sinners, who will have no place to hide when their day of reckoning comes. No one can escape him, as Jonah discovered. Yet this is also an encouragement, as each one who clings to him is guaranteed his closeness. 'As each one loves and keeps the words of Yeshua, no matter where he or she might be on the face of this earth, each one will be the object of the Father's love and both the Father and Yeshua will come and make their home with either him or her. His omnipresence is an encouragement by which to live with complete confidence and assurance.'[128]

David Stern compares ideas of God's transcendence and care for Israel described in the 11th century hymn the *Adon Olam* with the eternal nature and reconciling ministry of Yeshua in Col 1:13. 'The hymn moves from God as transcendent and eternal Creator and Ruler to God as personal Guide and Protector. The present passage moves from Yeshua as eternal Creator and Ruler to Yeshua as Head of the Messianic Community and Reconciler of persons.'[129]

For Stern the understanding of God's transcendence and otherness can overshadow an awareness of presence and nearness in traditional Judaism. An overemphasis on transcendence leaves many Jewish people 'feeling distant from God and his throne'. Yet '[n]ew believers are frequently amazed to experience God's warm and loving nearness. They find that they need not merely recite prayers from a prayer book; they find that God's love is not merely an abstract phenomenon without relevance to their heart's needs.'[130]

Stern and Goldberg engage with Jewish tradition in their discussion, whilst Maoz avoids this. The questions raised are evidence of their awareness of the issues, and rabbinic material is used to illustrate and confirm the argument. However, fuller and more sympathetic engagement with these materials is necessary for a developed Messianic understanding, and close interaction with the history of these debates in Judaism and Christianity.

---

[127] Ibid.

[128] Ibid., 62.

[129] Stern, *JNTC*, 604.

[130] Ibid.

The Eternal and Infinite God

In common with Jewish and Christian traditions, Messianic Jews affirm the eternal and infinite nature of God.

The Meaning of 'Eternal' (Maoz)

Baruch Maoz recognises some of the philosophical and theological problems when discussing the eternal nature of God. 'Because God has forever been like himself, he also exists forever. He existed before time began and will continue to be when time comes to an end. In reference to God, "eternal" means one who exists forever, without beginning and without end.'[131]

God's eternal nature is unlike anything that has been created. His existence had no beginning, cannot be explained, and has no cause. 'He is his own cause in every sense. That is to say, he exists because of himself, not because of anything that happened sometime somewhere.'[132]

His eternity leads to his power, self-sufficiency, freedom and sovereign activity in creation. 'God does not need anyone to help him, any food, water or air to live by, any companions to love or by which to be loved. He has in himself all he needs. He lives by his power, loves and is loved in an eternal Trinity and never needs to go outside himself.'[133] God's eternity results in his unchanging nature, his consistency, reliability, and stability. If God is perceived as changing, this is due to humanity's perception which is marred by sin. Our perception of God changes just as our perception of the earth changes when the sun is shining or is hidden behind a cloud.[134] Maoz here gives some classic formulations of the immutability of God, and is close to the Aristotelian formulations adopted by Maimonides in his 13 Articles of Faith, although this is not acknowledged.

The Eternal King (Stern)

David Stern understands God as the Eternal King. On the list of attributes of God found in 1 Timothy 1:17 Stern comments: '**King** – eternal, literally, "King of the ages", equivalent to the Hebrew words *"Melekh-ha'olam"* in many Jewish blessings, which are usually rendered, "King of the Universe", but can also be translated, "King of eternity".'[135]

---

[131] Maoz, *Lessons*, 25.
[132] Ibid., 26.
[133] Ibid.
[134] Ibid., 27.
[135] Stern, *JNTC*, 636.

God is the Alpha and Omega, 'the one who existed at the beginning and will exist at the end'.[136] But Yeshua is also referred to as 'the Ancient of Days', in the language used to describe 'God, the Father' in Dan. 7:9–10.[137] Yeshua's statement of Rev. 1:17 – 'I am the First and the Last' – takes up a title 'which the *Tanakh* applies only to *YHVH*' but is deliberately applied to Yeshua in the New Testament.[138]

Comprehending the Infinite (Goldberg)

Louis Goldberg adopts a biblical understanding of 'infinite', even though 'the English word only occurs once in the Torah, in Psalm 147:5.'[139] 'The Hebrew word is: *ein mispar*, meaning literally, without an end, or, without any limits. In this sense, the word is an apt term, highly suggestive of what "infinite" really means.'[140]

An 'abundance of the term' appears in the Psalms. God's thoughts about us are too numerous to count (Ps. 40:5). His loving kindness stands firm forever, and without end (Ps. 89:1, 2). God removes our transgressions 'as far as the east is from the west' (Ps. 103:12). 'As one reflects on the simile, the point is that as distant as the east is from the west, so when a person comes to faith, sins are taken an infinite distance away, so that no believer will ever have to face them again!'[141]

Yet there are problems in understanding God as Infinite. The existence of evil and God's seeming inability to control it has led some to question whether he has limitations and is not 'infinite'. In order to preserve divine goodness in the face of evil some have argued that God's power is limited – he wishes to stop evil but cannot. This leaves 'God' without omnipotence. Goldberg objects that, 'This would be no God at all. Rather, what should be recognized is that ever since the Fall of Adam and Eve, God has temporarily self-limited Himself to allow man to make his choices, for evil or good.'[142] We shall return to the problem of evil a little later.

The human mind has problems with the notion of 'infinity'. The question 'may seem insurmountable', yet by recognising that God has placed the notion of infinity in our hearts (Ecc. 3:11), we recognise that we have been created with some awareness of the notion. 'There is a two-pronged view of what is asserted: 1) Man does have the concept of certain intangibles,

---

[136] Ibid., 790 (Rev 1:8).

[137] Ibid., 792 (Rev 1:14).

[138] Ibid., 793 (Rev 1:17).

[139] Goldberg was a member of the translation panel for the New International Version.

[140] Ibid., 74.

[141] Ibid., 110.

[142] Ibid.

eternity, infinite, in his understanding so that the concept does have meaning. And yet, 2) man does not in this world ever attain to ultimate knowledge.'[143] Solomon tried to attain such knowledge, but 'rued the day when he realized he would never attain it'. We can understand something of what infinite or ultimate knowledge means, but only God has the capacity for such knowledge. But if 'infinity puts God so far above mankind, how then can finite beings ever reach Him?' This problem is similar to that of God's transcendence. Just as God moves in His universe and is present on earth as well, so 'we are finite, God knows it, and He has taken the steps to be present so that finite man can reach out to Him.'

Two practical benefits derive from understanding this attribute of God's infinite nature, those of *comfort* to God's people and *warning* to the wicked. A personal being who is infinite can still enter the creature's world and relate to their needs. And God takes note of the wicked throughout time. 'Because He is infinite, He can supervise their eventual judgment after this life and the punishment which calls for a suffering that will be infinite takes on new meaning since God Himself is also infinite. How terrible indeed will it be for those assigned to an infinity of suffering!'[144]

God's eternal nature is a corollary of his self-existence, and a wealth of biblical material 'attests to this facet of our God'.[145] God revealed himself to Abraham as 'the Everlasting God' (Gen. 21:33). Abraham must have evidently understood something about God's eternal nature because he called upon Him directly by that name. Moses expressed his faith in the God who is from everlasting to everlasting (Ps. 90:1–2).

Similarly the New Covenant writers 'had a good grasp on the God who is eternal'. Paul refers to the 'eternal power' of God, visible since creation (Rom. 1:20), and blesses God as 'to the ages of ages' (1 Tim. 1:17). 'Yeshua, likewise, is eternal, again because of composite unity with the Father, and so the writer to the book of Hebrews declared that God created the ages (literally) through the Messiah (Heb. 1:2). And finally, in the glory, the twenty-four elders 'fall down before' God 'who sits on the throne' and 'worship Him who lives forever and ever' (Rev. 4:10).'[146]

Because God dwells in eternity (Is. 57:15), God is above and beyond time. God sees all, not only within time, but also beyond time. The practical value of such understanding is that we can trust in a God who is eternal. He is our refuge and strength because 'underneath are His everlasting arms' (Deut. 33:27). 'We can trust Him because He is ever present, while here on earth, and certainly in a special relationship in the next world. This and

---

[143] Ibid., 112.

[144] Ibid., 73.

[145] Ibid., 58.

[146] Ibid., 59.

other promises can assure us, no matter what are our experiences in this life.'[147]

Omniscience and Omnipotence

The problems associated with the omnipotence and omniscience of God are biblical, philosophical and practical. Daniel Juster shows how God's omniscience and omnipotence are clear from the book of Exodus. 'God is one who identifies with the outcast and the dispossessed. He rescued a nation of slaves. We also see that God is sovereign, all knowing and all present.'[148]

The topics of God's omnipotence and omniscience challenge Messianic Jews to engage with the theological and philosophical traditions of Judaism and Christianity. Whilst familiarity with these traditions is apparent, full acknowledgement and use of them as sources is needed, before original proposals can be presented.

Foreknowledge and Predestination (Maoz)

Baruch Maoz assumes God's omniscience, and asks, 'Is God's knowledge different from that of man [as] a matter of quantity (what and how much he knows) or is it a different kind of knowledge (how he knows), that is to say a difference in quality? God's knowledge is most certainly different in its quality, just as everything about God is qualitatively different from anything he has made (Is. 55:8–11; Ps. 50:21). But what is the nature of that difference?'[149]

The difference lies in the way we acquire knowledge. God knows all things without having to learn them (Is. 46:10). 'He does not need to look into the past, the present or the future. He does not need to reason, analyse or commit to memory. He knows, period, because he is God, period. Hallelujah!'[150] He knows all things *because he determines everything that will 'happen'*. Also, he is not subject to time, so the future is as clear to God as the past. 'All the moments of history in the past, present and future are to God as a brief second because his eternity encompasses everything that is, was and will be.'[151]

Maoz follows a Calvinist line on predestination. There are no conditionals with God, as he determines all that will take place, and knows that which he determines. His knowledge includes the 'future free actions of man'.

---

[147] Ibid., 93.
[148] Juster, *Jewish Roots*, 27.
[149] Maoz, *Lessons*, 38.
[150] Ibid., 39.
[151] Ibid.

'That is what the Bible calls fore-ordination and it is the basis for all that God knows. The two [foreknowledge and fore-ordination] should not be confused. Things do not happen because God knew them in advance. Rather, he knew them advance in because he determined they were to happen.[152]

Men and women are still responsible for their free actions, though paradoxically God knows them already because he has determined what they will be. God's freedom defines the limits of man's freedom, as it does the limits of all creation. God's freedom is one aspect of his omnipotence, demonstrated in His creation through his Word, his rule over the nations, his gift of life, his power over nature and our will. Nothing can resist or change his will, and there are no limits to his power to do what he wills.[153] Does this mean that there are *limits* to humanity's freedom? Yes. 'Man is never free from God, not even in what we call his free actions'. So is *God* responsible for human sin? No. 'Man's freedom is the cause of man's sin, not God's rule over all.'[154]

Maoz reconciles the tension between divine sovereignty and human free will by appeal to scripture, but following a Calvinist reading on predestination. God moves humanity to do his will by turning their hearts to his purpose.

> Sometimes he works by an inner compulsion, by forming man's nature and will (Moses was prepared for leadership in the house of Pharaoh, David was prepared for his duties by his childhood experiences and by his many years of fleeing from Saul, Paul was prepared for his calling by his wide and thorough education) or by changing them forcefully (Jonah was forced to go to Nineveh, Nebuchadnezzar was humbled by a terrible experience, Paul was stopped on the way to Damascus). God is almighty. He can do all and anything he wants.[155]

Is God's power such that he can change the past? No, because his power is not a 'naked, abstract ability' but is consistent with his nature. He has determined the past and does not change his mind.

> It is not possible that the past ('Adam sinned') could exist side by side with a negation of the past ('Adam will not sin'). Changing the past involves changing the very nature of the world God has made. This would be a change in God's will and actions because the very logic of the universe comes from God (Is. 28:23–29). But God cannot deny or contradict himself (2 Tim. 2:13).[156]

---

[152] Ibid., 38.
[153] Ibid.
[154] Ibid., 40.
[155] Ibid., 42.
[156] Ibid., 41–42.

God is able to do all that is morally and logically possible. He thus cannot lie, or make a stone so heavy that he cannot lift it. But such theoretical possibilities are 'no more than games', as they contain an internal self-contradiction that 'removes them from the realm of what is actually possible'. It is not natural processes that limit God's power, but his own nature. Such limitation is not a weakness, but part of God's perfection, in that he cannot be forced to do something against his will or moral nature. He is sovereign and free to do anything he wants to do, and his perfection is such that he has no inner contradictions in his being. 'We rightly admire a person who is so honest that it is difficult to believe that he would lie. God is worthy of all our admiration because he can never lie, deny himself or act inconsistently with his perfect nature.'[157]

How is it possible then to resist God's will if he is all-powerful? In traditional Calvinist fashion Maoz distinguishes between two levels of God's will, his 'commanded and revealed will' and his 'intended and often unrevealed will'. The first is revealed in the commandments given to Israel and humanity which become the duty of those who are commanded to keep them. To resist his revealed will is not to resist his power, but to rebel against his authority. However, God's intended will cannot be resisted, as it is what God has determined will happen. Maoz cites the examples of Pharaoh and Judas to show how even evil actions are part of God's intended purposes, and yet humanity is free and responsible for them.

> God's intended will cannot change and has to do with all and every person. But neither is most of it revealed. God's commanded will is for men to obey. His intended will is not meant to guide mankind in moral and spiritual actions. To the extent it is revealed, it serves as a declaration of purpose on the part of God to the comfort, encouragement or warning of those to whom it is addressed.[158]

Further discussion is needed here, with some explanation of the overarching philosophical and theological frameworks assumed by such articulations, but Maoz does not proceed beyond the Protestant Reformed parameters of the discussion.

Beyond Human Understanding (Goldberg)

God's omniscience is 'mind-overwhelming' to Louis Goldberg, but is a most rewarding topic of study. God's knowledge is 'All-Inclusive', extending to past, present and future; this world and the next; and heaven and hell. God knows all the 'minute details of one's personal life', and 'all possible events under all possible combinations of circumstances'. 'That is why He is able to

---

[157] Ibid., 42.
[158] Ibid., 43.

pinpoint the accuracy of Messianic prophecy, exactly because He knows the multitude of the historical "bytes" of information in which prophetic fulfilment occurs (as for example in just one instance, Luke 2:1–7).'[159]

God's knowledge is 'Eternal, Perfect, and Complete' and such fullness of knowledge is beyond human understanding. Job could not answer even one of the forty questions God put to him (Job 38). The writer of Hebrews asserted that 'no creature is hidden from His sight, but all things are open and laid bare' to God who sees everything (Heb. 4:13). 'The point of these passages, as well as a host of other similar ones, is to remind everyone that his knowledge is perfect and complete, known to Him from the beginning. Such fullness of knowledge is awesome indeed.'[160]

God's knowledge involves a moral purpose, because the motives behind all knowledge and the ends to which such knowledge is put must always be morally justified. When God tests the hearts of his people to see whether they will keep his commandments (Deut. 8.2) it is not because God did not know what would occur; but the expression should be understood as an anthropomorphism, to show that testing focuses on the people involved and the decisions they will make. Taking a different line from Maoz, Goldberg maintains that, 'God certainly foreknows what man will do; He does not predetermine their actions!'[161]

The practical value of God's omniscience lies in the great consolation it gives, as Hagar (Gen. 16:3) and David (Ps. 56) discovered in the midst of suffering. God's omniscience also serves as a warning to the wicked. 'He will avenge the righteous for the deeds perpetrated upon them by the wicked, exactly because He knows what they are doing (Ps. 94:3–9). Who can escape His scrutiny and assessment of every evil thought, word and deed (Prov. 15:3)?'[162]

God's omnipotence similarly 'staggers the imagination as to its far reaching consequences'. The biblical title *El Shaddai* indicated to Abraham the nature of God's power (Gen. 17:1), and through the provision of the son of promise, Abraham and Sarah came to know its 'real meaning'.

God's omnipotence is always consistent with his moral nature and character, as he cannot deny himself (2 Tim. 2:13), lie (Titus 1:2), or be tempted by evil (Jas. 1:13). 'For example, the old adage question asks if God can even create some huge glob [*sic*] which He Himself can never lift. But this is totally inconsistent with His character; if He brought the universe into existence, He also is entirely capable of running it.'[163]

---

[159] Goldberg, *Messianic Jewish Theology*, 63.
[160] Ibid.
[161] Ibid., 62.
[162] Ibid., 101.
[163] Ibid., 67.

His omnipotence is manifested in creation (Jer. 10:12), nature (Jer. 10:13), history (Dan 4:17), his providential rule over the nations (Dan. 4:35), and in redemption. 'Sha'ul (Paul) had prayed the *hasidim* (saints) would know something of the greatness of the Messiah and that through His death, resurrection and enthronement at the right hand of God, He now has all things in subjection to himself and that he is also the head of this new body, the body of the Messiah wherein all are believers (Eph. 1:18–22).'[164] The 'practical value' again is that 'the believer can take heart and be encouraged as he or she lives for Yeshua every day and has the hope of eternal glory yet to come.'[165]

The Perfection of God

Messianic Jews recognise the perfection of God, but do not directly link their articulation of the doctrine with the traditional sources of Christian and Jewish discussion of the doctrine. Whilst they echo Aristotle, Maimonides, Aquinas, Calvin and Barth in their statements of the perfection of God, there is little direct acknowledgment or engagement with these primary sources.

Self-sufficiency and Perfection (Maoz)

For Baruch Maoz the notion of the perfection of God is both logically and morally self-consistent.

> God's self-sufficiency is an important aspect of his perfection. God is so perfect that he cannot change. Nothing can be added to or taken from him. That is in the nature of perfection: it cannot be changed, otherwise it is not real perfection. If you can improve it, it was less than perfect. If you can take anything away from it, then there is a higher, greater and therefore more perfect, power that can do so.[166]

God's self-consistency is an aspect of this perfection. He has limited himself by his own nature, not because of natural processes.

> This is not a shortcoming, it is actually a perfection. Man can be forced to do something contrary to his will and moral nature, God cannot. He always acts freely, out of the glory of his own person. He can do anything that he wants to do, and his perfection is such that there are no inner contradictions ... God is worthy of all our admiration because he can never lie, deny himself or act inconsistently with his perfect nature.[167]

---

[164] Ibid.

[165] Ibid., 68.

[166] Maoz, *Lessons*, 27.

[167] Ibid., 42.

This moral perfection is found in the sinless nature of Jesus, and is necessary for God's saving purposes. 'If Jesus had been born sinful, like all mankind, he could not have saved us or anyone else. His moral perfection is another important foundation for our salvation, and that is why he was born of Mary but not conceived through Joseph.'[168]

Perfection as Completion (Goldberg)

Louis Goldberg recognises that 'of all the facets of who God is, this one puzzles many and some even despair they can never be perfect as God is perfect.' He notes the biblical passages that speak of the perfection of God. 'In one of the greatest songs in the Torah, Moses ascribed greatness to the God of Israel, and as a result, the Rock, that is, God, is perfect, faithful and without any injustice in Him (Deut. 32:3, 4). David many times spoke of the God who is perfect and how His ways are blameless, or complete (Ps. 18:30) and that furthermore, the Torah is perfect, that is, complete, or whole (Ps. 19:7).'[169]

The New Covenant also witnesses to this perfection of God and Yeshua himself calls upon His followers to be 'perfect, as your heavenly Father is perfect' (Matt 5:48). Such divine perfection means that God is 'all that God ought to be, that is, He falls short in nothing' and is complete in everything. When scripture refers to created beings as 'perfect', such as Noah, Job and Lucifer, it means that

> As one saw them, they were a complete person. It does not suggest 'perfect' as God is perfect in His being and knowledge; for Noah and Job, they had a lot of maturing to do in order to continue in the completeness they had and for sure, they did. With Lucifer, however, when the test came in his experience, he made the wrong decisions, and therefore did not go on to further maturing, but rather, fell, from which there was no redemption, as there was with Adam and Eve. [170]

When we are commanded to be perfect (Matt. 5:48) there are two possible explanations, 'either Yeshua held forth the perfection of God for which we strive as our ideal, or, we strive but are limited by our failures and we continue to strive.' Goldberg refers to the Wesleyan explanation. We will never be as perfect as God, but at every stage of our maturity we aspire to perfection, in accord with what we know. 'When we do so, however, God will provide further knowledge by which to live. It is this incremental doing His will day by day, ever learning more about Him whereby believers mature in Him. This is the objective of being

---

[168] Ibid., 60.

[169] Goldberg, *Messianic Jewish Theology*, 68.

[170] Gen 6:9, Job 1:1, Ezek. 28:12.

perfect.'[171] The practical value of such a doctrine, for Goldberg, is that believers can 'be assured that his love, mercy, all power, all knowledge, and so on,
is perfect, complete in every way,' and that God will provide us with all that
is needed.[172]

Creation and Consummation

Messianic Jews affirm the doctrine of creation found in Christian and Jewish
tradition. Rather than discuss cosmology and *creatio ex nihilo* they are concerned with the role of the Trinity in Creation; the diversity in creation that
manifests itself in the creation of Israel and the nations; and the maintaining
of that diversity until the eschatological consummation of all things. Whilst
some are '6-day creationists', this is not an essential part of messianic teaching, and is not held by those discussed here.[173]

God the Creator and Sustainer (Maoz)

To Baruch Maoz it is clear from scripture that God created the universe. He
is the source, creator and sustainer, by whose will the universe came into
being. 'He is the independent creator on whom everything is dependent and
from whose will, power and action the universe came into being (Ex. 32:40;
Ps. 102:27; Is. 46:4; Eph. 1:4; 1 Tim. 1:17).[174] God is sovereign, free and independent in relation to the created order. 'Nothing in the universe exists or
happens of itself, except God. Everything that happens – a new star is born,
a blade of grass sprouts up, a wind blows, a leaf falls to the earth, a child
is born – God is the source and cause of it all.'[175] From many scriptural
passages Maoz affirms the doctrine of God as the unmoved mover. 'He is
self-existent, and he is their true cause (affecter). He affects all things
without being affected himself. He made all things (Gen. 1–2; Ps. 36:6–7;
Is. 40:12, 26–28; 45:7, 12; Acts 17:24–26; 1 Cor. 8:6) and keeps all things in
existence.'[176]

The work of creation is often ascribed to God the Father, the first person of
the Trinity.

---

[171] Goldberg, *Messianic Jewish Theology*, 70.

[172] Ibid.

[173] For 6-day creationism in Messianic Judaism, see Arnold Fruchtenbaum, *The Seven Days of Creation: Genesis 1:1–2:3* (Tucson: Ariel Ministries, 2005).

[174] Maoz, *Lessons*, 22, 25.

[175] Ibid., 25.

[176] Ibid.

When speaking about God, the Bible uses the term 'Father' in a number of ways: sometimes it simply means 'God', especially as he relates to mankind, of which he may be described as father because mankind was brought by him into being and he cares for it and maintains it constantly (Mal. 2:10; 1 Cor. 8:6; Eph. 3:14–15; Heb. 12:9; Jas. 1:17). Because creation is usually ascribed to God the Father, the first person of the Trinity, the term is especially appropriate in this context.[177]

Nevertheless the actions of creation and maintaining creation are also ascribed to the Son. 'Actions attributed to God are also attributed to him (Creation and maintaining creation – Jn. 1:3; Col. 1:16–17; Heb. 1:3, 10). Jesus is also given worship that should be given only to God (Jn. 5:23; 20:28; Acts 7:59; Rom. 10:13 {compare with Joel 3:5}; Phil. 2:10; Heb. 1:6; Rev. 5:12–14).'[178]

The Creator and his Creation (Goldberg)

Louis Goldberg affirms the divine freedom in creation: 'God … is active and therefore able to perform great works in creation when bringing it into existence, as well as in his relation to this universe as well as earth, in sustaining it, providing for every living creature, including man. One can say that activity is a mark and sign of life.'[179]

God's independence and self-consciousness removes the danger of pantheism. 'This truth – that God is entirely self-conscious of himself – has a practical value because it answers the pantheistic error … If God is locked into his creation where He is a part of it, He therefore cannot be self-conscious. No, He assures us that inasmuch as He is free, as already noted, He is not some dumb brute force.'[180]

The doctrine of creation teaches many important truths, confirming God's existence, omniscience, omnipotence and providence. 'His caring is also noted in that He has planned all things necessary for man and the animals to live in this environment which is suited for his creation of all living things. So much can be said that it staggers the imagination.'[181]

Creation and Science (Stern)

For David Stern the biblical doctrine of creation by word is a challenge to modern science. 'The Bible contradicts the philosophy of materialism. Incidentally, so does the "Big Bang" theory, which says that the entire universe began in an unimaginably great explosion some fifteen billion years

---

[177] Ibid., 52.

[178] Ibid., 55.

[179] Goldberg, *Messianic Jewish Theology*, 29.

[180] Ibid., 43–44.

[181] Ibid., 43.

ago, before which there was nothing.'[182] For Stern 'Scientism', a purely scientific approach to creation, cannot limit God's activity by claiming that the laws of nature are fixed, and that God cannot interfere with them or intervene in human history. 'Such a statement transgresses the limits of what science itself has a right to say; and responsible scientists do not abuse their profession to spread such ideas, even if they hold them. According to the Bible the "laws of science" are not forever fixed but are merely a human description of how God currently runs the universe.'[183]

Creation as a Personal Act of Divine Love (Kinzer)

Mark Kinzer's understanding of creation is focused on the Trinity. Creation is not 'an involuntary and necessary overflow of the superabundant life of God', but a free personal act of love.[184] There is an inherent connection between Yeshua as Wisdom, Torah and Logos of God that leads to the intelligibility of the created order. Kinzer's interpretation reflects a more sophisticated interaction with Jewish and Christian resources.

The focus of the biblical teaching is not 'the one-time, unrepeatable event in which something comes to be from nothing, but instead the nature of the perpetual bond inherent in the Creator-creature relationship'.[185] This means that the creature cannot be independent from the Creator; but must be continually sustained by the source of all being. Liturgical and biblical references support this.[186] However, the creature 'does not maintain its existence at the capricious whim of the Creator, nor does its need for God compromise its own integrity.' Rather, it exists as a stable and secure reality because the purpose of the Creator is stable. 'The Creator desired an "Other", something that was not himself, with which He could relate, and that "Other" is not a Divine fantasy, a dream in the mind of the Creator, but has a genuine, distinct, and integral reality.'[187]

Following R. Kendal Soulen, whose reconstruction of the biblical meta-narrative includes the election of Israel and eschews supersessionism,[188]

---

[182] Ibid., 708.

[183] Ibid., 761 (2 Pet. 3:3–9).

[184] Kinzer, *The Shape Of Messianic Jewish Theology* (Session #7: Creation, Covenant, & Consummation: Part I: Creator & Creation).

[185] Ibid., 1.

[186] Ibid.: 'Yotzer: "In his goodness He renews constantly and daily the work of creation" ' (*Ham'chadesh betuvo bechol yom tamid ma'aseh bereyshit*); Pesukei deZimra Berachot: *HaShem* praised as '*Chey HaOlamim*' (Life of the Worlds/Ages) [this world, and the world to come]; Apostolic Writings: 'In Him we live and move and have our being' (Acts 17:28); see also Neh. 9:6; Col. 1:17; Heb. 1:3.'

[187] Ibid.

[188] R. Kendal Soulen, *The God of Israel and Christian Theology*, (Minneapolis: Fortress, 1996).

differentiation is a crucial feature of both the divine and the created order. Divine differentiation within the Godhead is the archetype of created differentiation between male and female, and between Israel and the Nations. The elements of order, difference and mutual dependence that exist among human beings are a reflection of the life of the Godhead. Kinzer links God's plan and purposes in Creation with the national differentiation of Israel and the nations within the created order. The drama of the 'consummation and sanctification of the created order' gives an important place to the life of Israel, part of God's original creation purpose and not simply as a response to the Fall.

> If we accept the view of the incarnation suggested above, then, just as Genesis 1–2 indicates, Israel as a holy people would have arisen even if sin had never intervened, for the Heavenly Man needed to be born of some family, tribe, and people. This does not imply that Israel's *only* purpose is to be the means by which the Incarnation is realized (this is the battle which Soulen wages); just as Israel's emergence out of the nations does not annul the significance of the Nations but confirms it and gives it its true meaning, so Yeshua's emergence out of Israel does not annul Israel's significance but confirms it and gives it its true meaning.[189]

Kinzer speculates on the divine self-limitation in the act of creation, using the kabbalistic doctrine of the divine withdrawal (*tzimtzum*) to illustrate how God, in establishing a reality dependent upon but distinct from himself, imposed a limit on his being.

> Isaac Luria and the Jewish mystical tradition captured this truth in the doctrine of 'tzimtzum' or 'withdrawal': in order to create something that was other than Himself, God needed to withdraw somewhat into Himself, thus allowing 'space' in which that other could exist. The creation of humanity, a type of creature that in certain respects was like God, constituted an even more drastic act of Divine self-limitation, but it is simultaneously a way of bridging the chasm, since this particular creature was called to represent God in the world, to mediate between Heaven and Earth; it is a risky venture![190]

The ultimate example of this divine self-limitation is in Yeshua, the incarnation of the Word, where 'Divine Self-limitation is both embraced (as God is alienated from himself – Yeshua's *'Lama Sabachtani*?') and transcended (as God further realizes His purpose of taking the world into himself and filling the world with His Glory).'[191]

---

[189] Kinzer, *The Shape of Messianic Jewish Theology*, 1.
[190] Ibid.
[191] Ibid. ("Why did you forsake me?")

It is clear that Kinzer is processing Jewish and Christian materials on creation at some depth, although his presuppositions are not clear, and the parallels he draws between Jewish and Christian concepts are somewhat arbitrary. Nevertheless his exploration of the doctrine of creation attempts a coherent synthesis of the two streams of thought, and can be developed further.

Providence (Goldberg and Stern)

Messianic Jews believe in divine providence, the continuing preservation of creation and guidance towards its intended purposes. Louis Goldberg sees the outworking of providence in creation and in history as evidence that points to God's existence even though if falls short of proof. 'God has revealed himself in so many ways and means through His miracles and providential upholding of His creation.'[192] Numerous biblical passages point to God's providential activity throughout the history of Israel, such as the Exodus complex of events and the wanderings in the wilderness.

> On another note, when a generation of Judah came along where for the most part, no one would listen to God, He would bring pagan nations to discipline them so that His own people would know there is a God who really cared for them. While many would die in such circumstances, yet a remnant would come out of this pressure cooker of death in the homeland, and then banishment to a foreign land (Ezek. 11:9–10). Sometimes God had to work in such drastic circumstances so as to accomplish a positive purpose.[193]

Whilst these are only 'a very few of the miraculous and providential circumstances recorded in the Torah and New Covenant' there are enough there to reveal God as a 'special person, with power, who not only directs Israel but the nations as well'. Yet such revelations are limited in what they reveal. They are most meaningful to those who actually experienced them, but even then 'drawbacks to the totality of meaning are very apparent'. Providential events can be misinterpreted, and records of such events can become 'garbled, distorted and corrupted', as demonstrated by alternative accounts of Noah's flood in the Gilgamesh Epic and other Ancient Near Eastern literature. Ultimately, the working of providence cannot create faith. 'In the same way today, while God can do miracles today … yet, these same acts of God cannot make people believe God's message. God's directives must be accepted by faith, and while miracles can touch hearts open to receive truth, they by themselves are not the substitute for faith in God's Torah.'[194]

---

[192] Goldberg, 'A Messianic Jewish Theology', 47.
[193] Ibid., 48.
[194] Ibid., 50.

David Stern notes how God's providence towards Israel is recalled in the celebration of Sukkot,[195] and Shavuot.[196] Stern quotes the account of the death of Herod Agrippa in Josephus to show the workings of providence.[197] 'In God's providence, many have responded to the Good News of Yeshua the Messiah proclaimed by a hypocrite' quips Stern on Phil. 1:15,[198] and Phil. 4:19 gives the believer the 'ultimate assurance of God's providence and sufficiency'.[199] God's providence is ensured through the supremacy and rule of the Son over all things. '**He holds everything together** – the moment to moment existence of the physical and moral universe depend directly in his oversight and providence.'[200]

Evil and a Righteous God of Love

The nature of God's love and power, and the existence of evil and suffering, confront Jewish, Christian and Messianic Jewish theology with the problems of theodicy. In the light of the Holocaust, and Christian involvement in anti-Semitism and anti-Judaism, Messianic Jews have many questions to answer. A full discussion of the Holocaust is beyond the purpose of the present work, but some Messianic Jewish approaches to it will be briefly summarised.

Justice and Mercy (Juster and Maoz)

Daniel Juster describes God's holiness and his need to punish sin, as well as his love. 'God is *holy*. That is, He is *totally separated from evil, uncleanliness* and *immoral ways*. He is full of love and compassion.'[201] Sin leads to separation from the Holy God, yet humanity is made in the image of God, and to be created in the image of God means to be a 'reflection of God in function and attributes'. Thus humans are created to function as rulers over the earth as God is ruler over creation. They have attributes such as love, intelligence, freedom and intuition, which reflect God's nature and enable God to enjoy loving fellowship with humanity.

Baruch Maoz also discusses the nature of God's love. His love is first within his own Triune nature, an 'eternal community of love', and secondly

---

[195] Stern, *JNTC*, 175.

[196] Ibid., 219.

[197] Ibid., 266.

[198] Ibid., 594.

[199] Ibid., 602.

[200] Ibid., 505 (Col. 1:17).

[201] Juster, *Growing*, 27.

directed outward to his creation. His love for all people does not assure their salvation, for they must respond to it in repentance and faith.

> So you can see that God's love is not caused by anything. God does not love people because of what they have done or he was able to see that they would do in the future. God's love has no cause outside of himself. This is a wonderful comfort for weak, sinful and foolish mankind. It means that salvation is more than just possible. But it also means that we must love and obey God in return. If we despise his kindness and ignore his call to repent, believe and be faithful, we will bear the punishment of our sin (Rom. 2:4–5).[202]

God's truthfulness and righteousness are 'two sides of the same coin'. God is true to himself, his promises and his people. His righteousness is not a 'blind, rigid obedience to a standard' as 'God's righteousness is not caused in any sense, certainly not by maintaining any kind of standard. God is his own standard.'[203]

God's righteousness is not 'soft heartedness that is always ready to forgive and forget'. God has high regard for justice, and will treat all humanity fairly. He will give all what they deserve, and only by his grace will any be saved. For Maoz this is no small matter.

> Are you ready to stand before God in judgment? Everything you did is so well remembered it is as if it were written in a book (Rev. 20:11–13). Your most hidden secrets will be revealed (Matt. 6:4; Luke 12:3). God cannot be bribed, manipulated or swayed from his righteousness. Every man, woman and child will receive his just reward on the day of righteous judgment.[204]

Theodicy and the Holocaust (Goldberg et al)

Louis Goldberg is concerned with the issues of theodicy that arise from such statements.

> One major problem is that of reconciling the doctrine of a righteous God with the existence of a world filled with evil. The presence of this contrast is a major ethical problem as to how … God [can] permit such evil to exist, as for example, a Hitler who was responsible for the death of six million Jewish people as well millions of other people through waging his war of conquest.[205]

---

[202] Maoz, *Lessons*, 48.
[203] Ibid.
[204] Ibid., 50.
[205] Goldberg, *Messianic Jewish Theology*, 80.

Goldberg proposes several answers to the problem of innocent suffering as exemplified in the Holocaust, but finds none of them sufficient. Whilst God gave Hitler time to make his evil decisions on this earth, 'he will pay for his crimes for all eternity'. None can give a full answer to the problem of the Holocaust, although one 'notable piece' of the jigsaw is that the State of Israel came into existence shortly afterwards.

> Another piece is that God led some of His choice believers into the camps and because of the testimony of these special servants of God, many a Jewish person came to faith, either in the camps, or after being delivered. One more piece is that one might say that Hitler functioned much in the same way as did the Pharaoh of the Exodus. The more this Pharaoh hardened his heart, the more he became the vessel of wrath by which many Jewish people afterwards would be able to escape out of Egypt. In the same way, Hitler was also the vessel of wrath by which many of those who remained after the war would go to Israel.
>
> Does this fully satisfy the problem? No! We live in an imperfect world as it is today and believers, as Habakkuk of old, need again to realize that many times, all we can do is live by our faith in God's promises and seek to be used of Him as He leads us.[206]

Other Messianic Jews have dealt more directly with the problem of theodicy, especially in the light of the Holocaust. Arthur Katz sees the Holocaust as a judgement on the sin of Israel, and the founding of the state of Israel as a sign of the resurrection.[207] Tsvi Sadan sets the suffering of Job as the paradigm by which the Holocaust should be understood, and links this to the suffering of Yeshua, showing how the Jewish people are themselves unconsciously living through the sufferings of Christ.[208] Barry Leventhal surveys much Jewish thought on the Holocaust, and finds only the suffering of God incarnate can relate to the death of the six million.[209]

---

[206] Ibid.

[207] Arthur Katz, *The Holocaust: Where Was God?* (Pensacola, Fl: Mt. Zion Publications, 1998); 'Ezekiel 37: The Necessary Death and Resurrection of Israel: A Prophetic Scenario for the Last Days' (http://www.hearnow.org/ezek37.html, accessed 6th October 2007); 'The Holocaust As Judgement' (Paper presented at the Lausanne Consultation on Jewish Evangelism – North American Regional Conference, 1995).

[208] Tsvi Sadan, 'The Jewishness I Reject and the Jewishness I Embrace or: From Yavneh to Golgotha' in *Proceedings of the LCJE International Conference, New York, 12–17 August, 1999.*

[209] Barry Leventhal, *Holocaust Apologetics: Toward a Case for the Existence of God* (Paper presented at the Lausanne Consultation on Jewish Evangelism – North American Regional Conference, 1997).

Conclusion

It can be concluded that the Doctrine of God is a topic ripe for development by Messianic Jews. Whilst some groundwork in exposition of the biblical material has been covered, more reflection and theological depth is now required. At present Messianic Jews take for granted the common ground of Judaism and Christianity, but there is little discussion of methodology or the historical processes by which the formulations of Judaism and Christianity have influenced each other in antithetical and complementary ways. For Messianic Jews the particular areas of concern have been the personhood of God, the nature of his Triune unity, and the Incarnation, which will be discussed in the following chapter.

There is no established theological tradition or stream of theological discourse which links the biblical material to the contemporary Messianic movement. The writers who have contributed to the discussion would not be in agreement in all aspects of their understanding of God. Nevertheless it is clear that there is sufficient common ground amongst them to allow for a continuing discussion of the nature of God, within the parameters set by Judaism and Christianity. The task for a Messianic Jewish theology, however, must be to appropriately, sensitively, intelligently and self-critically engage with the two larger streams of tradition from which a Messianic Jewish perspective must develop, and produce a theological articulation that is fully cognisant, relevant and vibrant in its affirmation of the reality and nature of the one true and living God. Mark Kinzer stresses: 'All Messianic Jewish leaders require an ability to understand historic Jewish and Christian concerns regarding the nature of God, and to articulate a view of God which is faithful to revelation, respectful of both traditions, and framed in an idiom that is both Jewish and contemporary.'[210]

What would be needed for a Messianic Jewish doctrine of God? A theology that would engage with the developments of rabbinic, Aristotelian, mystical and modern thought in the Jewish tradition, and the developments of patristic, scholastic, reformation and modern thought in Christianity. Such a theology must engage with the biblical materials, the theological traditions of both faiths, up to their present expression in the context of postmodern reflection. This would present a sufficient challenge to most students of Judaism and Christianity. That Messianic Jews have *begun* to take up this challenge is apparent, but further reflection and exposition is needed to articulate a fully developed Messianic Jewish understanding of God.

---

[210] Mark Kinzer, *Course Outline, MJ518: God and the Messiah* (Messianic Jewish Theological Institute, Fuller School of Theology, 2004), 1.

Yet Messianic Jews potentially have much to contribute on the subject, combining and appropriating the insights and resources of two related but conflicting theological traditions. What they have to say on the nature of God has clear implications for their situating of themselves in relation to these two communities, and will have important consequences for their identity, rationale and apologetics. It remains to be seen how they will find the theological resources that will enable them to have something new to say on the subject, and are able to deal systematically and creatively with the tensions produced by the apparent clash of the two faith traditions. The present chapter represents one attempt to map out the territory. What emerges from this survey is the realisation of the need for an appropriate Christology in MJT. The chapter that follows addresses this question.

Chapter 5

Yeshua the Messiah: The Shaping of Messianic Jewish Christology

Introduction

> At the centre of the controversy between the Church and Synagogue stands the Christological question. This is not a question whether Jesus is the Messiah, but whether the Christian understanding of the Messiah is admissible in view of the Jewish concept of God. Here lies the dividing line between Judaism and Church. On this point neither can afford to compromise.[1]

Messianic Jews stand astride Jocz's 'dividing line', refusing to partition Judaism and Christianity into two mutually exclusive theological systems.[2] Nowhere is this more apparent than in the form of their belief in Jesus, which *seems* forced to choose between being either blasphemous to Judaism or heretical to Christianity; either clashing with the fundamental tenets of Jewish monotheism or compromising the uniqueness of Christ. However, the majority of Messianic Jews argue it is possible to have a theology of Yeshua which is completely Jewish and also compatible with orthodox Christian theology. The nature of Yeshua as Messiah and Son of God has always been a matter of controversy between Jews and Christians so it is bound to be a focal point for MJT.

The divine nature of Yeshua was again brought to prominence in the Messianic movement by the November 2002 articles in *Israel Today*.[3] In that issue 12 Messianic Jews were asked their views on the Divinity of the

---

[1] Jacob Jocz, 'The Invisibility of God and the Incarnation' in *The Messiahship of Jesus*, edited by Arthur Kac, rev. ed. (Grand Rapids: Baker, 1986), 189. Reprinted from *Canadian Journal of Theology* 4, no. 3 (1958).

[2] Cf. Daniel Boyarin, *Boundary Lines: The Partition of Judaeo-Christianity* (Philadelphia: University of Pennsylvania Press, 2004).

[3] A. Schneider, ed., 'Messianic Jews Debate the Deity of Jesus,' *Israel Today* 22 (November 2001): 21.

Messiah, and some of the answers given 'were made to seem to state that Yeshua is not God'.[4] Gershon Nerel comments: 'Like in ancient times, also the modern movement of Jewish Yeshua-believers is shaping its corporate identity through theological debates and doctrinal definitions. Particularly during the last two years we are observing unceasing discussions concerning the topic of Yeshua's divinity.'[5]

Tsvi Sadan notes the uncertainty that is found in the Messianic movement on the issue. 'As far as the Trinity is concerned, the truth is that there are as many opinions as there are people. I have talked to many and sometimes it was scary to find out what some of them believe in.'[6]

Joseph Shulam of *Netivyah* in Jerusalem is concerned at the level of heat generated by the controversy on the divinity of Christ.

> The question … is one of the hottest in all of Christianity and especially among the brothers and sisters in Israel. There have been inquisitory actions taken here by some brothers as if they were Savonarola or Torquemada during the darkest periods of Christian history, but with God's help we shall overcome this wave of tyrannical leadership with the love of the Lord and the Grace of the Cross.[7]

Elazar Brandt also expresses concern. 'Those who question the deity of Yeshua but serve him faithfully ought not to be labelled as heretics or unsaved for their ideas alone; likewise, Trinitarians ought not [to] be labelled idolaters by non-Trinitarians if their intent is to worship and serve one G-d. If we cannot grant each other some room for fresh thought, we will never advance beyond Nicæa in our concept of G-d.'[8]

David Stern recognises the need for Messianic Jews to develop their Christology: 'I challenge Messianic Jews, especially those of us who feel in our gut the need for staying Jewish, to get enough training in theology to deal seriously with the complex data underlying the Church's affirmation of Yeshua's deity – which can even be supported by material in the Talmud and other classical Jewish writings.'[9]

---

[4] David H. Stern, 'Israel's Messianic Jews and the Deity of Yeshua: An Update,' *Israel Today* 23 (July 2002): 23. http://mayimhayim.org/Academic%20Stuff/David%20 Stern/Article.htm accessed May 24th, 2007.

[5] Gershon Nerel, 'Eusebius' *Ecclesiastical History* and the Modern Yeshua Movement: Some Comparisons,' *Mishkan* 39 (2003), 80.

[6] Tsvi Sadan, e-mail message to author, June 5, 2003.

[7] Joseph Shulam, e-mail message to author, March 3, 2003.

[8] Elazar Brandt, e-mail message to author, March 10, 2003.

[9] Stern, 'Israel's Messianic Jews', 2.

The Need for Christology

Christology is concerned with the person, offices and work of Christ. This includes study of the life of Jesus (his virginal conception, birth, teaching, ministry, messianic claims, passion, atoning death, resurrection, ascension and second coming) and theological reflection on his pre-existence, Incarnation, uniqueness and divine nature. Messianism in Judaism discusses the appearance, identity, activity and implications of the *Mashiach*, the anointed one, who will occupy the particular office and future role of the expected heir of David. It deals with the signs of the Messiah's coming and what Israel must do to bring the Messianic Age. Jewish and Christian understandings of the concept of the Messiah have developed in interaction and opposition to one another in the light of Jesus' disputed claims. The widely divergent understandings of the Messianic idea in Judaism and Christianity challenge MJT to articulate a doctrine of the Messiah which addresses its own and its parent communities authentically, coherently, contemporaneously and relevantly.

Whilst there is strong and heated debate on the subject, there is little *written* material on the doctrine of the Messiah, especially on the relationship between the Jewish understanding of the Messiah and the Christian understanding of God. Messianic Jews have yet to address the topic in an organised and reflective way, and there are several reasons for this. There is the traditional Jewish reluctance to engage in the task of systematic theology, which appears overly abstract, conceptual, Hellenistic and accompanied by latent or overt anti-Judaism. Secondly, Messianic Jews often lack the theological training to engage competently in the disciplines of Jewish studies and Christian theology, and 'do not have the time for theology'[10] which they see as a Christian preoccupation. Those leading MJCs are caught up in pastoral and administrative activities. Few make the time to reflect on their theological methods and resources, and commit this to writing.

In addition, the Messianic movement has yet to develop the theological maturity to effectively speak on issues that have been the focus of controversy over many centuries. It is often divided on theological, cultural, geographical and generational lines, and there is no agreed mechanism or procedure for deciding key issues of theological orthodoxy. The presence of 'unorthodox views' is a matter of some embarrassment to leaders in the movement. David Stern comments on the lack of follow-up from the *Israel Today* article: 'So far as I know, there is no fuller report of these discussions. The sense of the meeting of the leaders that brought the problem to wide attention was that it would be better not to air our laundry (clean or dirty, as the case may have been).'[11]

---

[10] Verbal statement, Ruth Fleischer, 2002.

[11] David Stern, e-mail message to author, May 8, 2003.

Christology in Doctrinal Statements

The creeds and doctrinal statements produced by the Messianic movement reflect an orthodox Christian understanding of Jesus and the Godhead. All are uniformly Trinitarian, but expressed with varying degrees of Jewish content.[12] Michael Schiffman writes: 'Belief in the triune nature of God is not merely held by a group within the Messianic community, but is believed by every Messianic organisation of the community: the Union of Messianic Jewish Congregations, the Fellowship of Messianic Congregations and the Messianic Alliance of America.'[13]

For example, the Messianic Jewish Alliance of America (MJAA) *Basis of Belief* affirms the Triune nature of God and the deity of the Messiah.

> GOD – We believe that the *Shema*, 'Hear O Israel, the Lord our God, the Lord is one' (Deut 6:4), teaches that God is *Echad*, as so declared: a united one, a composite unity, eternally existent in plural oneness [Gen. 1:1 (*Elohim*: God); Gen. 1:26 'Let us make man in our image'; Gen. 2:24 Adam & Eve were created to be as one flesh (*basar echad*)], that He is a personal God who created us (Gen. 1 & 2), and that He exists forever in three persons: Father, Son, and Holy Spirit, as mentioned in Romans 8:14–17 (Father, Spirit, and Messiah – Son) and Matt. 28:18–20 (immersing in the name of the Father, Son, and Holy Spirit).
>
> A. GOD THE FATHER (*Abba*) – John 6:27b; 1 Cor. 1:3; Gal. 1:1; Rev. 3:5, 21; Jer. 3:4, 19; 31:9; Mal. 1:6; Matt. 6:9, 32; Luke 10:21–22; John 1:14; 4:23; 5:17–26; 6:28–46; Rom. 8:14–15.
>
> B. GOD THE SON (*HaBen*)
> 1. God does have a Son [Ps. 2; Prov. 30:4–6 (cf. Heb. 1); Luke 12:35–37; John 1:29–34, 49; 3:14–18].
> 2. The Son, called *Yeshua* (Jesus), meaning salvation, came to this world born of a virgin [Is. 7:14 (cf. Luke 1:30–35)].
> 3. The Son is God (Deity), and is worshipped as God, having existed eternally [Ps. 110:1 (cf. Heb. 1:13); Is. 9:6–7; Matt. 28:18–20; Phil. 2:5–11; Col. 1:15–19; Rev. 3:21 (Heb. 1 – worshipped by angels); Rev. 4:8, 5:5–14].

---

[12] Gershon Nerel, 'Creeds among Jewish Believers in Yeshua,' *Mishkan* 34 (2001), 61–79. Nerel examined the creeds of the Hebrew Christian Alliance of America (HCAA) (1915); the International Hebrew Christian Alliance (IHCA) (1925); the IHCA Hebrew Christian Church Commission (1932); Abram Poljak's 'Jewish Christian Union' (1939); and the Warsaw Hebrew Christian Community (published by Jacob Jocz) (1939).

[13] Michael Schiffman, *The Return of the Remnant: The Rebirth of Messianic Judaism* (Baltimore: Lederer, 1996), 93.

4. This One is the promised *Mashiach* (Messiah) of Israel [Is. 9:6–7; 11:1; Dan. 9 (esp. verses 20–26); Is. 53; John 1:17, 40–41, 45, 49; Mark 8:29].
5. He is the root and offspring of David, the bright and morning star [Num. 24:17; Rev. 22:16].
6. He is our Passover, the Lamb of God [1 Cor. 5:7; Rev. 5; John 1:29].[14]

Assent to Creeds in Messianic Judaism

However, not all Messianic Jews subscribe to creeds, for a variety of reasons.[15] Esther Dorflinger, in the case that was brought before the Israeli High Court in 1979, chose not to join a church or give her assent to any creedal statement. She declared: 'Theology and theological creeds are alien to the pure and simple New Testament faith in Jesus. The identity of Jesus is not simply an issue of theological definitions but one of divine revelation. My understanding of Jesus is not based on theological definitions but on God's revelation to me personally by his Spirit according to his word.'[16]

Joseph Shulam is similarly reluctant to affirm a particular creed (although willing to make his own personal statement of faith), seeing creeds as part of the 'plague of denominational sectarianism imported by "well meaning 'Christian' Missionaries" who have brought with them the divisions and religious rivalry from their home countries.'[17]

Jewish believers should not be 'infected with 'Creedalism' [*sic*] and sectarian attitudes, which basically are foreign to the very [s]pirit of Israel'. Instead they should 'be satisfied with the study of the Word of God' and allow it alone to be their constitution. Then they would not need a 'Statement of Faith'.

David Stern, whilst affirming the deity of Yeshua, was unwilling to sign the joint declaration recently proposed by leaders of congregations in Israel.

> I myself believe in the deity of Yeshua, and I can affirm the paragraph, but I would not have signed, because I don't believe others should require me to sign their creeds as a test of my faith ... I prefer to see Messianic Jews given room to express

---

[14] MJAA, 'MJAA Doctrinal Statement,' http://www.mjaa.org/statementOfFaith.html (accessed March 3, 2003).

[15] There is the traditional Jewish reluctance (with a few notable exceptions) to codify belief. Cf. Solomon Schechter, *Aspects of Rabbinic Theology* (New York: Schocken, 1969), 12: 'With God as a reality, Revelation as a fact, the Torah as a rule of life, and the hope of Redemption as a most vivid expectation, they felt no need for formulating their dogmas into a creed, which, as was once remarked by a great theologian, is repeated not because we believe, but that we may believe.'

[16] Quoted in Dan Cohn-Sherbok, *Messianic Judaism* (New York: Cassell, 2000), 196.

[17] Joseph Shulam, e-mail message to author, March 3, 2003.

their theological views within the framework of Jewish thought, rather than be required to sign on the dotted line of theological formulations that have a non-Jewish origin and a non-Jewish cast to them.[18]

Hugh Schonfield and the Divinity of the Messiah

Messianic Jews are well aware of the important episode in the history of the *International Hebrew Christian Alliance*, the forerunner of the contemporary Messianic movement.[19] Adherence to a creedal statement was used to ensure orthodoxy within the Alliance in 1937. Hugh Schonfield, who wrote *The History of Jewish Christianity* and the sensationalist *The Passover Plot*, was excluded from membership of the Alliance because of his dissent from its doctrinal statement.

Schonfield had originally affirmed an orthodox Christology, with Jesus as 'God's Son', the 'one mediator between God and man'. His own proposed basis of faith for the IHCA had expressed the Incarnation as 'God was manifest in the flesh and we beheld His glory – the glory as of the only begotten of the Father, full of grace and truth.'[20] But as his heterodox views developed, the matter was brought to the International Conference of 1937, where Schonfield's personal statement of his views was found 'inadequate'. A committee set up to investigate Schonfield's position insisted on a 'yes' or 'no' answer to the question, 'Do you believe in the Deity of Jesus Christ, as set forth in Article no. 9 of the Bye-Laws?'[21] Schonfield and his wife could not give assent to the article, and their membership of the IHCA was withdrawn.[22] As Harcourt Samuel reported in *The Hebrew Christian* magazine:

---

[18]   Stern, 'Israel's Messianic Jews', 2.

[19]   IHCA, now IMJA. For what follows see Richard Harvey, 'Passing over the Plot? The Life and Work of Hugh Schonfield,' *Mishkan* 37 (2002): 35–48.

[20]   Ibid., 41.

[21]   Ibid., 43. 'Persons eligible for membership must be Hebrew Christians who a) have made public confession of their faith; b) have accepted Jesus as their personal Saviour; c) believe in the Atonement and vicarious suffering which He has wrought on the Cross at Calvary; d) believe in His Deity and Resurrection; e) declare their adherence to the scriptures of the Old and New Testaments as the supreme rule of faith and life.'

[22]   His own position was summarised in *The Jew of Tarsus: An Unorthodox Portrait of Paul* (London: Macdonald, 1946), vii-viii: 'I am a Jew, and one, moreover, entitled to be termed a Nazarene, since Jesus is for me the Messiah. But I am not a Christian, if that name is to be applied only to those who have subscribed to the dogmas of the Church in their full orthodox form. I confess the Unity of God, not a Unity in Trinity.' (Harvey, 'Passing Over,' 47).

It was a most difficult matter that had to be decided. The fact that two Committees composed of men whose loyalty to the fundamental doctrines of our most holy faith is beyond question, should have reached different conclusions reveals its complexity. To some it may appear to be a mere matter of words, but the issue is much deeper than that. Believing as we do, in common with the whole Christian Church in all ages, that Jesus is God; we felt it imperative that we should not have in membership any who hold what we must regard as a lesser conception of Him and that there should be no doubt whatever as to the position of the Alliance. We are more sorry than we can say that we have lost the services of Mr and Mrs Schonfield. They have rendered invaluable service in many ways for a long period and are loved by us all. Nevertheless, we could do no other. One piece of solid satisfaction has come out of what was a most disagreeable necessity, and that is, that it has been established beyond doubt that the Alliance and all its members stand without compromise of any sort for the absolute Deity of our Lord Jesus Christ and the great doctrines of the evangelical faith.[23]

Schonfield's case has continued to strike chords in the Messianic move-ment,[24] and few have gone beyond or departed from an orthodox (Christian) formulation as a result.

The Development of Christology

Christological methods and resources in the Messianic movement are derived from previous approaches. Amos Funkenstein has identified five phases in the history of Jewish-Christian encounter and the presentation of the Messiahship and divinity of Yeshua.[25] The first stage was the early debate on the interpretation of the Hebrew scriptures, the *Tanach*. The use of *Testimonia*, collections of texts from the Hebrew scriptures confirming the Messiahship of Jesus, may be seen in some of sermonic material in the New Testament writings, and the *Dialogue of Justin Martyr with the Jew Trypho* is an example of this type of apologetic. A second phase developed with the use of Jewish sermonic material, the aggadah, in the context of mediaeval debate, as exemplified by Raymundus Martini's manual for Christian Preachers, the *Pugio Fidei*.[26] The debate between Paulus Christiani and Nachmanides in 1264 in Spain illustrates this approach. The third development was the use

---

[23] Harcourt Samuel, 'Editorial,' *The Hebrew Christian* 10 (April 1937–Jan 1938): 104–05.

[24] David Rausch, *Messianic Judaism*, 39–43; Richard Harvey, 'Passing Over the Plot', 48.

[25] Amos Funkenstein, 'Basic Types of Christian Anti-Jewish Polemic in the Middle Ages,' *Viator* 2 (1971): 373–82.

[26] Cf. Richard Harvey, 'Raymundus Martini and the Pugio Fidei: A Survey of the Life and Works of a Medieval Controversialist.' (MA diss., University College, London, 1991).

of the Jewish mystical tradition, the *Kabbalah*, to prove the Messiahship and divinity of Jesus. Tsvi Sadan is representative of this approach.

The fourth stage combined modern critical methods of study of scripture with changing views of the historical Jesus. In some cases this led to a liberal and rationalist perspective on Jesus, setting him within the Jewish context of his day, but not recognising his Messiahship or Divinity.[27] The Jewish reclamation of Jesus, and the loss of confidence in the uniqueness of Christ both emerged in the light of this development of 19th and 20th century critical studies. At the same time, the modern missionary movement developed, and Hebrew-Christian apologetics were developed and propagated by writers such as Joseph Christian Frey.[28]

A fifth 'Postmissionary' stage can be detected in recent presentations by Messianic Jews employing postliberal and postcritical readings of the biblical and rabbinic materials.[29] The term 'Postmissionary' is employed by Mark Kinzer, and typifies a less adversarial and apologetic approach to Jewish tradition. This approach is eclectic, and as yet undefined, but may allow for a rediscovery of Jesus as both Jewish Messiah and Incarnate deity. It is concerned with the construction of Jewish identity and 'Messianic Jewish social space' as much as with the nature and being of the Messiah. The materials of the Jewish tradition, *Torah*, *Talmud* and *Kabbalah*, are all resources from which a contemporary Jewish expression can be formulated. These are then filtered through the lens of modern and postmodern Jewish thought, which deconstructs, challenges and re-addresses age-old problems of Jewish existence.

Emerging Christologies

Previous studies have emphasised the uniformity of the orthodox (Christian) Christologies within Messianic Judaism.[30] The presence of heterodox views has caused some embarrassment within the movement.[31] It is clear that there is considerable variety within Messianic Judaism on the nature of

---

[27] Cf. Donald Hagner, *The Jewish Reclamation of Jesus* (Grand Rapids, MI: Zondervan, 1984).

[28] Joseph C. Frey, *Joseph and Benjamin: A Series of Letters on the Controversy Between Jews and Christians* (New York: Daniel Fanshaw, 1840), reprinted as *The Divinity of the Messiah* (Israel: Keren Ahavah Meshichit, 2002).

[29] Mark Kinzer, *Postmissionary Messianic Judaism: Redefining Christian Engagement with the Jewish People* (Grand Rapids: Baker Academic/Brazos, 2005). See below, 'The Hidden Messiah of Postmissionary Messianic Judaism'.

[30] E.g. Rausch, 'Messianic Judaism,' 125–26.

[31] John Fischer, 'Yeshua – The Deity Debate,' *Mishkan* 39 (2003), 27. The theme of the issue is 'The Divinity of the Messiah', with seven significant articles on the topic.

the Messiah. Five emerging Christologies can be identified which represent the spectrum of thought within the movement. The assumptions, resources, methods and content of each perspective are described, beginning with those closest to Christian orthodoxy, and concluding with those more in harmony with Judaism. The first reflects Protestant Reformed and Evangelical tradition. The second recontextualises the Nicæan formulation without losing its substance. The third articulates the deity of Christ in terms of the *Kabbalah* and the Jewish mystical tradition. The fourth attempts a new Christological method in its handling of the traditional materials. The fifth arises from Unitarian thought that denies the deity of Jesus and echoes adoptionist Christology. [32]

All these approaches accept that Yeshua (Jesus) is the Messiah, and are happy to base this on his fulfilment of prophecy in the Hebrew scriptures. They acknowledge his Jewishness, atoning work, and resurrection. The question is therefore what *kind* of Messiah he is, and how this is expressed in response to both Jewish tradition and Christian teaching. The focus of the current debate is the person of Yeshua in relation to the nature of God. [33]

Protestant and Evangelical

Theocentric Christology

Baruch Maoz warns of the dangers of compromise on Christology.

> It is very dangerous for us to choose to think of Jesus in terms that we might find more comfortable, or more understandable … It is wrong to give ourselves over to the rabbis, to allow them to wrest from our hearts increasing portions of our Faith, until they take us wholly captive, to do their will. We ought never to forget that precisely denials of Jesus such as are common to rabbinic Judaism today brought about the rejection and crucifixion of our Lord. [34]

---

[32] Developments in Christology outside the Messianic movement are not part of the present study except where their contributions have been adopted by MJT, eg. N.T. Wright, Larry Hurtado, Richard Bauckham and Oscar Skarsaune. Also not included are those who have written on Christology in the context of Messianic Judaism and Jewish-Christian relations, but are not actively part of the Messianic movement such as Rosemary Ruether and John Pawlikowski. Jewish scholars such as Geza Vermes, Pinchas Lapide are also not included.

[33] Other aspects of the person and work of the Messiah, such as Yeshua's self-consciousness, Jewish identity, revelatory presence, saving work (sin and atonement) and example for life are beyond the scope of the present study. Yeshua's relationship to Torah will be discussed in chapter 6.

[34] Baruch Maoz, *Lectures on The Person of Christ – Part Six – Other NT Texts and a Systematic Summary* (pre-publication copy, Rishon-le-Zion: Hagefen Press, 1999), 11.

Maoz argues for an orthodox Christology within a systematic theology framed by the Confessions of the Protestant Reformation. His exposition of the divine and human nature of Christ and his Trinitarian understanding of the nature of God are clear and unequivocal. His material, in the form of unpublished lectures and his book *Judaism is Not Jewish*[35] engages fully with Christological questions. He leaves little room for flexibility when it comes to expressing the nature of the Messiah or God outside the biblical frame of reference as interpreted by Christian orthodoxy. As a critical participant-observer Maoz takes the Messianic movement to task for failing to focus on the Trinity: 'The Messianic Movement has been far too tolerant of deviant views on central doctrinal issues … it is important to take note of the Unitarian tendency that finds acceptance among many non-Unitarian Messianics as expressed in a growing embarrassment with the Trinity and the deity of Christ.'[36]

In response to this trend Maoz has organised conferences 'to promote a courageous Gospel witness to the Jewish people that refuses to kowtow to rabbinic standards or place cultural matters where Christ should be'.[37] Topics for lectures include: the Deity and Centrality of Christ; the Trinity and Jewish Evangelism; Nicaea and Chalcedon. These show the clear emphasis of Maoz and others in this stream. Whilst labeling himself 'Jewish Christian' rather than 'Messianic Jewish' Maoz is clearly engaged in dialogue with the main positions and protagonists within the Messianic movement.

Maoz is clear about his presuppositions, acknowledging his debt to the tradition of Reformed Protestantism in which he has been nurtured. 'I know nothing but what I have been taught. I lay claim to no originality, so all you can read from me has been better said by others before me and can be found in all the major books on theology, particularly in this case on Christology. I see little wisdom in attempting to reinvent the wheel.'[38]

For Maoz, the deity of Christ is a *sine qua non*:

> Christianity stands or falls with regard to the identity, nature and accomplish-ments of Jesus. It has to do with his pre-existence, his birth, life, suffering, teach-ings, deeds, death, resurrection, ascension, reign and return. It is as dependent on him as is life on the existence of oxygen … If Jesus is not both God and man, and God and man in the fullest sense possible – equal to the Father in his deity, in all things but sin like us in our humanity – the Gospel is a vanity of vanities, a pursuit after the wind.[39]

---

[35] Baruch Maoz, *Judaism is not Jewish: A Friendly Critique of the Messianic Movement* (Fearn, UK: Mentor/Christian Focus Publications, 2003).

[36] Ibid., 252–54.

[37] 'Jewish Christian Conference', May 22–24, 2003 in Vienna, Virginia, USA.

[38] Baruch Maoz, e-mail message to author, January 10, 2003.

[39] Baruch Maoz, 'The Person of Christ' (Annual Lecture of the Israel College of the

Maoz expounds without argument the pre-existence and co-equality of the Son.

> Before Jesus was man, he was God. He had the very nature of God, that sum of essential, inherent characteristics that distinguishes God from all other beings. Whatever could be said of God could be said of Jesus. He was eternal, self-existent, perfectly holy, glorious beyond description. He knew all things, was present everywhere, could do all that was in his holy will. He is *equal to* God – yet God has no equal.[40]

Using any 'human grid' of understanding other than the formulations of the church fathers leads to a denial of Jesus' divinity, and should not be contemplated.

> There is no lower grade of deity. *Hear O Israel, the Lord our God the Lord is one.* Jesus is either very God of very God, the only begotten of the Father – begotten and not made – of the same and equal essence of the Father, or he is not our Saviour. Nor may he be considered divine in any sense. Only by distancing ourselves from Jesus as he appears in the scripture, only to the extent that we allow human grids and human interests to determine our understanding of who Jesus is, only then can we find cause to deny his utter deity. Only then dare we speak of him as in some sense divine yet not God, unequal to the Father in his deity.[41]

Maoz's doctrine of Christ is theologically orthodox, yet at the expense of any substantial engagement with Jewish thought or expression that goes beyond the biblical data. His matrix of interpretation leaves little room for new articulations of Trinitarian concepts or discussion of the divine and human natures of Christ. He stays deliberately within the mode of Chalcedonian thought, as interpreted through the Reformed tradition. What is lacking in Maoz's exposition is any discussion of the issues that arise in interpreting the divinity of Christ within a Jewish cultural or religious context, and the theological matrix with which Maoz works is the Reformed *sola scriptura, sola fide, solus Christus*.

For Maoz, the distinction between 'Judaism' and 'Jewishness' is crucial to his theological method.[42] Religious 'Judaism', the religion developed by the

---

Bible in Jerusalem, March 2002), reprinted in abbreviated form in *Maoz News*, May 10, 2002 (Volume 4.69), 1.

[40] Baruch Maoz, 'Lectures on The Person of Christ – Part Four (Philippians 2:1–11)', 5.

[41] Baruch Maoz, 'Lectures on The Person of Christ – Part Six – Other NT Texts and a Systematic Summary', 9.

[42] See Maoz, *Judaism is not Jewish,* and Richard Harvey, 'Judaism is Not Jewish: A Review' in CWI Herald (Summer 2003), http://www.banneroftruth.org/pages/ articles/article_detail.php?490 (accessed 6th October 2007).

rabbis, is a false path away from the New Testament revelation, and no use should be made of it in the attempt to articulate or legitimate Christian truth about the Messiah. 'Jewishness' is an ethnic, cultural and national identity, which should not be linked to an anti-Christian religious component. The error of the Messianic movement is the blurring of these two categories, at the expense of biblical revelation and a proper focus on the supremacy of Christ. Maoz's plea for a 'Jewish Christianity' retains its focus on the 'Christian' belief in Jesus, whilst allowing some 'non-religious' Jewish expression.

This argument restates a high Christology, but the underlying premise, that the 'Judaism' of the rabbis is not properly 'Jewish' is based on a negative construction of Judaism that arises from traditional Jewish-Christian polemics and a Reformation reading of Paul. This will not convince many, oversimplifying the complex interaction between religious, ethnic, cultural and other factors that make up Jewish identity. Furthermore, it is unlikely that the Messianic Jewish movement will fully accept the norms and criteria of Maoz's theological system, with its own Reformed Protestant perspective on the relationship between the gospel and culture, where culture is always subject to the gospel. Nevertheless the emphasis on the centrality of Christ, and a right understanding of his divine and human nature, is one that strikes a chord with many in the Messianic movement, and Maoz's position is a safe option for many in a complex area.

The Pre-Incarnate Christ

Arnold Fruchtenbaum argues for the doctrines of the Trinity, Incarnation and divine nature of Christ on the basis of the fulfilled prophecies of the Hebrew Bible.

> It has been shown that Jesus is the only person who could possibly fulfil all of these prophecies. Associated with a Christian interpretation of these Scriptures are certain doctrines which are consistently regarded under Judaism as being contrary to Hebrew Scriptures and therefore wholly unacceptable to any Jew. These are: 1. The belief that Messiah is God. 2. The belief in God as a Triune Being … It is commonly stated that these beliefs are thoroughly un-Jewish, being the invention of Christianity and originating in the New Testament … It can be shown that the doctrine of the Trinity actually originates in the Hebrew Scriptures and is merely developed and clarified in the New Testament.[43]

Fruchtenbaum illustrates his argument with a Christological exegesis of some thirty messianic prophecies, without discussion of alternative Jewish readings, hermeneutical principles or exegetical methods. Thus passages like Isa 9:6 'Teaches that: Messiah would be a king … Messiah would be both

---

[43] Arnold Fruchtenbaum, *Messianic Christology* (Tustin, CA: Ariel Ministries, 1998), 102.

God and Man ... Messiah must appear prior to 70 A.D. because of the requirements of the Davidic Covenant and the destruction of the Temple.'[44] Likewise Mic. 5:2 teaches that 'Messiah would be divine as well as human, having existed from eternity past'.[45]

> He is to be born in Bethlehem, but regarding His divine origin, He is said to be 'from long ago, from the days of eternity.' The Hebrew words for 'from long ago, from the days of eternity' are the strongest Hebrew words ever used for eternity past. They are used of God the Father in Psalm 90:2. What is true of God the Father is also said to be true of this One who is born in Bethlehem ... Again we have a passage which shows that Messiah is to be human – being born at some specific point in time and at some specific place – yet having existed since all eternity past, and therefore divine.[46]

Fruchtenbaum's proof-text method is derived from earlier apologetics, and is not open to question. He concludes: 'If the concept of the Trinity is not Jewish, then neither are the Hebrew scriptures. Jewish believers cannot be accused of having slipped into paganism when they hold to the fact that Jesus is the divine Son of God.'[47]

Recontextualised Nicene Christology

Louis Goldberg recognised the problems inherent in formulating a Messianic approach to Christology, and warned:

> Some Messianic Jews have sought to ingratiate themselves with the Jewish community and have spoken of God as simply a Unity. However, to this writer, this accommodates too much to the Jewish position of how to understand God as interpreted by the rabbis and therefore gives away what the Scriptures would assert. We must give a strong positive witness that God be considered as a *composite* unity thereby allowing for the possibility of the persons within the Godhead but yet at the same time, insisting that God is one. In that way, we have recontextualised the doctrine of God from that of Nicea and dealt primarily with what the Hebrew texts have to say, and at the same time, also considering what the Messianic Jews of the first century asserted regarding who God is.[48]

---

[44] Ibid., 41.

[45] Ibid., 64.

[46] Ibid.

[47] Ibid., 116.

[48] Louis Goldberg, 'Recontextualising the Doctrine of the Trinity as Formulated by the Council of Nicaea' (LCJE-NA Regional Conference, Chicago, 1996), 26. Italics added.

Robert Fischer, Daniel Juster, David Stern and Michael Schiffman also attempt to recontextualise Nicæa, by explaining the difficulties raised for Jewish and Messianic Jewish thought, yet engaging with the context and content of the Nicæan formulation, and finding ways to express this within a Jewish frame of reference.[49]

The Trinity in the Dead Sea Scrolls

Robert Raymond Fischer finds support for the divinity of Yeshua in the Dead Sea Scrolls. His aim is:

> First, to share in considerable detail the exciting presence of Yeshua as He can be seen deeply ingrained in the very fibre of the Dead Sea Scrolls; while offering as background an exposition of the little understood historical fact that the Triune nature of the Godhead is a solidly documented Jewish heritage (not some new derived 'Christian' theology that was dreamt up by the Church Fathers, then later codified by the Church itself) as many as eighteen centuries after it was first taught by mainstream rabbis as a central Jewish understanding. All of this will be focused on illuminating a much deeper revelation that the roots of the Christian Church are not simply Jewish but they are rather most pointedly deeply planted in the spiritually rich Nazarene/Essene soil of Qumran, Jerusalem and the Galilee as evidenced by the Dead Sea Scrolls and other historical reference.[50]

New discoveries, he claims, have confirmed an originally Jewish understanding of the Triune nature of God.

> These monumental new revelations [of the Dead Sea Scrolls] that point clearly to the actual Jewish roots of the Church are all the more exciting when taken together with the fact that the mainline ancient Jewish precursors of the Essene Sect held a clear and widely taught Triune understanding of the Godhead as central to their belief system, an understanding that may have stemmed as far back as to our father Abraham.[51]

In Jewish tradition, such understanding was handed down from Adam. 'There is another tradition, perhaps fanciful or perhaps not, that this ancient understanding that encompassed the Doctrine of the Trinity "– was first taught by God himself to a select company of angels – who most graciously

---

[49] Space does not permit consideration of Yellin, Frydland, Rosenthal, Harvey and many others.

[50] Robert Fischer, e-mail to author, March 10, 2003 and http://www. olimpublications.com/index.htm (accessed May 4, 2003).

[51] Ibid.

communicated this heavenly doctrine to (Adam) the disobedient child of earth – From Adam it passed to Noah, and then to Abraham –".[52]

Whilst Fischer's use of these materials is uncritical and his methodology questionable, his approach is of interest because of its appeal to Jewish materials in the promotion of a high Christology.

Transcending Hebrew and Greek Categories

Daniel Juster recognises that, 'To raise the question of Yeshua's divinity is to open one of the greatest debates between Jews and Christians. This question leads to the whole debate about the Trinity, since the Messiah is said to be divine as one part of the Triune God.'[53]

Juster rejects the 'widely held conclusion of modern scholarship' that sharply differentiates between Hebraic and Hellenistic modes of thought as functional and ontological. For him the real question is rather 'how a metaphysic that is implied by biblical teaching compares and contrasts with a Greek metaphysic. Because all human beings are created in the image of God, communication and evaluation with regard to metaphysical views is cross-culturally possible.'[54]

This recognition gives the debate on Christology a more fruitful foundation. The Nicæan statement is neither 'totally Greek and unacceptable' nor an absolutely 'accurate metaphysical statement of biblically implied truth'. The affirmations of Nicæa which are implied by the Bible, are that Yeshua is 'Son of God'; 'only begotten from the Father'; 'begotten not made (created)' and 'light from light'. Other dimensions of the Nicæan formula, although biblically defensible, are

> unhelpful in a Jewish context because they lend themselves to connotative misunderstanding. 'God from God' and 'true God from true God' are phrases that too easily lend themselves to misconception. These statements emphasize divinity to such a degree that the humanity of the Son and His submission to the Father are eclipsed (e.g., a danger of Docetism). New Testament Christology, at least with regard to the relationship of the incarnate Messiah to the Father, in all biblical language and in all apocalyptic pictures of the Father and the Lamb in heaven, reflect[s] subordinationist overtones. 'One substance' language is difficult philosophically even if there are reasons for its use. He is in His divine nature everlastingly one in being with the Father. Perhaps other language such as 'one in essence' or 'one in His divine being' could be more helpful.[55]

---

[52] Ibid.

[53] Daniel Juster, *Jewish Roots: A Foundation of Biblical Theology for Messianic Judaism* (Rockvillle: Davar Publishing, 1986), 181.

[54] Ibid.

[55] Ibid. It ought to be stressed that by 'subordinationist' Juster is not defending the

Juster reformulates the truths safeguarded by Nicæa in order to better communicate to the modern Jewish mind. He urges Messianic Jews to look to the original Jewish roots that influenced the Nicene Creed and from these roots speak afresh to our day. 'The basic question addressed to Jew and Gentile from the Messiah is "Whom do you say that I am?" That the New Testament scriptures reveal Him as the risen Messiah is at the centre of Christological controversy. The supernatural risen Messiah transcends the issues of Hebraic and Greek categories because His work was not conceived by the mind of man.'[56]

Juster defends the idea that the unified being of God in the *Tanakh* is a differentiated unity, and follows this with discussion of the Angel of the LORD, the superhuman nature of the Messiah (Isa 9:6–7) and discussion of New Testament passages that show the divinity of Yeshua. He then gives his own understanding of Yeshua's two natures.

> He is one person or aspect of that plural manifestation of God (from the *Tenach*) who became a human being. He, therefore, is a man who depends on the Spirit, prays to the Father, gets weary and dies. His divine nature never dies, but he is human as well as divine. As such, prayer in the New Testament is not primarily addressed to Yeshua but to 'Our Father' in the Name of Yeshua. For Yeshua is the human revelation of the Father.[57]

Juster warns against the Christomonism that loses sight of God the Father, calling for full recognition of Yeshua's divinity whilst recognising that God is more than just Yeshua. He then calls for a deeper expression of the Trinity in Jewish terms. 'Jewish ways of expression are needed, ways more consistent to the New Testament, if Jews are to penetrate Christian rhetoric to see the Truth of Yeshua's divine nature.'[58]

There are several reasons why it is important to accept the 'uni-plurality of God' and the divine nature of Yeshua. According to Juster, only a perfect man could bring a full revelation of God, as humanity is made in the image of God. The revelation of God's love in the form of a human being is the greatest way possible to show God's love. Such revelation has unique redemptive significance, as the Messiah's suffering is the revelation of the suffering love of God himself. Because the Messiah is divine his suffering has infinite redemptive value. So for Juster 'the divinity of the Messiah is not

---

kind of subordinationism judged by the Church to be heretical – namely that the deity of the Son is a lesser 'deity' than that of the Father (and hence, the Son is not *fully* divine). Rather, Juster's concern is to preserve the *order within* the Godhead to which scripture bears witness. (I owe this observation to my editor, Robin Parry)

[56] Ibid.

[57] Ibid., 187.

[58] Ibid., 188.

idolatry, but reflects the fullest revelation of God.' 'The scriptures thus communicate to us the impression of one great divine reality of three inseparable manifestations of God. The relationship of love and accord blends the three into eternal oneness beyond human comprehension ... The reciprocal *giving relationship* of love is eternally existent within the plural unity of God.'[59]

Antinomies and Mysteries

David Stern views the present debate on the Divinity of Yeshua as significant, but wishes it to be understood properly in context, rather than be misconstrued. Referring to the *Israel Today* article which reported the debate in Israel, Stern stressed:

> More importantly, whilst most of the twelve are concerned not to become 'Gentilized,' few have theological training; and this combination can distort theologising. In such cases the statements should be evaluated less as theology than as a heart cry to preserve Jewish identity. I think all twelve of the Messianic Jews quoted are believers who love God and his Messiah Yeshua with all their heart, even if some of their words about Yeshua deviate from what most Christians consider acceptable.[60]

Stern uses the concept of antinomies[61] because the biblical data underlying the theology of Yeshua's deity are too complex to be discussed in short magazine articles or debated in the form of slogans. The deity of Yeshua is a topic which refuses to 'submit to law', and is one of the 'paradoxes, mysteries, phenomena in which "A" and "not-A" both hold.'[62] In the *JNT* and *JNTC* Stern addresses such questions as 'Is Yeshua God?' and 'Is God a Trinity?' but ignores the reflex responses of 'Absolutely' (Christian) and 'Absolutely not' (Jewish) to discuss the substance of the matter – what positive and negative answers might mean, and whether both Christian and Jewish contexts might admit of 'less confrontational formulations without compromising the scriptural data.'[63]

God is the Alpha and Omega, 'the one who existed at the beginning and will exist at the end'.[64] Yet Yeshua is also referred to as 'the Ancient of Days',

[59] Ibid., 189–90.
[60] Stern, 'Israel's Messianic Jews and the Deity of Yeshua: An Update' *Israel Today* July 2002, (http://www.mayimhayim.org/Academic%20Stuff/David%20Stern%20Article.htm) accessed March 30, 2007.
[61] He ascribes this term to Geddes MacGregor, *Philosophical Issues in Religious Thought* (Boston: Houghton Mifflin, 1973); e-mail to author, March 20, 2003.
[62] Stern, 'Israel's Messianic Jews', 23.
[63] David Stern, *The Jewish New Testament Commentary* (Jerusalem: Jewish New Testament Publications, 1992), xiii.
[64] Ibid., 790 (Rev 1:8).

in the language used to describe 'God, the Father' in Dan. 7:9–10.[65] Yeshua's
statement of Rev. 1:17 'I am the First and the Last' takes up a title 'which the
Tanakh applies only to *YHVH*' but is deliberately applied to Yeshua in the
New Testament.[66] God's plans for Yeshua are from eternity.

> **God has made him Lord and Messiah**. From the viewpoint of God and eternity
> the Word became a human being (Yn. [John] 1:1, 14; Pp. [Phil.] 2:5–11). Under the
> aspect of time, in Kefa's [Peter's] experience, Yeshua had just been revealed as
> who he really is. Non-Messianic Judaism objects that the New Testament says
> Yeshua, who is only a man, became a god. But the New Testament never says such
> a thing, not even here. What it says is that God had, from eternity, made him who
> was already equal with God before the universe was created, **both Lord** of all
> humanity **and** the promised **Messiah**, king of the Jewish people.[67]

Yeshua is 'the same, yesterday, today and forever' which for Stern means
that 'he is still Jewish and will remain a Jew.'[68] Also, we learn that the
Messiah, like the Torah in Jewish tradition, has eternal origins. 'Just as no
human effort is needed to bring the *Torah* from heaven, where, according to
Jewish tradition, it existed from eternity past, before God gave it to Moses on
Mount Sinai; so likewise no one needs to **ascend to heaven**, where the
Messiah once was – even, according to Jewish tradition, from eternity past
(compare Micah 5:1(2)) – in order **to bring Messiah down**.'[69]

Jewishly Palatable and Theologically Precise

For Michael Schiffman, Chalcedonian orthodoxy must be expressed in
Jewish terms.[70] The terminology of the debate 'sounds very Catholic, and
hence, very non-Jewish' and there will always be a tension between finding
a word that is 'Jewishly palatable' and one that is theologically precise. The
Trinity is a theological concept that does not occur in scripture. If it were a
biblical term, or if there were a Jewish equivalent, it would be more acceptable. Schiffman nevertheless sees a theological development between the
Hebrew Bible's revelation of God and the doctrine of the Trinity. 'The reason
a formal [T]rinitarian concept does not exist in the Old Testament is not
because it is borrowed from Hellenism, as some suggest, but because as the

---

[65] Ibid., (Rev 1:14).

[66] Ibid., 793 (Rev 1:17).

[67] Ibid., 225 (Acts 2:36).

[68] Ibid., 721 (Messianic Jews [Hebrews] 13:8).

[69] Ibid., 400 (Rom 10:6–8).

[70] Michael Schiffman, 'Messianic Jews and the Tri-Unity of God,' in *The Enduring
Paradox: Exploratory Essays in Messianic Judaism,* edited by John Fischer, 93–104
(Baltimore: Lederer, 2000), 62.

revelation of God is progressive, so as with the nature of the Messiah himself, a full enough revelation did not exist in Jewish scripture until the New Covenant.'[71]

The conclusions of Nicæa are 'looked upon by some as having a distinctively anti-Jewish bias' such as the changing of the day of worship from Sabbath to Sunday, and the discouragement to celebrate Jewish festivals. But Schiffman also recognises the good that was achieved in facing the theological challenges affecting the *Ekklesia*, leading to the articulation of truth in response to the appearance of error. Schiffman challenges the view that the Nicæan Trinitarian formula is incompatible with the Jewish view of monotheism, showing this to be an anachronistic reading of the nature of early Jewish monotheism which was far more flexibly interpreted than that of today, in the light of later Maimonidean rationalism and anti-Christian polemic.

For Fischer, Juster, Stern and Schiffman expressing the Incarnation and Trinitarian thought in Jewish terms goes beyond the refusal to engage which Maoz and Fruchtenbaum adopt. Yet further is work is needed on the presuppositions and assumptions behind such undertakings, the need for critical reflection on the use of Jewish sources, and the method of argumentation. In the remaining three Christologies, proposals are made which go further in their use of Jewish resources but risk departure from the Chalcedonian norms.

Jewish Mystical Christology

A third Messianic Christology uses Jewish mystical ideas and exegetical methods to develop an understanding of Yeshua that is compatible with this stream of Jewish tradition, and to express the divinity of Christ in Jewish terms. Tsvi Sadan employs this method, which was developed by the Christian Kabbalists of the Renaissance and was taken up in the apologetics of the Jewish missionary movement.[72]

Christian Kabbalah

Pico della Mirandola (1463–94) argued that the *Kabbalah* confirmed the truth of Christian teaching, especially on the nature of the Trinity, believing that he could prove the dogmas of the Trinity and the Incarnation on the basis of kabbalistic axioms. In his 900 theses he claimed 'No science can

---

[71] Ibid.

[72] François Secret, *Les Kabbalistes Chrétiens de la Renaissance*, rev. ed. (Arché: Milan, 1985).

better convince us of the divinity of Jesus Christ than magic and the Kabbalah.'[73]

Under Pico's influence Johannes Reuchlin linked the doctrine of the Incarnation to kabbalistic speculation on the names of God. History could be divided into three periods, corresponding to the ages of Chaos, Torah and the Messiah.[74] In the first period, that of the patriarchs, God revealed himself as the three-lettered Shaddai (שדי). In the period of the Torah he revealed himself to Moses through the four letters of the Tetragrammaton (יהוה), and in the period of redemption and grace He revealed himself in the five letters of Yehoshua (Jesus) (יהושה) [*sic*]. This miraculous name contained the unpronounceable name of God (יהוה) with the addition of the letter *shin* (ש). Midrashic exegesis was here employed to prove Christian truth, despite the intentions and theological grid of the Aggadah.

The Christian Kabbalists continued throughout the Renaissance and Reformation, and their findings were used by the 19th century missions as apologetic resources. Christianising the mystical tradition was the goal of Johann Christian Jakob Kemper of Uppsala, a 17th century Jewish Christian who established the truths of Christianity on the basis of Jewish sources, particularly the *Zohar*, to show that the messianic faith of the Christians was, in fact, the truly ancient *Kabbalah* of Judaism.[75] His commentary on the *Zohar* published in 1711 begins with three initial chapters, on the Trinity, the divinity of the Messiah, and on *Metatron*, the embodiment of the Messiah. To this is added a series of defences of the Christian faith, and finally a translation into Hebrew and commentary on the Gospel of Matthew.[76]

Kemper shared the same strategy as other Christian Kabbalists of the Renaissance, and foreshadows that of later authors such as Pauli, and the modern generation of apologists. They had two related aims, the use of Jewish esoteric teachings to confirm Christian truth, and the Christian application of kabbalistic methods to construct new ideas and symbols. Wolfson

---

[73] Scholem, Gershom, *Kabbalah* (Israel: Keter, 1974; reprint, New York: Meridian, 1978), 197.

[74] Cf. Sanhedrin 97b 'There are three ages: two thousand years of chaos; two thousand years of the law beginning with the revelation on mount Sinai; two thousand years of the Messianic kingdom; and then finally the world with is only Sabbath, rest in eternal life.' When the 'days of the Messiah come', the 'days of the Torah' come to an end. Quoted in Jürgen Moltmann, *History and the Triune God: Contributions to Trinitarian Theology*, translated by John Bowden (London: SCM Press, 1991), 104.

[75] Elliot R. Wolfson 'Messianism in the Christian Kabbalah of Johann Kemper,' in *Millenarianism and Messianism in Early Modern European Culture: Jewish Messianism in the Early Modern World*, edited by Matthew D. Goldish and Richard H. Popkin (The Netherlands: Kluwer Academic Publishers, 2001), 1.

[76] On Kemper's translation see Pinchas Lapide, *Hebrew in the Church*, (Grand Rapids, MI: Eerdmans, 1984), 76.

describes the work of the Christian Kabbalists as part of the overall Christian attempt 'to subvert Judaism by means of appropriating it'.[77]

Kemper's reorientation of the Jewish mystical tradition to prove the truths of orthodox Trinitarian Christianity is to be noted for its dexterity in handling the Jewish sources, the creativity of its exegetical methods and the awareness shown of the Jewish context into which a Christological interpretation of the tradition is inserted. He distinguishes sharply between the false Oral Torah of the rabbinic tradition and what is for him the true Oral Torah, the sayings of Jesus as recorded in the gospels. Rabbinic tradition is used to confirm the truth of the gospel presentation of the Messiahship, pre-existence and divinity of Jesus, and of his membership of the Trinity.

Wolfson sees Kemper's approach as naturally reflecting 'the split consciousness of his own existential situation. He cannot divest himself completely of his rabbinic upbringing even though he is a fully committed Christian. On the contrary, the veracity of his Christian affiliation is confirmed most precisely by the rabbinic and kabbalistic sources with which he is so intimately familiar.'[78]

Kemper's approach has been influential in Jewish missions, the Hebrew Christian movement, and Messianic Judaism. Joseph Christian Frey, the initiator of the *London Society for the Promotion of Christianity amongst the Jews*, used similar material from the Talmud and Kabbalah to demonstrate the divinity of the Messiah, in addition to the material from the scriptures pointing to the plurality of God.[79] A second example of the Christian Kabbalist approach is Rev. C.W.H. Pauli's *How Can Three Be One?*[80] The title of Pauli's book is taken from the passage in the *Zohar* which suggests the

---

[77] Wolfson, 'Messianism,' 1.

[78] Ibid., 3.

[79] Joseph Christian Frey, *Joseph and Benjamin: A Series of Letters on the Controversy Between Jews and Christians* (New York: Daniel Fanshaw, 1840; reprinted as *The Divinity of the Messiah*. Israel: Keren Ahavah Meshichit, 2002). Frey argues that although the doctrine of the plurality in unity is a stumbling block, the Rabbis acknowledge the divine plurality of *Elohim*, give testimony to the divinity of the Messiah, equating the Angel of the Lord (*Malak YHWH*) with God himself, and accept the Divinity of the Holy Spirit as the third person of the Trinity (Vol. 2 Part II–IV, 122–252 on 'The Divinity of the Messiah').

[80] Hirsch Prinz, *How Can Three Be One?* (reprint, Jerusalem: Yanetz, 1974). Rev. C.W.H. Pauli was born Hirsch Prinz (Zevi Nassi) in Breslau in 1800. He was educated as a rabbi by his father, was given a New Testament by the London Society missionary C.G.Petri, and became a believer in Jesus. He studied at Cambridge, and went on to become Lecturer in Hebrew at Oxford. He served as a missionary in Berlin and Amsterdam from 1840 to 1874, then retired to the UK where he died in 1877. (A. Bernstein, *Some Jewish Witnesses for Christ*. London: Operative Jewish Converts Institution, 1909), 210–11.

Trinity.[81] Pauli argued that 'our sages of blessed memory, long before the Christian era, held that there was a plurality in the deity.' Whilst quoting from rabbinic literature, he asks the reader to bear in mind the fact that

> the Holy Scriptures, and nothing but the Holy Scriptures, are the foundation to which he holds, and upon which he claims that the Holy One, Blessed be He, is a divine and wonderful Tri-unity. Quotations from human writings, however old, venerable and reliable, are only presented in order to show my beloved brethren of Israel how inconsistent they are to reject such a thought regarding our great God and Saviour, while professing – as they do – to follow closely after their fore-fathers who, it is here proved, believed this wholeheartedly.[82]

Pauli uses Jewish tradition to explore the three-fold nature of God: the identity of the *Memra*, Angel of the Covenant and *Metatron* as descriptions of the Son of God, 'who is an eternal emanation from God, therefore called Jehovah';[83] and the divinity of the Holy Spirit. Pauli concludes by appealing to his readers 'Whether I am not right in maintaining that the Jewish church before the Christian era, and in the first two centuries of the same, held the Doctrine of the Trinity, as a fundamental and cardinal article of the true faith?'[84]

Pauli's method is not without its critics. His dating of the *Zohar* to the second century is now generally rejected in favour of a twelfth century origin, and his examples of rabbinic hermeneutics including *gematria*[85] as proofs for the Messiahship of Jesus 'bring no honour to Christianity and reflect badly against the one who uses them as well as the one convinced by them.'[86] William Varner decries such attempts as deeply flawed: 'Although their motives may have been sincere, their hermeneutical methodology was so defective that they did more harm than good in its implementation. Their writings serve to warn Christians today about how *not* to conduct the Jewish-Christian discussion.'[87] Yet this approach, which Varner decries as

---

[81] Harry Sperling, Maurice Simon and Paul Levertoff, trans., *The Zohar* Vol. 3 (London: Soncino Press, 1934, reprinted 1978), 134 (34b). '"Hear O Israel, YHVH Elohenu, YHVH is one." These three are one. How can the three Names be one? Only through the perception of Faith: in the vision of the Holy Spirit, in the beholding of the hidden eyes alone.'

[82] Prinz, *How Can Three Be One?*, preface.

[83] Ibid., 70.

[84] Ibid., 89.

[85] Mathematical computations involving the numerical values of the Hebrew letters.

[86] William Varner, 'The Christian Use of Jewish Numerology.' *The Masters Seminary Journal* 8, no. 1 (Spring 1997), 53.

[87] Ibid., 59.

'straying from a grammatical-historical hermeneutic', continues to have its proponents.

Contemporary Mystical Exegesis

A contemporary example of this approach is that of Tsvi Sadan, an Israeli Messianic Jew, whose views have been quoted in the recent debate on the divinity of Jesus.[88] Whilst Sadan does not wish to harmonise Judaism and Christianity, he believes that it is possible to preserve the integrity of both traditions and at the same time affirm that 'the Jewish image of the Messiah matches in many cases the image of Jesus. This allows me to 'keep the integrity' of these texts that do not speak about Jesus and at the same time say that with a change of mind about who the Messiah is, these texts can reflect, and even shed light on the Jesus of the New Testament.'[89]

In order to achieve this synthesis of truth across the two traditions, Sadan explores new materials from the resources of Jewish tradition and attempts to employ Jewish hermeneutical approaches and theological methods where there is little Messianic Jewish theological tradition.[90]

Sadan develops a 'high Christology' (although he rejects the Christian associations of the term) which includes the Incarnation of Yeshua and the unity of the Godhead, whilst retaining Jewish language and thought.

> If I can sum up my methodological assumption it will be this: anything a Jew needs to know about the Messiah (Yeshua) can be found within the Jewish

---

[88] Tsvi Sadan, 'Preliminary Sketches on the Divine Status of the Messiah' (private paper, June 2006), 1. Sadan disassociates himself from the examples of Frey and Kemper, which he labels 'a good example of a wrong approach' (Preliminary Status, 1, fn 2,) but he is using the same material with less polemical intent, and his methodology is similar. However, Sadan does not accept the comparison. 'I never, and refuse to use this kind of methodology that imposes later or foreign categories on earlier texts. This is what Kemper and Frey are doing. They impose the Trinity on Jewish texts. This, I would say, is even unethical approach, in addition to it being anachronistic. It goes without saying that Kemper and Frey-like people are not my predecessors. Though using the same material, I take exception to their approach. A glaring example is that I do not try to prove the Trinity from these texts since not only do I not accept this dogma but it is known to all that the Trinity is not the Jewish conception of the Godhead. It will be good if you can clarify that one can believe in the deity of the Messiah without succumbing to faith in the Trinity.' (Email to author, October 1, 2007).

[89] Tsvi Sadan, email message to author, October 7, 2007.

[90] Sadan draws from the *Hekhalot*, *Merkavah* and *Shiur Qomah* early mystical writings, employing the tools of contemporary scholarship on Jewish mysticism for their exegesis and theological interpretation.

tradition. This is a bold assumption but nevertheless, one that can be substanti-ated without violating this very tradition that stresses its incompatibility with Jesus. In 'Hundred Names of Messiah' I am trying to demonstrate how this is pos-sible. One of the more difficult things to do is my attempt to 'talk Jewish' rather than bring disguised Christian concepts.[91]

Sadan recognises the difficulty of this, not only in the misunderstanding that it can cause, but also the fact that the 'Jewish tradition' is not monolithic and could rightly include the Christian Jewish tradition of the New Testament and later Christianity. Sadan is reluctant to use a 'Christian grid'.

> Messianic Jews today understand Yeshua primarily through the Christian grid that itself was built around a particular interpretation of the Pauline Corpus. Whether or not we [i.e. Messianic Jews] should start from this assumption is not my concern here. However, at the outset, this needs to be clarified: If we approach relevant Jewish sources that deal with the divine status of the Messiah from that starting point, we carry the risk of imposing upon them Christian views. Instead, the discussion below agrees with the premise that 'to arrive at the Christian belief one must transfer the earlier [Jewish] symbolism through that of another theolog-ical system' (Daniel Abrams).[92]

Sadan recognises that Messianic Jews come to the topic 'loaded with Christian preconceived ideas' which they must be willing to re-examine. But he also asserts that the Divine Messiah is a 'Jewish concept' which Messianic Jews can accept without 'changing our religion'. Using Jewish inter-testamental literature and the resources of the Jewish mystical tradition, and employing Jewish theological and interpretive methods and approaches, confirms the divinity of the Messiah in a way that avoids Christian Trinitar-ian discourse as unnecessary and unhelpful.

Yet Sadan realises the need for controls on interpretation and the difficul-ties involved in handling esoteric materials with occult, Gnostic and panthe-ist influences:

> One of the more complex issues is that of mystical tradition. Beside the point that it is unaccepted in the Protestant world from which we Messianic Jews are so heavily influenced, it is an abused field since the very nature of mysticism is that of very loose boundaries. Nevertheless, I think it is possible to discern where valid interpretation ends. Characteristically the sign is when the text is aimed at the possibility to manipulate either divine or occult powers. I am not saying it is easy

---

[91] Ibid.

[92] Tsvi Sadan, 'Preliminary Sketches', 1. Sadan quotes from Daniel Abrams, 'The Boundaries of Divine Ontology: The Inclusion and Exclusion of Metatron in the Godhead,' *Harvard Theological Review*, vol. 87:3 (1994): 319.

and one needs to approach it with extreme caution. All I am saying is that it is usable and valuable, and by the way, to lesser degree, you can find elements of gnosticism, occult and you name it in almost any Jewish source, including *Talmud, midrashim* and what not. I don't think we need to respond to it but simply put it aside. No human source is a pure source. After all, don't we need to exercise discernment also when dealing with Christian material? The doctrine of the *sefirot* should be particularly intriguing for us since it deals with the very concept of the Trinity but instead of three godheads they have ten.[93]

Sadan affirms the Deity of Messiah, although he is reluctant to label himself a 'Trinitarian'. He addresses the Jewish objections to the plural nature of God from within the tradition itself. Judaism presents an 'outward face' which rejects the possibility of the Trinity, whilst in internal debate allows for the plural unity of God to be expressed in at times controversial ways.

> Among the Jews, the Trinity is bound to raise the question whether idolatry is in fact a feature of Christianity. In the Jewish discourse that is directed outside, toward Jewish unbelievers and Christians, it is clear that the doctrine of the Trinity provokes a strong negative reaction. In this discourse, Judaism presents a united front: Christianity (not to be confused with the New Testament) is an idolatrous religion because it teaches that Jesus and the Holy Spirit are gods on their own merit. The Christian theory of three entities – God the Father, God the Son and God the Holy Spirit – violates the command not to worship any other god. As such, the doctrine of the Trinity in its popular understanding – three gods who are one – violates one of only three commandments a Jew must die for and not transgress [idolatry, incest and murder]. This explains the strong Jewish reaction to it and why it presents an obstacle for any Jew who is willing to think seriously about his or her relationship to Jesus and the New Testament.[94]

Within Judaism itself, according to Sadan, there is more flexibility in expressing the plural unity of God.

> Within the internal Jewish discourse, matters are a little more complicated. Two examples will suffice to illustrate it. In his book *Aderet Elijahu*, the Gaon of Vilna, one of the greatest Jewish sages of all time, writes the following: 'The tabernacle was one [...]. One is something that encloses things in unity within itself, and such is with "Hear O Israel [our God is one Lord]."' The Vilna Gaon had no problem to see even in the most important declaration 'the Lord is one', an indication to

---

[93] Ibid.

[94] Ibid. It ought to be stated that the doctrine of the Trinity 'in its popular understanding' that Sadan outlines here is *not* the doctrine of the Trinity recognised as orthodox by the Christian Churches, but a heretical, tritheistic *mis*understanding of it. Sadan is right to critique it.

God's unity. And regarding the divinity of the Redeemer, in a discussion in the *Talmud* on the meaning of the term *Man of God*, the following was said: 'If it were not written, I would not be able to say it.' Here the difficulty inherent in the term *Man of God*, is acknowledged but not explained. Yet in the same *Midrash* (story) Rabbi Abin explains the difficulty: 'When he [Moses] went up, and did not eat or drink, he was called God, and when he came down, and ate and drank, he was called man. From halfway upwards he was God, and from halfway downwards he was man.' Moses, who is referred to in other places as 'the first redeemer,' is called both man and God hence *man of God*; albeit, nowhere does it say Moses is God! These few examples show that, in Judaism, the search for God's unity is not shaped through precise definitions. Instead, it is framed as a *Midrash* that is, imbedded in a story and therefore subject to an ongoing interpretation. As a result, the discussion on a sensitive topic of this kind produces a dynamic and tolerant understanding. On the other hand, to understand God's unity through attempts to figure out God's essence through strict definitions leads to a rigid and uncompromising dogma.[95]

Sadan seeks to avoid the confusion of the contemporary debate, which to him is a result not of the doctrine of the Trinity itself, but 'because a man-made doctrine was turned into the very living word of God.' 'If the Messianic Jews will decide to speak about the unity of God within the boundaries set by the Bible, they would not only be able to promote unity among themselves, but also improve their relationship with the Jewish community.'[96]

In his 'Hundred Names of the Messiah' Sadan elaborates on this method, showing how more evidence is found in Jewish sources for Jesus' assertion that Moses and the prophets explained things concerning himself.[97]

---

[95] Ibid.

[96] Ibid.

[97] Tsvi Sadan, 'One Hundred Names of the Messiah,' in *Israel Today* (January 2003), http://israeltoday/co/il/archives (accessed March 10, 2003). 'A name of the Messiah that begins with *vav* (ו), the sixth letter in the Hebrew alphabet is of great mystery. In Jewish mysticism, letters possess great importance since it is assumed that if God created the world by words and the words were spoken in Hebrew, each of the letters – its sound, shape and positions within the word – is significant. The letter *vav* thus is especially important since from it the name of God – the Tetragrammaton – is made. This fact makes the *vav* unique in that, along with *ha* (ה) and *yod* (י) it is not part of creation but of letters that create, as is befitting the name of God. Knowing this, the sages noted that the *vav* is positioned between two *ha* like so (יהוה). In other words, since *ha* is also the name of God, the positioning of the *vav* in the midst of God, in Hebrew: *bein elohim* (ביו אלהים) means a great deal because, due to the nature of the Hebrew language, where the vowel letters are not always pronounced, *bein elohim* can be easily read as *ben elohim* and in English, Son of God. Having learned this, the sages have reached the same conclusion John has reached, that *Vav*, the Son of God, creates and is not created.'

Not all will agree with this approach to Christology in the Messianic movement, but it is an exploratory one, which deserves consideration. If appropriate criteria for the use of the Jewish mystical tradition are given, the illustrative value of analogous formulations of the divine nature of the Messiah and the plurality within the Godhead may assist Messianic Jews as they formulate their own understanding. However, translating from the mystical tradition of Judaism back into a normative Christian orthodoxy is not an easy undertaking, and may do a disservice to the integrity of both traditions.

Raising the Bar of Devotion

David Rudolph sees the contemporary Lubavitch treatment of the deceased *Rebbe* as an aid and challenge to his own understanding of Jesus. Here statements about the *theosis* and occultation of the *Rebbe* as the hidden Messiah of Jewish mysticism can be similarly applied to Yeshua.

> Recently I've been reading the book *The Rebbe, the Messiah and the Scandal of Orthodox Indifference* by David Berger, who is an Orthodox rabbi and Professor of History at Brooklyn College. In this book, Professor Berger documents the extent to which Chassidic Jews today believe that the Lubavitcher Rebbe, Menachem Schneerson, is the Messiah and even the Creator of the Universe. These ultra-Orthodox Jews believe that the Rebbe bore their sins through his suffering and death in 1994 and will come again to establish the Kingdom of God on earth. One Chassidic publication that Professor Berger quotes states:
>
>> ... the Rebbe is the 'Essence and Being [of God] enclothed in a body', that a Rebbe is by nature 'omniscient' and 'omnipotent', that all material and spiritual blessings flow from the Rebbe.
>> ... the Rebbe can foresee and control and coordinate the finest details of someone's personal life effecting his powerful blessings over many years and many miles removed ... there is nothing shocking about the Rebbe's powers given that his nature is above the limitations of nature.
>> So who [is] *Elokeinu* [our God]? Who *Avinu* [our Father]? Who *Malkeinu* [our King]? Who *Moshianu* [our Redeemer]? Who *Yoshianu V'Yigaleinu Shaynis B'Karov* [will save and redeem us once again shortly]? The Rebbe, Melech HaMoshiach. That's who.
>
> The Lubavitch Chassidim place a great deal of emphasis on the exaltation of their Messiah. Pictures of him abound in their community. His teachings and miracles are the subject of constant discussion. Even their liturgy has been changed to reflect their belief that the Messiah has come. One addition to their Siddur is the *yehi* prayer, a declaration of praise to their Messiah. It proclaims – 'May our

Master, Teacher, and Rabbi [some add here 'Creator'], the King Messiah, live forever' (p. 81). In some yeshivas, students pray facing a picture of the Rebbe, their Messiah, their Creator. If this is how ultra-Orthodox Jews exalt their Messiah, even to the extent of worshiping him in the synagogue, it begs the question, 'How do we as Messianic Jews exalt Yeshua? Do we exalt Yeshua as high as the ultra-Orthodox exalt their Rebbe? How high should the bar of our devotion be to Yeshua?' [98]

Rudolph does not refer to the underlying assumptions of the Lubavitch claims for the Rebbe or the Christian influences which have led to this understanding of the Messiah.

The Hidden Messiah of Postmissionary Messianic Judaism

Mark Kinzer proposes a new paradigm for Christology within a Messianic Jewish theological framework. He realises that Messianics have much more work to do on thinking through their theology, and recognises the importance of Christology:

> As for written work being done within the Messianic Movement on this topic: I find very little of much substance. As I am sure you know, one can find articles in *Mishkan* and *Kesher*, but they are not really charting new territory. The tendency in our movement (lamentably) is just to recirculate worn-out Hebrew-Christian apologetics.
>
> I am sure you have read about the squabbles in Israel over the deity of Yeshua. Much heat, and not much light. The concerns of the non-Trinitarians are worth paying attention to. Their thinking may not be new in any absolute sense (their views clearly reflect past Christian positions), but their reasons for trying to break out of the 'Christian box' are somewhat new (i.e., a concern for operating within 'Jewish space'). I don't think they succeed in their goals, but I am also not satisfied with the response of their adversaries (which is largely a restatement of Christian orthodoxy – often poorly understood – without any serious attempt at Jewish reflection). [99]

Kinzer, who teaches a course on 'God and Messiah' at the Messianic Jewish Theological Institute at Fuller School of World Mission, suggests several creative lines of enquiry. His course

---

[98] David Berger, *The Rebbe, The Messiah, and the Scandal of Orthodox Indifference* (London: Littman Library of Jewish Civilisation, 2001) 83, quoted in David Rudolph, 'Raising the Bar of Our Devotion to Yeshua' (Sermon Preached at Congregation Ruach Israel, Boston, MA, April 27, 2002).

[99] Mark Kinzer, e-mail to author, March 28, 2003.

addresses the most important issue in the study of theology: the nature of God and His relationship to the created order. This has also been one of the most controversial of theological topics, both in the debates between Jewish and Christian theologians concerning the deity of Yeshua and the Triune character of God, and in the internal Christian debates that produced the first four ecumenical councils. This course shows how the high Christology of the early Messianic community emerged in the context of Second Temple Judaism and was reinterpreted in a Hellenistic milieu by the Church Fathers and Councils, and offers proposals about the restatement of this teaching in a contemporary Messianic Jewish context. The course will also give special attention to the topics of divine transcendence and personhood.[100]

Kinzer combines an 'examination of historical and sociological data with an examination of scripture in the light of historical and sociological realities.'[101] Kinzer's theme is 'the Divine Paradox',[102] the revelation of the invisible God in human form. Different models help to understand this revelation. The 'Eschatological Covenantal Monotheism' of the *Tanakh* and Second Temple Judaism eagerly expected the full revelation of the presence of God. Varieties of Judaism in the Second Temple period imagined this in different forms. The New Testament writers, describing how the Risen Jesus became the object of worship in the early church, bear witness to the 'early Christian mutation' whereby earliest Christian worship of Jesus emerged from the divine agency tradition in inter-testamental Judaism. Using the contemporary scholarship of Richard Bauckham and Larry Hurtado, Kinzer explains how this gave a distinctive place to the risen Messiah alongside God, and 'exhibited a sudden and significant difference in character from Jewish devotion,' resulting in a binitarian conception of God.[103]

The 'Divine Paradox' is then traced in the rabbinic writings, early Jewish mysticism, medieval philosophy, *Kabbalah*, Chabad Messianism and 21st century Judaism. This is set alongside the incarnational and Trinitarian theology of the Christian Tradition, especially looking at the second century

---

[100] Mark Kinzer, 'MJTI Syllabus,' (July 2002), 21. http://www.mjti.org/docs/mjticatalog.pdf (accessed June 29, 2007).

[101] Kinzer 'God and the Messiah: Course Outline, MJ518,' (paper presented at Messianic Jewish Theological Institute, Fuller Theological Seminary, 2002): 44.

[102] Mark Kinzer, email to author (June 6, 2003): 'The tension found in *Tanakh* and Jewish tradition between descriptions of God as infinite, transcendent, and ineffable – in later Kabbalistic terms, as *Eyn Sof* – and descriptions of God that refer to a spatially localized presence, an anthropomorphic appearance, and an anthropopathic personality.'

[103] Larry W. Hurtado, *One God, One Lord: Early Christian Devotion and Ancient Jewish Monotheism* (London: SCM, 1988), 99. Cf. Richard Bauckham, *Jesus and the God of Israel* (Milton Keynes: Paternoster, 2008).

transition from Jewish to Gentile Context, the third century Fathers, the Church Councils and their Protagonists, and an assessment of the patristic achievement. This survey allows for discussion of Messianic Jewish Models for exploring the paradox, and discussion of how to develop Trinitarian worship of God 'through the Messiah in the *Ruach* [Spirit].' Kinzer's focus is on the 'Jewish Models of the Differentiated Godhead.' 'The fundamental reality we must be concerned with is not that of theological propositions, but instead the worship practices that express and shape our actual relationship with God.'[104]

Yeshua is the human image and representation of God, and also the representative of Israel and all humanity. Whilst worship of Yeshua is biblically sanctioned, outside a proper context it can lead to a 'skewed relationship with the Godhead.' Yeshua's life of self-emptying love reveals in definitive manner who God is. The honouring of Yeshua by submission, acclamation of his self-emptying love and obedience, and confession that he bears the Divine Name is still 'to the glory of God the Father.' For Messianic Jews such worship of Yeshua is consistent with their identity in Christ, the representative of Israel, the High Priest for Israel, the one who mediates between God and Israel. Messianic Jews can therefore pray the traditional prayers of the Synagogue without having to alter those prayers ('though we probably need to supplement them') as they pray them *through the Son, in the Ruach.* Kinzer gives the examples of wearing the *Tallit* as 'putting on Yeshua'; saying the *Shema* as 'identification with Yeshua's obedient love of the Father, summed up in his death'; and using the *Amidah* as 'identification with Yeshua's priestly intercession on behalf of Israel and the world'.

Kinzer finds earlier Jewish 'triadic models' are instructive but not so helpful today, (such as the Angel of the LORD and *Metatron).* He refers to the kabbalistic view of the Torah as the Name of God that is one with God, and its later expressions which saw Israel also as a heavenly reality that embodies the Torah and therefore also is a Divine archetype, quoting Moses Hayyim Luzzatto's statement in the 18th century that 'The Torah, God, and Israel are one'.

The mystical understanding of the relationship between God, the Written Torah and the Oral Torah provides a possible model for the incarnation, but it is difficult to understand and apply this model directly to the Trinity. Kinzer's attempt to re-formulate incarnational thinking within the Jewish tradition can be challenged. Whilst some would question whether Judaism does use incarnational language, Kinzer quotes the contemporary Jewish philosopher Michael Wyschogrod: 'In the broadest sense, the Jewish people is the incarnation of the Torah. If the Torah is demand, the Jewish people is the embodiment of that demand. A *talmid chacham* ('rabbinic scholar') is

---

[104] Mark Kinzer, 'Jewish Models of the Differentiated Godhead' (Session 17, MJTI, March 2003), 1.

considered a living Torah. We merely extend this to the people of Israel, of whom the *talmid chacham* is but an outstanding member.'[105]

Kinzer also considers Yeshua as the *Shekinah*, the one who accompanies Israel, 'entering fully into our experience and suffering, who as the presence of God actually suffers with us (it would be proper to give this notion of Divine suffering a prominent place in our theology); the one who even (like the *Shekhinah* of the *Kabbalah*) experiences in his total identification with us a separation from God (on the execution stake – "My God, My God, why have you forsaken me?").'[106]

The unity of the Deity needs to be understood eschatologically as a matter of His lordship being established throughout creation, so that all 'accept the yoke of His Kingship'. The resurrection of Yeshua and the gift of the *Ruach* are anticipations of that final *Echad*. The revelation of the Triune nature of the Godhead in the Apostolic Writings and in the life of the body of Messiah is not just a fuller manifestation of the Divine nature; paradoxically, this definitive demonstration of the inner differentiation of the Godhead has as its purpose the eschatological realisation of His unity when 'God will be all in all.' Thus for Kinzer the Jewish mystical tradition is crucial for our formulating an authentic 21st century Messianic Jewish understanding of God and of Messiah.

The heart of Kinzer's Christology is to be found in his ecclesiological formulation. Yeshua unites both *ekklesia* and Israel, participating in both. Kinzer's important book *Postmissionary Messianic Judaism* proposes that the Messiah Jesus is hidden in the midst of the Jewish people. Kinzer proposes a 'bilateral ecclesiology' made up of two distinct but united communal entities: '(1) The community of Jewish Yeshua-believers, maintaining their participation in the wider Jewish community and their faithful observance of traditional Jewish practice, and (2) The community of Gentile Yeshua-believers, free from Jewish Torah-observance yet bound to Israel through union with Israel's Messiah, and through union with the Jewish *ekklesia*.'[107]

Kinzer's stress on the inherent 'twofold nature' of the *ekklesia* preserves 'in communal form the distinction between Jew and Gentile while removing the mistrust and hostility that turned the distinction into a wall'. Kinzer argues that a bilateral ecclesiology is required if the Gentile *ekklesia* is to claim rightfully a share in Israel's inheritance without compromising Israel's integrity or Yeshua's centrality.

Kinzer turns to the Jewish people's apparent 'no' to its own Messiah. Kinzer argues that Paul sees this rejection as 'in part providential, an act of

---

[105] Michael Wyschogrod, *The Body of Faith: God and the People Israel*, 2nd ed. (Northvale: Jason Aronson, 1996), 211.

[106] Kinzer, 'Jewish Models,' ibid.

[107] Mark S. Kinzer, *Postmissionary Messianic Judaism: Redefining Christian Engagement with the Jewish People* (Grand Rapids: Brazos, 2005), 5.

divine hardening effected for the sake of the Gentiles'. Paul, according to Kinzer, even implies that this hardening involves Israel's mysterious participation in the suffering and death of the Messiah.

> In the light of Christian anti-Semitism and supersessionism, the Church's message of the Gospel comes to the Jewish people accompanied by the demand to renounce Jewish identity, and thereby violate the ancestral covenant. From this point onward the apparent Jewish "no" to Yeshua expresses Israel's passionate "yes" to God – a "yes" which eventually leads many Jews on the way of martyrdom. Jews thus found themselves imitating Yeshua through denying Jesus! If the Church's actual rejection of Israel did not nullify her standing nor invalidate her spiritual riches, how much more should this be the case with Israel's apparent rejection of Yeshua![108]

The Jewish people's apparent 'no' to Jesus does not rule them out of God's salvation purposes, any more than the Church's *actual* 'no' to the election of Israel. Both are within the one people of God, although there is a schism between them. The New Testament 'affirms the validity of what we would today call Judaism'.[109]

Kinzer recognises that the presence of Yeshua is necessary in order to affirm Judaism. 'Those who embrace the faith taught by the disciples will be justifiably reluctant to acknowledge the legitimacy of a religion from which Yeshua, the incarnate Word, is absent.'[110]

Judaism's validity can not be demonstrated if Jewish people have a way to God that 'bypasses Yeshua'. However, Kinzer argues that in some mysterious and hidden way 'Yeshua abides in the midst of the Jewish people and its religious tradition, despite that tradition's apparent refusal to accept his claims'.[111] This divinely willed 'disharmony between the order of knowing and the order of being' means that Yeshua is present with his people without being recognised. The *ontic* is to be distinguished from the *noetic*, what exists from what is known. The New Testament affirms that Yeshua is the representative and individual embodiment of the entire people of Israel, even if Israel does not recognise Yeshua and repudiates his claims. Even this rejection testifies to his status as the despised and rejected servant. Echoing Karl Barth's doctrine of the Church in relation to Israel, Israel's 'no' is answered by the Church's 'yes' to Jesus, and in Jesus himself both 'yes' and 'no' are brought together, just as Jesus is both divine and human, and accepted and rejected.[112]

---

[108] Ibid., 5.

[109] Ibid., 215.

[110] Ibid., 217.

[111] Ibid.

[112] For a summary of scholarship on Barth's view of Jesus and Israel, see Mark R. Lindsay, *Barth, Israel and Jesus: Karl Barth's Theology of Israel* (Aldershot: Ashgate, 2007).

Both Church and Israel are 'bound indissolubly to the person of the Messiah', one in belief, the other in unbelief. Therefore 'Israel's no *to* Yeshua can be properly viewed as a form of participation *in* Yeshua!'[113] 'If the obedience of Yeshua that led him to death on the cross is rightly interpreted as the perfect embodiment and realisation of Israel's covenant fidelity, then Jewish rejection of the church's message in the second century and afterward can rightly be seen as a hidden participation in the obedience of Israel's Messiah.'[114]

Kinzer's paradox draws from earlier thinkers like Lev Gillet, the friend of Paul Levertoff. 'His [Gillet's] entire notion of 'communion in the Messiah' presumes that faithful Jews and faithful Christians can have communion together in the one Messiah. In fact, he seems to hold that the Messiah is also hidden for Christians to the extent that they fail to understand or acknowledge the ongoing significance of the Jewish people in the divine purpose.'[115]

Gillet views the Jewish people as a *'corpus mysticum* – a mystical body, like the church'. The suffering of the Jewish people is to be understood in the light of Is. 53, as both 'prophetic and redemptive,' but Gillet does not, according to Kinzer, lose 'his christological bearings'.[116] Gillet's aim is to build a 'bridge theology' that links the mystical body of Christ with that of the mystical body of Israel. 'The *corpus mysticum Christi* is not a metaphor; it is an organic and invisible reality. But the theology of the Body of Christ should be linked with a theology of the mystical body of Israel. This is one of the deepest and most beautiful tasks of a "bridge theology" between Judaism and Christianity.'[117]

Gillet aims to heal the schism between Israel and the Church, showing that both Christian and Jew are united in the Messiah. 'The idea of our membership in Israel has an immediate application in all the modern questions concerning Jewry. If we seriously admit the mystical bond which ties us, as Christians, to the community of Israel, if we feel ourselves true Israelites, our whole outlook may be modified, and our lives of practical action as well.'[118]

However, Gillet's argument relies on 'the mystery of the [future] restoration of Israel, who are still, in Paul's words, experiencing "Blindness in part".'[119] The Messiah is hidden from them, because of the blindness of unbelief. Whilst he is hidden within his people, he is also hidden from them by their partial hardening.

---

[113] Kinzer, *PMJ*, 223.

[114] Ibid., 225.

[115] Ibid., 280.

[116] Ibid., 281.

[117] Lev Gillet, *Communion in the Messiah: Studies in the Relationship Between Judaism and Christianity* (London: Lutterworth Press, 1942), 215, quoted in Kinzer, *PMJ*, 281.

[118] Gillet, *Communion in the Messiah*, 215.

[119] Kinzer, *PMJ*, 281.

Kinzer's concept of the 'hidden Messiah' derives not from the idea of 'anonymous Christians' proposed by the Roman Catholic theologian Karl Rahner, but from Karl Barth and Franz Rosenzweig, and later Jewish-Christian relations thinkers such as Paul van Buren. Kinzer also refers to Edith Stein, the Jewish philosopher who became a Carmelite nun, who conceived of the sufferings of the Jewish people as 'participating in the sufferings of their unrecognised Messiah'.[120] Thomas F. Torrance lends support to this Christological understanding of the suffering of Israel as participation in the suffering of the Messiah, albeit unconsciously.

> Certainly, the fearful holocaust of six million Jews in the concentration camps of Europe, in which Israel seems to have been made a burnt-offering laden with the guilt of humanity, has begun to open Christian eyes to a new appreciation of the vicarious role of Israel in the mediation of God's reconciling purpose in the dark underground of conflicting forces within the human race. Now we see Israel, however, not just as the scapegoat, thrust out of sight into the despised ghettos of the nations, bearing in diaspora the reproach of the Messiah, but Israel drawn into the very heart and centre of Calvary as never before since the crucifixion of Jesus.[121]

Kinzer echoes Bruce Marshall in arguing that the Jewishness of Jesus implies his continuing membership of, and participation in, the Jewish people. God's incarnate presence in Yeshua thus 'resembles God's presence among Yeshua's flesh-and-blood brothers and sisters'.[122] Quoting Marshall, the doctrine of the incarnation of God in Christ is analogous to the doctrine of God indwelling carnal Israel, as articulated by Michael Wyschogrod, the Jewish thinker. 'The Christian doctrine of the incarnation is an intensification, not a repudiation, of traditional Jewish teaching about the dwelling of the divine presence in the midst of Israel.'[123] If God is 'present in Israel, Yeshua is also present there', and according to Robert Jenson, the 'church is the body of Christ only in association with the Jewish people'.

> Can there be a present body of the risen Jew, Jesus of Nazareth, in which the lineage of Abraham and Sarah so vanishes into a congregation of gentiles as it does in the church? My final – and perhaps most radical – suggestion to Christian theology ... is that ... the embodiment of the risen Christ is whole only

---

[120] Ibid., 227.

[121] Thomas F. Torrance, *The Mediation of Christ* (Colorado Springs: Helmers and Howard, 1992), 38–39, quoted in Kinzer, *PMJ*, 227.

[122] Kinzer, *PMJ*, 231.

[123] Bruce Marshall, *Trinity and Truth* (Cambridge: Cambridge University Press 2000), 178, quoted in Kinzer, *PMJ*, 231.

in the form of the church *and* an identifiable community of Abraham and Sarah's descendants. The church and the synagogue are together and only together the present availability to the world of the risen Jesus Christ.[124]

Kinzer covers much new ground here, painting in broad brushstrokes an ecclesiology developed by postliberal Christian theologians in dialogue with contemporary Jewish thinkers. The discussion draws from Karl Barth's Christological doctrine of the election of the one 'community of God' as Church and Israel, and seeks to navigate between universalism on the one hand, and a continuing supersessionism on the other. Whilst Karl Barth withdrew from participation in Rosenzweig's 'Patmos group' because of its perceived Gnosticism, there is also a danger of Gnosticism in this doctrine of the Hidden Messiah incarnate in his people Israel.[125] Kinzer, following Bruce Marshall, relies on a 'divinely willed disharmony between the *ontic* and the *noetic*'. 'For most Jews, Paul seems to say, there is at this point a divinely willed disharmony between the order of knowing and the order of being which will only be overcome at the end of time.'[126]

But if the mystery of God's dwelling in Christ is known to the Church, it can not be equally true that Israel can be approved by God for affirming that the opposite is the case, and that Yeshua is not the risen Messiah. Whilst Messianic Jews recognise a continuing election of Israel (the Jewish people) and thus a continuing commitment of Yeshua *to* His people, most will be reluctant to admit that this commitment *in itself* is salvific, or that the hidden presence of the Messiah *with* His people is the means by which he is revealed to them. The Hidden Messiah of *PMJ* owes more to a Christian re-orientation of perspective on Jesus and the election of Israel than on a Jewish recognition of a hidden Messiah.

Whilst Kinzer uses contemporary New Testament scholarship and the works of modern Jewish scholars to illustrate the possibilities of incarnational theology within the Jewish tradition, his approach awaits consolidation into a definitive statement on the humanity, divinity and work of the Messiah. However, he provides a suggestive 'road-map' for future progress on the issues, steering the debate into more profound theological reflection whilst also recognising the weaknesses of previous approaches.

---

[124] Robert W. Jenson, 'Towards a Christian Theology of Judaism,' in Carl E. Braaten and Robert W. Jenson eds., *Jews and Christians* (Grand Rapids: Eerdmans, 2003), 9–11, quoted in Kinzer, *PMJ*, 232.

[125] Lindsay, *Barth, Israel and Jesus*, 28.

[126] Kinzer, *PMJ*, 217.

Adoptionist Christology

A fifth Christology, reminiscent of Ebionite Christology, denies the divinity of Jesus. According to Ray Pritz, 'An extremely small minority of congregations in Israel (I would estimate no more than 5%) would hold a formal doctrinal position that does not affirm the divinity of Jesus.'[127]

Pritz adds that of the twelve Messianic Jews reported in the November 2001 issue of *Israel Today*, one third of those quoted came from two of the congregations who take this position, and their comments were given undue prominence.[128] Uri Marcus, a member of the *Heftzibah* congregation in Israel, summarises his position.[129] 'Myself as well as our entire congregation of Believers in *Ma'aleh Adumim*, completely reject the Trinitarian notions of plural unity, and will not acquiesce to any theology which challenges the ONEness of *HaShem* in any fashion ... Yeshua is the Son of the living G-d, never G-d the Son, in our view.'[130] David Tel-Tzur and Emanuel Gazit, also leaders in the same group, deny Yeshua's pre-existence and deity.

> John (the Evangelist) is not teaching that the Son (of God) was living prior to his birth. The Son appeared for the first time as an entity when he was miraculously created as the 'Second Man' in his mother's womb. The 'Word' (*Logos*) in Scripture never appears in the meaning of an entity or a person ... The Trinity is paganism, contrasted with 'Hear (*Sh'ma*) O Israel our God is One'. Yeshua is not the creator of the world, but the world was created for him. [131]

Marcus argues against the deity of Jesus on the grounds that the Hebrew scriptures and Jewish tradition forbid idolatry; the Christian understanding of the incarnation is idolatrous, and Trinitarian doctrine is a Hellenistic misreading of the biblical data. Trinitarians misread scripture without taking into account their original Jewish background and frame of reference.

---

[127] Ray Pritz, 'The Divinity of Jesus,' *LCJE Bulletin* 69 (August 2002): 3.

[128] Ibid. Estimates vary as to what proportion of Israeli believers hold such a position. David Tel Zur claims that 'more than half of all Jewish believers in Israel' would informally hold his views, a claim that is difficult to verify. (Robert Fischer, email to author, March 5, 2003).

[129] Marcus is founder of the *Nehemiah Fund*, a relief and development fund that assists Messianic Jews in Israel. Through his aid work and well-publicised activities, he is well-known throughout the Messianic movement.

[130] Uri Marcus, e-mail to author, March 21, 2003.

[131] Letters to the Editor, *Kivun* no. 30, quoted in Nerel 'The Trinity and the Contemporary Jewish Believers in Yeshua,' *Nachrichten Aus Israel* (Beth-Shalom) no. 5 (May 2003): 1.

This is given by rabbinic tradition, which provides the authoritative understanding of the nature of God, the meaning of idolatry and the nature of the Messiah. Only with the use of this interpretive tradition can the early Church's excessive reliance on an 'anti-Semitic' Hellenistic influence be avoided.[132]

Monotheism and Idolatry

Marcus is clear about his assumptions: 'I love discussing theology. It can be lots of fun, if people follow basic rules, like: "What the Scripture presents as a mystery should not be made into Dogma".'[133] However, Marcus is quite dogmatic about the nature of idolatry, assuming that any representation of the deity or suggestion of a plural nature should be seen as idolatrous. He uses Maimonides' *Thirteen Principles of Faith* to affirm the incorporeality of God.

> In addition to his law code, Maimonides penned the famous 'Thirteen Articles of Faith' whose words speak about the attributes of G-d and the beliefs that were intended to map out the borders between Judaism and other then acceptable belief systems (such as Christianity and Islam). Why was this necessary?
>
> In the 12th century, Jews had already suffered a significant amount of persecution by the 'min', a term used in the *Talmud* to refer to early Christians, which meant 'heretic.' A need arose for Jews exiled in Christian Europe, to set forth a definitive basis, upon which a person might know if he or she was diverging from the basic tenets of the Torah. Already, a plethora of polytheists, deists, atheists, those who believe one should worship demigods (middle-men), and those who say that G-d has a body, were vying for social and religious supremacy.
>
> Rambam [Maimonides] took the challenge seriously. To him, putting G-d in a body was tantamount to polytheism, since it was just a verbal difference between talking about a god who has parts and a pantheon of multiple gods. After all, pantheism is belief that G-d, or a group of gods, is identical with the whole natural world.

---

[132] Marcus strongly rejects this interpretation of his position: 'You stated that I see Rabbinic tradition as the authoritative understanding of the nature of G-d, and that I employ an interpretive tradition in my reading of the *Tanach* … All I can do is deny your allegations. I do not accept Rabbinic Tradition as authoritative interpretations, when I read my Bible! I find them useful. I find them helpful. I find them in many cases wise. But I also find them stupid, and ridiculous and completely false, in many other cases.' (e-mail June 10, 2003). I have given quotations at some length, to allow the reader to decide whether my interpretation is fair.

[133] Marcus' views are to be found at 'Adonai Echad: Deity of Yeshua Debate: Why Yeshua is NOT G-d: An Internet Course from a Jewish Perspective,' http://groups.yahoo.com/group/AdonaiEchad (accessed 3rd June 2003).

Anyone who wants to find out how the Jewish People, to whom were committed the oracles of G-d for the past 4000 years, are going to define who G-d is, and consequently who He is NOT, should study this prayer. Regardless of the failure of our people to remain faithful to *HaShem*, and to His Torah, as history records, it in no way invalidates the primary revelation that the Jewish People received at Sinai and held onto, which we later transmitted to the rest of the world.[134]

Maimonides' rationalist and Aristotelian formulation of the divinity is here equated with Sinaitic revelation, allowing the authority of later Jewish tradition to set the normative framework for the conceptualising of the divine nature. The *Yigdal*, a prayer reflecting the *Thirteen Principles*, implies that '*HaShem* is indivisible, unlike humans, who have many different body parts' but does not acknowledge that this position reflects the same Hellenistic currents of thought which Marcus opposes. For Maimonides, in seeking to introduce Aristotelian thought into Jewish understanding, could do no other than deny the possibility of pre-existent parts in an uncreated Creator. For Maimonides belief that God might have corporeality or is liable to suffer affection went against the Aristotelian notion of the Perfection of God, a more serious intellectual error than that of idolatry.[135]

Hebraic and Hellenistic Thinking

Marcus allows rabbinic tradition to define the nature of the Messiah, giving it an authority equal to the New Testament. On the pre-existence of the Messiah he refers to the Talmudic passage concerning the seven things that were created before the world was created, including the name of the Messiah.[136] Because tradition ascribes this teaching to the period of Hillel and Shammai (c.10 C.E.), its origins can be traced back perhaps even earlier, 'to Moses and David'. The New Testament writers would have used this as the basis for their own teaching, but the Church Fathers refused to consider

anything about what the Jewish mind had to say, the same which birthed the concepts of the Messiah, redemption and the belief in ethical monotheism, as they

---

[134] Marcus, 'Lesson 3 I'll take ONE please,' http://groups.yahoo.com/group/ AdonaiEchad/message/16 (accessed 3rd June 2003).

[135] 'For the idolater does not deny the existence of God; he merely makes the mistake of supposing that the image of his own construction resembles a being which mediates between him and God ... How much more serious is the error of him who thinks God is body! He entertains an error regarding the nature of God directly, and surely causes the anger of God to burn.' (Maimonides, *Guide to the Perplexed* (Bk. II, ch.36), summarised in Isaak Husik, *A History of Medieval Jewish Philosophy* (New York: Temple, 1916, 1969), 261.

[136] Tractate *Pesachim* 54a.

[the Church Fathers] formulated their wording of the creeds which the Church to this day stands upon, and enforces with furious intolerance … I don't think they considered any of this. I think rather, that these Church Fathers did everything possible to avoid any contact with 'Hebraic Thinking' or 'Hebraic Thinkers' and instead embraced the common Greco/Roman Hellenistic philosophical understandings of who G-d was in the world, as they set out to determine what defined Christian beliefs. After that, it was just a simple matter of superimposing those ideas onto the Gospel accounts, in order to arrive at a palatable form of Christianity for the Gentiles.

So, with our agendas clearly exposed, and our two approaches to tackle the text in front of us, as a fork before us in the road, I'll tell you what I've told you in the past … I'm taking the road to Jerusalem, rather than that which leads to Rome.[137]

Marcus reads the Talmudic material of the 5th and 6th centuries as accurately reflecting the views of the 1st century, and assumes that the gospel writers followed these. He excludes the possibility of different understandings of the Messiah in the 1st century, and does not consider the hypostasisation of the divinity discussed by Kinzer. Nor does Marcus consider the impact of the resurrection on the development of Christology.

Other Messianic thinkers such as Daniel Juster respond to this by arguing that Marcus' distinction between Hellenistic and Hebraic thought is oversimplified. In reality, the interaction and interdependence of Jewish and Hellenistic thought is complex and varied.

The bifurcation of Hebraic thinking and Greek thinking as respectively functional and metaphysical-ontological is a widely held conclusion of modern scholarship (cf. O. Cullman, *Christ and Time*, also Bishop J.S. Spong, *The Hebrew Lord*). Yet, in my view, this absolute separation of functional thinking as Hebraic and metaphysical thinking as Greek can not be maintained. Functional thinking at least implies statements about the nature of being or it would lend to relativism in questions concerning the nature of reality. (This distinction has been used to bolster relativism in theology.) The real question is rather one which raises the issue of how a metaphysic that is implied by biblical teaching compares and contrasts with a Greek metaphysic. Because all human beings are created in the image of God, communication and evaluation with regard to metaphysical views is cross-culturally possible.[138]

---

[137] Marcus, 'Lesson 3,' ibid.

[138] Daniel Juster, 'The Christological Dogma of Nicaea – Greek or Jewish?' *Mishkan* Vol. 1, no. 1 (1984), 54. It ought to be noted in this connection that most contemporary biblical scholarship has moved away from the neat division between Hebrew and Greek thinking so popular in the 1950s and 1960s. The different Jewish cultures of the Second Temple period all reflect differing degrees of influence from Greco-Roman culture and one simply cannot make a *neat* division between them.

Christian Unitarianism

Marcus reads scripture from a Unitarian perspective, acknowledging his debt to the writings of Anthony Buzzard.[139] His paraphrase of John 1 retranslates material that would otherwise be problematic to his argument. He writes:

> Yochanan [John], who wrote his account of the life of Yeshua, and whose pro-
> logue of that account (Yochanan 1:1–18), we are now studying, certainly under-
> stood that the 'Name of the Messiah' … existed as the centerpiece of G-d's plan for
> the world, and for the redemption of mankind. This fact would not have escaped
> his mind, as he began to write …

> In the beginning was the Torah,
> and the Torah was with G-d,
> and godlike was the Torah.

> It was with G-d in the beginning.

> All things came to be through it.
> and without it nothing made had being.

> In it was life,
> and the life was the light of mankind. (Yochanan 1:1–4)

> The above is a basic assumption we must make, as we approach the text of
> Yochanan's gospel. And if you really want to be honest with yourselves, you must
> realize that you only have two approaches from which you can draw near to
> Yochanan's text. Either 1) You must approach the text with the assumptions that
> Gentile Church Fathers had in their minds about redemption and beliefs in deity,
> taken from their own foreign cultures, apart from ANY KNOWLEDGE of these
> key Jewish Talmudic concepts, or 2) You must approach the text with the assump-
> tion that Yochanan was a Jew, communicating to Jews, in Jewish terms, using
> Jewish concepts that were common knowledge, and regularly taught by the
> Rabanan.[140]

---

[139] Anthony Buzzard and Charles Hunting, *The Doctrine of the Trinity: Christianity's Self-Inflicted Wound* (New York: International Scholars Publications, 1998). Marcus also refers to Richard E. Rubenstein, *When Jesus Became God* (New York: Harvest Books, 2000).

[140] Uri Marcus, 'Lesson 6 – 'And the Word was G-d?' Yochanan 1:1–3' (September 6, 2002), http://groups.yahoo.com/group/AdonaiEchad/message/23.

It is clear that Marcus makes significant hermeneutical assumptions as he reads scripture, framing it within his own anti-Hellenistic theological grid. His use of rabbinic materials does not deal with questions of dating, or context, and this leads to certain questionable conclusions about the intent of both the rabbinic tradition and the writers of the New Testament. Similarly, the complex landscape of Jewish views about the Messiah in the first century, including the apocalyptic and mystical speculation about the hypostasisation of the divine attributes, are not considered. This results in a simplistic contrast between Judaism and Hellenism. In effect, Marcus is reading the New Testament in the light of a form of Judaism that developed after the Second Temple period – sometimes in direct reaction to Christian theology – rather than in the light of forms of Judaism that existed at the time in which the New Testament was written.[141]

Marcus' position appeals to the Messianic movement because of the temptation to disassociate itself from the later Church councils and creeds, with their Hellenistic and Gentile influences that are linked to anti-Judaism. It points to the need for MJT to address the theological formulation of such councils with greater attention and consideration, if it wishes to avoid this path. Jacob Jocz, expressing an earlier Hebrew Christian position, anticipated such a Christological option, but rejected it.

> This is the reason why a Unitarian form of Christianity is a contradiction in terms; at best it can be a Gentile Synagogue, but it can never be a Church. It is important to remember that Christology to the Church is not an abstract theological subject which can be discussed on purely theoretical lines. It is not that Christology was first formulated and then adjusted to fit the case of Jesus of Nazareth. The process was the reverse; the Church defined her Christology in view of Jesus Christ. He must remain at the centre of Christian thinking, otherwise it ceases to be Christian.[142]

---

[141] In this regard it is interesting to consider Richard Bauckham's new book, *Jesus and the God of Israel* (Milton Keynes: Paternoster, 2008) which argues that when the New Testament texts are read against the background of 1st century Jewish monotheism we realise that Jesus was believed by his early Jewish followers to share in the divine identity of the one God of Israel without in any way compromising that oneness. Bauckham seeks to articulate the high Christology of the New Testament texts *in 1st century Jewish categories* and to avoid the later Hellenistic categories used by the creeds (whist recognising that the later creeds express the same ideas as the New Testament using different conceptual schemes and language). In this respect his work shares concerns with that of MJT.

[142] Jacob Jocz, 'The Invisibility of God,' 189.

Conclusion

How a Messianic Jewish Christology will locate and develop an incarnational Christology that reflects classical Trinitarianism remains to be seen, but it is of vital significance for the future of the Messianic movement, and remains a high priority for its theology. Lev Gillet stated the need for a 'translation of meanings' for a Messianic Jewish Christology. 'What is needed is a "translation of meanings". A re-thinking of Christology in Jewish terms, *i.e.* not only in Hebrew words, but in Hebrew categories of thought.'[143]

The challenge for a Messianic Jewish Christology is to express 'Christian' truth in 'Jewish' terms with biblical integrity, theological accuracy and intercultural sensitivity because arguably such 'Christian' truth is, at its root, actually 'Jewish' truth. Baruch Maoz's theocentric Christology chooses not to engage at any depth with a Jewish religious tradition, and imports a Protestant Reformed position into a secular Israeli context. Arnold Fruchtenbaum similarly employs a Dispensationalist doctrinal system and hermeneutic, with little regard for Jewish midrashic exegesis of scripture or the speculations of Jewish religious tradition about the nature of the Messiah.

Daniel Juster, David Stern and Louis Goldberg attempt to re-contextualise Nicaean orthodoxy in Jewish terms, engaging in debate with current New Testament scholarship on the Jewish background of incarnational Christology, the influences of Hebraic and Hellenistic modes of thought, and the need for a rapprochement between the creeds and councils of the patristic period and the development of rabbinic tradition. This approach will continue to gain support from the emerging scholarly position on the 'Ways that Never Parted.' Advocated by scholars such as Daniel Boyarin and Paula Fredericksen, this work has yet to be appropriated into Messianic Jewish streams, but will contribute further scholarly material for their Christology.[144]

Tsvi Sadan incorporates Jewish religious and mystical tradition into his articulation of Trinitarian thought and incarnational language. His method draws on 'Jewish' theological resources such as mystical exegesis and inter-testamental materials without recourse to 'Christian' tradition. Whilst this

---

[143] Lev Gillet, *Communion in the Messiah: Studies in the Relationship Between Judaism and Christianity* (London, Lutterworth Press: 1942), 73.

[144] Daniel Boyarin, *Border Lines: The Partition of Judaeo-Christianity* (Philadelphia: University of Pennsylvania Press, 2004); Paula Fredericksen, 'What Parting Of The Ways? Jews, Gentiles, and The Ancient Mediterranean City,' in Adam H. Becker and Annette Yoshiko Reed, eds., *The Ways That Never Parted: Jews and Christians in Late Antiquity and the Early Middle Ages,* (Minneapolis: Fortress, 2007), 35–64.

approach has not been systematically developed, and exhibits some unwarranted antipathy to the methods and materials of the Christian tradition of Christology, it breaks new ground in voicing a distinctive and new approach to Messianic Jewish Christology.

Mark Kinzer also employs resources from Jewish tradition within a 'high Christology'. His bilateral ecclesiology of the Church and Israel (the Jewish people) united as the People of God in Christ allows him to see the 'hidden Christ' incarnate in the Jewish people. This has challenging soteriological implications – the Jewish 'no' to a wrongly presented Jesus of supersessionist and anti-Jewish Gentile Christian tradition is in fact a faithful 'yes' to God. Kinzer's Christology is fully orthodox in Christian terms, but his embedding of the incarnate Messiah within the people of Israel's covenant fidelity and Torah-observance recasts the nature of the gospel and poses further challenges to a Messianic Jewish Theology, in terms of the nature of the gospel it proclaims and the manner of its presence within the Jewish community.

Uri Marcus's position reflects the Arian and adoptionist Christologies of the early Church, and is influenced by the need to assert the singularity of God's oneness without compromise. This position, whilst attractive to some, remains a minority position. In contrast to Marcus, the UMJC position paper on the Tri-Unity of God summarises the biblical data for the plurality of God, the basis in Jewish tradition for plurality in the divinity, then goes on to state:

> It has also been pointed out that traditional Judaism has always rejected the concept of the tri-unity of G-d, interpreting the Shema in a narrower sense as an absolute oneness. This traditional view is in no way monolithic. The biblical data is also [part of] Jewish thought. Within Jewish thought, albeit mystical, the Zohar contains a trinitarian concept of G-d. While the Zohar is not our authority, it does demonstrate that the trinitarian understanding of G-d is NOT non-Jewish. Regardless of traditional views, we must not look to traditional Jewish teaching to tell us what is proper for us to believe. Our authority is the Word of G-d. Traditional rejection of the tri-unity is not based upon what we believe, but based upon their erroneous interpretation of what we believe. We in no way affirm the existence of three gods, but ONE G-d eternally existent in three persons. [145]

It concludes with the strong affirmation of the deity of Jesus and the plural unity of God: 'Because the tri-unity of G-d has a central bearing upon the rest of our theology and the scriptures do support it as a biblical doctrine,

---

[145] UMJC, 'The Tri-Unity of G-d from a Messianic Perspective', UMJC position paper, http://www.umjc.org/aboutumjc/theology/triunity.htm (accessed March 12, 2003).

Messianic believers need to affirm the tri-unity of G-d as a central part of our faith and not relegate it to secondary importance or opinion for the sake of palatability to others.'[146]

Messianic Jews need to avoid both an 'arid biblicism and a shallow Trinitarianism'[147] in their search for an appropriate Christology and Trinitarian theology. Jacob Jocz stated the challenge for MJT clearly some fifty years ago.

> The Synagogue has a right and an obligation to ask ... 'How is Jesus of Nazareth God?' The Christian answer cannot be evasive. It must not fall back upon the authority of Church Councils. To refer a Jew back to the Council of Nicæa is an admission of our own helplessness and lack of conviction. It is the task of theology to attempt a *contemporary* answer, but with a view to the past. The Jewish questioner today is not edified by the historical information [about] what Christians in the fourth century thought about Jesus; he wants to know what we think about him in the intellectual context of our own time.[148]

The task for MJT is thus to appropriate and re-express a Jewish expression of belief in the Messiah which allows room for Trinitarian and incarnational thought. Without that possibility discussion of the nature and outworking of Torah, which occupies the following two chapters, will inevitably control understandings of the divinity of Yeshua, and prevent the development of a comprehensive theological system which holds the continuation of the Torah in creative tension with its radical fulfilment brought by the arrival of the Messiah.

---

[146] Ibid.

[147] A phrase borrowed from N.T. Wright.

[148] Jocz, 'The Invisibility of God,' 62.

Chapter 6

Torah in Theory

Introduction

> We have seen how theological error and misinterpretation of the *Brit Chadasha* [New Testament] have led to an outright neglect of the Torah at best, and a stiff-necked rejection of it at worst. Let us now attempt to do what no other generation has ever done. Let us be the first generation of Jewish believers since the early days of our history to begin turning back the tear-drenched pages of our history and again to follow the covenant which the Holy One made with Moshe Rabbenu.[1]

The Hebrew word 'Torah' means more than just 'law'. It includes teaching, instruction and revelation. The term is used by Jewish people to refer to both the Pentateuch, the Hebrew scriptures and to the "Oral Torah" (the Mishnah, Talmud and other rabbinic writings).[2] Thus the word 'Torah' serves as a general term for revelation or teaching and in some contexts the intended sense of 'Torah' is not always clear.

Jewish religious groupings interpret Torah differently. Orthodox Jews are strict in their observance of the laws of the Pentateuch, which are further expanded, interpreted and applied by rabbinic tradition. Conservative Jews modify this traditional observance in the light of modern thought. Reform, Liberal and Reconstructionist Jews adopt a humanist and revisionist position that looks to the Torah for moral principles and cultural norms, but these may be renegotiated and there are few absolutes. Whilst many Jewish people observe some aspects of the Mosaic Law as customary and traditional rather than out of the conviction that God commands them, the

---

[1] Ariel Berkowitz and Devorah Berkowitz, *Torah Rediscovered: Challenging Centuries of Misinterpretation and Neglect*, 3rd ed. (Littleton, CO: First Fruits of Zion, 1998), 144.

[2] The Jewish order of the Hebrew Bible is Torah (Genesis to Deuteronomy), Neviim (the Prophets) and Ketuvim (the Writings). These comprise the acronym 'TaNak'. The Talmud (Teaching) is composed of the Mishnah ('Repetition') and Gemara ('Completion'). These are known as the 'Oral Torah'. The Jewish mystical tradition, the Kabbalah, is known as the 'Hidden Torah'.

importance of Torah has never been in doubt, and has often been contrasted with the alleged lack of emphasis in Christianity on the need for Law. 'The laws of the Torah are to Judaism the quintessence of permanent goodness. Christianity, on the other hand, advances its claims on the strength that the 'Law' is superseded and abrogated by 'Faith' in Jesus.'[3]

It is frequently claimed that Messianic Jews do not have a place for Torah, or that their understanding of Torah is inconsistent. David Berger and Michael Wyschogrod accuse Messianic Jews of inconsistency bordering on hypocrisy.

> We have already explained why Judaism rejects the belief that Jesus was the Messiah. But the claims of these groups to Jewish identity are made even more dubious by the fact that they are generally quite unclear about their commitment to Jewish practices and even Jewish survival. Some of them practice various Jewish customs, such as wearing *tsitsit* (fringes) and lighting candles on Friday nights. But do they believe that a Jew is obligated to obey the whole Torah?[4]

Messianic Jews recognise some accuracy in these charges, and look to develop an integrated theory and practice of Torah.

> The relationship between Messianic Jews and the law is an important issue in the Messianic movement because the law is not solely a theological issue to be debated, but part of Jewish culture, heritage and worship. At the same time, Messianic believers recognise their relationship to the law is not the same as that of traditional Jews because the centre of a believer's life is not the law, but the Messiah.[5]

David Stern recognises that there is much work to be done on a theology of the Law: 'The lack of a correct, clear and relatively complete Messianic Jewish or Gentile Christian theology of the Law is not only a major impediment to Christians' understanding of their own faith, but also the greatest barrier to Jewish people's receiving the Gospel.'[6]

In developing their understanding and practice of Law, Messianic Jews are 'Torah positive'.[7] They deny both the charge of legalism that comes from the Church, and the accusation that they have 'abandoned the Law' levelled

---

[3] Trude Weiss-Rosmarin, *Judaism and Christianity: The Differences* (New York: Jonathan David, 1943), 81.

[4] David Berger and Michael Wyschogrod, *Jews and 'Jewish Christianity'* (New York: KTAV, 1978), 65.

[5] Michael Schiffman, *Return from Exile: The Re-emergence of the Messianic Congregational Movement*, 2nd ed. (New York: Teshuvah Publishing Co., 1991), 72.

[6] David Stern, *Messianic Jewish Manifesto*, (Israel: JNTP, 1988), 125.

[7] A phrase used by Daniel Juster but not found in his published work.

by the Jewish community. Yet their understanding and practice of Torah
varies widely. The MJM is deeply divided on what the Torah is and how it
should be lived out. This chapter surveys the Messianic Jewish reclamation
and appropriation of the Torah in the light of Yeshua. It assesses the role and
significance of the Oral Torah and Jewish tradition, examining the construction of Messianic *halacha*[8] and surveying attempts to formulate it. Finally
some reflections on the future of Torah in Messianic Judaism will be offered.
The practical outworking of the different understandings of Torah will be
noted in the following chapter.

'Torah' is a both a key concept and a matter of controversy within the
Messianic Jewish movement. There is no agreed-upon definition, and this
leads to a lack of clarity in the discussion. 'Torah' may mean one or several of
the following in Messianic Jewish discussion: the Pentateuch (the Mosaic
Law); the Hebrew scriptures (the Old Testament); the Written and Oral Law;
Jewish tradition (including its Orthodox, Conservative, Reform, Liberal and
Reconstructionist expressions); the New Testament and the teaching of
Jesus; 'Law' as opposed to 'Grace'; and individual statutes and commandments. The term 'Torah' thus functions as a theological shorthand for
various understandings of Jewish law, from the most flexible to the most rig-
orous halachic requirements. The relationships between 'Law' and 'Grace',
between Yeshua and the Torah, and between the practice of the early Jewish
Yeshua-believers and today, are all matters of debate.

Several rationales are given for Torah observance. It has value in witness
to, and cultural identification with, the Jewish people. It sheds light on the
life and teaching of Yeshua. For some it has a validity of its own, in that
the Torah remains in effect as the grounds for the life of the covenant people,
leading to ethical and spiritual wholeness, and preserving the distinct
witness of Israel to her God. For others, there is deep concern that all talk of
'Torah observance' may lead to legalism and 'bondage to the Law'. At
present there is no normative view of Torah, although all seek legitimacy for
their position.

'Torah Negative' Views

There are several strands within the Messianic movement that distance
themselves from the 'Torah positive' approaches. Their influence is significant, although they are not always accepted as truly 'Messianic'.
Nevertheless they are participants in the debate on the nature of Messianic
Judaism, especially as it revolves around the issue of Torah-observance. It
is necessary to consider their views if we are to represent the full range of

---

[8] *'Halacha'* is from the Hebrew verb 'to walk'. It refers to the practical and authoritative rulings setting out the way in which Jews should live.

opinion in the MJM, and to show how the more Torah-positive approaches respond to them. We will briefly survey their views before paying more careful attention to those who advocate Torah observance and the construction of Messianic Jewish *halacha*.

Messiah, not Moses (Fruchtenbaum)

Based on a Dispensationalist theological system that sharply distinguishes between the Dispensation of Law (Moses) and of Grace (Christ), Arnold Fruchtenbaum sees the Mosaic Torah as 'inoperative' since the coming of the Messiah. However, Jewish believers in Jesus are still free to observe those aspects of the Mosaic law that Yeshua affirmed. 'Messianic Jewish practice can not be based on the Law of Moses as an *obligation* for the law has been rendered inoperative and is no longer in effect.'[9]

Fruchtenbaum is clear that the Mosaic law as a unit of 613 commandments is no longer the 'rule of life for Jewish believers'[10] and argues that 'No Messianic Jew who claims to be "Torah Observant" accepts his own thesis since he must believe in the doing away with, in some form, of many of the commandments of the law of Moses, if not most.'[11]

For Fruchtenbaum the major laws of the Sabbath and dietary laws have been annulled by the New Covenant,[12] and the believer in Messiah is 'free from the law of Moses'.[13] However, Fruchtenbaum adds 'On the other hand, he is also free to keep parts of the law of Moses that do not violate the law of Messiah if he so desires.'[14] Fruchtenbaum illustrates this from the life of Paul, 'the greatest exponent of freedom from the law' who took a Nazirite vow, desired to be in Jerusalem for Pentecost and lived as an observant Jew. There is freedom to observe commands that are 'New Testament-neutral, meaning they do not violate any New Testament principle or command.'[15]

---

[9] Arnold Fruchtenbaum, *Israelology: The Missing Link in Systematic Theology*, Rev. ed. (Tustin, CA: Ariel Ministries, 1993), 759, italics added: 'The Practice of Hebrew Christianity/Messianic Jewishness'. Cf. *Hebrew Christianity: Its Theology, History, and Philosophy* (Grand Rapids: Baker, 1974), 83; 'Messianic Congregations May Exist within the Body of Messiah, As Long As They Don't Function Contrary to the New Testament,' in *How Jewish Is Christianity? 2 Views on the Messianic Movement*, ed. Louis Goldberg (Grand Rapids: Zondervan, 2003), 116–25, 'The Role of the Mosaic Law'.

[10] Fruchtenbaum, 'Messianic Congregations May Exist,' 119.

[11] Ibid.

[12] Ibid., 121.

[13] Ibid., 122.

[14] Ibid.

[15] Ibid.

Those who impose an obligation of keeping the Mosaic law are divisive legalists.

> A recent strong trend in the Messianic movement is that of 'Torah Observance'. Adherents of this trend *do* see the law as an obligation, and they have, in fact, been splitting Messianic congregations in many different places. It has been my observation that many in the 'Torah observant movement' are not even Jews but Gentiles – the kind of Gentiles to whom Paul's letter to the Galatians was written.[16]

Fruchtenbaum chides the Messianic movement for not being clear on the role of the Mosaic law, which has led it into turmoil on the issue. With 'no real parameters', and 'since it is obvious that no one is really "Torah observant" in the way Moses prescribed', there is now much disagreement, unnecessary division and confusion within the movement. To Fruchtenbaum those who claim to be 'Torah positive' or 'Torah observant' are not 'really and truly observing Torah in the way Moses commanded. Their lives are simply full of inconsistencies and contradictions along this line.'[17]

For Fruchtenbaum the 'simple, yet biblical, solution' is to recognise that the Mosaic law has been rendered inoperative and is no longer an obligation on the believer. They are then free to observe 'New Testament neutral' commandments in a 'variety of different ways', either in the way prescribed by Moses, or they can 'observe them rabbinically',[18] provided they do not judge the Jewish loyalties or identity of those who may 'choose to follow these laws differently or not follow them at all'. Despite the strong dispensationalist theological basis which Fruchtenbaum uses, the plea for variety and mutual tolerance within the movement strike a chord that most Messianic Jews generally affirm. A more 'Torah observant' Messianic Judaism must critique Fruchtenbaum's theological basis if it is to effectively promote Torah observance. It must also accommodate itself to less observant forms of Messianic Judaism if it is to remain accepted within the MJM.

'Jewishness', not 'Judaism' (Maoz)

Baruch Maoz writes from a Protestant Reformed theological tradition, calling himself a 'Jewish Christian' who sees 'Jewishness' as a valid cultural, national and ethnic identity but not accepting any form of 'Judaism' as having authority in the life of the believer in Jesus.[19] He is scathing of those

---

[16] Ibid., 123.
[17] Ibid., 124.
[18] Ibid., 125.
[19] Baruch Maoz, *Judaism is Not Jewish: A Friendly Critique of the Messianic Movement* (Fearn, UK: Mentor/Christian Focus Publications, 2003).

who import 'legalism' into their faith by allowing 'Rabbinic Judaism' to have normative value. Maoz bases his critique of rabbinic Judaism on Matt. 23, where Jesus criticises the Pharisees for departing from the true path. 'Already at this relatively early stage, rabbinicism had hardened into a system that was in direct conflict with the fundamental principles of God's revelation.'[20]

For Maoz there is nothing to be gained from following the path set by rabbinic Judaism, which sets Law against Gospel. 'Pharisaism is a total worldview that shuts out the light of the Gospel by inculcating concepts that run directly contrary to those of the Gospel. The Gospel says that no man [*sic*] can meet God's just and perfect requirements. Judaism says that a man's good deeds can outweigh his evil ones.'[21]

Maoz argues further that there is 'no biblical evidence' to support the view that the apostles 'continued to keep rabbinic tradition', apart from 'some within the early church who continued to think in rabbinic terms', although this group did not succeed in persuading the apostles or 'prominent others' of their opinion.[22]

Maoz challenges 'Torah positive' views. Everything is now 'kosher', and the dietary requirements imposed on Israel by the commandment of God are no longer binding.[23] Paul missed being present in Jerusalem for many of the Jewish festivals. He did not keep Jewish practices because of a so-called 'glorious and beneficial dimension to some of the traditions of Judaism' as many modern-day Messianic Jews insist, but rather on grounds of expediency. 'Paul circumcised Timothy because his mother was Jewish (Acts 16:1–3) and *because of the Jews who were in those parts* (v.3), not for any religious or spiritual purpose.'[24]

Because rabbinic traditions form a large part of Jewish culture and national identity, such as setting the calendar, they are of value, as 'Rabbinic customs play a large role in the formation of that tradition which constitutes the national and cultural consensus among Jewish people, and which distinguishes them as such.'[25] However, such practices must be subject to careful scrutiny so that they do not 'conflict with the gospel, or permit any part of its message to be less than crystal clear'. Whilst Messianic Jews 'make much of quoting the Bible, Messianic Judaism is in fact not guided by truly biblical standards in its attitude to Jewish tradition. The extent to which I have succeeded in proving this is the extent to which Messianic Judaism should be rejected.'[26]

---

[20] Ibid., 163.

[21] Ibid., 165.

[22] Ibid., 168.

[23] Ibid., 169.

[24] Ibid., 170.

[25] Ibid., 172.

[26] Ibid., 173.

It is clear that Maoz is following a different agenda, assuming that the 'Judaism' of the rabbis is a false path, and that the only value of 'Jewishness' is in national and cultural matters. Religious truth is only found in the gospel of Christ, not the Law of rabbinical Judaism. This leaves little room in the life and faith of the believer for any form of 'Judaism', let alone a 'Messianic Judaism'. So when Messianic Jews appreciate aspects of rabbinic tradition or practice them they choose a false path, taking the believer away from true faith in the Messiah. Maoz summarises his position:

> Like all Christians, Jewish Christians are free from the Mosaic covenant, as we are from rabbinic tradition.
>
> • We are free to maintain our national identity and should maintain it, if we wish to further the best interests of our people.
> • The only way to do so is to maintain that cultural consensus by which the majority of contemporary Jews express and maintain their Jewishness.
> • But we must do so in a manner that is consistent with the Scriptures: the issues of the gospel may never be obscured.
> • Nothing but God in Messiah and his finished work on Calvary may be the focal point of congregational life, worship or evangelism.
> • The unity of the church should be maintained, and rabbinic tradition should never be accorded religious authority.
> • God reigns among his redeemed by his word.[27]

Maoz notes that Messianic Jews place high value on the Torah, quoting Dan Juster, Ariel Berkowitz and David Stern as representatives of this view,[28] claiming that they do see 'spiritual advantage' in keeping the Torah. To Maoz they confuse 'national and religious identity', as does the whole Messianic movement, who consider Judaism as a means of righteousness. 'So, it is not by believing in and obeying Jesus that the righteousness of the law is fulfilled in us (Rom. 8:3–4), but as we keep the Law, we partake of Jesus, who is seen in us!'[29]

Maoz is determined that the Mosaic law and Rabbinic observances should have no place in the lives of the believer or their congregation, unless it can clearly be shown that they have no 'religious' value, and in no way obscure the nature of saving faith in the gospel. The Reformation principles Maoz employs of *sola fide, sola scriptura* and *solus Christus,* inevitably repudiate any other religious system, and there can be no room for compromise.

---

[27] Ibid., 229–30.
[28] Ibid., 108–10.
[29] Ibid., 109.

Biblical *Halacha* Without Rabbinic Tradition (Nerel)

Gershon Nerel recognises amongst Jewish believers in Yeshua (JBYs)[30] a variety of attitudes to the Oral Law.[31] 'Today too, the issue of observing Torah is often the cause of divisions between Jewish and gentile believers, as well as within the inner circles of JBY themselves.'[32] Whereas Joseph Shulam[33] regrets the lack of a continuing tradition of Jewish Christian practice from Apostolic times to the present, for Nerel this provides a significant opportunity. 'The very fact that *congregations of JBY lack a two-millennia tradition* helps them easily to find the bridge between themselves and the first-century model of JBY as portrayed in the New Testament.'[34] Nerel similarly challenges the approach of those who wish to construct Messianic *halacha*, seeing this as confusing the nature and identity of 'Jewish Believers in Yeshua' (JBY), his preferred term to describe himself.[35] Whilst the Torah is still valid for Jewish Believers in Yeshua, we should not be legalistic in our approach to it, seeing that 'the ultimate and supreme authority lies in the teachings of Messiah Yeshua – the Son of God – together with the constant guidance of the Holy Spirit.'[36] Too many Messianic Jews 'overestimate [overesteem] the *Halacha* and fail to observe the scriptural Torah according to the teaching of the New Testament'.[37] They need to recognise that 'the *Halacha* stands apart from the sacred collection of the Bible' and 'assumes an authority that was not given to it, aspiring to overmaster the authority of the Holy Bible'.[38]

---

[30] Gershon Nerel prefers this term and uses it consistently, refusing the associations inherent in the terms 'Messianic Jew/Judaism' or 'Jewish Christian.' He explains his position in 'Modern Assemblies of Jewish Yeshua-Believers Between Church and Synagogue' in *How Jewish Is Christianity? 2 Views on the Messianic Movement*, ed. Louis Goldberg (Grand Rapids: Zondervan, 2003), 96–99, 'The Trap of Mixed Nomenclature and Praxis'.

[31] Nerel, e-mail message to author, October 10, 2006.

[32] Gershon Nerel, 'Eusebius' *Ecclesiastical History* and the Modern Yeshua-Movement' in *Mishkan* 39 (2003), 65–86, 68.

[33] See below for Shulam's position.

[34] Nerel, 'Modern Assemblies,' 106.

[35] Gershon Nerel, 'Torah and *Halacha* Among Modern Assemblies of Jewish Yeshua-Believers' in *How Jewish Is Christianity? 2 Views on the Messianic Movement*, ed. Louis Goldberg (Grand Rapids: Zondervan, 2003), 152–65; 'Observing the Torah according to Yeshua,' *CHAI: The Quarterly Magazine of the British Messianic Jewish Alliance* 212 (2001), 5–8. http://www.bmja.i12.com/chai_page_5/htm (accessed May 5, 2003).

[36] Nerel, 'Observing the Torah,' 5.

[37] Nerel, 'Torah and *Halacha*,' 152.

[38] Ibid.

Because Judaism and synagogue continue to maltreat the name of Yeshua and still excommunicate his Jewish disciples, it is not only out of context but even pathetic that congregations of JBY wish to follow rabbinical culture and institutions. Therefore, when JBY confuse their Jewish ethnic and national identity with synagogue patterns of thinking and behaviour, they fail to appreciate the centrality of Yeshua and his message.[39]

The central question is not 'should we observe the Torah?' but 'How should we observe it?' – whether this be following Orthodox, Reform or Conservative Judaism, or choosing an 'independent track of our own'. Nerel recognises that the JBY has a 'distinct and legitimate Jewish identity', and that keeping the Torah where it is 'spiritually reasonable and practically possible' such as in regards to marriage and burial practices in Israel is perfectly acceptable, although these rights are often denied JBYs living in Israel. The practice of circumcision,[40] the Sabbath and the biblical calendar,[41] Kashrut (but allowing the mixing of milk and meat),[42] even men not completely shaving the beard,[43] are all examples of following biblical Torah, without need for later rabbinic *halacha*.

The key principle that distinguishes 'major' and 'minor' issues is the teaching of Yeshua that explains how to observe the Torah. This does not mean observing the Torah according to rabbinical traditions and restrictions.

In keeping the Shabbat, for example, Yeshua is telling us that 'it is lawful to do good on the Sabbath' (Matt. 12:12). Our Messiah also demonstrates that: 'The Sabbath was made for man, and not man for the Sabbath' (Mark 2:27). Therefore, to mention a contemporary example, it is right for us to use a car and to travel on the Shabbat to a Bible study or worship.[44]

Today, it is completely clear that it was Yeshua who gave the Torah to Israel on Mount Sinai, and therefore Yeshua is the authority who interprets His own Torah. Obviously Yeshua can alter the Torah and even add to it new guidelines. Consequently, Jewish believers in Yeshua, are free of keeping the *Torah ba'al peh*, the Oral Law, those customs and decrees originating from non-believers in Yeshua. Therefore, Jewish believers in Yeshua are not obliged to keep the *Halacha*, the rabbinical habits, because the *Halacha* intentionally ignores Yeshua.[45]

---

[39] Nerel, 'Modern Assemblies,' 97.
[40] Nerel, 'Torah and *Halacha*,' 157.
[41] Ibid.,158–61.
[42] Ibid., 161–62.
[43] Nerel, 'Observing the Torah,' 5, cf. Lev 19:27.
[44] Nerel, 'Observing the Torah,' 7.
[45] Ibid.

Therefore there is no need for a 'Messianic *Halacha*',[46] as the JBY is 'totally free of keeping the *Torah shebe'al peh*, the oral law' and should not develop his own *halacha* based on 'those customs and decrees originating from non-believers in Yeshua', the 'so-called *hazal*, the Jewish sages' who still 'reject Yeshua and oppose his teachings'.[47] There are clashes between the New Testament and rabbinic *halacha* on issues such as the wearing of *kippot* (head coverings for men), which Nerel sees as biblically forbidden for men.[48] Messianic Jews should not follow the traditional Haggadah but should 'Celebrate *Pesach* by reading and by interpreting only the narratives of the relevant biblical texts and, particularly, to focus on the Lamb symbolism and the Lord's Supper.'[49]

It is ultimately only practical to live out such a biblical Torah life-style within the modern State of Israel. Attempts to shape a 'Messianic Jewish identity' in the Diaspora are doomed to failure.

> Within the Jewish State it is our daily life that enables us to maintain and preserve our Jewish identity. This happens alongside our permanent witness for Yeshua. Thus, for example, our children normally attend the Israeli State schools, like in any other Jewish family in Israel, and we do not need to establish separate 'Ghetto schools' of our own. We also serve as soldiers and officers in the Israeli Army. This we are doing, not only for the three years of obligatory military service, starting at the age of 18, but also during the reserve military service, which lasts for almost two additional decades. Such pragmatic matters enable us to identify with our nation as an integral part of our people.
>
> Therefore, there are evidently two different ways to shape the Jewish identity in Messiah Yeshua: either in the Diaspora or in Israel. 'Messianic Judaism', as it is currently shaped mainly in America and exported from there to other places, is a product of the Diaspora for the needs of the Diaspora. 'Messianic Judaism' is a tool for those who actually wish to remain in the Diaspora and do not want to come and settle in Israel. They wish to safeguard and to perpetuate Jewish life in the Diaspora. For achieving this aim, they adopt rabbinical Judaism under the new slogan of 'Messianic *Halacha*'. The tools they choose for that survival in the Diaspora, are the rabbinical traditions and rites.[50]

Messianic Judaism, by constructing *halacha*, 'replaces the message of the Kingdom of God' and Messianic Judaism 'becomes an aim in itself', threatening to 'take the place of the teachings of Yeshua Himself'. JBYs should recognise that their theology and nationality are both based on the Old and

---

[46] Nerel, 'Torah and *Halacha*,' 163–64.

[47] Ibid., 164

[48] Nerel, 'Observing the Torah,' 7, cf. 1 Cor 11:7.

[49] Ibid.

[50] Ibid., 8.

New Testaments, and should not try to prove that they are Jews or Israelis. Nor do they need to 'strictly observe all rabbinical traditions', as this 'will not help them to be considered by the authorities – secular or religious – as Jews'. They should consider the changed situation in Israel today. 'In the Jewish State we are full citizens – and not members of the synagogues. Practically, it is only in Israel that Jewish believers in Yeshua can redefine Jewishness outside the rabbinic institutions and still remain an organic member of Jewry, within the national Jewish commonwealth.'[51]

Nerel arrives at a cautious approach to *halacha* on the basis of his reading of scripture, with tradition, whether Jewish or Christian, playing a minor role.

> When Yeshua himself went to the synagogues he quoted only scripture and interpreted it with a fresh insight and a divine authority. It is also my understanding that we, contemporary JBY, should come with the same approach because only this scriptural basis is a solid foundation. Of course we do interpret the text, yet we should do that with the guidance of the Holy Spirit and with the other parts of the text itself. Namely, our interpretation of the Bible should be done with and through the canonical biblical verses! This is what I find that Yeshua did after the devil tempted him (Matt. 2; Luke 4).[52]

Nerel represents a significant number of Israeli JBYs who are unhappy with both the nomenclature and the tendencies of the American Messianic movement. Torah observance should only be used to support the cultural norms of Israeli secular identity. Any religious meaning is derived primarily from the teaching of Yeshua and the New Covenant, not from either Jewish or Christian tradition.

'Torah Positive' Views

Fruchtenbaum, Maoz and Nerel provide a series of caveats to 'Torah observance' and the construction of Messianic Jewish *halacha*. However, the Messianic movement, particularly in the USA, is paying increasing attention to the subject. The approaches of several more 'Torah positive' positions are surveyed, in the light of the concerns expressed.

'Torah Incognita' (Stern)

Despite its significance in Judaism, according to David Stern, 'Torah' is the great 'terra incognita' for Christians and Messianic Jews alike, and

---

[51] Ibid.
[52] Nerel, email message to author, 10th October 2006.

'Christian theology's greatest deficiency'.[53] Christians have a simplistic understanding of the Law, and little to say of relevance about one of the three fundamental issues [God, Torah and Israel] of Jewish faith.[54] Stern maps out his theology of Torah. Referring to C.E.B. Cranfield, W.D. Davies and E.P. Sanders, he presents a more positive and less disparaging understanding of νομος in the New Testament than is typically held. 'The works of the Law' (τα 'εργα του νομου) opposed by Paul are better understood as 'legalistic observance of particular Torah commands'.[55] The New Testament clearly states that Torah has not been abrogated. Rather Yeshua inaugurates the New Covenant as Torah, in 'exactly the same sense' as that which was given to Moses on Sinai. The gospel does not bring the Torah to an end ('termination'), but rather is the end ('goal, purpose, consummation') to which the Torah aims. Torah continues in force, renewed, established and fulfilled by Yeshua, and now inaugurated as the new Torah of the Messiah that rabbinic speculation anticipated.

Stern is well aware of the complex mental gymnastics he has performed to come to this position, but denies that he is being theologically evasive.[56] Not only is a reassessment of the theology of Torah necessary, but once it is properly understood, it will be clear that the Torah continues in force.

> When I say this, I am not making a concession to Judaism, as some Christian critics might suppose. Nor am I somehow expressing anti-Torah theology in hypocritical, deceptive and confusing pro-Torah language, an accusation I could expect from a few non-Messianic Jews. Rather, I am stating as clearly as I can what I believe the New Testament teaches. It will prove to be neither a concession nor a confusion, but a challenge – to both Jews and Christians.[57]

So if legalism is not the problem, 'the question that resonates in this conflict the loudest is: should Messianic Jews observe the Torah?'[58] Messianic Jews suffer from an identity crisis that is not of their own making but a 'result of historical developments over the past 2000 years'.[59] The question of Torah observance raises acutely the question of how to 'put together and express' the Jewish and Messianic elements in their lives. Just as Orthodox, Reformed, Conservative and other non-Messianic Jews hold differing understandings and applications of Torah, a similar breadth of options is to

---

[53] David Stern, *Messianic Jewish Manifesto*, 125. Stern devotes 65 pages (ch. 5, 125–89) to Torah, more than 20% of the book. Cf. *JNTC*, 566–70.

[54] Ibid., 126.

[55] Ibid., 130.

[56] Ibid., 135.

[57] Ibid.

[58] Ibid., 137.

[59] Ibid., 138.

be expected within the Messianic community, which will have its own *Bet Hillel* and *Bet Shammai*.

It is only here that Stern defines 'Torah', giving five possible understandings. First, the Orthodox understanding of the five books of Moses, the *Tanakh,* the *Talmud* and Codes, and contemporary *Halacha*, provides one conception,[60] which can be clearly seen in the teaching of the *Shulchan Arukh*. Conservative Jews 'hold generally to the overall framework' but 'differ on specific judgments', adapting to the needs of modern society. Reform 'generally holds that only the ethical commands are binding', with the civil and ceremonial as optional. The two remaining views of Torah are what Stern calls 'Biblical Law' and his own unnamed understanding, which are explained with less clarity than could be desired. 'Biblical Law' is the 'Written Law' held by some Messianic Jews and some Christians, such as Seventh-Day Adventists, who consider 'the Oral Law not inspired and not binding'. Biblical *Kashrut* for them consists of not eating pork or shellfish, but allowing milk to be mixed with meat, since that aspect of *Kashrut* is not taught in the Bible.[61] Stern sees this approach as similar to that of the Sadducees and the Karaites in their rejection of the oral tradition of the Pharisees.

Stern states his own position: 'My own view is that the Torah is eternal, and the New Testament has not abrogated it. But in its totality the Torah must be understood and interpreted in the light of what Yeshua the Messiah and the rest of the New Covenant scriptures have said about it.'[62]

Whilst not explaining how his view differs from the 'Biblical Law' approach, one is left to assume that it has something to do with acceptance of the Oral Law as in some sense inspired, and to be included in the meaning of Torah, although this is not made explicit. For the purposes of discussion Stern then defines Torah as 'what Orthodox Judaism understands it to be', so that he can proceed to further analysis.[63] This less than satisfactory step in the argument is taken because 'discussions of whether Messianic Jews should observe the Torah generate more heat than light when there is disagreement over what is meant by "the Torah" [so] we shall for the purpose of this section define the *Torah* arbitrarily as what Orthodox Judaism understands it to be, so that we can progress to analysis.'[64]

Five possible answers to the question 'should Messianic Jews keep the *Torah* as understood in Orthodox Judaism?' are given, ranging from an 'absolute yes' and 'desirable', to 'indifferent', 'undesirable', and 'absolutely not'.[65] But realising that this definition of Torah is unsatisfactory Stern abandons it.

---

[60] Ibid., 139.
[61] See chapter 7 below for discussion of 'biblical *kashrut*'.
[62] Ibid.,139–40.
[63] Ibid., 141.
[64] Ibid., 140.
[65] Ibid., 140–45.

Any Messianic Jew who thinks that following the Orthodox or Conservative Jewish version of the Torah will increase his credibility before non-Messianic Jews ought to disabuse himself of the idea at once. He will never be 'Jewish enough' to prove that Yeshua is the Messiah, and there is the risk that he will become the issue, rather than Yeshua. Furthermore, non-Messianic Jews who consider him no longer Jewish will not be convinced otherwise by his law-keeping.[66]

The true Torah is that taught and fulfilled by Yeshua and his disciples, and this should be observed by both Jews and Gentiles. 'We conclude that under the New Covenant the *Torah* remains in force and is as much for Gentiles as for Jews, although the specific requirements for Gentiles differ from those for Jews.'[67] The Gentiles follow the Noachide commandments as adopted in Acts 15. Jewish believers in Yeshua continue to live according to the Mosaic Covenant, fulfilled in Messiah.[68] Thus the true Oral Torah is that taught by Yeshua's disciples, the Apostles, as they give instructions in the book of Acts.

> This is the first time the New Testament portrays the emissaries' teaching, giving out the true *Torah sh'be 'al peh* ('Oral Torah') … What traditional Judaism calls the Oral Torah can certainly be mined for its treasury of truths. But as it stands the Oral Torah cannot be authoritative; because its writers and expositors have ignored the Messiah's coming, his interpretations of *Torah* and the interpretations of those he appointed, as well as the New Testament itself, which constitutes one-quarter of the written Word of God.[69]

Stern's understanding of the nature of Torah reflects the formative stage of the Messianic movement of the 1980s. He writes as one liberated from a traditional Protestant Evangelical 'anti-Torah' attitude by the new awareness of New Testament scholars at that time of the 'Jewishness of Jesus' and the 'new perspective on Paul'.[70] It became clear at that time that the New Testament itself was not as against 'legalism' as later Reformation teaching would become in its polemic against Roman Catholicism, and Messianic Jews gladly affirmed such scholarship. However, Stern stops short of a rationale for appropriating Jewish tradition in the form of the Oral Torah, using it as a reference point in his discussion but remaining ambivalent as to what

---

[66] Ibid., 144–45.

[67] Ibid., 157.

[68] Ibid., 154–57. The Noachide laws are seven moral principles given to all nations.

[69] David Stern, *Jewish New Testament Commentary* (Jerusalem: Jewish New Testament Publications, 1992), 227, on Acts 2:42.

[70] Cf. Geza Vermes, *Jesus the Jew* (London: SCM Press, 1974) and E.P. Sanders, *Paul and Palestinian Judaism* (London: SCM Press, 1979).

authority and respect to give it, and at times expressing an adversarial rather than accommodating position towards it.

Stern explains that an interpretative mechanism is needed to apply the 'Written Torah' of the Old and New Testament similar to the operation of the United States Constitution.[71] Congress can interpret and apply the Constitution, and even repeal its own legislation where necessary, although it does not have power to revoke the original Constitution.[72] Stern argues that the rabbis took over what was intended to be a flexible system of *cohen* (priest) and *shofet* (judge), and that 'ossification set in as the precedents of the Oral Torah came to be regarded as decreed by God for all time and just as binding as the Written Torah.'[73]

Whereas Congress can pass laws that do not violate the Constitution and modify these, the 'Oral Torah has come to be "set in stone" so that its decisions can not be revoked'. This makes the Oral Torah 'unworkable', because if it had more flexibility, Yeshua 'might not have had to scold the scribes and Pharisees, "With your tradition you nullify the word of God" (Mark 7:13)'. However, there is still value in the Oral Torah, and those Messianic Jews who 'reject everything added to the Written Torah by the rabbis as unbiblical' in order to arrive at a 'supposedly "biblical Judaism"' are themselves creating a new 'Oral Torah'. A better way of relating to the existing Oral Torah is to see it 'not as divine command but as religious and cultural tradition, much of which can guide us toward holiness and toward making congregational life both satisfying for ourselves and useful for showing non-Messianic Jews the gospel in the context of who and what we are. Also relating to the Oral Torah will better prepare us to dialogue with the Jewish religious world if the opportunity arises.'[74]

So for Stern there are grounds for recognition of the Oral Torah such as cultural identification and witness. Its 'religious component' stops short of 'divine command' but leads to personal holiness and congregational integrity. Rather than allow the oral to be the authoritative interpreter of the written, it is the written Torah of Old and New Testament combined that must be used to correctly interpret and apply the Oral Torah.

'My Law on Your Heart' (Powlison)

Arye Powlison, a Messianic teacher based in Israel, recognises a certain level of authority in the Oral Torah, as would be given to secular powers. He

---

[71] David Stern, 'Summary Essay: The Future of Messianic Judaism' in *How Jewish Is Christianity? 2 Views of the Messianic Movement*, ed. Louis Goldberg (Grand Rapids: Zondervan, 2003), 184.

[72] Ibid.

[73] Ibid.

[74] Ibid., 184–85.

maintains allegiance to Yeshua as the 'only rabbi who can teach the inner purity of heart and the life of service that his disciples are called to follow'. He summarises his position as follows:

> There are several areas of rabbinic teaching which Yeshua rejected out of hand as unacceptable. Usually, the reason was that they contradicted fundamental logic based on the Scriptures, or even that they contradicted the Scriptures directly. However, neither Yeshua nor His disciples rejected rabbinic teaching with the argument that the rabbis lacked the authority to decide *Halacha* (the applicable Law of Moses for the Jewish people); nor did they reject rabbinic additions to Jewish practice merely because they were rabbinic additions.[75]

Yeshua accepted rabbinic authority but did not regard it as absolute, teaching that certain rabbinic interpretations transgressed biblical requirements such as the laws of divorce, support of parents and observance of the Sabbath. For Powlison the key method and motivation for living life according to the Torah is to follow the example of Yeshua as the servant of others.

> Finally, the way that we live Torah will be greatly influenced by such an approach. Your Judaism will hardly be recognisable when compared with that which is practised by most people today. You will not be studying in order to become known; you will use what you have in the service of others; you will not be trying to attract attention to yourself; you will not be afraid to suffer, or to be in need. Most of all, you will not be afraid for it to be known that Israel did not recognise her Messiah, and that she hung Him on a tree.[76]

The requirement in the Torah of 'circumcision of the heart' is more important than fulfilling the external requirement of a *Beth Din* (the religious court), and following the Divine Torah of 'inward cleanliness' is more important than following the human Torah of outer cleanliness. 'This is the secret of the Torah of the heart. It is a way which was made possible by the Lamb of G-d from the beginning of creation, by the willing sacrifice of Himself for us, for the forgiveness of our sins.'[77]

For Powlison the rabbis still have authority over us, but in the same way as secular authorities, rather than as revealers of divine truth.

> Therefore, even though we accept rabbinic authority over Jewish believers, just as we submit to all those in authority over us (Rom 13:1–2), we nevertheless do not

---

[75] Arye Powlison, 'Rabbinic Judaism as a Background to Scripture,' *Tishrei* 32, no. 2 (May 2003), under 'Yeshua and Limits of Rabbinic Authority,' http://www.familyrestorationmagazine.org/tishrei032.htm (accessed June 7, 2007).

[76] Ibid.

[77] Ibid.

accept that authority according to rabbinic rules. They are subject to the authority of Heaven, and of our Messiah Yeshua, and of the Scriptures, including the New Testament. Rabbinic teaching which contradicts any of these is false teaching, and must be ignored. On the other hand, *Halacha* which follows from any of these three sources, but which is not supported by the rabbis, is nevertheless *Halacha* to be obeyed by us.[78]

Whilst this position appeals to the Protestant view of the authority of scripture and the freedom of individual conscience and call to personal inner piety, it does give some degree of respect to rabbinic tradition as the cultural ambit within which Messianic Jewish life and observance is to be outworked. Powlison acknowledges the positive and negative values of the Orthodox Jewish tradition, and seeks to identify himself within it, with certain reservations, as an act of commitment and service to the Messiah.

Variety With Guidelines (Goldberg)

Louis Goldberg summarises Messianic Jewish attitudes to Torah. 'Messianic Jewish believers have identified three principles in relation to the oral law: (1) some of it can definitely be used; (2) some of it can be adapted for use; (3) using it indiscriminately is unwarranted.'[79] There are clear principles for the use of the Oral Law.

> Can we use the oral law in our teaching and practice? The guidelines for its usage are clear enough. As long as biblical support for it is present, from either the written law or the New Covenant or both, *if* Yeshua said nothing against it, and if it does not violate a basic neutrality between Scripture and the function of everyday life, it is appropriate to use the traditions. We need then to relate these practices to Yeshua so that we are enabled to grow into his full stature.[80]

Four elements make up the Mosaic covenant: the moral law of the Ten Commandments; the five Levitical sacrifices; the civil and criminal laws; and 'lifestyle' laws, which includes dietary codes and a 'multitude of other guidelines'.[81] Only the first two elements are carried over into the New Covenant; the moral law which is universal, and the sacrificial system, which is

---

[78] Ibid.

[79] Louis Goldberg, 'Testing How Jewish We Should Be: A Response to Arnold Fruchtenbaum' in *How Jewish Is Christianity? 2 Views of the Messianic Movement*, ed. Louis Goldberg (Grand Rapids: Zondervan, 2003), 142.

[80] Ibid., 144.

[81] Louis Goldberg, 'Living the Messianic Jewish Lifestyle: A Response to William Varner' in *How Jewish Is Christianity? Two Views of the Messianic Movement*, ed. Louis Goldberg (Grand Rapids: Zondervan, 2003), 90 (fn 14).

'subsumed in the one offering by the Messiah'.[82] Goldberg does not question the arbitrary nature of these divisions nor the implicit Dispensationalist theological grid that brings such hermeneutical procedures to the text, but rather accepts them as the basis for the working out of Messianic practice. Whilst 'the Mosaic covenant *as a total package* is no longer in force today',[83] some of the Mosaic covenant is 'still in force because of the strong imprint of the moral code on the new covenant'.[84] This gives the Jewish believer in Yeshua freedom to adopt, adapt or abandon Jewish practices as 'biblical theology guides the process to mark the acceptable choices'.[85] On the basis of these guidelines Goldberg quotes Sam Nadler's statement that those who involve themselves in Messianic Congregations will 'accept the cultural distinctions, the language issues, the appreciation of Torah, the Messianic standards and garb that become the identity of the congregation, and so on. The Jewish believer does this, not because of legalism, but because of a calling based on a liberty which the New Covenant encourages.'[86]

New Covenant *Halacha* (Juster)

Daniel Juster's 'New Covenant Halachic Approach' (NCHA) addresses the nature of the Church's relationship to Israel, the relationship of Law to Grace and the nature of Messianic Jewish practice based on Torah.[87] The New Testament does not abrogate the Law or segment it into 'rigid categories' of the ethical and ceremonial, but rather sees the spiritual and ethical purpose of the whole Law. Rabbinic Judaism sometimes provides helpful natural extensions and applications of Torah, but can also be found to be 'seriously wrong'. The Talmud is often, for all its wisdom and insight, 'a childish book in many regards'.[88] The New Testament provides ample evidence of 'New Covenant *Halacha*' (NCH), and also supplies the principles

---

[82] Ibid.

[83] Ibid., 146.

[84] Ibid., 147.

[85] Ibid., 148.

[86] Sam Nadler, 'What is Legalism? What is Liberty' (unpublished paper) quoted in Goldberg, 'Testing How Jewish We Should Be,' 148.

[87] Daniel C. Juster, *The Torah And Messianic Jewish Practice*, LCJE Third International Consultation Conference Paper (Easneye: LCJE, 1986), 3. Cf. 'Covenant and Dispensation' in *Torah and Other Essays*, ed. Ronald Lewis (Ramsgate: International Hebrew Christian Alliance, 1983), 42–58; *Jewish Roots: A Foundation of Biblical Theology For Messianic Judaism* (Rockville: Davar, 1986), 191–226, 259–88; *Growing to Maturity: A Messianic Jewish Guide* 2nd ed. (Rockville: UMJC, 1985); 'Messianic Judaism and the Torah' in *Jewish Identity and Faith in Jesus*, ed. Kai Kjær-Hansen (Jerusalem: Caspari Centre, 1996), 113–21.

[88] Juster, *The Torah and Messianic Jewish Practice*, 4.

for developing a 'Halachic approach to the commands of the Tenach'. One must understand the context of each command, know the underlying principle behind it and to whom the command is given, then work out how to apply the command in a 'New Covenant order'.[89]

The NCHA gives a practical method for applying the laws as part of Israel's life and witness, yielding a 'Jewish life in fulfilled form'.[90] Juster illustrates with the examples of the festivals, the Sabbath, *Tallit* and *Tefillin*, and with other examples of Jewish culture, identity, history and nationhood.[91] Juster sees the NCHA as the most fruitful approach to the Torah (which includes both Old and New Testaments, but not, apparently, oral tradition). With suitable peroration he concludes:

> It is a Jewish approach rather than a foreign theological system imposed on the Scriptures. It reflects the unity of the Bible and the continuity of salvation history. This approach frees us from legalism, but not from the proper role of law. It emphasises the Spirit so as to avoid the childish and soulish. It solves problems in exegesis and debate from the impasse between Covenant Theology and Dispensational Theology. It is my hope that this approach will be more firmly established among Jewish believers in Yeshua in the days ahead.[92]

However, it is not clear how this approach will be worked out in detail, and how a corpus of New Covenant *Halacha* will be developed, codified and accepted as authoritative. Juster does not discuss further the significance of rabbinic tradition. Whilst he affirms the priority of scripture, it is not clear how his reading strategies and theological assumptions situate New Testament material in the light of Jewish cultural contexts and the nascent Rabbinic Judaism of the period.

Juster argues that the Torah (by which he means the Pentateuch) is foundational for Judaism, and that any Messianic Jewish perspective must be 'clear in its understanding of Torah and the early covenants God made with Israel'.[93] Messianic Jews must 'gain an accurate understanding of Torah in general if they are to know how to relate their Jewish heritage to Christian theology'.[94] Then they will integrate the *Tanakh* with the New Testament in a 'balanced understanding' in which biblical revelation is seen as a whole. The Torah should not be 'dismissed because of debates which arose from new contexts' [those between Paul and his opponents]. Only by understanding the Torah's legislation in its own context can the Messianic Jew avoid the

---

[89] Ibid.

[90] Ibid., 5.

[91] See chapter 7 below for Juster's approach to Sabbath and *kashrut*.

[92] Ibid., 6.

[93] Juster, *Jewish Roots*, 1.

[94] Ibid., 14.

extremes of Dispensationalism and Adventism. The former distinguishes between the Mosaic Law and the 'law of Christ' and limits believers in Jesus to only keeping those commands of the Torah which are repeated in the New Testament.[95] The latter holds the Sabbath command to be as important as the other Ten Commandments.[96]

The New Covenant is not an abrogation of Torah but an 'ability to walk *in* Torah'. The Mosaic Torah reflects 'God's universal and eternal moral standards'. Once we understand the Torah's 'accommodations to its age' and bear in mind 'New Testament truth',[97] we can still accept the instructions of the Torah as inspired scripture. We do not fulfil Torah to 'gain merit before God, but as those who are led by the Spirit to do God's will in response to His grace'.[98] Yeshua 'never confutes the intended meaning and purpose of the Torah if properly understood'.[99] His quarrel was not with the Law, but with his contemporaries' *misinterpretations* of the Law.[100]

Juster calls for an understanding of biblical Law in its original context, a thoughtful application in the light of Yeshua's teaching and example, and flexibility in addressing contemporary needs and practice. The 'spirit of the Torah' must be followed rather than the strict letter. Rabbinic tradition should not have normative authority. Whilst Messianic Jews value the traditions of Judaism they are 'not bound by tradition as a legalistic straitjacket', but follow the Holy Spirit's leading as they reflect carefully on each practice.[101] They respect rabbinic *halacha* whilst at the same time reserving the right to 'criticize it in love', without allowing traditions to 'blind us to the heart intent of the Word'.[102] For Juster the application and development of *halacha* calls for constant reflection on the original purpose of the commandments, and a relevant contemporary application in the light of their intended purpose.

Rabbinic tradition for Juster is a mixed bag, which can produce unnecessary and burdensome legislation such as the 'extra-biblical' command to separate milk from meat.[103] It may yield illustrations of the 'wrong road to take' or give a 'brilliant application that helps us to appropriate the teaching in our day'.[104] Rabbinic tradition can be no more than a guideline and a resource to be used with careful evaluation, and within the norms of

---

[95] Ibid., 15.
[96] Ibid., 17.
[97] Ibid., 41.
[98] Ibid., 42.
[99] Ibid., 50.
[100] Ibid., 51.
[101] Ibid., 227.
[102] Ibid., 228.
[103] Ibid., 231.
[104] Ibid., 230.

scripture. As an aid for further study Juster includes a listing of the *Taryag Mitzvot,* making provisional assessment of their relevance to the life of Messianic Jews today. In a suggestive proposal he categorises the 613 commandments into 8 categories.[105] This provides a basis for a complete analysis of the Mosaic Torah in the light of Jewish traditional interpretation, but the project is not developed further.

The Messianic Taryag Mitzvot (Michael Rudolph)

Michael Rudolph, a colleague of Daniel Juster, has examined each of the 613 commandments (the *Taryag Mitzvot*), explaining his exegetical methods and producing his own halachic recommendations. As both a lawyer and a Messianic rabbi, his insights are practical and pastoral. The work is intended to be something upon which others can build. Rudolph notes that the Bible can be appreciated from several points of view, and his approach is to see it as a 'book of law, containing God's instructions for holy, moral and victorious living'.[106] He defines the Torah as the Pentateuch, the law of Moses, which the rest of the *Tanakh,* whilst also divinely inspired, seeks to 'merely historicize, exemplify and embellish'. Rudolph see two categories of commandments contained in the *Tanakh,* both of which are to be viewed as 'divine statutory law'. There are 'Those whose literal compliance depends on the [Mosaic] Covenant's continued existence, and those whose literal compliance does not. We shall call the first of these, "covenant-dependent", and the second of these, "covenant-transcendent".'[107]

Rudolph derives these organising categories from the New Testament Book of Hebrews, understanding that Heb. 8:13 'suggests a diminishing literal role for covenant-dependant statutes, whilst it is the premise of this book that those which are covenant transcendent become adopted into the New Covenant law along with their literal applications.'[108] For Rudolph the 'Mosaic statutes per se' are not part of the New Covenant, rather 'It is the essential teaching (*torah*) of these statutes, and not the statutes themselves, which are adopted into it.'[109]

Rudolph adopts a spiritualising exegesis, extracting the 'essential teaching' as it is re-defined in the New Covenant, and applying literally those commands that are re-asserted in the New Covenant, a development of Daniel Juster's approach in a systematic and methodical fashion. 'A rule-of-

---

[105] Ibid., 259–87. Juster's categories are 'Temple (T)'; 'Moral Universal (UM)'; 'Universal but *revised* (UR)'; 'Jewish (J)'; 'J – Ancient'; '? – unclear'; 'Combination (C)'; and 'N.A. – No longer applies'.

[106] Michael Rudolph, *The Law of the Messiah* (unpublished paper, 2001), 1.

[107] Ibid.

[108] Ibid.

[109] Ibid., 2 (footnote 5).

thumb test is to ask; "Can or should this statute be complied with in the New Covenant era exactly and literally as commanded?" If the answer is "yes", it is "transcendent". If not, it is "dependent".'[110]

Biblical Torah Without Rabbinic Tradition (Berkowitz)

Ariel Berkowitz argues for a fresh and positive understanding of the Torah.[111] For Berkowitz the primary sense of 'Torah' is the Mosaic law, and his chapter on 'Jewish Misconceptions of the Torah' distinguishes the written from the oral.[112] The claim that *Torah she biktav* is part of the 'dual Torah' is a 'fraudulent attempt by an impostor to pass itself off as the true Torah'.[113] This essential concept of both ancient and modern traditional Judaism, stated by the *Mishnah* in Pirke Avot 1:1,[114] clarified by Maimonides in the *Mishneh Torah*[115] and codified in the *Shulchan Aruch* of Joseph Karo and *Mishnah Brura* of the *Chafetz Chaim*,[116] whilst both fixed and fluid in their origin and transmission through the centuries, is not truly binding or authoritative.[117]

Whilst it is reasonable that Moses gave some of his teaching orally, and there are traces of oral tradition within the *Tanakh*, Berkowitz questions how accurately such a tradition could have been passed down by 'scores of mouths over a period of hundreds of years'.[118] Berkowitz refutes the possibility of a 'divinely inspired oral tradition', stating that 'the Holy One was careful to ensure that all necessary and binding revelation was written down and preserved accordingly'.[119] Arguing from Josh. 8:31–35 and 23:6–8 he rejects the Maimonidean distinction between Torah as the teaching of the written Law and *mitzvot* as the accompanying Oral Law, stating that 'each generation was to follow the Written Torah under the direction of the Spirit of God, and not with a fixed, established interpretation called Oral Torah.'[120]

---

[110] Ibid.

[111] Ariel Berkowitz, and Devorah Berkowitz, *Torah Rediscovered: Challenging Centuries of Misinterpretation and Neglect*, 3rd ed. (Lakewood: First Fruits of Zion, 1998); Ariel Berkowitz, *According to God's Heart: A Biblical Case for a Torah Lifestyle* (Portland: Torah Resources International, 2003).

[112] Berkowitz, *Torah Rediscovered*, chapter 6, 93–115.

[113] Ibid., 94.

[114] Ibid., 95.

[115] Ibid., 96.

[116] Ibid., 98.

[117] Ibid., 99.

[118] Ibid.

[119] Ibid.

[120] Ibid., 101.

Berkowitz's critique of the Oral Torah is based on Yeshua's attitude to the developing *halacha* of his day. Whilst he was familiar with it and in certain respects followed it,[121] he did not accept its claim to divine origin or follow it in every case. Yeshua distinguished between the 'commandments of God' and the 'traditions of men' in his debate with the Pharisees on hand-washing.[122] Yeshua thus rebuked those who criticised him for breaking the Oral Torah, stating that he did not consider the Oral Torah to be 'authoritative for the man of God, the man of Torah'. Nevertheless, the Oral Torah does have value, as it gives us the best detailed understanding of Jewish life and religion at the time of Yeshua. It helps Christians appreciate the depth of care which Jewish people have devoted to the preservation and transmission of the scriptures, and gives valuable practical advice and illustrations on how the Torah is to be applied in everyday life. It provides a healthy corrective to Christian anti-Semitism by giving insights into the minds of the Sages and Jewish sensibility throughout history.

Berkowitz concludes his discussion of the Oral Torah with two heavily-loaded questions: 'Does the written Torah permit us to assume an Oral Torah, given by God to Moshe but authoritative for every generation? Or are we to depend on the leading and teaching of the Spirit of God to apply Torah's precepts to our generation?'[123]

Whilst Berkowitz appreciates some value in the Oral Torah, he clearly denies its authority and inspiration, allowing it to have illustrative value without being prescriptive. He does not develop his own proposals for how Messianic Jewish *halacha* should be developed. His work is mainly addressed to non-Jewish readers wishing to regain a positive approach to Law, and he does not enter into the debates within the Messianic movement on the halachic issues directly affecting Messianic Jews.

Biblical Re-Appropriation of Torah (Schiffman)

Michael Schiffman's chapter on 'Messianic Jews and the Law' includes a detailed section on Jewish tradition.[124] Biblical, rabbinic Jewish and Pauline understandings of Torah are given. 'Torah' forms the basis for the life of the Covenant people of God. It is the Law of Moses, fulfilled in Yeshua and reflected through some aspects of Jewish heritage and tradition (but without the normative claims of the rabbis). Several misunderstandings are corrected: that the Law is necessary for salvation; that Paul denied that Jewish

---

[121] Ibid., 103, quoting David Flusser, *Jewish Sources in Early Christianity*, (Tel Aviv: MOD Books, 1989), 21.

[122] Berkowitz, *Torah Rediscovered*, 104–5 on Mark 7:1–8.

[123] Ibid., 107.

[124] Michael Schiffman, *Return From Exile* (New York: Teshuvah, 1990), 72–96.

believers in Jesus were still free to observe the Law; and that rabbinic tradition in the *Mishnah* and *Talmud* are to be understood as biblical Torah. Torah
observance has positive value in cultural identification and witness, and in
providing the model for right conduct. Schiffman's understanding of Torah
in the life of the Messianic believer thus reflects a composite and eclectic perspective typical of the movement. 'Similar to Inaugurated Eschatology's
concept that the Kingdom of God is here and at the same time, yet to come;
so the law is fulfilled, and at the same time, is yet to be fulfilled in believers
living a godly life of faith.'[125]

Schiffman distinguishes between 'divine law' and 'human tradition',
which may be in agreement or in tension. Just as the oral tradition of the
rabbis is intertwined within Jewish culture, so Messianic Jews may integrate
tradition into their lifestyle and religious expression without accepting
the whole theological system behind it.[126] It is important that if such tradition is incorporated into Messianic observance it has 'a clear meaning
regarding biblical truth, and that it not be practiced merely because it seems
a Jewish thing to do'. According to Schiffman, Messianic believers are not
obligated to keep the Law but have the freedom to do so, provided they do
not fall into the trap of seeking to justify themselves by the works of the Law.
Rather they should affirm the purpose of the Law as a guide for godly living.
Schiffman concludes

> We are not under law, and consequently compelled to observe its precepts,
> but are over law and under grace, and have the freedom in Messiah to celebrate
> his faithfulness through the rich heritage God has given. It is important for
> Messianic Jews to point out to Jewish people that we may indeed be practicing
> the same customs and celebrating the same holidays but for very different
> reasons.[127]

For Schiffman the observance of Torah for Messianic Jews has the additional
purposes of cultural identification and witness to Yeshua, in addition to
providing the means to live a godly life.

Yeshua Kept *Halacha* – So Should We! (Fischer)

According to John Fischer, because Yeshua himself supported the traditions
of the Pharisees that later became rabbinic *halacha*, Messianic Jews today
should not only take note of rabbinic tradition but incorporate it into
Messianic Jewish *halacha*. 'Yeshua, the Apostles, and the early Messianic

---

[125] Ibid., 88.
[126] Ibid., 89.
[127] Ibid., 90.

Jews all deeply respected the traditions and devoutly observed them, and in so doing, set a useful pattern for us to follow.'[128]

Fischer outlines the principles for development of contemporary Messianic *halacha*. Only the Bible has authority for Messianic Jews, and anything that contradicts scripture should have no place in Messianic Judaism.[129] Such teachings were never intended to promote 'justification by works'. Rather, the rabbis themselves condemned the 'calculating Pharisee' who did good deeds to compensate for his sins.[130] The outlook and world-view of the rabbis must be understood just as we seek to understand the context of scripture, and this prevents a misrepresentation of rabbinic Judaism common in Protestant and Catholic thought. Understanding the 'Semitic mind set' helps us appreciate 'how the rabbinic mind functions' without the 'inadequate and highly inaccurate' interpretations seen through 'the eyes of the Twentieth Century or the glasses of the Western world and the lenses of modern philosophy and philology'.[131]

It is not clear what method Fischer proposes to better understand the rabbinic worldview apart from the use of the historico-critical method. Against the anti-Judaism of some Protestant scholarship, he asserts a more positive approach to Rabbinic Judaism. Not only do rabbinic traditions give us the basis for understanding and celebrating the biblical holidays,[132] but Yeshua and his disciples accepted them in matters of liturgy, belief and practice. Ninety percent of the *Siddur*, the prayer book, is composed of scripture.[133] The use of rabbinic tradition does not violate the biblical command to 'go outside the camp'[134] if rightly understood by Messianic Jews. Nor is 'rabbinic' Judaism a 'Babylonian religion that is un-godly and man-made'[135] or a product of 'Greek philosophical speculation and sophistry that pervert and distort God's revelation'[136] but was in fact developed to oppose Fischer's ultimate *bête noire* – Hellenism.

For Fischer the centrality of faith '*must* remain squarely on Yeshua', but this does not mean disregarding the traditions. Only the Bible is

---

[128] John Fischer, 'Would Yeshua Support Halacha?' in *Kesher: A Journal of Messianic Judaism* 5 (Summer 1997), 51–81. Messianic Jewish *halacha* is the main subject of the issue.

[129] Ibid., 76.

[130] Ibid., 78, referring to Jerusalem Talmud Berachot IX, 14b.

[131] Ibid., 79.

[132] John Fischer, 'The Place of Rabbinic Tradition in a Messianic Jewish Lifestyle' in *The Enduring Paradox: Exploratory Essays in Messianic Judaism*, ed. John Fischer (Baltimore: Lederer, 2000), 156–58.

[133] Ibid., 164.

[134] Heb. 13:13.

[135] Fischer 'The Place of Rabbinic Tradition,' 164.

[136] Ibid., 165.

authoritative, and we are not 'under "the authority" of the Rabbis', which is frequently a 'badly distorted and a poorly understood concept some believers share, often due to the influence of the Western World's Protestant and Catholic views of authority'.[137] The *halacha* in fact reinforces and refocuses the nature of Yeshua and his teaching. It has also been used by God to preserve the Jewish people throughout the centuries, and can claim in some sense (which Fischer does not clarify) the status of divine revelation. Therefore Messianic Jews should build on and supplement the *halacha* in the same way that classical Judaism has done, in order to develop a 'sound, biblical *halacha* after the pattern of Yeshua and his followers'.[138]

So Fischer has cleared the groundwork for the development of Messianic *halacha* by reassessing the relationship between Yeshua and Pharisaic Judaism as one of complementarity rather than antithesis. Jesus operated within the realm of nascent *halacha*, although he was critical of it at times. Now, Messianic Jews can learn from rabbinic *halacha* how to understand better Jesus and his ministry, and how the Torah can be applied in everyday life. The depth and beauty of the rabbinic tradition is there for Messianic Jews to explore and appropriate for themselves, providing they stay focused on Yeshua and under the authority of scripture. Fischer clarifies his presuppositions when approaching *halacha*:

> Above all, the traditions are not authoritative for Messianic Jews – only the Bible has that role. Anything that contradicts Scripture does not belong in Messianic Judaism. However, the traditions are usually beneficial and elevating. Messianic Judaism can learn and appreciate much through them. Not that the traditions have no shortcomings, but they possess a great deal of richness, beauty and depth.[139]

Whilst Fischer reclaims *halacha* for the Messianic Jew, and gives positive affirmation to the place of Oral Torah in the formulation of Jewish and Messianic Jewish identity, his procedure for deciding on the relevance of *halacha* is based on the authority of scripture and the centrality of Yeshua. Fischer brings a more 'Jewish-friendly' approach to the scriptures and a greater awareness of the Jewishness of Yeshua within his own context, and uses these as hermeneutical tools for the examination of rabbinic *halacha* and its adoption by Messianic Jews. However he has yet to propose a way forward for the construction of Messianic *halacha*, and to state more fully how the 'authority of the rabbis' should be correctly understood once the negative presuppositions of anti-Judaism have been removed.

---

[137] Fischer, 'Would Yeshua Support Halacha?' 79, cf. 'The Place of Rabbinic Tradition,' 170 (footnote 58).

[138] Ibid., 80.

[139] John Fischer, 'The Place of Rabbinic Tradition,' 156.

Messianic Halacha not easy to define (Sadan)

For Tsvi Sadan[140] the question of the Torah is a 'fish-bone stuck in the throat of many who have been brought up in the tradition that G-d's "grace" has superseded the commandments and made the Torah obsolete'.[141] To release Jewish and Gentile believers in Jesus from the 'unclean heritage' which repudiates the whole of the Torah, Sadan gives 'Torah' the broadest sense of 'teaching'. The Church inconsistently and selectively appropriates aspects of Torah, using the Augustinian categories of moral, ritual and civil law which fail to do justice to its holistic nature and are based on the negative assumption that the Law is merely a preparation for grace.[142] Paul's statement in Galatians that the Law is a schoolmaster (*paidagogos*) to bring us to the Messiah is re-interpreted to allow for a transformation of the relationship between the believer and the Torah in the light of their coming to Christ rather than a termination of it.[143] Paul 'could not, and did not, teach the Jews to stop observing the Law of Moses'.[144]

---

[140] Tsvi Sadan, e-mail message to author, November 24, 2003. 'Dealing with the issue of *halacha*, as I am sure you are aware, is very, very problematic for it assumes a positive approach to both Torah and Jewish tradition. It also stands in sharp opposition to the traditional attitude of both the Catholic and Protestant churches toward anything Jewish. Add to it the fact that most Messianic Jews are heavily influenced by the negative attitude of evangelicalism to tradition as such and you begin to realize that those Messianic Jews who advocate for *halacha* are pressed tight against the corner where anti-Judaism and anti-tradition attitudes meet. On top of it all, given that the halachic process is one of the most demanding skills that exists in Judaism and the lack of knowledge of most Messianic Jews of the material leads to a very hesitant steps toward it, and rightly so (I doubt if there are even a handful of Messianic Jews who can read a Gemara page, let alone arriving to proper halachic decision). You also may think of another aspect why Messianic Jews are hesitant. Once you say that you are for *halacha*, you must begin to build the proper institutions for it. In other words, you must begin to build a community where halachic decisions are considered obligatory. It means that you must have people with authority, call it a *Beit Din*, the council of the wise, or whatever. However, in an environment polluted by Protestantism where "you do whatever you want and I do whatever I want" rules supreme, in such an environment, *halacha* cannot exist. This explains somewhat why you will find very little written material on the issue.'

[141] Tsvi Sadan, 'The Torah: what do we do with it?' *Teaching from Zion* 5 no. 2, ed. Joseph Shulam (Jerusalem: Netivyah Bible Instruction Ministry, May-June 1994), 17–44.

[142] Ibid., 24.

[143] Ibid., 27.

[144] Ibid., 29.

Sadan applies this new understanding of Torah to the life of believers. For Gentiles who believe in Yeshua, only the specific commandments mandated by the Apostles in the book of Acts are obligatory and they should not attempt to obey the whole of the Mosaic law. But Jewish believers in Jesus should follow the example of Paul, the Apostles and the rest of the early Messianic community, and live their lives in obedience to the Torah of Moses.[145]

Sadan states firmly that he is not suggesting the Torah 'possesses the power to save'. Obedience to the Torah does not compromise the redemption we have through Yeshua's death and resurrection. But it is not clear how this is to be outworked in the life of the Jewish believer. Nor does Sadan specify what part or authority oral tradition should play in formulating such lifestyle. Yet for Sadan the reasons for such a position are compelling. Rather than appeal to arguments about cultural sensitivity or missiological expedience, the arguments for Torah observance are clearly based on 'good *scriptural* grounds' – even if this position is at times inconsistently applied by some Messianic Jews who 'claim to be "law-keepers" on the one hand, while eating ham sandwiches on the other'.[146] Scripture, not history, must be our guide, as we commit ourselves to 'vigorous study of the Word, accompanied by the attempt to live out our convictions'.[147]

'Yes!' and 'No!' to Messianic *Halacha* (Shulam)

Joseph Shulam looks for the development of Messianic *halacha* but recognises the difficulties this causes in the Messianic movement.[148] A 'serious approach to doing *halacha*' must avoid the Roman Catholic elevation of Canon Law above scripture. Messianic Jews should instead follow the rabbis who, whilst occasionally taking 'their authority a little too far', generally gave 'strict adherence to the text of the Torah according to the exegetical rules of interpretation'. The 'battles' between the rabbis on the interpretation of every detail of scripture's meaning and application 'kept the making of *halacha* a very serious and laborious task and away from a dictatorial, ex-cathedra attitude that prevailed in the Church.'[149]

Several further difficulties face the construction of Messianic *halacha*. Messianic Jews at this stage of their history have neither the 'heritage nor the equipment' to do *halacha*. They are divided on the lines of the traditional Christian denominations, and would become still more divided if *halacha* was constructed prematurely. Messianic Jews do not command approval in

---

[145] Ibid., 30.
[146] Ibid.
[147] Ibid., 31.
[148] Joseph Shulam, 'The Halachic Process' in *Kesher* 5 (Summer 1997), 23–34.
[149] Ibid., 25.

the eyes of the Jewish, Christian or even other Messianics for their integrity or knowledge of Torah and Judaism, and would not be able to win acceptance for their halachic decisions because of this lack of credibility. The context in which *halacha* is to be developed is one where 'we have needs that are too hot and the situation is an infected tooth. One does not make *halacha* in the heat of an infection. We have to make *halacha* when we are as detached from internal politics and power plays as possible.'[150] Furthermore, many in the MJM do not appreciate Jewish tradition and 'do not care for Judaism nor for what is already clearly *halacha* written in the Scripture. Why should they care about what some leaders have decided to bind upon them?'[151]

The construction of a distinctively Messianic Jewish *halacha* may 'take us out of the fellowship of the people of Israel' by making a particular set of rules and regulations that are either in conflict or opposition to the Jewish tradition, widening the division between Messianic Jews and the Jewish community. Finally, Shulam recognises that the majority of those attending Messianic fellowships in the USA 'may be non-Jewish' and asks rhetorically, 'What kind of *halacha* will you make that will be bound upon these people?'[152]

The argument for continuing adherence to rabbinical authority is based on Jesus' challenge in Matt. 23:1–4 to 'do whatever they tell you to observe'.[153] Therefore: 'We must discover a *modus vivendi* that will allow us to respect and accept the traditional interpretation of Orthodox Judaism, and at the same time add to it elements of life, the guidance of the Holy Spirit, and a good measure of God's love and grace in the spirit of Yeshua's teaching. I suppose that is our greatest challenge as a Jewish Messianic Movement.'[154]

But Shulam is still ambivalent. 'Should the Messianic movement do *halacha* now? To answer the above question I must say both, "Yes!" and "No!" Perhaps it is the right time to consider doing Messianic Jewish *halacha*. Or, as a movement that is still in a transitional stage, perhaps it is the right time to prepare for doing Messianic Jewish *halacha* some time in the future.'[155]

To begin, perhaps it would be possible to 'just accept the traditional *halacha* on every subject that does not directly pertain on the person and character of Yeshua the Messiah?'[156] Or should we 'just forget about doing *halacha*' and settle for the Protestant model, 'succumbing to the weight of American Christian culture'? It is clear that Shulam, who leads the most

---

[150] Ibid., 26.
[151] Ibid.
[152] Ibid., 27.
[153] Ibid., 27–30.
[154] Ibid., 30.
[155] Ibid., 30–31.
[156] Ibid., 31.

Orthodox-style Messianic group in Israel, is reluctant to dip his toe in the sea of halachic deliberation.

Despite this ambivalence, Shulam gives five 'suggestions and rules' for doing Messianic Jewish *halacha*. First, all the halachic rulings and apostolic examples found in the New Testament should be observed, as the basis on which to build further rulings. Shulam cites 1 Tim. 2:9–12, calling for women to dress modestly and keep silence rather than have authority to teach, a ruling that he observes is not kept in the USA Messianic movement.[157] This requires an honest assessment of ourselves, and a serious commitment to follow Yeshua's own instructions to the disciples to study and understand the teaching of the Pharisees. Secondly, we must take time to explain our position to the rest of the Body of the Messiah who are 'still stranded on the unbalanced shores [sic] of Luther's understanding of God's grace'.[158] Thirdly, we must commit ourselves to unity and fellowship, as 'in doing *halacha* all the possible disagreements and personality clashes that can arise do arise'.[159] A fourth principle is to commit ourselves to the teaching of scripture rather than 'words of prophecy' or feelings and experiences. Finally we must allow sufficient time to develop

> the kind of respect and prestige that is necessary for the community to abide by the rulings of a committee. If we are going to have a Messianic Jewish *halacha* in the future, which I hope we will have, it will take much time, some people who will work hard to gain the respect and the authority of God, and of the movement. It will take scholarship, and scholarship takes time to build and develop.[160]

Shulam concludes on a positive note: 'I have been negative enough in this article! It is time now to take the positive attitude. It is my firm conviction that with much good will from the part of the movement, and a broad enough base of people who are willing to think independently, Biblical and Jewish *halacha* can be built up for the future generations of Messianic Jews.'[161]

Shulam's advocacy represents a positive but cautious approach, pointing out the need for Messianic *halacha* but showing the embryonic stage of the MJM in its development.

---

[157] Ibid., 32.

[158] Ibid., 32.

[159] Ibid., 33.

[160] Ibid.

[161] Ibid., 33–34.

Halacha – Messianic and Conservative (Kinzer)

For Mark Kinzer, the leading voice in the *Hashivenu* group and the author of *Postmissionary Messianic Judaism,* 'there are two basic questions: (1) Is the Torah foundational for Messianic Jewish life? (2) If so, what is the role of Rabbinic tradition in determining how the Torah is to be lived out?'[162] The streams within the MJM give different answers to both questions. The Israeli Messianic movement and what he calls the 'missionary movement' in the Diaspora would generally not see the Torah as necessary whereas the congregational movement in the Diaspora would see it as normative.

> Someone like Gershon Nerel or David Chernoff or Daniel Gruber would proba-
> bly answer 'yes' to question number one (in contrast to Baruch Maoz or Arnold
> Fruchtenbaum or Moishe Rosen), but would not see Rabbinic tradition as having
> any significant role in Messianic Jewish life. For those who are more open to the
> relevance of Rabbinic tradition, some are respectful but cautious (e.g., Dan
> Juster), others assert the necessity of serious engagement with the tradition but
> emphasize even more strongly the need for a distinctive Messianic halachic
> approach (e.g., David Stern), whereas others think that our approach to *halacha*
> should in most cases resemble that found in the wider Jewish community (either
> modern orthodox or conservative, or sometimes reform). In this latter category,
> I would put the Hashivenu/New England Halachic Council.[163]

Kinzer also asks whether the biblical text is sufficient for understanding and applying the Torah, and what role post-biblical Jewish tradition has in the process of interpretation and application. For those who think that post-biblical Jewish tradition must be factored into Messianic Jewish understanding and practice of the Torah, what level of authority does that tradition have, and which contemporary expressions of Jewish life (e.g., in American terms – Orthodox, Conservative, Reform, etc.) can best exemplify the principles determining conformity and freedom in dealing with the tradition? Kinzer realises that

> how one answers these questions is as important as the actual answers given.
> What does the Torah say about itself? What role has it played in Jewish history,
> and what importance does this have for us? How is the Torah related to Jewish
> peoplehood (i.e., Israel's life as a *goy kadosh* [holy people])? And most crucially for
> us: how do we interpret Yeshua's teaching and action in regard to the Torah, and
> the teaching and action of his emissaries?[164]

---

[162] Mark Kinzer, email message to author, May 10, 2004.

[163] Ibid.

[164] Mark S. Kinzer, 'Messianic Judaism and Jewish Tradition in the 21st Century: A Biblical Defense of "Oral Torah"' (paper presented at the 2003 Hashivenu Forum, Pasadena, January 2003), 1.

Messianic Jewish teachers in the past who upheld the importance and even the authority of rabbinic tradition tended to apply 'Biblical fundamentalist' principles to their reading of the rabbis, treating rabbinic materials uncritically and unhistorically, and looking to Orthodoxy and ultra-Orthodoxy as their models. Kinzer himself belongs to the newer generation who are developing their approach to *halacha* using Conservative and Reform perspectives. This approach has led to the formation of the New England Halachic Council (NEHC), a group of Messianic Jewish leaders who 'for the first time' are developing a common approach to Messianic Jewish *halacha*.[165]

Kinzer addresses concerns Messianic Jews have about the Oral Torah.[166] The unique authority of the written Torah neither requires nor permits any supplement. Some argue that the rabbinic doctrine of the Oral Torah was invented 'not just to supplement the Written Torah but to supplant it'.[167] Others note the attitude of the New Testament in its treatment of the Pharisees and Yeshua's apparent reservations towards the Pharisaic 'Traditions of the Elders' – which is read as a direct rejection of any notion of the Oral Torah. They see Yeshua's bestowal of halachic authority on the apostles as a precluding of Pharisaic or rabbinic claims to such authority. A final suspicion regarding the Oral Torah is based on the fact that the Pharisees and later rabbis rejected the claims made for Yeshua, and persecuted his Jewish followers. Kinzer raises and deals with these concerns so that the Oral Torah will 'no longer be off limits for us as Messianic Jews'.[168]

Kinzer then provides evidence within the *Tanakh* for a developing oral tradition of interpretation of the Pentateuch which provided an interpretive framework to the original Mosaic legislation. This leads him to conclude:

(1) Because of its lack of legal detail and its abundance of apparent legal inconsistency, the Torah requires supplemental legal instruction; (2) the Torah itself recognizes this fact, and envisions a Mosaic teaching office whose role is to interpret and apply the Torah's regulations to new circumstances; and (3) this Mosaic teaching office, while having its ultimate authority from God, receives its immediate sanction from the affirmation of the Jewish people as a whole. While the Torah itself nowhere uses the term, there is no reason why the tradition of supplemental instruction in the Mosaic succession should not be called 'Oral Torah'. It is thereby both distinguished from the Written Torah, and identified with it – just as the high court of Deuteronomy 17 and the seventy elders of Numbers 11 are both distinguished from Moses and identified with him.[169]

---

[165] See below on the NEHC, renamed as the MJRC.
[166] Kinzer, 'Messianic Judaism and Jewish Tradition,' 1.
[167] Ibid., 2.
[168] Ibid.
[169] Ibid., 12.

Kinzer rejects the 'naive version' of the giving of the two Torahs to Moses on Sinai, which has little grounding in the tradition itself. He prefers a less rigid and Orthodox understanding, although this is a minority and more recent view.[170] Following David Weiss Halivni and David Novak,[171] Kinzer argues for a more reflective understanding of the relationship between the oral and written Torah. He uses Conservative and Reform perspectives which allow a flexible reinterpretation of the Oral Torah that will be acceptable to Messianic Jews.[172]

Recent New Testament interpretation sees Matthew's teaching on the Pharisees positively, and Jewish believers today can similarly defer to rabbinic *halacha*. 'Just as Matthew develops a first-century form of Messianic faith that builds upon the distinctive traditions of the Pharisaic movement, and even (though perhaps grudgingly) acknowledges their ongoing role as halachic authorities, so we can develop a 21st century form of Messianic faith that builds upon the distinctive traditions of the Rabbinic movement that emerged out of Pharisaism, and acknowledge its ongoing role in halachic development.'[173]

Yeshua's relationship to the Pharisees, as seen by Kinzer, steers between the two extremes of outright rejection and uncritical acceptance, and is fraught with implications for the development of Messianic *halacha*.

> The Apostolic Writings present Yeshua as standing in an ambivalent relation to the Pharisaic predecessors of the Rabbinic tradition. On the one hand, he offers prophetic criticism of Pharisaic practice, finding fault with what he saw as their privileging of ritual minutiae over relational obligation, and their preoccupation with their tradition at the expense of the Biblical witness. Close reading of the relevant texts shows this criticism to be a correction of emphasis rather than a rejection of basic convictions. But it nonetheless demonstrates a tension between Yeshua and his followers and the Pharisaic movement. On the other hand, Matthew and Luke-Acts present a picture of Yeshua and his followers that implicitly and at times explicitly expresses their affinity for the Pharisees.[174]

The challenge for the Messianic movement in the 21st century is to 'go beyond mere Biblical analysis and examine the historical developments of the past two millennia'. Then it will be possible to 'acknowledge the authority of a tradition that has emphatically denied the Messiahship of Yeshua'

---

[170] Ibid.

[171] Cf. David Weiss Halivni, *Revelation Restored* (Boulder: Westview, 1997); David Novak, *The Election of Israel* (Cambridge: Cambridge University Press, 1995).

[172] Cf. John D. Rayner, *Jewish Religious Law: A Progressive Perspective* (New York: Berghahn Books, 1998).

[173] Mark Kinzer, 'Messianic Judaism and Jewish Tradition,' 30.

[174] Ibid., 31.

and see it as the tradition that embodies 'Oral Torah', and carries on the work of Moses from one generation to the next.[175] A Messianic Jewish version of the Oral Torah must therefore recognise 'two legitimate halachic authorities in tension' – those recognised by the Jewish community as a whole, and those presiding over its Messianic sub-community.

The 'halachic authority' of the Messianic community will be prophetic in character, reflecting Yeshua's own authority which came not from institutional office but from his Messianic empowerment. If the requirements that follow from faith in Yeshua 'conflict with the norms of Rabbinic tradition and the institutions of the wider Jewish community', then a way must be found 'to be true to Yeshua while maintaining respect for the community and its tradition'. Kinzer acknowledges that this is an 'excruciatingly difficult task', but sees this as following the example and challenge of Yeshua himself.[176]

Kinzer argues for a conclusion that would be merely 'the starting point for other forms of Judaism', recognising that 'one could develop an Orthodox, Conservative, Reform, or Reconstructionist Messianic approach to Jewish tradition' if this starting point is allowed. Despite the little work that has been done in the movement to take the development of *halacha* further, Kinzer looks forward to further discussion. 'We cannot expect to engage in such a discussion fruitfully if we do not begin where all other modern Judaisms begin – with explicit acknowledgement of the validity of Rabbinic tradition, the Oral Torah, as providing the necessary context for all practical interpretation and application of the Written Torah to contemporary Jewish life.'[177]

This philosophy of *halacha*, influenced by Conservative Judaism, is more aware of the social context in which Jewish identity is grounded and formed and is less theologically dogmatic. It maintains sympathy and sensitivity to the Jewish tradition in which the *halacha* has developed. New philosophical insights, and more complex legitimation and rationalisation are employed, to situate the neo-orthodox Messianic Jew in the variegated world of Judaisms and Christianities. Kinzer approaches the need for Messianic *halacha* as one influenced by the Conservative movement's understanding of oral tradition. He also brings Christian reflection into performance of the *mitzvot*. Kinzer's approach to *halacha* is both profound and programmatic, involving a re-evaluation of Jewish sources and a new reading of the New Testament materials, suitably engaged in the fabric of Christian post-liberalism and postmodern Jewish identity. Whether his post-formative Messianic Jewish approach to Torah will carry conviction and win assent within the broader Messianic movement remains to be seen.

---

[175] Ibid., 32.

[176] Ibid., 34.

[177] Ibid.

A Reflection of Yeshua's Heart (Hashivenu)

The Hashivenu group of Messianic leaders, a post-formative network within the UMJC, adopts a positive approach to Torah. [178] Hashivenu's core values state:

> 1. Messianic Judaism is a Judaism, and not a cosmetically altered 'Jewish-style' version of what is extant in the wider Christian community.
> 2. God's particular relationship with Israel is expressed in the Torah, God's unique covenant with the Jewish people.
> 3. Yeshua is the fullness of Torah.
> 4. The Jewish people are 'us' not 'them'.
> 5. The richness of the Rabbinic tradition is a valuable part of our heritage as Jewish people. [179]

Messianic Jews should live a Torah-observant life, as God's particular relationship and unique covenant with Israel is expressed through Torah.

> We in Hashivenu believe that the specific observances of the Torah serve as signs of the distinctive character and calling of the Jewish people: 'You must keep my Sabbaths, for this is a sign between me and you throughout the ages, that you may know that I, *HaShem*, have consecrated you' (Ex. 31:13). It is emphasized time and again throughout Jewish tradition that the Torah is G-d's special gift to the people of Israel: 'Blessed are You … who chose us from all nations and gave us Your Torah'. [180]

The keeping of Torah is that which distinguishes Jews and Messianic Jews from Gentiles and Gentile Christians:

> We in Hashivenu believe that this truth requires emphasis within the Messianic Jewish movement. Though Messianic Jews never cease to attack 'replacement theology' (usually known outside our movement as 'supersessionalism' [*sic*]), we are in danger of falling prey to a more subtle form of the same error. If, in all its ordinances, the Torah addresses Gentiles as much as it does Jews, if it defines the

---

[178] Hashivenu, 'Who is Hashivanu?' http://www.hashivenu.org/who_is.htm (accessed June 1, 2003). 'Hashivenu – Towards a Mature Messianic Judaism,' lists Stuart Dauermann as President, with Mark Kinzer, Rich Nichol, Paul Saal, Michael Schiffman, Ellen Quarry and Robert and Susan Chenoweth as committee members.

[179] Hashivenu, 'Towards a Mature Messianic Judaism,' http://www.hashivenu.org/core_values.htm#top (accessed June 1, 2003).

[180] Ibid.

life of the Church as much as it defines the life of the Jewish people, then what remains of Israel's unique character and calling?

In the past Jews who entered the church were compelled to surrender Jewish observance and identity and, as a result, they were assimilated and they and their children lost any sense of being Jews. If, contrary to the Apostolic decree and the Pauline injunction, Gentiles in the church are now encouraged to live just like Messianic Jews, will not the same result occur? And what of the Jews who do not believe in Yeshua? What need is there for them? G-d now has a people who are truly keeping his Torah – the Church! We are left with a Messianic Jewish movement without any Jews, a movement that loves Jewish things but not Jewish people.[181]

This somewhat tortuous logic expresses the concern that the Messianic movement, at least in the USA, is composed of a majority of non-Jewish members, who see no problem in adopting a form of Torah observance.[182] Seeing Yeshua as 'the fullness of Torah', Hashivenu reclaims Torah from the false antithesis of the 'Christian worldview' that has accepted the 'distorted view' that 'Torah is bad, the Gospel is good'. Rather, Yeshua is the source of Torah, who himself 'gave the Torah' to Israel.

The real problem with the Torah is not the Torah but the human misunderstanding of Scripture. The Torah was given by G-d at Mt. Sinai. Yeshua was more than a latter born Moshe. He is the Word who was in the Beginning, through whom the world was created. He is the G-d of Israel, the G-d who gave the Torah to the sons of Israel through the hand of Moshe. The commandments of the Torah are Yeshua's commandments, not an arbitrary set of rules or rituals. They are a revelation of the heart of G-d; they are a reflection of Yeshua's heart.[183]

Those who wish to be like Yeshua must therefore follow his Torah, recognising the Torah as the sufficient revelation of God's will.

The Torah is not a lesser revelation of Yeshua, like an uncompleted puzzle. Simply attaching an addendum to a prayer or commandment does not make it any more complete than it was prior to the addendum. The mitzvah is already complete in that it reflects the heart of Yeshua. When a mitzvah is completed as it

---

[181] Ibid.

[182] It is beyond the purpose of this book to quantify the proportion of Jewish and non-Jewish members of the Messianic movement, nor to include those 'Torah Observant' Messianic Gentiles who have their own similar groupings, but they represent a growing number, challenging the nature and character of the Messianic movement. For the purposes of this study Messianic Jewish leaders have been quoted, unless indicated otherwise.

[183] Ibid.

was intended when given, it reflects the heart of G-d. Our goal should not be to amend every prayer, commandment, and ritual with Messianic nomenclature. Rather, our goal should be to follow Torah, having faith and a desire to connect with G-d through the act of following. Surely, this was the life Yeshua lived and the life He desires His people to live. Every act of observance is an opportunity to connect with Him. He is the fullness of Torah. Our lives should be so full.[184]

The statement stops short of explaining how to keep Torah in the light of the New Testament and Rabbinic tradition, stating merely the principle that keeping the Torah is sufficient in itself. Further clarification is necessary, and several examples of this approach follow.

Messianic Jewish Rabbinical Council

Mark Kinzer's argument for the construction of *halacha* has been taken up by the Messianic Jewish Rabbinical Council of New England of which he is a member, a federation of Messianic Jewish Synagogues in the North East of the United States.[185] The MJRC has produced significant rulings on halachic matters.[186] Whilst such rulings have no authority beyond those congregations which participate in the MJRC, they signal an increasing tendency for Messianic Judaism to develop a 'Torah-observant' Messianic Judaism. The MJRC emphasises the primacy of scripture.

> In Jewish tradition as a whole, Scripture is of paramount importance and author-ity in the development of *Halacha*. In principle, issues become 'Halachic' because they are connected to some area of life in which Scripture reveals certain authori-tative norms. In addressing those issues, Scripture is not the only resource consulted. However, it is always the source of greatest sanctity. Thus, when Rabbinic literature distinguishes between laws that are *d'oraita* (ordained by Scripture) and those that are *d'rabbanan* (established by Rabbinic authority), precedence is always given to those that are *d'oraita*.[187]

There are degrees of a 'sanctity' within Scripture itself, with the Pentateuch having the greatest authority. Then the New Testament, the teaching of Jesus, and the practice of the first Messianic Jews, provide 'crucial halachic guidance'.

---

[184] Hashivenu, 'Towards a Mature Messianic Judaism,' http://www.hashivenu.org/core_values.htm#value2 (accessed June 1, 2003).

[185] Previously known as the New England Halachic Council (NEHC).

[186] See chapter 7 for Kashrut and Sabbath.

[187] Rich Nichol, ed., *Collected Halachic Decisions of the Messianic Jewish Rabbinical Council* (Boston: MJRC, May 2006), 1; 'Section 1.0 – Authoritative Sources in Halachic Decision Making'.

In addition to Tanakh, we as Messianic Jews have another authoritative source for the making of Halachic decisions: the Apostolic Writings. Yeshua himself did not act primarily as a Posek issuing Halachic rulings, but rather as a prophetic teacher who illumined the purpose of the Torah and the inner orientation we should have in fulfilling it. Nevertheless, his teaching about the Torah has a direct bearing on how we address particular Halachic questions. As followers of Messiah Yeshua, we look to him as the greatest Rabbi of all, and his example and his instruction are definitive for us in matters of *Halacha* as in every other sphere.

In addition, the Book of Acts and the Apostolic Letters provide crucial halachic guidance for us in our lives as Messianic Jews. They are especially important in showing us how the early Jewish believers in Yeshua combined a concern for Israel's distinctive calling according to the Torah with a recognition of the new relationship with God and Israel available to Gentiles in the Messiah. They also provide guidelines relevant to other areas of Messianic Jewish *Halacha*, including (but not restricted to) areas such as distinctive Messianic rites, household relationships, and dealing with secular authorities.[188]

In addition to scripture, Jewish tradition plays an important role.

In principle, Scripture always has highest authority in the Halachic process. However, in practice other sources play as significant or a more significant role. While all *Halacha* is rooted in Scripture, the text usually provides limited information on how the *mitzvot* are to be lived out and how they are to be adapted to new circumstances. In order to add concrete substance to Halachic decision making, we must have recourse to the way the *mitzvot* have been understood and observed by Jews throughout history and in the present.[189]

Traditional Jewish leadership in the form of the rabbinate is a God-given means for outworking the corporate life of the people of Israel in accordance with scripture. Yeshua himself recognised this role and authority of the rabbis.

This principle finds support in Yeshua's teaching in Matthew 23:3 which urges obedience to the decisions of the Pharisaic Torah-teachers. This verse echoes Deuteronomy 17:10, the key text in Rabbinic tradition undergirding the authority of Israel's sages. Thus, while we may critique traditional rulings, and argue for alternative positions, we should be reluctant to depart from Halachic rulings accepted by Jews throughout the centuries and held today by most of the branches of Judaism and most committed Jews.[190]

---

[188] Ibid.

[189] Ibid., 2.

[190] Ibid.

However, Yeshua also instituted a new body with a new authority to derive *halacha*.

> At the same time, Yeshua did found a new sub-community of Jews (i.e., the *ekklesia* of the Circumcision) whose life is marked by an anticipatory experience of the powers of *Olam HaBa* [The age to come], and who are to have a special relationship with a body of Gentile worshipers of the G-d of Israel (i.e., the *ekklesia* of the Uncircumcision). As such, he imparted to this sub-community and its leaders Halachic decision making authority for its common life (Matthew 18:18). Thus, when the Apostolic Writings and the Good News warrant it, we may need to strike out in new directions.[191]

The aims of Messianic *halacha* must be to welcome and include those of uncertain halachic status and without a traditional Jewish upbringing.

> As followers of a Messiah whose mission took him more to the sick than to the healthy, and who, while welcoming the righteous and the pious, eagerly pursued the *am ha'aretz*, we recognize that our Halachic orientation must be toward inclusion of those Jews who have been alienated from their own heritage. Eager to heal the wounds of Israel, we also seek to lead those of ambiguous Jewish status back to the way of their ancestors. While we are committed to not diluting the demands of the Torah, we want to bring many near to Torah who are now far from it.[192]

A Messianic halachic process will therefore be reflective and open to the needs of contemporary realities.

> Therefore, like Conservative, Reform, and Reconstructionist branches of Judaism, we recognize that the new circumstances of the modern world require adaptation in traditional practices. Our Halachic decision making will require thoughtful reflection on these new circumstances, and the changes they may require. In this process, we should pay special attention to the Halachic analysis and rulings of these branches of Judaism, and learn from them.
>
> Responsible engagement in the Halachic process places enormous demands on Jewish leaders. We will need to devote ourselves to serious study, prayer, discussion, and corporate decision-making. At the same time, we believe that the Resurrected Messiah dwells among us and within us, and we rely upon his ongoing guidance as we seek to carry on his work of raising up the fallen booth of David within the people of Israel.

The MJRC then gives some 15 pages of rulings which include Sabbath, Festivals, Kashrut, Niddah, Prayer and Blessings. The rulings follow

---

[191] Ibid.

[192] Ibid.

Conservative Jewish practice, and have yet to be adopted by a wider group in the UMJC or elsewhere. The halachic process is in its early stages, and the wider movement will respond as the rulings are publicised more generally. Mark Kinzer admits, 'the lack of material available represents the little work that has been done'.[193] No Messianic scholar has yet published a collection of *Responsa*, yet alone a full-orbed commentary on the Mishnah, or the Taryag Mitzvot. Whilst Messianic Jews discuss the guidelines and preliminaries for such an endeavour, and some have adopted the practice of living in varying degrees according to *halacha* as interpreted by different strands within Judaism, the practice of Torah by Messianic Jews has yet to be realised and articulated to any great degree.

Rabbinic *Halacha* for Messianic Jews

Elazar (Larry) Brandt is the most outspoken advocate in the Messianic movement for a return to Orthodox *halacha*. Brandt's main complaint about the Messianic movement, in which he has been involved since the 1970s, is that the movement has 'never really got out of the gate when it comes to embracing our Jewish heritage and responsibilities.'

> As I like to put it, in over 30 years, we keep repeating the first generation, and never advance to the next and beyond. We are still arguing about the same things, making the same mistakes, refusing to get educated, avoiding participation in the Jewish community, and shunning rabbinic 'authority' (for lack of a better term). In the last analysis, our movement is a product of its time. Our leaders were rebels and outcasts, and they just refuse to allow anyone in the 'establishment' to tell them what to do. We have people calling themselves 'rabbi' who don't know how to light a Shabbat candle, who have no training beyond dropping out of their bar mitzvah classes, and who have never read a page of Talmud or Rashi or Rambam, who for the most part cannot read the Torah in Hebrew. How can we even begin to think about messianic *Halacha* under these conditions?[194]

For Brandt it would be a mistake to construct an alternative 'messianic *Halacha*' as an alternative to rabbinic *halacha*, and would be a new form of 'replacement theology'. He would rather see Messianic Jews becoming Orthodox or Conservative rabbis themselves, learning how to apply Torah in the everyday lives of their congregations, possibly becoming qualified to be judges on a *Bet Din*, and constructing Messianic *halacha* within the Jewish establishment, rather than as an alternative to it. This is the only possible future for Messianic Jews. The alternative option, a distinct Messianic

---

[193] Mark Kinzer, e-mail message to author, November 26, 2003.
[194] Elazar Brandt, e-mail message to author, November 19, 2003.

Jewish identity with its own Messianic *halacha*, will 'lead us down a separatist path and into obscurity'.

Messianic Jews should retain their connection with, and observance of, traditional Orthodox rabbinic *halacha*, as this has preserved the Jewish people. 'What has kept our people together against all odds from generation to generation through history's worst storms and onslaughts has been our tenacious clinging to that sacred trust committed to our ancestors – our Torah, our *Halacha*, our Laws and customs, our Tradition.'[195]

Torah observant Judaism is the only form of Judaism that has survived, and Messianic Jews should hold fast to it.

> There is only one type of Judaism that has consistently stood the test of time, and that is the type that is fully Torah compliant and Tradition compliant ... I do not call this type of Judaism 'Orthodox' because that puts a modern polemical spin onto an ancient way of life. There is a Judaism that traces its roots back through the Rabbis, through Ezra, through the prophets, and Kings, and all the way back to Moses and the Patriarchs. There is a Judaism that transcends sectarian boundaries, that is recognized and recognizable in all times and places as the normative way of life for Torah and Tradition compliant Jews.[196]

Unless Messianic Jews observe the Torah as interpreted by Orthodox Judaism, they will suffer the penalty of assimilation and being 'cut off' from their people.

> Departure from this norm – whether because of brazen sinful rebellion, or the desire to conform to the surrounding culture, or because of intermarriage, or lack of interest, or because one finds his 'messiah' in one place or another – always yields the same result. The intention of one's heart doesn't much matter. Departure from the norm begins a process that works swiftly and efficiently to guarantee that one to three generations hence, your children or grandchildren will not know or not care that they are Jewish, will not identify themselves as Jews, will not affiliate with the Jewish community in any of its forms, and ultimately will not be recognizable as Jews. I believe this is the very penalty the Torah speaks of in the language of the 'soul being cut off from its people'.[197]

In Brandt's understanding, his belief in Yeshua should not have prevented him from observing Torah. But when he became part of Church life, he felt under pressure to abandon Jewish practice.

---

[195] Elazar Brandt, 'Response to "The Value of Tradition" by Daniel C. Juster' (paper given at Hashivenu Forum, *Messianic Judaism and Jewish Tradition in the 21st Century*, Pasadena, California, February 2003).

[196] Ibid., 2.

[197] Ibid., 3.

But of course it didn't take long before I began to be told, much to my surprise and disappointment, 'Larry, we're not under the law anymore. Jesus delivered us from all that. We don't need it. We're saved by grace' ... By my second year walking with Yeshua I had allowed the church to convince me that it was no longer necessary to engage in Jewish practices except for their educational value as illustrations of Biblical culture and practices.[198]

For Brandt the 'test case' was failing to fast on *Yom Kippur*, and being noticed by friends from his synagogue as he 'slinked down the street to the Taco Bell and had lunch'. 'Somehow in my naïveté I understood that I could not continue to call myself a Jew and cease to live as one at the same time. That *Yom Kippur*, I repented. I repented of my rejection of Torah in the name of the Gospel. And I have tried from then onward to keep myself from repeating that mistake.'[199]

Brandt's views are controversial within the movement, and have met with strong negative response from those who oppose the practice of Torah and rabbinic traditions, and who do not wish to assign any authority to rabbinic tradition or 'non-messianic rabbis' of today. In various forums of Messianic Congregations and amongst their leaders he has been shouted down. 'As soon as I explained that I observe Shabbat and Kashrut according to orthodox *halacha* (to the best of my ability), I was unable to continue speaking because of the literal shouts of opposition rising from the audience. And I only spoke of what I do. I said nothing about anyone else doing it.'[200]

Whilst Brandt has much to say on the topic, he finds few that are willing to listen to him, and has become disillusioned with the broader movement. It remains to be seen whether his views will be published and become more widely circulated, or whether, as some fear, he will situate himself more within Orthodox Judaism at the expense of his visibility as a believer in Yeshua as the Messiah, and be less involved in the Messianic movement.

Conclusion – Abandon, Adapt, Adopt or Accept?

Messianic Jews believe that the Law has been fulfilled by Yeshua (Matt. 5:17) and that He is the 'goal of the Law' (Rom. 10:4). Just as there are different understandings of Torah in the Jewish community, so too among Messianic Jews. Some (Baruch Maoz and Arnold Fruchtenbaum) see the Law of Moses as obsolete. Yeshua has inaugurated the *new* covenant. The old has gone. The laws of sacrifice have been fulfilled in Christ. The civil laws were only

---

[198] Ibid.

[199] Ibid.

[200] Elazar Brandt, e-mail message to author, November 19, 2003.

relevant to ancient Israel. Only the universal moral law as exemplified in the Ten Commandments is still applicable. It is therefore misguided to observe aspects of the Mosaic Law that lead back to bondage in legalism. If Messianic Jews observe the Mosaic Law they are denying the grace of God and justification by faith alone. They rebuild the 'middle wall of partition' (Eph. 2:14), attempting to justify themselves by works of the Law.

A second view (Gershon Nerel) affirms the cultural and social practices of the Mosaic Law yet this is not for 'religious' reasons. Customs that make up Jewish identity have been incorporated into Jewish life by tradition over the centuries, such as the calendar, circumcision and the food laws. These are still normative for ethnic, cultural and national identity but have *no theological merit* and do not add to righteousness. Consequently they are not prescriptive on Jewish believers in Jesus, who are free to observe them if they choose.

A third approach (Daniel Juster, David Stern and several others) recognises the continuing validity of Jewish tradition as the interpretative context for understanding the biblical Torah of the *Tanakh* and New Covenant. Yeshua, in His teaching and example, and the practice of the early church, defined a new *halacha* for the new covenant community. This *halacha* is developed today following the first Messianic Jews' example in the book of Acts. They observed Jewish lifestyle and practices, adapted some, abandoned others and applied only a few to the nations. Messianic Jews who observe Torah in this way both acknowledge its value but challenge its interpretation by the main branches of Judaism. They propose a new interpretation of Torah based on the teaching and practice of Yeshua and the first disciples.

A fourth position (Mark Kinzer, Hashivenu and the MJRC) argues that Messianic Jews should observe the Torah according to Orthodox or Conservative tradition, with only a few exceptions. Torah observance is a necessary response of gratitude and obedience in the light of God's election of Israel, which has not been abrogated, diminished or substantially altered with the coming of Yeshua. Torah observance preserved the Jewish community through its rabbinic leaders over the centuries, and Messianic Jews should accept their normative authority and work within this. This will enable them to develop their primary identity within the Jewish community rather than the mainstream Church. They should see themselves as members of the community of Israel, even if others do not accept them.

This challenges Messianic Jews to identify fully with their cultural and religious heritage rather than deny, ignore or approach it in an adversarial manner. A few (such as Elazar Brandt) would extend this approach to a complete identification with non-Messianic Judaism in its observance of Torah. The Jewish tradition is itself the inspired, God-given vehicle for the preservation of the Jewish people, and should not be criticised except from within, by those who already adhere to it. The problem raised by this approach is the potential compromise on the significance of Yeshua, and his soteriological role. Whilst such an option may be attractive for those wishing to receive a validation of their identity from the Jewish community, it can lead to a diminishment of effective testimony. The self-understanding that may be gained from such an approach leads to isolation from other believers. Torah observance at the cost of the visible unity of the Body of Messiah made up of Israel and the Nations can only result in loss of fellowship and faith.

MJT has yet to reflect seriously on these options, which are still at an early stage of presentation and debate. The manifold values behind some form of 'Torah observance' will continue to challenge and inspire the movement. Living a godly life, following the example of Yeshua, having a culturally sensitive lifestyle and witness, demonstrating the freedom given to observe or not observe aspects of *halacha*, taking up the responsibilities of Israel, reacting against assimilation, are all motivations to be integrated in 'taking up the yoke of Torah'. What is needed for the future development of MJT is further reflection on the theological assumptions, hermeneutical methods and exegetical processes that Messianic Jews bring to the subject of Torah. Also needed is a systematic development and working out in detail what a Messianic *halacha* will look like. It is with that question in mind that the next chapter considers Torah in practice, focusing on the specific aspects of Sabbath, *Kashrut* and Passover.

Chapter 7

Torah in Practice

Introduction

> One who studies Torah in order to teach, is given the means to study and to teach; and one who studies in order to practice, is given the means to study and to teach, to observe and to practice.[1]

'Torah' has little significance without practical application. This chapter examines how the different understandings of Torah in theory find practical expression in Messianic Jewish life. Messianic Jews make significant theological statements through their lifestyle, liturgy and culture. Their outward, practical expression of Messianic Jewish identity gives coherence to their theology. The core affirmations of Messianic Judaism that Yeshua is the Messiah, and that it is appropriate for Jewish people to believe in and follow Him, are embedded in their practice. A rich and colourful diversity of practice has developed, reflecting the diversity of practice found within other branches of Judaism.[2]

Pauline Kollontai surveys the range of Jewish practice in the Messianic movement. Celebration of traditional Jewish lifestyle and life-cycle events plays a key role in the construction of Messianic Jewish identity.

> *Brit milah* (Covenant of circumcision) is observed within Messianic communities because it is commanded by God as symbolic of the covenant with the people of

---

[1] Pirkei Avot 4:6 in Nosson Scherman (ed.), *The Complete Artscroll Siddur,* 2nd ed. (Brooklyn: Mesorah Publications, 1986), 567.

[2] Daniel Juster, *Jewish Roots: A Foundation of Biblical Theology for Messianic Judaism* (Rockville: Davar, 1986), 191–226, 'Messianic Jewish Practice'. Juster treats Jewish identity; Sabbath; the festivals; fringes, *tephilin*, head-covering; biblical food and cleanliness laws; the importance of Messianic Jewish Congregations; life in a Messianic Congregation; and Rabbis, schooling and authority. Barney Kasdan's *God's Appointed Times* (Baltimore: Lederer, 1993) and *God's Appointed Customs* (Baltimore: Lederer, 1996) select the biblical and post-biblical Jewish festivals, and the lifecycle events of circumcision, redemption of the firstborn, *bar mitzvah* and *bat mitzvah*, marriage, death and mourning. *Mezuzah, kashrut, mikveh,* fringes, headcovering, and *tephilin* are discussed as part of Messianic Jewish lifestyle.

Israel. Circumcision of the flesh is placed alongside spiritual circumcision of the heart. *Bar mitzvah* is also observed, and weddings and funerals are mainly Jewish in form but have some "Christian" – that is, culturally Christian, rather than specifically religious – aspects.[3]

The Sabbath and Festivals are seen as 'a valid and important aspect of their belief and practice' yet Messianic Jews, like non-Orthodox Jews, 'avoid an overt legalistic approach to the Sabbath and festivals'.

The key difference is that traditional Jewish blessings are accompanied by other blessings that refer to Jesus, and passages are read from the Torah and the New Testament, which they call the Torah of the Messiah. Other aspects of Jewish life-style practised in the Messianic Jewish community include observance of *kashrut*, the wearing of the *kippah, tallit*, the laying of *tefillin*, and having a *mezuzah* and other Jewish artefacts such as a *menorah* and *seder* plate in the home. Maintaining some, if not all, aspects of Jewish lifestyle is considered to deepen and enrich a Messianic Jew's faith and Jewish identity. Generally, whilst all key aspects of Jewish lifestyle and life-cycle events are recognized by the Messianic Jewish community, there is variation in observance and practice that is determined by the individual.[4]

Previous studies such as Kollontai's have observed Messianic Jewish practice from a phenomenological perspective, or as examples of how such practice illustrates beliefs.[5] Yet none have assessed the *diversity of practice* within the movement as indicative of its *differing theological emphases*. The present chapter does not attempt a comprehensive survey of every aspect of Messianic Jewish practice. It focuses on the three key topics of Sabbath, *kashrut* and Passover. These three observances serve as significant and representative indicators of the diversity of practice and the accompanying variety of theological understandings of Torah, tradition and culture. The selection of these three practices in particular is based on the importance of Sabbath and *kashrut* as boundary markers within Judaism, and of Passover as *'the* major Messianic feast'[6] because of its distinctively Christological emphasis.[7]

---

[3] Pauline Kollontai, 'Messianic Jews and Jewish Identity,' *Journal of Modern Jewish Studies* 3 no. 2 (July 2004): 197. Kollontai is inaccurate in her interpretation here. Messianic Jews import Christian *theological* understandings into their practices, whilst generally eschewing 'culturally Christian, rather than specifically religious aspects'.

[4] Ibid.

[5] E.g. Feher, Harris-Shapiro, Cohn-Sherbok, op.cit.

[6] Gershon Nerel, 'Torah and *Halakhah* Among Modern Assemblies of Jewish Yeshua-Believers: An Israeli Response to Arnold Fruchtenbaum' in *How Jewish Is Christianity? 2 Views of the Messianic Movement,* ed. Louis Goldberg (Grand Rapids: Zondervan, 2003), 160.

[7] Male Circumcision is universally observed within the Messianic movement, and

The majority of those involved in Messianic Judaism would define themselves in some sense as 'Torah observant' or 'Torah positive'. The present chapter follows the spectrum of Messianic Jewish thought from the most 'Torah negative' to the most 'Torah positive'. How do differing understandings and Jewish tradition work themselves out in practice, and how do Messianic Jews formulate their own *halacha* and *minhag* to accompany these understandings?

The Diversity of Messianic Jewish Practice

Natalia Yangarber-Hicks observes that 'Significant diversity characterises the extent to which Messianic Jewish congregations and individuals implement traditional Jewish practices into their life and lifestyle.'[8] Whilst Messianic Jews recognise the importance of Messianic Jewish practice, there is much debate within the movement on the subject. 'There is considerable divergence among Messianic Jews about which scriptural laws are binding.'[9] External observers of the movement have noted the degree of confusion on the topic.

> One series of sessions was designed for Messianic leaders to learn the appropriate ways to celebrate Jewish life-cycle events. The overriding concern of the Messianic spiritual leaders teaching the sessions was that Jewish events should be Jewish events, and not every event should be an occasion to preach the gospel. There was considerable disagreement among those present about how these events should be celebrated, so it seems that Jewish practice in the movement is still in a state of flux.[10]

Such confusion is not surprising when the Jewish community itself reflects many different understandings of the place of Torah and its practical outworking.

---

there is general agreement on its practice and theological significance as a sign of entry into the Abrahamic covenant and a defining mark of Jewish descent which continues to be valid today. Cf. Daniel Juster, *Jewish Roots*, 191–93.

[8] Natalia Yangarber-Hicks, 'Messianic believers: reflections on identity of a largely misunderstood group', *Journal of Psychology and Theology* 33, no. 2 (2005):127.

[9] Cohn-Sherbok, *Messianic Judaism*, 159.

[10] Francine K. Samuelson, 'Messianic Judaism, Church, Denomination, Sect or Cult?' *Journal of Ecumenical Studies* 37, no. 2 (2000): 183. Samuelson adds in a footnote: 'Though non-leaders were repeatedly asked to leave by the session chairs, this author did not leave. Apparently, their concern was that lay members of the U.M.J.C. not see how unresolved the movement still is over Jewish practice' (footnote 24, page 183).

Surveys of Messianic Jewish Practice

Jeffrey Wasserman found considerable diversity when he examined the practice of over 200 Messianic Congregations in North America. Half of the congregations surveyed asserted that 'not only was observance of elements of the Mosaic Law permissible and recommended for Messianic Jews, but between 13 and 23 percent thought it mandatory'.[11]

> What portions of the Torah are to be observed? Once again there is no clear consensus. Like the Jewish community itself, with its Orthodox, Conservative and Reform interpretations or rabbinic Judaism, the Messianic community has varying attitudes with regard to the application of the Torah to daily life and congregational worship. There are those who keep a few select portions of the Law and others who not only strictly observe the Law according to the Orthodox rabbinic mandates, but believe that the Talmud (rabbinic commentary) is inspired and therefore binding on Messianic Jews.[12]

David Stern recognised a similar variety of practice as he estimated the practice of 300 Messianic Congregations in the USA, and some 90 in Israel. He recognises a considerable variety of practice:

> Data evidencing the Jewish aspects of the Messianic Jewish congregations are harder to come by. I would guess that 10 to 20 percent of them have Torah scrolls. A much larger percentage celebrate the major Jewish holidays in some fashion. A significant number of their members light *Shabbat* candles. Observance of *kashrut* (the dietary laws) varies from not at all to the fairly careful separating of meat and milk (a rabbinic ordinance).[13]

Detailed information on the degree of practice found in the movement is not available. The variety of practices found are a result of different emphases on liturgy and the use of the *siddur*, different attitudes to worship styles (such as different responses to the influence of the charismatic movement), different theological emphases on the nature and place of Yeshua within

---

[11] Jeffrey S. Wasserman, *Messianic Jewish Congregations: Who Sold this Business to the Gentiles?* (Lanham, Maryland: University Press of America, 2000), 97. See also Jeffrey S. Wasserman, 'Messianic Jewish Congregations in North America,' *Mishkan* 27 (1997): 31. Bulend Senay found similar results in the UK amongst individual members of the two Messianic associations, the BMJA and MJAGB; Bulend Senay, 'The Making of a Tradition: Jewish Christianity,' *Mishkan* 27 (1997): 39.

[12] Jeffrey S. Wasserman, *Messianic Jewish Congregations*, 62.

[13] David H. Stern, 'Summary Essay: The Future of Messianic Judaism' in *How Jewish Is Christianity? 2 Views of the Messianic Movement*, ed. Louis Goldberg (Grand Rapids: Zondervan, 2003), 176.

worship, and linguistic and cultural issues (the place of Hebrew and the role of Diaspora Judaism in creating Jewish identity).

A plethora of organisations produce a multiplicity of resources. These include liturgies, guides to Jewish practice, and guides to Messianic Jewish life. Each grouping has its own liturgy committees, and many individuals have developed their own resources in the hope that these will be taken up and used by others.[14] Although it is not possible to quantify the range of observance of Messianic Jewish practice, its leading thinkers are clear in their advocacy of Messianic Jewish practice, and their understandings of Sabbath, *kashrut* and Passover are examined in the following sections.

The Sabbath

The Sabbath is foundational in Jewish life, and Messianic Jews meet for worship on the Sabbath. Bodil Skjøtt surveyed Sabbath worship and observance in Israel.[15] She found that whilst the majority of congregations met on the Sabbath, few members were 'Sabbath observers', choosing not to travel, cook or do other forms of work prohibited by *halacha*. Senay found similar results in the UK, as did Wassermann in the USA. He found only 14 percent considered that keeping the Sabbath was 'mandatory' and 33 percent considered it 'recommended' for Jewish believers.[16]

Many families observe the lighting of the candles and the blessings before the meal on Friday night. Some congregations meet on Friday evenings, but the majority meet for a Sabbath morning service as their main weekly meeting. Some follow the Orthodox practices of not driving to Synagogue, and doing no forbidden work, but the majority of Israeli and North American congregations are less strict. As Joseph Shulam notes: 'The major problem which keeping the Sabbath raises for contemporary Jewish believers is not whether we should keep the Sabbath, but how to keep it.'[17]

---

[14] The range of resources for Messianic Jewish practice is extensive. The survey of materials by Karl Pruter, *Jewish Christians in the United States: A Bibliography* (New York: Garland Publishing, 1987) has not been updated. There are directories of Messianic Jewish Resources published by the Messianic Alliances in the USA, UK and Israel. http://www. Messianicjewish.net lists several links (accessed June 12, 2007).

[15] Bodil Skjøtt, 'Sabbath and Worship in Messianic Congregations in Israel – A Brief Survey,' *Mishkan* 22 (1995), 29–33. See also Kai Kjær-Hansen and Bodil Skjøtt, *Myths and Facts about the Messianic Congregations in Israel* (Jerusalem: UCCI,1999), 27.

[16] Bulent Senay, 'The Making of a Tradition – Jewish Christianity,' *Mishkan* 27 (1997): 36–42. Wasserman, *Messianic Jewish Congregations*, 96–97.

[17] Joseph Shulam, 'The Sabbath Day and How to Keep It,' *Mishkan* 22 (1995): 26. The issue is devoted to the Sabbath in Judaism, Christianity and Messianic Judaism.

The reason for this difficulty, according to Shulam, is that both Judaism and Christianity have developed many 'strata of traditions' which over the 2000 years of exile have meant that the 'biblical way of looking at the Sabbath, and indeed the whole Torah, has been lost.'

Sabbath with Gusto, But Not According to the Rabbis (Maoz)

Baruch Maoz is critical of Messianic Jews who 'pick and choose' which aspects of Judaism they will observe. 'Few if any really avoid travel or the use of any form of electric power on the Sabbath.'[18] He knows of none who 'avoid tearing toilet paper on the Sabbath'[19] yet are happy to wear the *tallit* on Friday evening services in contrast to 'true Jewish tradition'.[20] He notes that 'something is wrong here'. 'If we empty Jewish tradition of its original meanings and pour into them distinctly Christian content, to which content none of our nation subscribes, we are hardly treating our tradition with respect. Indeed, to what extent can we say that we are really following Jewish tradition?'[21]

Maoz is against the reinterpretation of Jewish observance to give the outward symbols a Christian content and meaning. Nevertheless he observes the Sabbath in his own way. 'I love being Jewish. My family greets the Sabbath each Friday night with a traditional Sabbath meal and we celebrate all the biblical and traditional feasts with gusto.'[22] The Sabbath is part of the Mosaic Law which has eternal moral value, reflecting the nature of God himself. 'Sabbath was an eternal duty in which man [sic] was instructed to emulate his Creator, resting in the finished work of the Eternal One who loved him so freely. The day was blessed and sanctified to God from the sixth day of creation. The principle of one day in seven remains our joy and duty today, and so shall be for all eternity.'[23] But the 'civil and ritual aspects' of the Mosaic Law 'are not essential to the law itself', and pass away, as 'shadow, not substance'.[24] This is why 'ritual was never a crucial part of the Law. Priests could work on the Sabbath in the tabernacle and in the temple without being charged with doing what is unlawful. They trimmed the lights, cleared the ashes from the altar, carried wood to renew the fire and generally watched over their charges.'[25]

---

[18] Baruch Maoz, *Judaism is not Jewish: A Friendly Critique of the Messianic Movement* (Fearn, Scotland: Mentor, 2003), 241.

[19] Ibid., 146.

[20] The *tallit* is only worn in morning services.

[21] Ibid., 147.

[22] Ibid., 34–35.

[23] Ibid., 117.

[24] Ibid., 125.

[25] Ibid.

Whilst the specific forms of Sabbath observance form 'part of our national culture', they have now been fulfilled and 'no longer have the religious value they had in the past'.[26] Maoz finds the lighting of Sabbath candles objectionable. It is an example of 'rabbinic practice, adhered to on the wrong grounds, not biblical custom'.[27] Maoz notes how Jesus kept the traditions of the Judaism of his day because

> He lived among a people that had not yet been enlightened by the gospel and at a time when the gospel was not yet fully made known. He also openly transgressed those traditions by healing on the Sabbath and defending the disciples' right to pluck grain, peel and eat it on the Sabbath – contrary to tradition – and to eat without the ritual washing of hands. He castigated the Pharisees for their customs because those customs transgressed the Word of God (Mark 7:6–13).[28]

Yet because rabbinic customs 'play a large role in the formation of that tradition which constitutes the national cultural consensus among Jewish people', the traditional 'festive meal on Sabbath eve, when the family meets together at the table' is acceptable.[29]

Preaching Law Whilst Practising Grace (Fruchtenbaum)

Arnold Fruchtenbaum also finds a discrepancy between 'Law' and 'grace' in the teaching and observance of the Sabbath amongst Messianic Jews.

> Another example has to do with the proper way of observing the Sabbath. Most Messianic Jews are under the misconception that the Sabbath was observed as a mandatory corporate day of worship. Actually, Moses commanded the Jews to stay home and observe the Sabbath as a day of rest rather than a day of corporate worship. Sabbath corporate worship was mandated for the priesthood in the tabernacle/temple compound but not for individual Jews elsewhere. So if a Messianic Jew gets into his car, starts the engine, and drives to his congregation on Friday night or Saturday morning, he is actually breaking the Sabbath in the way Moses prescribed it. Once again, he is preaching [L]aw while practicing grace. Grace permits one to stay home and rest on the Sabbath, it permits one to have corporate worship on the Sabbath, it permits one to have corporate worship on any other day of the week.[30]

---

[26] Ibid., 127.

[27] Ibid., 154.

[28] Ibid., 161.

[29] Ibid., 172.

[30] Arnold Fruchtenbaum, 'Messianic Congregations May Exist Within the Body of Messiah, as Long as They Don't Function Contrary to the New Testament' in *How Jewish Is Christianity? 2 Views of the Messianic Movement*, ed. Louis Goldberg (Grand Rapids: Zondervan, 2003), 124.

Fruchtenbaum dismisses Daniel Juster's remark – 'I am not particularly inspired by the Jewish identity of one who gives up the Sabbath' – with:

> Juster certainly has the freedom to observe the Sabbath and observe it in the way he chooses, even if the specific way is not in Scripture (i.e. *challah*, wine, and candles). There are no biblical grounds for denying him this privilege. However, to deny the Jewish identity of another Jewish believer who chooses not to observe the Sabbath is out of order and contradicts New Testament teaching. Since from Abraham to Moses Jewish identity remained intact apart from observing the Sabbath, there are no grounds for making Sabbath observance the key element to determine Jewish identity or loyalties after Jesus.[31]

Similar concerns are voiced about the blessing said over the Sabbath candles. Messianic Jews using the traditional Orthodox Jewish service have often unknowingly developed statements and practices which are 'quite contrary to biblical truth'.

> This practice was never commanded in the Law of Moses, but is of rabbinic origin. However, it is not forbidden by the New Testament, it is biblically neutral. The Jewish believer is free to kindle the Sabbath lights, but he [*sic*] is also free not to. However, the prayer that goes with it states: 'Blessed art Thou O Lord our God, King of the Universe, Who has sanctified us with His commandments and commanded us to kindle the Sabbath candles.' The truth is that no such command is found anywhere in Scripture.[32]

Because the prayer is not 'biblically neutral' and the Jewish believer would be 'wrong to recite this prayer', it leaves three options.

> First, he [*sic*] may choose to dispense with the prayer altogether. Second, he can reword the above prayer to bring it into conformity with biblical truth; the last phrase could read, 'permitted us to kindle the Sabbath candles.' Third, he may choose to make up his own prayer. Messianic Jews are free to participate in these things, but the guiding principle is that of conformity with their faith in Jesus the Messiah and the Scriptures.[33]

Fruchtenbaum is determined that Messianic Jews should have freedom to observe the Sabbath in any way they choose, provided they do not impose this on others, and do not themselves come under a bondage to legalism.

---

[31] Arnold Fruchtenbaum, *Israelology: The Missing Link in Systematic Theology* (Tustin: Ariel Ministries, 1992), 761.

[32] Fruchtenbaum, *Israelology*, 761; 'Messianic Congregations,' 126–27.

[33] Fruchtenbaum, *Israelology*, 761; 'Messianic Congregations,' 127; 'The Use of the Siddur by Messianic Jews,' *Mishkan* 25 no. 2 (Jerusalem, UCCI, 1996), 44.

Biblical Sabbath Without Rabbinic Additions (Nerel)

For Gershon Nerel the Sabbath, along with the other Levitical feasts, has not been rescinded, and 'is therefore valid for JBY to observe'.[34] Nevertheless JBY should 'carefully discern between what *the* Rabbi [Jesus] says in the New Testament' and what 'the establishment rabbis say'. 'Only the guidelines of Yeshua should be considered by JBY for the observance of the seventh-day Sabbath, since "the Son of Man is Lord of the Sabbath." (Matt. 12:8).'[35]

In Israel it is natural for JBYs to observe the Sabbath rather than Sunday, as it is the nation's day of rest. The principle should be that we follow Yeshua's practice and teaching, and be careful to apply this to the 'current rabbinical establishment with its restrictions concerning the *Shabbat* observance'.[36] 'For example, because 'the Sabbath was made for man, not man for the Sabbath' (Mark 2:27), it is fully right for JBY to use a car and travel on the Sabbath to a Bible study or worship. Similarly, because 'it is lawful to do good on the Sabbath' (Matt. 12:12), it is right for JBY to use fire and electricity for elementary activities. The same would apply for using money discreetly when circumstances require it.'[37]

Nerel has little patience with 'imposed *Shabbat* traditions' such as the lighting of candles on Friday night or the *Havdalah* service, which have 'no biblical foundation whatever, although rabbinical traditions introduced "divine" prayers and blessings as though they were ordained by God'.[38] 'Contrary to the *Halakhah* blessings during the lighting of candles, God did not command any JBY to perform these acts. Needless to say, traditional East-European food, like *gefilte* (stuffed) fish, has nothing to do with the observance of the Sabbath.'[39]

Whilst Nerel personally enjoys eating *gefilte* fish, he gives this as an illustration, to distinguish between *Yiddishkeit* and Judaism. A problem he sees in the USA Messianic movement is its failure to distinguish between a Jewish cultural veneer and biblical Judaism.

> In fact, personally I *do* like *gefilte* fish very much, but within the Gundry article I just gave this as an illustration, as I also could add, and perhaps should have done so, about peppery fish prepared for Shabbat by Jews from Northern Africa. My real point was/is that *Yiddishkeit*, characterized by this or that traditional food, is irrelevant for our Messianic Jewish and biblical identity. Indeed, I should again

---

[34] Nerel, 'Torah and *Halakhah*,' 158.
[35] Ibid.
[36] Ibid.
[37] Ibid., 159.
[38] Ibid., 159.
[39] Ibid.

underline that *Yiddishkeit* is not Judaism. And in fact, *Yiddishkeit* is not just a matter of Jewish culture, but rather a combination of issues around Jewish *folklore* and myth.[40]

The priority of the Sabbath is not the enjoyment of leisure activities, but physical and spiritual renewal. 'The major issue of the seventh-day Sabbath is to rest from weekly obligations and to worship God. This holy day is to be used for the Lord and not for exhausting oneself through shopping, sports, or sightseeing at the expense of taking quality time for spiritual growth and edification.'[41]

Freedom, Not A Requirement (Kasdan)

Barney Kasdan describes the key features of Shabbat as observed by Messianic Jews.[42] He reminds his readers that 'Of utmost importance is the emphasis upon our freedom in the Messiah. These days, as with any other biblical custom, are not meant to lead us into legalistic bondage. Messiah Yeshua is our total sufficiency when it comes to our spiritual standing before God (Gal. 5:1).'[43]

The two-fold theme of the Sabbath is to 'remember the creator and set the day aside to rest in him'.[44] The Sabbath preparation begins on the Friday afternoon, with the lighting of the Sabbath candles and the blessings over the wine and bread. Kasdan uses the traditional blessing, *'asher kidshanu b'mitzvohtav v'tzi-vanu l'hadleek ner shel Shabbat*, "who has sanctified us by your commandments and commanded us to light the Sabbath light".'[45]

This emphasises the rabbinic understanding that the lighting of the Sabbath candles is a commandment, rather than simply a tradition. The bread is broken by hand, not sliced with a knife, to 'symbolise the day when all weapons of war will be done away with at the coming of the Messiah (Is. 2:4)' and the *challah* is eaten with salt as a reminder of the salting of the sacrifices in the days of the Temple. Blessings are said for the children and the *aishet khayeel* is recited in the wife's honour. 'Shabbat is meant to be a wonderful time of worship to the Lord God and a time of family sharing'.[46]

---

[40] Gershon Nerel, e-mail message to author, October 10, 2006.

[41] Nerel, 'Torah and *Halakhah*,' 159.

[42] Barney Kasdan, *God's Appointed Customs* (Baltimore: Lederer Books, 1993), ch. 1, 1–24.

[43] Kasdan, *God's Appointed Customs*, vii-viii.

[44] Ibid., 2.

[45] Ibid., 3. Others use more Messiah-centred or New Testament inspired blessings. E.g *Asher kidd'shanu b'Ruach Hakodesh v'natan lanu et-Yeshua Hamashiach l'hiyot or l'olam*, 'who has sanctified us by the Holy Spirit and given us Yeshua the Messiah to be the Light of the world'.

[46] Kasdan, *God's Appointed Customs*, 5.

After the meal, with its accompanying *zemirot* and grace after the meal, most messianic synagogues have an *Erev Shabbat* service. The main service occurs on the Sabbath morning, as 'an important part of Shabbat observance is attending corporate worship services'.[47] The services that took place in Tabernacle and Temple in biblical times have continued in the synagogues of the Diaspora, providing the Jewish people with a time of rest, and allowing a 'corporate focus' on the God of Israel. Kasdan describes the elements of a typical service, following the basic structure laid down from the time of Ezra and Nehemiah (Neh. 8). The opening praise, hymns and psalms are followed by the public reading or chanting from the Torah and *Haftarah*, which are based on the annual or triennial lectionary cycle. The third major section of the service is the sermon on the passage for the week. The service concludes with the *Oneg Shabbat*, after which the congregation returns home for lunch and a leisurely afternoon of visiting friends or resting.

The Sabbath closes with *havdalah*, a service which the rabbis created to distinguish Shabbat from all other days, which consists of 'interesting symbolic elements',[48] the lighting of the *havdalah* candle, the passing round of the *b'sameem* (spice) box, and the extinguishing of the candle in the cup of wine. The singing of a 'significant song', *Eliyahu Ha-Navi* (Elijah the Prophet) closes the service. It is 'strongly Messianic in content' and Kasdan notes that 'Having enjoyed the refreshing rest and worship of Shabbat, it is appropriate to consider the ultimate fulfilment of Shabbat, when Messiah will come with his kingdom of peace and rest.'[49]

The place of the Sabbath in the New Testament and the teaching of Jesus is emphasised. 'Because of its centrality in Jewish tradition, we would naturally expect to find the observance of Shabbat mentioned throughout the New Testament.'[50] And this is the case, as 'the most detailed account in scripture of such a service is found in the Gospels', where Kasdan refers to the Nazareth sermon of Luke 4:16–21. 'Yeshua made it his habit to worship at the weekly Shabbat service. What else would he do? He was born a Jew and lived a life consistent with much of traditional Judaism of his day. Likewise, the first disciples continued in the traditional forms of synagogue worship.'[51]

This does not mean that Yeshua 'agreed with every detail' or every rabbinic attitude to Sabbath observance, and he 'tried to correct imbalances in rabbinic perspective' by reminding that 'Shabbat was made for mankind, not mankind for Shabbat (Mark 2:27).' The potential for legalism when the

---

[47] Ibid.
[48] Ibid., 6.
[49] Ibid., 7.
[50] Ibid.
[51] Ibid., 8.

Sabbath is observed must be avoided. 'Sadly, too often the people forget to make Shabbat a delight, relegating it to a list of rules instead. Yeshua challenged the people of his day to remain biblically balanced, to enter into the true rest of God's spirit. The same appeal goes forth in this generation.'[52]

From the book of Hebrews Kasdan gives a Christological understanding of the Sabbath. The Sabbath has been 'prophetically fulfilled' through the coming of the Messiah, and 'spiritual rest is the prophetic fulfilment of the biblical observance of Shabbat'.[53] Kasdan adds his own premillennial understanding. The coming '1000 year Kingdom of Yeshua' will be a 'beautiful time of rest' and corporate worship of the King, and believers in Yeshua should long for its arrival. Until then the Messiah 'bids us to experience the truth of Shabbat in our daily walk ... As we celebrate Shabbat, may spiritual rest in Yeshua constantly be our experience!'[54]

Kasdan provides a practical guide for the observance of the Shabbat, complete with handcrafts, recipes and songs.[55] Examples are given of Messianic modifications of the liturgy, such as the alternative blessing for the lighting of the candles that is used in many congregations. This avoids the sanctioning of rabbinic tradition, and emphasises Yeshua as light of the world.

Baruch atah Adonai Elohenu melek ha-olam, asher kidshanu b'mitzvotav l'hayot or l'goyeem v'natan-lanu Yeshua m'sheekhaynu ha-or la-olam.

Blessed art thou, O Lord Our God, King of the universe, who has sanctified us by thy commandments and commanded us to be a light unto the nations and has given us Yeshua, [our Messiah,] the light of the world.[56]

Apart from such occasional modifications, Kasdan urges Messianic Jews to adopt the rhythm and practice of the Sabbath, both congregationally and personally, as a way to celebrate the spiritual rest brought by the Messiah, and as a 'graphic reminder of the coming day when Messiah Yeshua will establish his true Shabbat light and the sweetness of his coming kingdom! May we, his followers, appreciate the foretaste of this truth as we observe this rich holy day, Shabbat.'[57]

---

[52] Ibid.
[53] Ibid., 9.
[54] Ibid.
[55] Ibid., 12–23.
[56] Ibid., 9–10.
[57] Ibid., 11.

Celebration Without Legalism (Juster)

For Daniel Juster, because the Sabbath is a special 'sign of the covenant' between Israel and God, failing to observe the Sabbath is to 'cast doubt on whether or not we uphold the continuing covenant of God with Israel'.[58] Daniel Juster affirms the foundational role the Sabbath plays.

> The Sabbath is a central pivot of Jewish life. As taught by Yeshua, 'the Sabbath was made for man, and not man for the Sabbath' (Matt. 12). It was never meant to be a day of legalistic conformity. However, Sabbath is a day of crucial significance to Jewish identity. The principle of *weekly rest, worship and renewal has universal significance*. In this sense the Sabbath principle is a *spiritual and humanitarian guide for all peoples*. Christians are free to incorporate this principle on Sunday or other days.[59]

Messianic Judaism looks to Yeshua, who proclaimed Himself 'Lord of the Sabbath' for the principles and details of Sabbath observance. As a memorial of creation and redemption, the day should be celebrated as an 'essential faith principle,' but without the 'legalism' found in the practices of the New Testament Pharisees. 'Yeshua knew such legalism caused people to be concerned with restrictions, thereby missing the true meaning of the day: joy, refreshment, and renewal. As Lord of the Sabbath, Yeshua set the record straight.'[60]

The first Jewish believers continued to observe the Sabbath, but the early church moved from Sabbath to Sunday.[61] Sunday-keeping was not introduced as an 'authoritative apostolic practice' but originated in communities of Gentile believers in Jesus.

As rules should not be 'imposed ad infinitum' Juster gives two basic principles for the Sabbath. Whilst there can be exceptions for emergencies and for those in certain professions, the day should be a 'day of freedom from work'. Secondly, it is valuable to 'mark the day off from other days' by a Friday evening meal, with the lighting of candles and prayer. Messianic Jews should mirror traditional Jewish observance of the Sabbath as a day for worship and the exposition of scripture, and make a time for fellowship with family and friends. 'It is a wonderful time for restful, quiet activities we might otherwise overlook. Reading biblical stories together, quiet games,

---

[58] Daniel C. Juster, *Growing to Maturity: A Messianic Jewish Guide* (Denver CO: UMJC Press, 1996), 181.

[59] Juster, *Growing to Maturity*, 181; cf. *Jewish Roots*, 195.

[60] Juster, *Growing to Maturity*, 182–83.

[61] Ibid., 183. Juster uses the thesis of Samuele Bacchiochi, *From Saturday to Sunday* (Rome: The Pontifical Gregorian University Press, 1977).

sharing with friends, even just napping, can all be interwoven to make Sabbath a joy.'[62]

Juster adopts 'traditional (rabbinic) practices that are in keeping with the Spirit of the New Covenant and the beauty and joy that is our inheritance' such as the *havdalah* service, but stresses that 'of primary importance' is that all Sabbath activity should be a 'true renewal of life in God'.

> The rule of the New Testament is to engage in activity that is spiritually renewing or redemptive for ourselves or others. Sabbath should be a *real contrast* from other work days. Congregations with Sabbath schedules ought to be careful they do not tax their people with too much activity. To make Sabbath a delight, our celebration should be creatively expressed, not rote.[63]

Juster's approach combines flexibility with respect for tradition, but does not allow the imposition of legislation to affect the atmosphere and spirit of rest. His theology of the Sabbath is based on his understanding of Yeshua as 'Lord of the Sabbath', but he does not go into greater detail about the precise practice of the day, leaving it to the individual and their community. Whilst he does not consider the Sabbath mandatory, he regards it as an important part of Messianic Jewish identity. 'I am not particularly inspired by the Jewish identity of one who gives up the Sabbath.'[64]

Following the Pharisaic Pattern (Fischer)

For John Fischer the Sabbath is still in force, as observed by Yeshua. 'To argue that the Sabbath has been abolished by the coming of Yeshua, as many do, contradicts not only Yeshua's own words in Matthew 5:17–20 ... but also Paul's statement in Romans 3:31, that faith by no means nullifies the [L]aw.'[65]

Fischer challenges the view that Yeshua's attitude to the Sabbath 'appears lax'.[66]

---

[62] Juster, *Growing to Maturity*, 184.

[63] Ibid., 185.

[64] Daniel Juster to Arnold Fruchtenbaum, letter dated September 29, 1984, quoted in Arnold Fruchtenbaum, *Israelology: The Missing Link in Systematic Theology* (Tustin, CA: Ariel Ministries Press, 1992), 762.

[65] John Fischer, 'Messianic Congregations Should Exist and Should Be Very Jewish: A Response to Arnold Fruchtenbaum' in Louis Goldberg (ed.), *How Jewish Is Christianity: 2 Views on the Messianic Movement* (Grand Rapids: Zondervan, 2003), 136.

[66] John Fischer, 'The Place of Rabbinic Tradition in a Messianic Jewish Lifestyle' in *The Enduring Paradox: Exploratory Essays in Messianic Judaism*, ed. John Fischer (Baltimore: Lederer, 2000), 149.

The religious leaders had criticized Yeshua for his disciples' actions in picking grain on Shabbat [Mark 2:23–28; Matt. 12:1–8]. Yeshua's response is often presented as evidence that he disregarded the regulations for Shabbat observance. However, at this time in history, there was an ongoing discussion over the picking and eating of grain on Shabbat. Even the Talmud points out: 'Bundles which can be taken up with one hand may be handled on the Sabbath ... and he may break it with his hand and eat thereof' (Shab.128a). This is exactly what the disciples were doing. Further, Yeshua's reasoning concerning his position on this issue follows the same patterns used by the Pharisees to demonstrate that the needs of life are paramount, even over the Sabbath regulations ... Even Yeshua's concluding statement is found in the Talmud: 'Sabbath was made for man, not man for the Sabbath' (Mark 2:27; Yoma 85b). In neither case are the Sabbath regulations being set aside.[67]

Fischer also reviews Yeshua's healing on the Sabbath and concludes with a quotation from Shmuel Safrai: 'Jesus' Sabbath healings which angered the head of the synagogue were permitted by tannaitic law.'[68] Yeshua remained an 'observant, traditional Jew, both in his life and in his teachings'. [69] Fischer challenges Fruchtenbaum's assertion that corporate worship on the Sabbath was not part of the original biblical teaching.

As for the critique that the Sabbath is a day of rest, not a day of corporate worship, it is both unjustified and anachronistic. Exodus 20:10, by noting that this day is a 'Sabbath to the LORD,' clearly implies the notion of response and therefore worship, an idea also suggested by Isaiah 58:13–14 ('if you call the Sabbath a delight and the LORD's holy day honourable, and if you honour it by not going your own way ...'). Further, by the time of the second temple the Sabbath clearly was a day of corporate worship and one in which Yeshua (Matt. 9:35; Luke 4:16–30) and Paul (Acts 17:2) regularly participated.[70]

Details of observance are not given, but Fischer expects the example of Yeshua to be followed, as Sabbath-keeping is a fundamental principle, and not just a body of legislation. The Sabbath should be appreciated in the light of the 'covenant pattern of the [Ancient] Near East, which shows that all Torah material reflects God's grace'.[71] The principles of 'keep it holy', 'no

---

[67] Ibid., 149–50.

[68] Ibid., 151, quoting S. Safrai, 'Religion in Everyday Life' in S. Safrai and M. Stern (eds.), *The Jewish People in the First Century*, vol. 2 (Philadelphia: Fortress Press, 1976) (no page reference).

[69] Ibid.

[70] Ibid., 138. See above, section 2.2.

[71] John Fischer, *Siddur for Messianic Jews* (Palm Harbor, FL: An Adventure in Faith, 1984), 202.

labour', 'unto the Lord' and 'a delight' are the underlying themes. 'To keep something holy means to set it apart, separate it, *for* God and *from* other things. So Shabbat should be different from the other days, separated *from* the ordinary purposes of the week. It's to be set apart *for* God in order to build up and renew our life with God. Worship and instruction play an important role in this.'[72] For Fischer this means synagogal worship, the congregation meeting as a community, but with 'two important constructs' that undergird the significance of the Sabbath – rest and anticipation.[73]

> It is a day for not working, i.e. not interfering with or changing the natural order, not disturbing the harmony of creation. We don't work on this day because work is a symbol of conflict, disharmony and struggle (cf. 'cursed is the ground for your sake; in the sweat of your face will you eat of it'); it reminds us of man's [*sic*] fall (Gen. 3), not God's *shalom*. By not working we free ourselves from our weekly struggle with the world in order to make a living.[74]

The second construct, 'anticipation', is linked to the world to come, and the second coming of the Messiah.

> The time of harmony Shabbat looks forward to is the *Olam Ha-Ba* (the world to come), i.e., the time of the Messiah. This explains why we call the Messianic age the time of 'continuous Shabbat.' The Messianic strains of Havdalah heighten this sense of anticipation each week. So for us, Shabbat serves as a symbolic expectation of our Messiah's second coming, as well as an opportunity to experience *now* in a small way the rest and harmony that will exist *then*.[75]

Keeping the Sabbath Holy and Wholly (Kinzer)

Mark Kinzer examines the practice of Yeshua and his disciples, challenging traditional readings that assume observance of Jewish practice is no longer valid, and in fact 'legalistic' for Messianic Jews.[76] Yeshua observed Sabbath, *kashrut* and the festivals, and for Kinzer such norms still apply today. They are God's provision and providential ordering for the survival of the Jewish people up to the present.

---

[72] Ibid., 203.

[73] Ibid., 205.

[74] Ibid.

[75] Ibid.

[76] Mark Kinzer, *Postmissionary Messianic Judaism: Redefining Christian Engagement with the Jewish People*, (Grand Rapids: Brazos, 2005), ch. 2, 'The New Testament and Jewish Practice,' 49–96.

Yeshua and his followers were born and raised within a Jewish world where such practices (i.e. circumcision, Sabbath and holiday observance, and dietary laws), commanded in the Torah, were presumed rather than disputed. Fierce disputes arose over *how* these commandments were to be interpreted and applied – but not over *whether* they were to be interpreted and applied. Nevertheless, according to conventional Christian readings of the New Testament, Yeshua and his followers ultimately rejected or transcended these basic Jewish practices. The purpose of this chapter is to examine this conventional assumption in order to determine if the evidence warrants it. We will find that it does not.[77]

The outworking of this approach to Shabbat is found in the Collected Halakhic Decisions of the MJRC (Messianic Jewish Rabbinical Council) of New England, in which Kinzer is a leading voice. The stipulations for Sabbath observance run to several pages, and follow closely Conservative Jewish practice.[78] The principles behind the Sabbath are outlined from a quotation from Morris Joseph.

> The Sabbath is a sacred day and there are certain kinds of enjoyment which by their very nature are out of harmony with its inherent holiness. Participation in them on the Sabbath is like a sudden intrusion of a shrill street organ on a beautiful melody sung by a lovely voice. It is difficult, almost impossible, to lay down a definite rule on this point, to say 'This sort of amusement is allowable, that sort improper, on the Sabbath.' The matter must be left to the individual conscience, to each person's sense of what is seemly.[79]

The MJRC follows the traditional commencement of the Sabbath, beginning an hour before sunset and ending an hour afterwards. '3.1.1 Shabbat begins and ends according to the times determined and accepted by the wider Orthodox and Conservative Jewish world. This means that we are accepting the Rabbinic fence around the law, with an earlier time for starting and a later time for ending.'[80]

Candle lighting is expected, and should be done before the beginning of the Sabbath. This is in contrast to most Messianic Jews, who do not follow this practice but light candles at services which often begin after the Sabbath.

---

[77] Kinzer, *Postmissionary Messianic Judaism*, 50.

[78] MJRC, 'Collected Halakhic Decisions (May 2006)', (draft pre-publication paper of the Messianic Jewish Rabbinical Council of New England, email attachment from Mark Kinzer, June 20, 2007), 3–7.

[79] MJRC, 6, quoting Morris Joseph, *Judaism as Creed and Life* (New York: Bloch, 1920), 89–90.

[80] MJRC, 'Collected Halakhic Decisions,' 3.

3.2.1 *If it is not possible to light candles before Shabbat begins, traditional halakhah* would strictly prohibit lighting the candles at a later time. We respect this traditional halakhic decision, and the honor it shows to the objective temporal boundaries of Shabbat built into the natural order. At the same time, given the symbolic importance Shabbat candlelighting has assumed in modern Jewish family life, our own basic practice will not prohibit lighting Shabbat candles after Shabbat begins by transferring a fire from a candle lit before the beginning of Shabbat. In this case the original candle should not be extinguished on Shabbat, nor should the *mitzvah berachah* be recited.[81]

A traditional blessing should be used, but a Messianic one may be added if wished. This emphasis reflects a desire to follow orthodox/conservative tradition rather than use the opportunity for a Christocentric exegesis of the custom, as would be the case in the majority of Messianic groups that practice candle-lighting on Friday evening.

3.2.3 The *berachah* recited at the lighting of the candles will be the traditional *mitzvah berachah*. If one wants to use an additional Messianic berachah, one may do so.[82]
The Sabbath meals should be accompanied by the traditional graces in Hebrew.
3.4.1 Friday night meal. The basic practice includes saying *kiddush, hamotzi* (over bread), and an abbreviated *birkat hamazon* (all prayers in Hebrew).[83]

The meals should take place with the traditional features such as 'handwashing, use of two loaves of bread, salting the bread, recitation of *ayshet hayil*, blessing of the children, singing of *zemirot*, full *birkat hamazon* and discussion of Torah.' The traditional *havdalah* service should also be observed at the end of the Sabbath.

Normal professions, trades, and daily occupations should cease, 'except in the following occupations: health care workers and care-givers, police, military, emergency personnel, and synagogue personnel who are involved in the synagogue activities of the day'.[84] One should not light a fire, although 'Halakhic authorities disagree about whether the use of electrical devices and the combustion involved in starting and running an automobile violate this commandment of the Torah. Our basic practice will follow the more lenient interpretation.'[85] According to Neh 13, buying and selling should be avoided. ' "Buying and selling" here includes both the selling of goods for

---

[81] Ibid., 3–4.
[82] Ibid., 4.
[83] Ibid.
[84] Ibid., 5.
[85] Ibid.

profit and the selling of goods that are not sold for profit (e.g., religious articles). Thus, we will not sell items (such as books or CD's) in our synagogues
on Shabbat. "Buying and selling" here includes payment for food or enter-
tainment. Credit card purchases are "buying".[86] However, offerings and
tzedakah on Shabbat 'do not constitute buying and selling' and are permitted. 'Dining out or other recreational activity that involves spending money
is inappropriate on Shabbat'.[87]

Travelling is permitted in some circumstances.

> In general, travelling on Shabbat conflicts with the spirit of the day. Nevertheless,
> limited travel may be appropriate to uphold certain values that are themselves
> associated with Shabbat. Thus, our basic practice does not prohibit travel on
> Shabbat to attend services at the synagogue, to visit the sick, and to sustain
> contact with the synagogue community and with one's family, though such travel
> should not occupy a substantial portion of the day. Normally one should avoid
> travelling on Shabbat for other purposes.[88]

Food should be prepared in advance, or kept on a slow cooker, where it may
be kept warm or reheated. 'On Shabbat we do not manipulate and alter the
world but receive and enjoy it. Cooking alters the composition of food'.[89]

The MJRC recognises the difficulty of some traditional requirements.

> Due to the demands of modern life, the traditional prohibition on writing and
> drawing places an excessive burden upon the Messianic Jewish community in
> our contemporary situation. Therefore, our basic practice will not include prohi-
> bitions of the sort of writing and drawing that enhances the community's ability
> to experience Shabbat and that does not violate the spirit of Shabbat. At the same
> time, we appreciate the reasons for these prohibitions and recognize their great
> value, and therefore commend them as part of our expanded practice.[90]

In order to maintain the 'spirit of Shabbat' it is best to avoid all activities that,
although not strictly work, are not in keeping with the spirit of the day, and
this includes avoiding Shabbat activities 'that involve the general public'.[91]
Television is best avoided due to 'the socially fragmenting effect on families', especially commercial television. Letters should be left unopened and
unread, email should not be read or composed, and the telephone should
only be used in emergencies. Computers, videos and mobile phones should

---

[86] Ibid.
[87] Ibid.
[88] Ibid., 5–6.
[89] Ibid., 6.
[90] Ibid.
[91] Ibid.

be switched off.[92] Kinzer and the MJRC thus provide a guide to the Sabbath which would not be out of place in any observant community.

Summary

For both Maoz, Fruchtenbaum and Nerel, traditional observance of the Sabbath is problematic. Maoz does not accept a theological rationale for observance of Jewish 'religious' customs or attempt to give them new meaning in the light of Yeshua. There is no room for contextualisation, and no possibility of adapting rabbinic practices as vehicles for expression of faith in Jesus. Maoz's Protestant Reformed principles disallow the adoption of practices that are not clearly scriptural, and his construal of 'religious Judaism' is that it is antithetical to 'the gospel'. Here he represents one pole of the Messianic movement, with others more willing to engage with 'religious' elements of Jewish culture.

Fruchtenbaum and Nerel also issue caveats. For Nerel, only the biblical forms of Judaism are permissible, and for Fruchtenbaum neither Mosaic (Pre-Yeshua) or Rabbinic (post-Yeshua) legislation can interfere with the believer's freedom in Christ, to observe the Sabbath as the Lord of the Sabbath intended.

For Kasdan, Fischer, Juster and Kinzer the Jewish tradition is to be accepted, either with adaptations, or with as few modifications as possible. Questions of the relationship between the Law and grace, between freedom and observance, are not so threatening, as their hermeneutic reads scripture as affirming Yeshua's own Torah-observance, and they are willing to give rabbinic tradition a degree of legitimacy and normative influence, without seeing this in conflict with their allegiance to Yeshua. A similar breadth of opinion is to be observed in the discussion of the food laws that follows below.

Kashrut

On *kashrut* Messianic Jews explain the biblical and rabbinic traditions, consider the practice and teaching of Jesus and the first Messianic Jews, and make practical recommendations about how and to what degree Messianic Jews should keep the food laws today. As in the Jewish community, there is considerable variety of interpretation and implementation of these practices. In addition, for Messianic Jews, the balancing of the principles of the liberty of the individual over matters that are not essential to faith, the need to maintain unity in the *ekklesia*, and the call to a Torah-observant lifestyle produce a variety of responses on the issue.

---

[92] Ibid., 7.

A Sign of Weakness (Maoz)

For Baruch Maoz observation of the food laws is a sign of a weakness of faith. 'Paul addresses Gentiles in these chapters [Rom. 14:16–15:13] calling them to bear with the weakness of those among their Jewish brethren who still had qualms about certain aspects of Jewish tradition.'[93] Paul, according to Maoz, is *'convinced that nothing is unclean in itself* (Rom. 14:14)' [emphasis his].

> Everything is kosher, everything is acceptable to be received and eaten with thanks to God, the gracious Provider (see 1 Tim. 4:4). The dietary restrictions imposed upon Israel by the commandment of God and as an integral part of the Mosaic covenant are no longer binding (see also Mark 7:14–19). Whoever thinks something to be unclean, it is unclean in his own mind (not in and of itself, Rom. 14:14). So, do not wound the oversensitive and misinformed conscience of your brother by demonstratively partaking of foods that offend his conscience (14:15).[94]

Maoz is critical of those Messianic Jews who do observe a form of *kashrut*. 'Messianic Jews pick and choose aspects of Judaism to which they will adhere … Few maintain a truly kosher kitchen. If they keep kosher, most keep what they describe as a "biblical *kashrut*".'[95] For Maoz this is highly unsatisfactory. Citing the study by Feher,[96] he concludes:

> In what sense can such practice be construed as traditional Judaism, which rejects such a version of *kashrut* and insists that only traditional Jewish practice – the *Halacha* – may determine what is to be eaten, when and how. Feher is right (page 83) when she says 'They keep kosher in order to identify with Judaism, and yet, because they choose to keep biblical *kashrut* they end up by not belonging. Messianics' attempts to achieve balance creates a contradiction: in seeking to offend no one, they potentially offend everyone.'[97]

---

[93] Maoz, *Judaism Is Not Jewish*, 168.

[94] Ibid., 169.

[95] Ibid., 241. 'Biblical kashrut' allows for the mixing of milk and meat dishes, but still forbids pork, shellfish and other foods.

[96] Shoshana Feher, *Passing Over Easter: Constructing the Boundaries of Messianic Judaism* (Walnut Creek: Alta Mira Press, 1998), 83.

[97] Maoz, *Judaism Is Not Jewish*, 241, quoting Feher, 83. Maoz does not reflect Feher's main point, which would go against his own argument. 'Thus Messianic Believers place themselves in a unique position toward Jewish ritual that gives them a private symbolic ethnicity.' According to Maoz, Messianic Jews keeping 'biblical kosher' are seeking to be construed as keeping traditional Judaism, because he does not wish to accept the creation of a new possibility, a Messianic Jewish identity which is neither rabbinic nor Gentile Christian. For Feher, this is the very purpose for which the notion of 'biblical kosher' exists.

This unsystematic and insensitive approach does more harm than good. 'Repeated efforts by Messianic Jews to force Christian meanings into Jewish traditions are as much an offence to Orthodox Jews as any one could imagine. It certainly does not convey a sense of honest loyalty to those traditions.'[98]

Maoz himself does not keep kosher.[99] His own Israeli identity does not require it, and he is not impressed by those who argue for a modified *kashrut*. He notes the range of *kashrut* observance reflects that of the Jewish community. Some keep kosher strictly; some keep kosher in the home but not when eating out; others advocate a 'biblical *kashrut'*. An additional group, probably the majority of Messianic Jews, do not observe *deliberately and for theological reasons*, stressing their freedom in Christ and that they are no longer 'under the law.'

A Ham Sandwich in Harlem (Fruchtenbaum)

Arnold Fruchtenbaum argues that the ritual laws are no longer in effect because, with the coming of the Messiah, the Mosaic covenant has been rendered inoperative. He can see no useful function for the food laws. The dietary laws no longer apply to a believer in Jesus, but there is freedom to keep them if appropriate. '*This he said making all foods clean.* Can it be any clearer than this that at least the dietary commandments have been done away?'[100] For practical purposes Fruchtenbaum urges sensitivity. 'I would not eat a ham sandwich in the Mea Shearim (ultra-Orthodox) quarter of Jerusalem. But here even total abstention is not the answer. Eating meat sacrificed to idols was permissible in certain situations, and I have no problem eating a ham sandwich in Harlem where the culture is not against it.'[101]

'Biblical *Kashrut'* (Kasdan)

Barney Kasdan observes a 'biblical *kashrut'* which is 'not overburdened with rabbinic legislation'. He notes the variations found in the Jewish community on the topic, and admits 'as with the traditional Jewish community, there is also a great deal of diversity among believers in Yeshua when it comes to *kashrut*. Many follow what might be described as a "biblical kosher" approach. This lifestyle shows deference to the biblical dietary laws. Hence, only kosher animals are eaten: the *tareyf* animals are avoided.'[102]

---

[98] Maoz, *Judaism Is Not Jewish*, 241.
[99] Personal interview and meal with author, September 9, 2006.
[100] Fruchtenbaum, *Israelology*, 648.
[101] Fruchtenbaum, *Hebrew Christianity*, 131.
[102] Kasdan, *God's Appointed Customs*, 110.

Kasdan questions the traditional reading of Mark 7 that 'these words of Yeshua negate all of *kashrut*'. Yeshua clearly upheld the Torah (Matt. 5:17). What is at issue is not whether all foods have now become *kosher*, but whether the 'higher principle' behind the dietary laws was 'always to be spiritual. God is always looking at the heart before the diet.'[103]

> The question was *not* one of non-kosher foods. Presumably, the food under discussion was considered biblically kosher. The main question was whether or not this kosher food would be rendered as *tareyf* because the disciples did not follow the rabbinic practices. Contrary to popular belief, Yeshua was not pronouncing the arrival of 'kosher bacon,' but was simply affirming the priority of the Scriptures over the authority of the rabbis.[104]

Kasdan then challenges the later rabbinic injunctions on the mixing of milk and meat.

> A question is often raised as to what to do with the extra-biblical customs the rabbis have included. There is broad consensus, considering the teaching of the New Testament, that Messianic believers are not *bound* by the traditions of man [*sic*]. The mixing of milk and meat, for example, while an Orthodox Jewish tradition, is not a biblical law. This means that the laws pertaining to separate dishes, silverware and pots are really not an issue in seeking to live a biblical lifestyle.[105]

Kasdan is willing to allow flexibility.

> Of course, there are those who may choose to follow elements of rabbinic tradition. This is fine as long as it does not contradict Scripture and is done in the right spirit. A Messianic believer may want to buy meat from a kosher butcher and/or keep separate dishes. Some believers may prefer some modifications. Whatever approach a Messianic believer takes to *kashrut*, it is wise to walk in love and to heed the New Testament's council: 'whatever you do, whether it's eating or drinking or anything else, do it all so as to bring glory to God' (1 Cor. 10:31).[106]

Kasdan, Juster and Schiffman reflect the majority preference of the movement for a modified, 'biblical kosher' or Karaite form of *kashrut*, although there is little evidence that this form of *kashrut* was observed by Yeshua and his disciples. The rationalisation to an easier, more flexible system retains a modified form of the food laws. But Maoz's critique, whilst based on the debatable premise that Mark 7 invalidates the food laws, nevertheless highlights the difficulty of maintaining such a position.

---

[103] Ibid., 107.
[104] Ibid.
[105] Ibid., 110.
[106] Ibid.

Cleanliness Laws Superseded? (Juster)

Daniel Juster has only a brief section in *Jewish Roots* on the 'Biblical Food and Cleanliness Laws'.[107] Without prescribing how much Messianic Jews should still observe these laws today, he notes three possible explanations for them in the biblical material: the health benefits; the distinction between clean and unclean; and the anthropological theories of Mary Douglas. He concludes 'Perhaps these three explanations for the clean-unclean distinctions and the forbidden food all have some value. The evidence is certainly not so clear as to justify dogmatism.'[108] Yet Juster is reluctant to conclude that the food laws are still to be kept in the same fashion today, and challenges the rabbinic development of such traditions. Such clean-unclean distinctions were relevant at the time of the Temple, but 'In some aspects, therefore, the clean-unclean distinctions are for the age of the Temple which has been superseded for us in Yeshua during this age.'[109]

On the matter of *kashrut* there should be flexibility.

> As for *Kashrut* in this Rabbinical sense, we believe that everyone should be led by the Spirit. Is God leading the person to a special level of identification whereby he or she will practice the full rules of Rabbinic *Kashrut*? Or would this be too restrictive even for our general social relationships in the Jewish community to which we minister? Everyone must seek God in this. Certainly there is no requirement in these matters for Messianic Jews.[110]

Michael Schiffman is similarly flexible. 'Messianic believers may choose to avoid meats forbidden in the *torah* as a lifestyle and cultural identification, and yet eat cheeseburgers forbidden by Rabbinic traditional law but not by scripture.'[111]

Torah Still Valid – According to Yeshua (Nerel)

For Nerel *kashrut* is observed for both religious and practical reasons. The *kashrut mitzvoth* in the Torah are ratified by Yeshua himself in Matt. 5:17, and are still valid for modern JBY. 'Before any "Practical/Cultural consideration

---

[107] Juster, *Jewish Roots*, 219–20.
[108] Ibid., 219.
[109] Ibid., 220.
[110] Ibid., 231.
[111] Michael Schiffman, *Return From Exile* (New York: Teshuvah, 1990), 72–96; 68. Revised edition published as *Return of the Remnant* (Baltimore: Lederer, 1996), 55–79. The revised edition has expanded the section on Jewish tradition (1990:90–96) to a separate chapter 'Jewish Believers and Jewish Tradition', 71–79.

in Israel", I always underline my axiom that the Torah is still valid – according to Yeshua.'[112]

In the State of Israel it is easier to keep *kashrut*, because issues of *shechita*, certification of shops and restaurants, and supervision are controlled nationally by the State Chief Rabbinate, and most shops and restaurants offer kosher food.

> In Israel the *kashrut* is almost a non-issue for those that want to keep it as Torah observant according to Yeshua. So, then, *kashrut* does have religious/theological grounds, but practically in Israel it can be observed more conveniently and handily than in the Diaspora. The general conclusion in my view is, as the Apostle Shaul/Paul said, that we as Yeshua-believers shall not become a stumbling-block for our neighbors and our brethren on 2 sides, neither to the Jew nor to the Gentile (1 Cor. 10: 27–28). For the Jew we in principle keep the Torah and the *kashrut*, for the Gentile who invites us to his home we shall not quarrel about the food he puts on the table, unless it belongs to idol worship (Rom. 14). We must be both wise and spiritual and sometimes just choose to become (even ad-hoc) vegetarians … This I found very effective when I did not want to embarrass my hosts or to avoid unnecessary questions and debates. Time is life![113]

The food laws of the Old Testament also have some application to Gentile believers in the New. 'Whereas the Old Testament dietary laws were primarily given for the Jews, the New Testament also instructs Gentile believers to distinguish between food that is *kasher* (permissible) and *terefah* (forbidden). The council of the apostles at Jerusalem decided that even Gentile believers should 'abstain from things sacrificed to idols, from blood, from the meat of strangled animals' (Acts 15:29).'[114] From this Nerel derives the general principle. 'Basically, and wherever possible, JBY should keep the dietary laws of *kashrut*, avoiding meat such as pork, seafood and creeping animals. In the State of Israel it is no problem for JBY to keep the elementary dietary laws of *kashrut*, although obviously such abstaining has nothing to do with salvation or achieving a higher spiritual status.'[115]

Nerel is clear that 'one should not be legalistic in these matters' and that both 'logic and the guidance of the Spirit' must be used. Likewise, JBY should not make the issue of food a 'source of arguments and quarrelling'. For Nerel the 'proper principle' has to be the words of 1 Cor. 10:25 – 'Eat anything sold in the meat market without raising questions of conscience.'

---

[112] Gershon Nerel, e-mail message to author, May 20, 2007.

[113] Ibid.

[114] Nerel, 'Torah and *Halakhah*,' 161.

[115] Ibid.

Reinterpreting Mark 7:19b (Rudolph)

David Rudolph's advocacy of *kashrut* challenges the reading of Mark 7:19b: 'thus he declared all foods clean' (NRSV). According to Rudolph, the alternative minority reading of 'the body purging itself of all food' better accounts for the original sense of the passage. The primary intention of the writer was not to declare that *kosher* food is the same as *treif*, but to release the Gentiles from the necessity of observing the food laws of the Torah, which are still incumbent on Israel.[116] Jesus' parable in Mark 7:14–19a and Mark's comment in 7:19b uphold the 'validity of the Torah purity system', and that Jesus' aim was 'prioritisation, not abrogation' of the food laws. 'Mark's parenthetical comment was specifically intended for Gentile Christians (an important nuance), and may have served to establish theological justification for the Apostolic decree that exempted Gentile Christians from the food laws.'[117]

Rudolph assumes that Messianic Jews retained *kashrut*, and recognition of this 'Jew-Gentile ecclesiological variegation is essential to understanding the early Church's reading of Mark 7'. It is clear that 'Jesus was a Torah faithful Jew who observed the biblical dietary laws and that his disciples (all Jews!) did the same as well. The continuing validity of Israel's dietary laws for Jewish Christians raises a number of compelling questions for modern Christian theology, which continues to associate clean/unclean food distinctions with legalism for Jewish Christians.'[118]

Rudolph's exegetical study affirms the importance of the food laws for Jewish believers in Jesus, in the light of later Christian anti-Judaism.

> The preponderance of evidence, therefore, suggests that the later Gentile Church teaching that Jewish Christians were 'freed' from these laws on the basis of Mark 7:19b (and that eating unclean food was even a test of their fidelity to Jesus!), is spurious. Such a break with Judaism – on the part of Jewish Christians – would have been a 'distortion of Jesus' own vision and intention.'[119]

Although Rudolph does not develop a rationale and guide for contemporary observance of the food laws, his arguments have been taken up by others in the movement.[120]

---

[116] David J. Rudolph, 'Jesus and the Food Laws: A Reassessment of Mark 7:19b,' *Evangelical Quarterly* 74/4 (October 2002): 311.

[117] Ibid., 310.

[118] Ibid.

[119] Ibid.

[120] E.g. Stern, *JNTC*, 93–94.

Preventing the Abolition of the Jewish People (Kinzer)

Mark Kinzer builds on Rudolph's work.[121] He resituates the first Jewish believers in Yeshua in the Jewish context of their day, and restructures the biblical metanarrative in such a way that the continuing election of Israel makes Torah observance for Messianic Jews a normative requirement. *Kashrut* is a cornerstone of Torah observance and Jewish identity. Kinzer argues for a reading of scripture which accepts this continuing validity. 'If Yeshua abolished the dietary laws, then why did his Jewish followers (such as Peter in Acts 10) require special divine intervention before they would even sit at table with non-Jews?'[122]

Kinzer's hermeneutics favours 'plausible readings of the New Testament that support the ongoing validity and spiritual significance of the Jewish people and its distinctive way of life'. He is therefore emphatic: '*The abolition of the dietary laws is in effect an abolition of the Jewish people itself* [emphasis his].'[123] Like circumcision, Sabbath and the festivals, the Torah's dietary regimen 'serves as a fundamental sign of the particular vocation and identity of the Jewish people',[124] and this in itself provides 'strong theological grounds' for a 'non-abolitionist reading' of passages such as Mark 7:19.

Kinzer adopts Conservative *halacha* on the issue of *kashrut*.[125] As a member of the MJRC (Messianic Jewish Rabbinical Council) of New England, a loose federation of Messianic Jewish Synagogues in the North East, he and others have produced rulings on a number of halachic matters. Whilst such rulings have no authority beyond those congregations which participate in the MJRC, they signal an increasing tendency for Messianic Judaism to mirror in its practices, if not its beliefs, the canons of contemporary Conservative Judaism.

The fundamental requirements of *kashrut* are clear from scripture. Pork, shellfish, and food containing their elements such as lard are to be avoided. Fruits, grains and vegetables are permitted, as are fish with fins and scales. The MJRC follows Conservative *halacha* in considering swordfish and sturgeon acceptable as part of 'our basic practice'. Meats (except from the hind quarters) from cattle, lamb, goat, or deer, and from most common fowl (e.g., chicken, turkey, goose, duck) may also be eaten. The same applies to gelatin, cheese and wine. '5.2.1 For our basic practice we will adopt the standards of the Conservative Movement that treat all gelatin and cheese as

---

[121] Kinzer, *PMJ*, 57 (footnote 15).
[122] Ibid., 58.
[123] Ibid.
[124] Ibid.
[125] Gilbert S. Rosenthal, *The Many Faces of Judaism: Orthodox, Conservative, Reconstructionist and Reform* (New York: Behrman House, 1978), 113.

acceptable.'[126] However, wine need not be prepared under supervision except for liturgical purposes. '5.2.2 All wines or other alcoholic beverages are acceptable. In the case of Jewish ceremonies only kosher wine or grape juice should be used.'[127]

Shechitah is a preferred requirement, and ideally all meat shall be prepared in the traditional way, but where this is impractical, other means may be used.

> 5.3.1 The most basic Biblical dietary law, addressed not only to Israel but also to the nations of the world in Noah, involves avoiding the eating of blood (i.e., foods that are cooked in or with blood). Concern to guard this core dietary law led to the institution of *Shechitah* – the Jewish ritual slaughter of animals and preparation of meat. Therefore, ideally it is recommended that meat be purchased from a kosher butcher.
>
> However, given the difficulty in many places of obtaining kosher meat, our basic practice will not involve eating only meat from a Kosher butcher (i.e., meat slaughtered and prepared according to the laws of *Shechitah*). It will involve urging that we avoid meat from the hindquarters of permitted four-legged animals (a practice rooted in Jacob's injury in Genesis 32).[128]

The separation of milk and meat products should be observed, again following a more lenient Conservative practice. 'Our basic standard should urge that people avoid eating meat products (including fowl) and obvious dairy products (or foods containing obvious dairy products) together in a given meal. Meat may be eaten after eating obvious dairy foods without any time interval, though they should not be present together at the same table. After eating a meat meal, the minimum time interval before eating obvious dairy products should be one hour.'[129]

Eating in restaurants that are not kosher is permitted, but should be done with discernment. 'When eating out, the above standards may be relaxed, but one should continue to avoid all meat (and meat-products) from unkosher animals (e.g., pig, shellfish). Beyond this basic practice, we commend the eating of non-meat meals when eating in non-kosher facilities.'[130]

---

[126] MJRC, 'Collected Halakhic Decisions (May 2006)', (draft pre-publication paper of the Messianic Jewish Rabbinical Council of New England, email attachment from Mark Kinzer, June 20, 2007), 11.

[127] Ibid.

[128] Ibid., 11–12.

[129] Ibid., 12.

[130] Ibid.

Summary

A number of theological concerns are at work in the various practices of *kashrut*. The development of Messianic *kashrut* must reckon with the orthopraxy advocated by the Jewish religious establishment; the different interpretations of the New Testament practices and teaching of Yeshua and the first century Messianic Jews; the need to be culturally appropriate and sensitive; and the possibility of variety rather than uniformity in such issues. What is missing from the present discussion is a more systematic theology of Torah which confirms and justifies the validity of the food laws, not simply as boundary markers, but with their own inherent theological rationale. This might be developed from a more historical, anthropological and theological reading of the Pentateuchal legislation, and a more detailed discussion of the place of the food laws within Jewish history and identity formation. Without more adequate justification for *kashrut's* continued validity, the majority of the Messianic movement will not be convinced by Kinzer's statement that the *'abolition of the dietary laws is in effect an abolition of the Jewish people itself'*.[131] A systematic MJT will surely have to address such issues with greater rigour.

Passover

Whilst there is considerable diversity on the observance of *kashrut*, there is greater unity and uniformity in the observance of Passover, and its significance for Messianic Jews cannot be overestimated.

> The secular nature of American Jewish life means that many of the participants in Messianic Congregations had little exposure in their childhood to any of these holidays other than Passover, *Rosh Hashanah* and *Yom Kippur* ... Consequently, it is common for these holidays to be a time of instruction (and often redefinition) of their Jewish meaning. An example of this redefinition to conform to Messianic belief is the Passover celebration.[132]

Passover is a *locus classicus* for the practical outworking of MJT, demonstrating the creativity of its exegesis of scripture and its interpretation and modification of Jewish tradition. 'As a great feast of remembrance, Passover is a feast without equal. It is full of meanings which relate to all followers of the Messiah. The Exodus is a type or image pattern of all God's redemptive acts and even of the final redemption and the establishment of God's Kingdom.'[133]

---

[131] Kinzer, *PMJ*, 58.

[132] Wasserman, *Messianic Jewish Congregations*, 94.

[133] Juster, *Jewish Roots*, 200.

Many issues are raised when Messianic Jews come to celebrate Passover, as they decide how to adopt, adapt, or abandon the Jewish and Christian accretions that have developed and been incorporated in the haggadah. 'Passover is only one example of the constant decoding and recoding of Jewish ritual by Messianic Judaism. This decoding and recoding – the constant infusion of Jewish ritual and cultural norms with Christian symbolism and, to a lesser extent, the infusion of Christianity with Jewish symbolism – is a central theme.'[134]

Messianic observance of Passover reflects the variety of understandings within the Jewish community. Rich Robinson states:

> With Jewish observances, questions arise about whether or not particular observances are proper for a follower of Jesus, and these questions have been debated among Jewish believers. One problem is that it is often hard to separate cultural from religious expressions. For an Orthodox Jew, celebrating Passover is a fulfilment of divine command, and is done in accordance with the accretions of 2,000 years of rabbinic tradition and rabbinic law. For a Reform or secular Jew, celebrating Passover is often simply an opportunity to enjoy doing something Jewish: having a get-together with the family, going though a few traditions familiar from childhood and sharing a meal. Is Passover then a cultural expression or a religious one? Similar questions arise pertaining to other aspects of Judaism, because Judaism today is not a monolith when it comes to religious and cultural expression.[135]

Whilst the *haggadah* is replete with symbolic elements open to Messianic interpretation,[136] it is with the tradition of the *afikoman* that a distinct Christological interpretation becomes the key to the understanding of the connection between the sacred meal in Judaism and the Christian Last Supper and Holy Communion.

> The breaking of the middle *matzah* and the wrapping of the middle *matzah* and the hiding it away represents death. Death is separation. Physical death is a

---

[134] Feher, *Passing Over Easter*, 20.

[135] Robinson, *Fieldguide to the Messianic Movement*, 102–03.

[136] See Feher, chapter 1, 'Exodus and Communion,' 13–24, for analysis of the Seder service as celebrated by Messianic Jews, and the Seder as 'metaphor' for Messianic Judaism (14–24, 'The Seder as Metaphor'). For the influence of Christianity on the development of the Passover liturgy see Israel Jacob Yuval, *Two Nations in Your Womb: Perceptions of Jews and Christians in Late Antiquity and the Middle Ages* (Berkeley: University of California Press, 2006), 68–91; 205–56. Yuval demonstrates that celebration of the Christian Mass had a significant influence on the construction of the Passover Seder, particularly in the symbolism of the *afikoman*. Messianic Judaism detects and exploits these influences, although Yuval's scholarship has yet to be appropriated by Messianic Jews.

separation of the material part of man from the immaterial, the flesh from the soul and the spirit. Spiritual death is eternal separation from God. The Bible tells us that the wages of sin is death – that it was through Adam that death came upon mankind. As long as the *matzah* remained hidden it symbolised that death reigned. But when the broken *matzah* was found and returned it symbolised life and resurrection.

The origin of the broken *matzah* is unclear, but many scholars believe it was instituted by Yeshua (Jesus) Himself at his last Passover. Even the tradition of the word '*Afikoman*' is lost in antiquity. Jewish tradition says that it means 'dessert.' However, other scholars believe it comes from a root word meaning 'I have come.'

Is it not significant that it is this middle *matzah*, which was broken and then hid away, finally to be brought back, broken and distributed, that Jesus points to and says, 'this is MY body which is given for you'? Is it not significant that '*Afikoman*' means – 'I have come'?[137]

With such strong Christological statements concerning the *afikoman*, the focus of this section will be on its interpretation in Messianic Judaism.[138]

The *Afikoman* Not Inspired (Maoz)

Maoz objects to the use of Christian symbolism in Messianic Jewish celebrations of Passover. 'A further example is the now popular attribution of Christian symbolism to purely rabbinic custom, such as certain features in the Passover Seder. The rabbis who invented the *afikoman*, for example, were not inspired by the Spirit when they did so and Messiah is not hidden in the *afikoman*.'[139]

David Stern's unbelievable insistence that many scholars believe that these customs were started by Messianic Jews and invested with the meanings we have noted here, but somehow the customs were absorbed into non-Messianic Judaism (*Manifesto*, p. 171) is wholly contrary to fact. There are no such scholars and there are no grounds for such an assertion except wishful thinking and a certain

---

[137] Harold A. Sevener, ed., *Messianic Passover Haggadah* (Charlotte, NC: Chosen People Ministries, n.d.), 36–37, quoted in Wasserman, *Messianic Jewish Congregations*, 95.

[138] The number of Messianic Jewish Passover *Haggadot* available is too great to quantify. Each Messianic ministry and organisation produces its own version. Examples are: Janie-Sue Wertheim (ed.), *Messianic Family Haggadah* (San Francisco: Purple Pomegranate Productions, 2007); Barry Rubin and Steffi Rubin, *The Messianic Passover Haggadah* (Baltimore: Lederer Messianic Publications, 1990).

[139] Maoz, *Judaism Is Not Jewish*, 174.

(welcome) discomfort with the attribution of Christological intimations to a central Jewish tradition.[140]

Maoz is so concerned to distance the traditional Jewish Passover from any Christian associations that he goes as far as denying that *any* scholars suggest that Jewish believers in Jesus may have influenced the development of rabbinic Passover customs. However, in this he goes too far.[141] Critiquing Kasdan's reading of the Seder, he states:

> Again, Barney Kasdan writes in *Passover and the Feast of Unleavened Bread* … that there are 'spiritual lessons' to be found in the rabbinic traditions surrounding the Passover feast. 'These customs may seem strange to the uninitiated but the deep spiritual truth will be evident to discerning believers in Yeshua.' (*Messianic Jewish Life*, Vol. LXXII, No. 2, p. 6). Discerning believers and Orthodox Jews alike know this not to be true.[142]

Maoz denies the possibility of any Messianic Jewish interpretation of the rabbinic material of the traditional haggadah, seeking to drive a wedge between traditional Jewish practice, and Christian affirmation of the Messianic claims of Jesus.

Lamb, not Chicken (Fruchtenbaum)

Arnold Fruchtenbaum chides Messianic Jews for not being sufficiently biblical.

> The simple fact is this: Regardless of whether they claim to be 'Torah positive' or 'Torah observant,' no one really keeps the Torah the way Moses actually required it to be kept. Even the most zealous 'Torah observant' Messianic Jews, while teaching [L]aw, are actually practicing grace. For example, they would require Messianic Jews to keep the Passover. On what basis must we keep the Passover? Their answer is, because Moses said so. What else did Moses say? For one thing, he said that Passover is not to be observed at home, but 'in the place [God] will choose as a dwelling for his name' (Deut 16:6), which ultimately became Jerusalem. If there is any Messianic Jew who celebrates Passover … at home or in the country where he lives … he is not observing the Torah but is practicing grace. Grace permits a Messianic Jew to observe Passover anywhere.[143]

---

[140] Maoz, *Judaism Is Not Jewish*, 174–75.

[141] On the *Afikoman* as a Messianic symbolic incorporated into the Haggadah due to the influence of Jewish Christians, see David Daube, *He That Cometh*, (London: Council for Jewish Christian Understanding, 1966); Yuval, *Two Nations*, 205–56.

[142] Maoz, *Judaism Is Not Jewish*, 175.

[143] Fruchtenbaum, 'Messianic Congregations,' 123.

Fruchtenbaum's literalist exegesis does not take into account the fact that for other Messianic Jews the 'Torah' includes rabbinic tradition (of which the haggadah is a product) and is not merely the Mosaic covenant, which he, as a Dispensationalist, believes is now inoperative. He continues:

> Furthermore, at every Messianic Jewish *seder* I have ever attended (except my own) the main course was roasted chicken. But what does the Torah require as the main course for Passover? Roasted lamb. This is what I serve in my own *seder* at home. Messianic Jews choose to serve chicken because this is what Ashkenazi rabbis required. This is *not* being Torah observant. Once again, they are preaching [L]aw while practicing grace, because grace allows you to serve any type of meat at Passover.[144]

Fruchtenbaum's point about lamb rather than chicken, (which unintentionally follows the North African Sephardic menu), concerns the relationship between the Mosaic and the New Covenant. Passover, for Fruchtenbaum, is celebrated in the light of the New Covenant. The Mosaic covenant has no more than symbolic value. Likewise the haggadah of Rabbinic Judaism is also not sufficiently Christ-centred to be used, and Messianic Jews must construct their own haggadah. Fruchtenbaum's own version omits the rabbinic material, focusing on the biblical passages from the Hebrew Bible and New Testament, with emphasis on the New Covenant communion service.[145]

The 'Biblical *Pesach*' (Nerel)

Gershon Nerel calls for the celebration of the 'biblical *Pesach*'. It is not acceptable to use the traditional rabbinic format of the service, as the focus should be on the biblical material without the interpretive matrix of Jewish tradition imposed on it. Whilst Nerel sees Passover as '*the* major Messianic feast', it should not have as its focus the reading of the traditional haggadah. Whilst it is significant to remember Israel's redemption from Egypt, it is 'even more important to remember the redemption through Yeshua from the bondage of sin'. Therefore 'the *Pesach* should primarily be a reminder of the Last Supper of Yeshua and his command to commemorate his death and resurrection.'[146] Because 'time-management' is important when there are young children present 'thus the *Pesach* ceremony must not relate to marginal issues considered important by tradition, such as reading of lengthy portions from the Talmud or singing Aramaic songs like *Had Gadya* (meaning 'An Only Kid'), hardly understood by children.'[147]

---

[144] Ibid., 123–24.

[145] Arnold Fruchtenbaum, *A Passover Haggadah for Jewish Believers* 5th ed. (Tustin, CA: Ariel Ministries, 1991).

[146] Nerel, 'Torah and *Halakhah*,' 160.

[147] Ibid.

For Nerel the service should be stripped of Jewish traditional elements that are not fully in accord with his own reading of scripture, particularly the New Testament focus on the crucifixion, death and resurrection of Yeshua. He does not recognise any theological significance or powers of narration of the traditional Haggadah which are not firmly rooted in the biblical texts themselves.

> In other words, as JBY celebrate *Pesach*, it is sufficient to use only the relevant texts from Scripture. For example, such texts are clearly found in Exodus 12, where the connection is quite clear between the blood of each Passover lamb on each Jewish home and the death of Messiah. Here, with the blood of the lamb on the lintel and the two doorposts of each house, one can also observe the symbol of the cross. Another text may relate to the fulfilment of Isaiah 53. Eventually, the whole celebration should be connected with the Lord's Supper, reminding the people of Yeshua's victory over sin.[148]

Joyous Celebration Without Legalism (Juster)

Juster notes four 'salient facts' about Passover. Firstly, the sacrifice of the Passover lamb is used in the New Testament as the basis for understanding the death of Yeshua.[149] Yeshua is the lamb who was slain (1 Cor. 5:7), and this passage commands the purging of the 'leaven of malice and wickedness' as a parallel to the cleansing of leaven from the home. Second, the feeding of the Israelites with manna in the wilderness is linked to the feeding of the 5,000 Israelites who ate the loaves which were 'multiplied by the supernatural power of God in Yeshua' (John 6).[150] Thirdly, the early believers, both Jew and non-Jew, celebrated Yeshua's resurrection on Passover, seeing him as the replacement for the sacrifice of the paschal lamb. And fourthly, Yeshua's taking of the third cup (the cup of redemption) and the *afikoman* to symbolise his broken body and shed blood showed the disciples how to make the Passover meal a 'pointer to His redemption and a participation in its power and meaning'.[151]

Therefore Messianic Jews rejoice with their people for their deliverance from Egyptian bondage, and incorporate 'all of the meanings of Yeshua's life in us' in their celebration. All of the sacrificial images which were part of Passover can be seen in Him. For Juster Passover is a 'great celebration of God's grace in both Old and New Testament times'. No-one should be prevented from attending, as 'the proscription of guests who are not circumcised at the meal is not applicable to any believer who is clean (circumcised

---

[148] Ibid.
[149] Juster, *Jewish Roots*, 200.
[150] Ibid., 201.
[151] Ibid.

in heart) in Yeshua (Acts 10). 'There is no legalism involved in this joyous celebration.'[152]

Redemption Typified (Kasdan)

For Barney Kasdan Passover illustrates both the past, present and future redemption of the Jewish people. 'Passover clearly typifies redemption in a dramatic way. It is a holy day commemorating God's deliverance of Israel from the slavery of Egypt. Yet Pesach also holds a greater prophetic picture of God's plan for world redemption.'[153] Kasdan describes the historical background and traditional Jewish observance of Passover, adding Messianic interpretation to the symbols and activities.

> A particularly intriguing element incorporated by rabbis is called the *matzah tash*. This is a linen pouch or plate with three different sections. A piece of *matzah* is placed within each section, individually set apart yet united in the one container. Rabbinic commentaries don't give the exact origin of this custom. They speculate that the *matzah tash* represents unity – perhaps the unity of the people of Israel through the forefathers (Abraham, Isaac and Jacob) or the unity of the families of Israel (Aaron, the Levites, the common people).[154]

Kasdan allows his readers to draw their own Trinitarian interpretation of the *matzah tash* as he unfolds the meaning of the middle *matzah*.

> During the first part of the seder, the middle piece of *matzah* is taken out and broken in half. Half of the *matzah* is placed back in the *matzah tash*. The other half is wrapped in a napkin and hidden somewhere in the room by the leader of the seder. The hidden *matzah* is called the *afikoman*, a Greek word meaning 'that which comes last.' Rabbis say it alludes to the fact that the *afikoman* is the last thing tasted at the seder, the dessert. Others have suggested the translation 'he will come again.' This sense of the word has much meaning to the Messianic believer since it pictures the resurrection and return of the Messiah.[155]

Kasdan's association of the *afikoman* with the Messiah is clear, leading to a Trinitarian reading of the three-fold matzah pouch as representing the unity of God as Father, Son and Holy Spirit. That Jesus took the *afikoman* and used it to refer to his offering of himself (Matt. 26:6) as he instituted communion at the Last Supper is also clear. He is the Bread of Life (John 6), unaffected by

---

[152] Ibid., 202.
[153] Kasdan, *God's Appointed Times*, 26.
[154] Ibid., 27.
[155] Ibid., 28.

the leaven of sin, and also the bread of affliction, in that as the suffering Messiah he was pierced and striped, as is the *matzah*, for the sins of the world.[156]

Misuse of Jewish Sancta? (Stern)

Stern is aware of the controversy that arises from Messianic celebration of the Passover with a Christological interpretation. 'Messianic Jews are accused by some in the Jewish community of "misusing Jewish sancta"... I said the sancta are ours to use, since we are Jews too; but they are not ours to misuse out of ignorance, nor are they ours to use to put on a show with; rather they are ours with which to express and enhance our Messianic faith.'[157] Nevertheless Messianic Jews are fully justified in their celebration of Passover from a Messianic perspective.

> So if we use the found half of the *afikoman* and the third cup of the Passover *Seder* for communion, non-Messianic Jews may object; but we can defend ourselves on the ground that this is what the Messiah did. If we point out that the three *matzot* represent Father, Son and Holy Spirit, and that the broken middle *matzah* represents Yeshua's body, broken for us, we have theological grounds for what we do. In fact, many scholars believe that these customs were started by Messianic Jews and invested with the meanings we have noted here, but somehow the customs were absorbed into non-Messianic Judaism and stripped of their Messianic significance.[158]

Certain general principles of contextualisation should be employed. 'It would be wise for us to make such modifications only after much thought and prayer. For we are dealing with ceremonies weighted with intellectual, emotional and spiritual meaning. *Ad hoc* changes are likely to prove tasteless, offensive, theologically erroneous, or all three.'[159]

Stern deals further with the accusation of misuse of 'Jewish sancta'.

> The fourth aspect concerns 'Christianizing' Jewish *sancta*. That is, for example, revising the Passover *Haggadah* so that the *afikoman* and the lamb shank refer to the Messiah, the third cup to communion, the deliverance from Egypt to the believer's deliverance from sin through the sacrifice of the Messiah, and so on. My answer is based first on the fact that Yeshua not only used Jewish *sancta* but often endowed them with new significance. Also, since they are part of the heritage of

---

[156] Ibid., 28–30.
[157] Stern, *Messianic Jewish Manifesto*, 171.
[158] Ibid.
[159] Ibid., 172.

Messianic as well as non-Messianic Jews, we have the right to invest them with meanings conforming to the truth of God as expressed in the New Testament – indeed, I would say we have more right than non-Messianic Jews have to exclude that truth.[160]

Stern thus calls for care and sensitivity in the adaptation and reinterpretation of traditional Jewish symbols.

Messianic Judaism in its present experimentalism, is introducing New Testament meanings in various ways. For example, there are a number of Messianic versions of the *b'rit milah* ceremony and literally dozens of *Haggadot* for Passover. The one thing one might ask from all these experimenters is that they increase their knowledge of Judaism and of the New Testament's Jewish background, so that the revisions they make will draw deeply from the heart of the materials they are working with and not be merely superficial adjustments. There are signs that those concerned with Messianic Jewish liturgy are taking their task with increasing seriousness.[161]

The use of Passover symbols, especially the *afikoman*, to represent Messianic affirmations about Yeshua, provide Messianic Jews with a rich opportunity for material illustrative of their beliefs. Israel Yuval's insights into the mutual influence of Christian and Jewish practice have yet to be integrated into Messianic thought, but the connections are already clear.[162]

Conclusion

Daniel Juster reflects the controversial nature of the place and manner of Messianic Jewish practice.

During the last several years an undercurrent of disagreement concerning the place of Jewish ritual has existed among Messianic Jews. On the mild side the disagreement is expressed in non-judgemental terms – 'The Spirit of God has led us to include (or exclude) these traditional rituals as part of our life and worship expression.' The more radical opinion is sometimes voiced that ritual is idolatry.[163]

---

[160]　Stern, *JNTC*, 504–5.

[161]　Ibid., 505.

[162]　Yuval, *Two Nations in Your Womb*, ch. 5, 'Inverted Ceremonies: The Host, The Matzah, and the Quarrel,' 205–56.

[163]　Daniel C. Juster, *Jewish Roots: A Foundation of Biblical Theology for Messianic Judaism.* (Rockville, MD: Davar Publishing, 1986), 299.

This chapter has surveyed three examples of the Torah in practice, and identified a variety of Messianic approaches. Whilst there is general agreement on the significance and celebration of the Passover, there is a considerable diversity of practice. With Sabbath and *kashrut* the different ways of observance are more easily traced to the theological assumptions behind such practice. Baruch Maoz is deeply suspicious of any 'religious' elements that come from rabbinic Judaism. Arnold Fruchtenbaum allows some rabbinic and traditional elements, as long as they are 'biblical'. Gershon Nerel calls for a biblical observance of Sabbath and *kashrut*, but without rabbinic encumbrances.

Barney Kasdan, Daniel Juster and David Stern are more relaxed in the application of rabbinic observances, allowing a New Testament Halachic Approach to control the permissibility of rabbinic custom in the light of their freedom in the Messiah to celebrate the fulfilment of Jewish life. John Fischer, Mark Kinzer and the MJRC, working within the parameters of the Conservative Judaism, identify with what they see as the normative influence of the Jewish community in defining practice.

The variety and diversity of Messianic Jewish practice observed in relation to Sabbath and *kashrut* is to be found in every area of Messianic Jewish life. Such pluralism of practice and interpretation reflects the Jewish and Christian influences in the Messianic Jewish movement. The Diaspora nature of much of the movement emphasises the religious expression of Judaism as a means of cultural identification, whereas in the Land of Israel the majority of Israeli Messianic Jews do not need to assert their 'Jewishness' in such 'religious' ways, and react against the Orthodox influence.

Practical application of the Torah includes adoption without change, various degrees of adaptation and, in some cases, complete abandonment. Whilst there is a basic agreement that the Torah should be lived out in practice, there is no consensus on how this should be done. For the formation of a Messianic Jewish theological tradition that encompasses practical expression of faith, further examination is needed of the methods and assumptions behind the formation of Messianic *halacha*. In the concluding chapter the pluralism of interpretive approaches and practical applications of Torah will be further classified and characterised.

Messianic Jewish practice is influenced by the various approaches to Torah found within Judaism and the variety of attitudes to 'Law' found within Christianity. Two attitudes to 'Law' are in competition here, that of Orthodox Judaism which tends to conservatism in matters of *halacha*, and that of a certain type of evangelical Christianity which reacts against such a view, proclaiming 'grace' rather than 'works'. Most Messianic Jews have not yet evolved a coherently articulated and well-reflected position, but find themselves somewhere between the two extremes.

It is unlikely that conformity of practice will develop, or a Messianic *minhag* emerge, until the theological debates on the nature and authority of Torah have been clarified and some conclusions drawn that win the approval of a substantial section of the movement. At present the views of Kasdan, Juster and Stern would appear to have the most popular appeal. But the dynamics of demographic, generational and geographical changes in the constitution of the Messianic Jewish movement worldwide may influence the movement in the directions of either greater 'orthopraxy', or less concern with observance, or continuing the flexibility and diversity of practice that characterise it at present.

Chapter 8

The Future of Israel

Introduction

> A Messianic Jew who lives in Israel often sees his [sic] presence in that land as both fulfilment of prophecy and as an eschatological sign. The Messianic Jew's identity is integrally related to being part of the Jewish people who have returned to the Promised Land to fulfil their final destiny.[1]

The present chapter focuses on the pressing theological question of the place of Israel in prophecy, and the practical implications this has for them.[2] Messianic Jews are deeply concerned for the future of Israel and thus eschatology is a topic of much speculation. Dan Juster notes: 'In the charismatic world and to a lesser extent in the messianic Jewish world, an ungodly war rages over these issues.'[3]

Discussion of Israel combines politics and identity, hermeneutics and recent history. The movement exhibits a breadth and variety of views reflecting those found in the wider Jewish and Christian communities within which, and in response to which, Messianic Judaism develops and

---

[1] Lisa Loden, 'Messianic Jewish Views of Israel's Rebirth and Survival in the Light of Scripture,' (paper presented at Director's Conference: Christian Perspectives on the Israeli-Palestinian Conflict, International Baptist Theological Seminary, Prague, Czech Republic, November 14, 2006), 1.

[2] The third main subject area of Jewish theology, 'Israel', incorporates several sub-topics which should be included in a comprehensive MJT. These include: the nature, definition and identity of the Jewish people; the inter-relationship of Land, State and people; conversion to Judaism and Messianic Judaism; Messianic Judaism's mission to Israel, and Israel's mission to the nations; the relationship between religion, society and politics; and the relationship of the Church to Israel. These are beyond the scope of the present study. *Voices of Messianic Judaism*, edited by Dan Cohn-Sherbok (Baltimore: Lederer, 2001) includes several essays on these topics.

[3] Dan Juster and Keith Intrater, *Israel, the Church and the Last Days* (Shippensburg, PA: Destiny Image Publishers, 2003), 70.

articulates its theology. There is general agreement that the present and future of Israel has great theological significance, but no clear consensus. Lisa Loden observes:

> There are ... a small number of issues on which the vast majority of Messianic Jews find themselves substantially in agreement. This is the case with the subject of this paper ['Messianic Jewish Views of Israel's Rebirth and Survival in the Light of Scripture']. Although some of the positions held are more nuanced than others, the general trajectory is that the rebirth of Israel as a nation and her subsequent survival, have come about and will continue by divine intervention in history.[4]

To understand how Messianic Jews construct their 'Israelology',[5] familiarity with the main Christian eschatological schemes is needed. They influence Messianic understanding by providing conceptual schemes used by Messianic Jews to develop a self-understanding of the eschatological significance of the Jewish people and Messianic Jews in particular. Whereas Christians have looked *at* Israel, Messianic Jews see themselves as part *of* Israel, and their understanding of prophecy impacts them personally as part of the Remnant (Rom. 9–11). Dispensational Premillennialism, Historic Premillennialism and Amillennialism are the main influences on Messianic Jewish eschatologies.[6] In addition, but with less impact, are deliberate agnosticism, Jewish eschatological thinking and the more complex eschatologies of Karl Barth and Jürgen Moltmann.[7]

Discussion is often based around the millennium, the thousand-year reign of the Messiah with the resurrected martyrs.[8] This is an intermediate period between the destruction of the present age that is evil and ruled by Satan, and the creation of new heavens and earth in an eternal age. The

---

[4] Lisa Loden, 'Messianic Jewish Views', 1.

[5] Arnold Fruchtenbaum, *Israelology: The Missing Link in Systematic Theology*, 2nd ed. (Tustin, CA: Ariel Ministries Press, 1993), 2. 'The term refers to a subdivision of Systematic Theology incorporating all theological doctrines concerning the people of Israel.'

[6] A detailed survey of Christian Eschatology is beyond the purposes of this dissertation. For a survey of the history of Eschatology see Robert Doyle, *Eschatology and the Shape of Christian Belief* (Carlisle: Paternoster, 1998).

[7] For Karl Barth's eschatology of Israel see Mark R. Lindsay, *Barth, Israel and Jesus: Karl Barth's Theology of Israel* (Aldershot: Ashgate, 2007). For Jürgen Moltmann, *The Coming of God: Christian Eschatology*, trans. Margaret Kohl (London: SCM Press, 1996); Richard Bauckham, 'Must Christian Eschatology Be Millenarian? A Response to Jürgen Moltmann' in *'The Reader Must Understand': Eschatology in Bible and Theology*, eds. K.E. Brewer and M.W. Elliott (Leicester: Apollos, 1997), 263–78.

[8] Rev 20:4. Robert Clouse, ed., *The Meaning of the Millennium: Four Views* (Downers Grove, IL: InterVarsity Press, 1977).

millennium combines the prophetic ideal of a Messianic kingdom with a range of apocalyptic features. The major question in the history of interpretation of the millennium has been whether it should be understood literally or figuratively. Dispensational and Historic Premillennialists understand it 'literally', and then concern themselves with the issues raised; the timetable and scenarios leading up to the millennium; the present state of the world, the church and the Jewish people. Amillennialists understand the millennium symbolically, although there is no consensus as to how the biblical material should be interpreted.

Dispensational Premillennialism

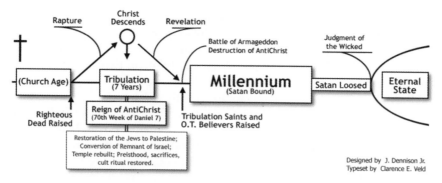

Figure 1 Dispensational Premillennialism[9]

Dispensational Premillennialism (figure 1) reads the biblical material with a 'literal hermeneutic' based on the teachings of J.N. Darby and the Scofield Reference Bible.[10] According to Ryrie the threefold '*sine qua non* of dispensationalism' is that:

(1) A dispensationalist keeps Israel and the Church distinct … the basic premise of Dispensationalism is two purposes of God expressed in the formation of two peoples who maintain their distinction through eternity …
(2) This distinction between Israel and the Church is born out of a system of hermeneutics which is usually called literal interpretation … the word

---

[9] James T. Dennison, 'Dispensational Premillennialism,' http://blueletterbible.org/faq/dispre.html (accessed October 20, 2007).
[10] Charles Ryrie, *Dispensationalism Today* (Chicago: Moody Press, 1965); Stephen R. Sizer, 'Dispensational Approaches to the Land' in *The Land of Promise: Biblical, Contemporary and Theological Approaches*, eds. Philip Johnston and Peter Walker (Leicester: Apollos, 2000), 142–71.

literal is perhaps not so good as either the word *normal* or *plain*, but in any case it is interpretation that does not spiritualize or allegorize as nondispensational interpretation does ...

(3) A third aspect ... concerns the underlying purpose of God. The covenant theologian in practice makes this purpose salvation, and the dispensationalist says the purpose is broader than that, namely, the glory of God. To the dispensationalist the soteriological or saving program of God is not the only program but one means God is using in the total program of glorifying Himself. scripture is not man-centred as though salvation were the main theme, but it is God-centred because His glory is the centre.[11]

Baruch Maoz summarises the distinctive features of *Dispensational* Premillennialism as the way in which they develop the standard premillennial idea that Jesus will return before the establishment of a millennial kingdom. Dispensationalists believe that Jesus' return will be in two stages: 'First he will descend to the air, dead believers will be raised (the first resurrection) and they, with the living believers then on earth, will be taken up to meet the Lord in the air (raptured) and then return with him to the earth, there to reign. The bodies of the dead will be glorified, made spiritual and united with their spirits.'[12] Then follows the establishment of a physical kingdom on earth in which Jesus is physically present and reigning from Jerusalem. This is the Kingdom of God on earth, and in the course of Jesus' 1000-year reign Satan is bound.

Before the kingdom is established a very large number of Jews will be brought to faith in Jesus, and they will preach the gospel to the world. Israel's restored political reality will also become the world centre for a restored Temple and Temple worship, including sacrifices. During this reign of peace carnivores will become herbivores, wars will cease, and universal peace will prevail. At the end of this time Satan will be released and will deceive the nations into a rebellion, which will be 'quashed by divine intervention'. Finally, 'the faithful will be raised to eternal life (the second resurrection). The sinful dead will be raised to judgment. A new heavens and a new earth will be created. Sin will be banished forever. Satan, his angels and all sinners will be cast into the eternal pit, which is the second death. The redeemed will enjoy the eternal presence of God and the eternal state will thereby be ushered.'[13]

---

[11] Ryrie, *Dispensationalism Today*, 44–46.

[12] Baruch Maoz, 'A Review of Premillennialism' (paper presented to the Elders of Grace and Truth Christian Congregation, Rehovot, December 2003), 4.

[13] Ibid., 4–5. 'All premillennial schemes believe in a time of persecution of the Church that is to precede the Millennium. They differ strongly as to whether the coming of Christ and the resurrection of believers precede the great persecution (pre-

The hermeneutics of Dispensationalism are criticised by some Messianic Jews, but they acknowledge its role in preserving an interest in the literal Israel (the Land and the Jewish people) in Christian circles, and as the major theological influence in Christian Zionism. Messianic Jews are also grateful for the Dispensationalist emphasis on the expectation of imminent fulfillment of God's purposes for Israel. Although they may not agree with all aspects of the conceptual schema, they approve of the place given to the restoration of Israel in Dispensationalist thinking as a healthy reaction and corrective to the 'replacement theology' they discern in much Covenant theology.

Historic Premillennialism

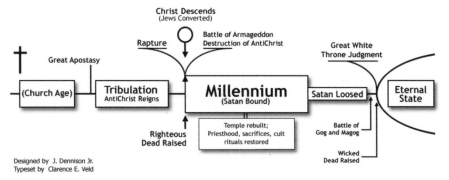

Figure 2 Historic Premillennialism[14]

Historic Premillennialism (figure 2), the earlier form of Premillennialism held by the early church fathers Papias, Irenaeus and the early Augustine, reappeared in the chiliasm of Joachim de Fiore and in the writings of Charles Spurgeon, D.L. Moody and George Eldon Ladd.[15] The historic

tribulationist rapture), occurs in the course of it (mid-tribulationist rapture) or follows it (post-tribulationist rapture). Some versions of Premillennialism draw a clear distinction between Israel and the Church in the sense that their destinies differ. Jewish believers until the coming of Christ are part of the Church. Jewish believers who live following the coming of Christ are to be part of Israel. Our discussion is not affected by these differences of opinion but it is worth noting that these are distinctive features of Dispensational Premillennialism'. Early Church Historic premillennialists such as Irenaeus did not discuss what modern pre-millennialists call the rapture. I am indebted to Father Peter Hocken for this observation.

[14] James T. Dennison, 'Historic Premillennialism,' http://blueletterbible.org/faq/hispre.html (accessed October 20, 2007).

[15] George Elton Ladd, *The Last Things* (Grand Rapids: William B. Eerdmans, 1982); *The Gospel of the Kingdom* (Grand Rapids: William B. Eerdmans, 1981).

premillennialist position holds to a literal millennium, and hence a physical restoration of the Jewish people to the Land of Israel in some way related to their spiritual restoration through recognition of Jesus as Messiah. But the Historic Premillennialist avoids the systematisation of this position found in Dispensationalism.[16] Messianic Jews are attracted to this position as it appears to avoid the excessive systematisation in Dispensationalism, does not rigidly separate the Church and Israel as two peoples of God, and is more cautious about the timetabling of future events. Daniel Juster advocates this eschatological system as midway between Dispensationalism and Covenant theology.

Postmillennialism

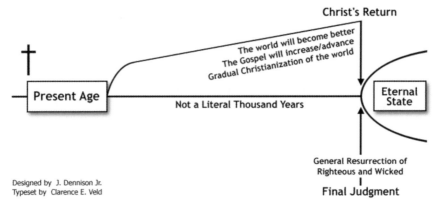

Figure 3 Postmillennialism[17]

---

[16] Alistair McGrath, *Christian Theology: An Introduction*, 3rd ed. (Blackwell: Oxford, 2001), ch. 18, 'The Last Things: The Christian Hope', 552–77. Peter Hocken comments: 'When you say that "the historic premillennialist position holds to a literal millennium, and hence a physical restoration of the Jewish people to the land of Israel in some way related to their spiritual restoration through recognition of Jesus as Messiah", this is no doubt true of today's Evangelical pre-millennialists, but is very misleading concerning the early church fathers. Irenaeus for example believes in the return of Israel to the land after the resurrection. It is a totally different thought world to the modern Evangelical. What this really suggests to me is that the phrase "historic premillennialism" is itself problematic. It has been coined by Evangelicals repudiating Dispensationalism to give their position an historical pedigree, but they probably haven't really studied the early church fathers!' (email correspondence with author, January 10th 2009).

[17] James T. Dennison, 'Postmillennialism,' http://blueletterbible.org/faq/post.html (accessed October 20, 2007).

Postmillennialism (figure 3) interprets the millennium symbolically as already begun through the coming of the Messiah and the inauguration of the Church. A period of unprecedented revival will take place before the Messiah's return. The Church will be characterised by unusual spiritual vitality and will grow numerically. Israel will turn back to the Messiah towards the close of the period, during which the world will experience peace and economic improvement until Jesus' return. During this millennial period, Christian values and principles will dominate, but not every person will become Christian. There will be a brief time of apostasy (particularly of nominal Christians) when the Man of Lawlessness is revealed, but this will be brought to an end through the return of Christ.

Postmillennialism emphasises the victorious reign of Christ in the Church and the world, actively extending the kingdom of God in this world through the power of the Word and the Holy Spirit. It also recognises the power of God to change the world in many of its key areas.[18] Owing to its triumphalist nature in proclaiming the dominion of the Church as the kingdom of God on earth, this view has fallen out of popularity in recent years, and few hold it within the Messianic movement, as it sees the Church as the New Israel.

Amillennialism

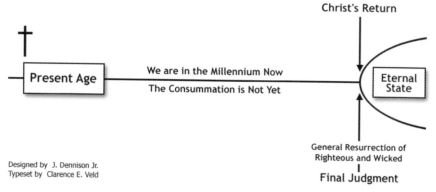

Figure 4 Amillennialism[19]

Amillennialism (figure 4) holds that the symbolic Millennium began with the first coming of the Messiah and will end with his return. Satan is bound by the death of Christ; the souls of dead believers are now alive with Him in heaven. The resurrection of believers and unbelievers will take place at

---

[18] Key biblical passages referred to in Postmillennialism are Pss 2; 22; 72; 110; Is. 2:2–4; Matt. 28:18; Eph. 1:19–23.

[19] James T. Dennison, 'Amillennialism,' http://blueletterbible.org/faq/nunc.html (accessed October 20, 2007).

Christ's return, at which time also the Last Judgment will take place and there will be a new creation. Augustine, Aquinas, Calvin, the Puritans and Charles Hodge held this view. Some Puritans were amillennialists who also believed in the restoration of Israel. Some contemporary amillennialists, such as John Stott, Colin Chapman and Stephen Sizer, see no future for literal Israel, whereas others, like Errol Hulse and Richard de Ridder, do not rule this out. This stream influences Baruch Maoz and Rich Nichol.

Previous Studies of Messianic Jewish Eschatology

Bodil Skjøtt surveyed Israeli Messianic Jewish beliefs on the Land of Israel.[20] Ninety-four Messianic Jews of mixed age, gender and education living in Jerusalem, the West Bank, and throughout Israel were asked a series of questions to ascertain their views on what the Bible teaches about the Land and the Jewish people; the significance of the return of the Jews to the Land; its proper boundaries; how Messianic Jews should relate to Palestinian Christians; and how Messianic Jews relate to the Palestinian people and their demand for a State. Whilst small, the survey sample represents a significant proportion of Messianic Jews in the land.[21]

Skjøtt found that the majority of respondents believe that the biblical promises of the Land apply to the Jewish people forever.[22] However, whilst 95 per cent understood that the Bible clearly promised the Land to the Jewish people, only 20 per cent saw this as an essential part of the teaching of Jesus. Only one in five saw the message of the gospel as incomplete without a clear statement of the right of the Jewish people to the Land. Whilst the eternal validity of the promises of the Land to the Jewish people was accepted by 90 per cent, it was not regarded as an essential element of the gospel.

The majority of respondents saw the return of the Jews to the Land as the fulfilment of God's promises, and understood Zionism not just 'as a secular movement but rather as a necessary instrument in the fulfilment of prophecies and in God's programme to bring the Jewish people to faith in Jesus'.[23] However, this percentage varied amongst male and female respondents (72 percent and 62 per cent respectively) and only 57 per cent believed that

---

[20] Bodil Skjøtt, 'Messianic Believers and the Land of Israel – a Survey,' *Mishkan* 26, no. 1 (1997): 72–81.

[21] According to Kai Kjær-Hansen and Bodil F. Skjøtt, *Facts and Myths about the Messianic Congregations in Israel,* Mishkan Double Issue 30–31 (Jerusalem: United Christian Council in Israel/Caspari Centre for Biblical and Jewish Studies), 94 respondents represents 3 per cent of Israel's Messianic Jewish congregational members.

[22] Skjøtt, 'Messianic Believers,' 75.

[23] Ibid., 76.

the Jewish people would never again be exiled from the Land, with one in 12 disagreeing with the statement, and a third unsure.

As regards the ideal boundaries of the modern State of Israel, 76 percent saw Judea and Samaria (the Occupied Territories) as included. 59 percent included the Golan Heights, and a surprising 49 percent believed areas to the east of the Jordan River should also be part of the State. Skjøtt suggests that this view is derived from the respondents' eschatological scheme that sees the boundaries of Israel in the 'last days' as extending beyond those of the present state, although only 50 percent believed that the Bible gives clearly defined borders. Skjøtt also suggests that most respondents, from the confused nature of their responses to this question, 'are not sure whether we are living in the last times'.[24]

As regards relationships with Palestinian Arab Christians, 94 percent thought that there should be more fellowship between Messianic Jews and Arab Christians, and 85 percent believed that developing this fellowship was more important than Land issues. On the political rights of the Palestinians, the majority of respondents believed that Palestinians living in the Land have as much rights as Jews to remain there, but nearly half the respondents did not wish to grant Palestinian refugees the right of return to the Land in which they or their family had once lived.[25]

The survey found areas of uncertainty amongst Messianic Jews, particularly regarding the borders of the Land and the right of Palestinians to return. These levels were higher amongst women and those under 35. The most agreement was found on the biblical teaching on the rights of the Jews to the Land, and on the need for fellowship with Palestinians. As Skjøtt wryly comments: 'Presumably, in order to achieve greater fellowship, someone is going to have to back down on the question of ownership of Judea and Samaria/West Bank.'[26]

Skjøtt interprets the results as showing that Messianic Jews inconsistently both support the peace process with a willingness to share the Land on one hand, whilst also maintaining the claim of ownership of the West Bank. Whilst the majority of Messianic Jews in the survey upheld the promises of the Land to the Jewish people as permanently valid, this did not necessarily affect whether they voted for a particular political party whose program was to hold on to all Land. Nor is it straightforward how the biblical promises of the Land are to be interpreted and applied in the contemporary situation. 'The certainty with which the Bible speaks is not easily translated into a clear understanding of the present political situation in which we all have to act and react.'[27]

---

[24] Ibid., 77.
[25] Ibid., 78.
[26] Ibid., 79.
[27] Ibid., 80.

Skjøtt concludes by noting that whilst respondents agreed that the teaching of the Bible on the Land was clear, they disagreed as to the importance of the Land in the teaching of Jesus. Messianic Jews could be taking this in one of two ways. Either its lack of prominence in the teaching of Jesus has little significance, as Jesus did not 'negate or nullify the promises,' or else the lack of importance it had to Jesus should lead his followers to 'look at the question through the teachings of Jesus and not put emphasis on issues that Jesus did not speak about, perhaps even avoided'.[28] Whilst Messianic Jews choose the first option, Skjøtt, whose aim in doing the survey was to 'provide a tool for positive and constructive self-evaluation' that would 'provide direction and inspiration' for the building up of the Messianic community in Israel, clearly implies that they should also consider the second.

Building on Skjøtt's findings, and anticipating future trends in the Messianic movement in Israel, Kai Kjær-Hansen observed continuing 'millennial fever' and a strengthening of right-wing political attitudes strongly tied to Dispensational Premillennialism.[29]

> I have to say that I consider the end-times fever – all other things being equal – much more dangerous and destructive for Jewish believers in Israel and for a sound development of the Messianic movement than, for example, a tightening of the anti-mission legislation or increased harassment, opposition or downright persecution of Jewish believers in Israel … Jewish believers in Israel would do themselves and the rest of us an enormous favour if they disassociated themselves from this day's speculative prophecy teachers![30]

Kjær-Hansen reviews the trend of eschatological speculation, recognising it as an unhelpful focus when it distracts from the practical realities of living in the Land, relating with other Messianic believers and engaging in the quest for peace, justice and reconciliation with the Palestinians. 'I also hope that the movement as such will not become so much involved in the eschatological drama of the future that it does not take the present challenges seriously.'[31]

---

[28] Ibid.

[29] Kai Kjær-Hansen, 'Upside-down for the sake of Yeshua: Challenges and pressures on Israeli Jewish believers in Jesus' (paper presented at the Seventeenth North American Consultation of the LCJE, Atlanta, March 13–15, 2000). http://www.lcje.net/papers/2000/LCJE-kai.pdf (accessed June 7, 2004).

[30] Ibid., 1.

[31] Ibid., 15.

Development of a Messianic Jewish Eschatology

Within the messianic movement itself the main Christian eschatological positions are adopted with little critical examination or development. As with Christian Zionism, the Dispensational Premillennialism predominant in North America is expressed in political support for Israel and the Zionist programme.[32] Joseph Rosenfarb notes this pattern in his chapter on eschatology:[33]

> It is difficult for many in the Messianic Jewish Movement to recognize how particular theologies impact on us. This is due to the pioneer nature of the movement, coupled with the relatively short history for plentiful Messianic Jewish congregations, in modern times. We have not had time and, in some cases, the ability to investigate how particular theologies have been absorbed and/or deflected.[34]
>
> Understanding where people are coming from in their view of eschatology will give us tremendous awareness if we accept the premise that a person's (group's) eschatology will determine their philosophy and method of ministry ... Thus, the need to understand people's theologies of the last days becomes both a theological and practical necessity.[35]

David Stern represents the majority opinion when arguing for the Jewish right to the Land and future expectation of deliverance, advocating a strong Zionist political position in the light of present day realities:

> In this I think I can safely claim to be speaking for virtually all Messianic Jews in Israel. Zechariah 12 and 14 proclaim the day when all nations will come against Jerusalem and the Lord (that is, the Messiah Yeshua) will fight and defeat them. The Jewish people will be saved as they recognize and mourn for their Messiah, 'whom they pierced' (Zech 12:10). He, the Messiah, will be standing on the Mount of Olives, 'with all his holy ones', repelling and defeating all the nations battling the Jews. And where will you be, O Christian? Will you be opposing the Jewish people as they defend their land? Or standing with Yeshua? There seems to be no other option.[36]

---

[32] Cf. Dan Cohn-Sherbok, *The Politics of Apocalypse: The History and Influence of Christian Zionism* (Oxford: Oneworld, 2006).

[33] Joseph Rosenfarb, 'Eschatology: Views Which Effect/Affect Messianic Jewish Philosophy of Ministry', in *Israel and the People of God* (Virginia Beach, VA: Kochav Publishing, 1989), 245–62.

[34] Ibid., 246.

[35] Ibid., 248.

[36] David Stern, 'Making the Issues Clear: The land from a Messianic Jewish Perspective' in *The Bible and the Land: An Encounter*, ed. Lisa Loden, Peter Walker, and Michael Wood (Jerusalem: Musalaha, 2000), 54.

Dan Cohn-Sherbok summarises the prevailing eschatological tendency in the North American side of the Messianic movement: 'Like the mainstream fundamentalist churches, many Messianic congregations are pre-tribulationist in orientation, holding to the view that all believers in Yeshua will be raptured at the beginning of the Great Tribulation.'[37] David Stern expresses the difficulty of the topic: 'Since so many of the biblical prophecies about the *acharit-hayamim* ('the end of days') involve the Jewish people, it is not surprising that there is intense excitement among many Messianic Jews awaiting their imminent fulfilment. Likewise, the arguments which can emerge between those who differ on the interpretation of these prophecies can be intense.'[38]

Messianic Jews have yet to realise the potential of their unique role in the various eschatological scenarios. They need to develop their thinking 'outside the box' of the inherited Christian schemes, and find their own tools, methods and resources for an eschatology which expresses their own perspective. The sections below survey four representative streams within the movement, viewed from the perspective of their acceptance of, and responses to, the influence of Dispensationalism.

Messianic Dispensationalism *(Fruchtenbaum)*

The most developed eschatology within the Messianic movement is that of Arnold Fruchtenbaum.[39] His views are modelled on the Dispensationalism of Charles Ryrie as taught in Dallas Theological Seminary where Fruchtenbaum studied, with additional details and variations developed by Fruchtenbaum himself. Whilst Fruchtenbaum's position is not without its critics, few have matched his depth of study of eschatology, and his positions may be taken as representative of the majority of Messianic Jews, and those who have written on the subject.[40] Fruchtenbaum pays particular

---

[37] Dan Cohn-Sherbok, *Messianic Judaism* (London: Cassell, 2000), 171.

[38] David H. Stern, *Messianic Manifesto* (Israel: JNTP, 1988) 119–20. Stern adds 'This book is not the place for me to enter the fray'.

[39] Arnold Fruchtenbaum, *Israelology: The Missing Link in Systematic Theology*, revised ed. (Tustin, CA: Ariel Ministries Press, 1993), *Footsteps of the Messiah: A Study of the Sequence of Prophetic Events* (Tustin, CA: Ariel Ministries Press, 1982); 'Eschatology and Messianic Jews: A Theological Perspective' in *Voices of Messianic Judaism*, ed. Dan Cohn-Sherbok (Baltimore, MA: Lederer, 2001), 211–19.

[40] See for example the articles in *Mishkan* 26:1 (Jerusalem: UCCI/Caspari Centre, 1997) on 'The Land', esp. Chaim Urbach, 'The Land of Israel in Scripture', 22–31; David Miller, 'Messianic Judaism and the Theology of the Land', 31–38; Louis Goldberg, 'The Borders of Israel according to Ezekiel', 44–48; Gershon Nerel, 'Zion in the Theology of L. Averbuch and S. Rohold', 64–71; Louis Goldberg, 'Israel and

attention to the role of Israel, which is the 'missing link' in systematic theology.

Dispensationalism's two 'sound hermeneutical principles' guide interpretation of prophecy.[41] The principle of literal interpretation means that the 'normal, plain sense is assumed rather than assuming a figurative, spiritual or allegorical meaning – unless the text itself reads otherwise.' Secondly, 'Israel' in the New Testament always applies to the Jewish people, not the Church.[42] From these two assumptions eschatology and 'Israelology' flow smoothly and programmatically, following the classic Dispensationalist sequence of tribulation, rapture, armageddon, millennium and eternal state (see Figure 1).

The present age, a 'parenthesis' in God's originally announced intention, will soon come to an end with the secret 'rapture' of believers to meet the (invisible) descending Messiah in the air. Dead believers will be resurrected and living believers will be transformed; they will return to heaven with him for the judgment seat of Messiah at which their deeds will be judged. Meanwhile on earth the last seven years of Dan. 9 begin. The leader of a ten-nation grouping will make a seven-year alliance with Israel; for three and a half years there will be peace, but Israel will then be attacked by this leader (usually identified with Russia). The attack will be supernaturally defeated but oppression will continue from a Middle-East dictator, who will eventually rule the world. However, he will be defeated in a great battle when the Messiah returns visibly. At the same time, the martyred dead from the tribulation period will be resurrected and will share in Christ's thousand-year reign on earth from Jerusalem.[43]

Messianic Jews are members of both the Church and Israel, and have a dual role in the unfolding of future events. As the believing remnant Messianic Jews represent the 'spiritual Israel' that has not failed in being faithful to the promises of God. By accepting Yeshua as Messiah, they hold a vital role that continues to the present: 'The present day Jewish believers in Yeshua, regardless of what title they go under (Messianic Jews, Jewish believers,

---

Prophecy' in *The Enduring Paradox: Exploratory Essays in Messianic Judaism*, ed. John Fischer (Baltimore MA: Lederer, 2000), 105–21. Also papers by David Stern, Menachem Benhayim and Joseph Shulam in *The Bible and the Land: An Encounter*, eds. Lisa Loden, Peter Walker, and Michael Wood (Jerusalem: Musalaha, 2000); Paul Lieberman, *The Fig Tree Blossoms*, 3rd ed. (Indianola, IO: Fountain Press, 1980) ch. 12, 'The Future of Abraham's Seed', 111–20.

[41] Arnold G. Fruchtenbaum, 'Eschatology and Messianic Jews: A Theological Perspective' in *Voices of Messianic Judaism: Confronting Critical Issues Facing a Maturing Movement*, ed. Dan Cohn-Sherbok (Baltimore MA: 2001), 211–19.

[42] Ibid., 211.

[43] The principal Biblical passages used are: Dan. 7–9; Ezek. 38–39; Jer. 30:3–7; I Thes. 4:13–18; Rev. 7–21.

Hebrew Christians or Jewish Christians), make up the present day remnant of Israel. There cannot be an adequate eschatology without recognising the role of the remnant of Israel.'[44] Messianic Jews are thus recipients of both the physical promise of the Land, and the spiritual promises of blessing and salvation.

The Church is defined, using the terms *k'hillah* and *ekklesia* 'to help take the edge off' the negative nuances that the term 'Church' has for many Jewish people. Fruchtenbaum opposes 'replacement theology' which teaches that 'the Church has always existed, comprises all who have believed since Adam, and that the Church is true Spiritual Israel'.[45] The Church is the new and third entity made up of believing Jews and Gentiles that came into being by 'Spirit-baptism' on the day of Pentecost. It is not, according to Fruchtenbaum's reading of Eph. 2:11–3:6, 'incorporated into the common-wealth of Israel. Rather, what the text clearly says is that God made of the two (Commonwealth of Israel and the Gentiles) a third new entity which is the Body, and the Body has already been defined as being the *k'hillah/ ekklesia*. Two plus one equals three, and it is obvious that there is a third new entity comprised of Jewish believers and Gentile believers.'[46] By keeping these three groups separate, but allowing Jewish believers to be part of both Israel and the Church, Fruchtenbaum's eschatology flows clearly. There will be a rapture of all who believe, both those alive and those who have died, before the tribulation period. Then the Messiah will return to set up his mil-lennial kingdom. The Jewish people will believe in him in totality when he returns. Messianic Jews who believe before the rapture, including the 'Old Testament saints', will return with the Messiah as rulers over the millennial kingdom of Israel according to its biblical boundaries, which present-day Israel has not yet fully possessed. Only in the Millennial Kingdom will the Land promises be fulfilled completely, and the Promised Land be fully enjoyed by the Jewish people, as a centre of universal peace for all the nations.[47]

According to Fruchtenbaum the literal millennium will end with the release of Satan, a final revolt against God, and then the resurrection of all believers will take place. Judgement will be given before the Great White Throne, the damned will be thrown into the lake of fire, and the destruction of the present heavens and earth will be followed by the creation of the new heavens and earth, and the eternal state.[48]

Fruchtenbaum's eschatology is attractive to those looking for a concep-tual scheme that can be easily applied once its presuppositions and methods

---

[44] Fruchtenbaum, 'Eschatology and Messianic Jews,' 212.

[45] Ibid., 213.

[46] Ibid., 214.

[47] Ibid., 215–18.

[48] Fruchtenbaum, 'Israelology,' 330.

are accepted. It allows a theological justification for the return of Messianic Jews to the Land, and political support for the State. But it proves to be a procrustean bed on which MJT may find itself constrained, and some change is necessary if the movement is to develop its own theology. The 'Progressive Dispensationalism' of Darrel Bock and Craig Blaising allows a more nuanced and hermeneutically sophisticated approach, whilst still seeing the continuing purposes of God at work in the present-day situation of Israel and the Jewish people.[49] However, Messianic Jewish thought has yet to adopt this revision of Dispensationalism.

Messianic Historic Premillennialism

A 'Millennium of Sorts' (Stern)

Whilst Fruchtenbaum's views are clearly articulated and influential within the movement, there are dissenting voices that are indebted to him but that part company with Dispensationalism. Thus David Stern writes:

> In the 19th century **Dispensationalist Theology,** attempting to present a more balanced and less anti-Jewish view [than Replacement Theology], one that would see that the Jews have not become merely another nation, portrayed them as God's earthly people and the Christians as God's heavenly people. This strict separation of roles did not deal with the problem of Messianic Jews – do they ascend at the Rapture with the Church or remain below, loyal to their Jewish people? Either profoundly unsatisfying answer demonstrates the absurdity and inadequacy of this theological solution to the question of God's people.[50]

It is not clear that Stern has correctly understood Fruchtenbaum's form of Dispensationalism, which includes the believing remnant of Israel in those of the body of Christ who will be raptured, then return with Christ after the seven-year tribulation period. Nor is the strength of Stern's objection clear, as he notes that dispensationalists who hold to a pre-tribulation rapture still accept that Messianic Jews will be present on earth.

---

[49] Craig A. Blaising, and Darrell L. Bock, *Progressive Dispensationalism* (Grand Rapids: Baker, 1993, 2000).

[50] David H. Stern, 'Making the Issues Clear: The Land from a Messianic Jewish Perspective' in *The Bible and the Land: An Encounter*, eds. Lisa Loden, Peter Walker, and Michael Wood (Jerusalem: Musalaha, 2000), 39–40. See too 'The Significance of Jerusalem for Messianic Jews' in John Fischer (ed.) *The Enduring Paradox: Exploratory Essays in Messianic Judaism* (Baltimore MA: Lederer, 2000), 95–104; 'Messianic Jews Should Make *Aliyah*' in *Voices of Messianic Judaism: Confronting Critical Issues Facing a Maturing Movement*, ed. Dan Cohn-Sherbok (Baltimore MA: 2001), 193–201.

Pre-Tribulation Rapture. The event of [1 Thes. 4:15–17] takes place prior to the Tribulation. Believers are removed so that they will not have to experience the time of the greatest trouble since the earth began, and they return with the Messiah to rule on earth in glory. During the Tribulation itself, 144,000 Messianic Jews evangelize the world (Rev. 7).[51]

Stern's own view is more tentative. Having discussed the amillennial and postmillennial positions, he looks at the range of options for premillennial teaching on the timing of the rapture in relation to the tribulation, the seven-year period that precedes the millennium. He too holds that Messianic Jews will remain on earth during the tribulation, a view he found 'profoundly unsatisfying' when held by Dispensationalists. But he adopts the *Post-Tribulation Rapture* position, equating this with the Historic Premillennialism of George Elton Ladd[52] and Dan Juster.

Post-Tribulation Rapture. The Rapture takes place after the Tribulation, so that the Church experiences it too. This is my own position, although I am not so dogmatic about it. To me it is unthinkable that what New Testament faith offers is escape from suffering; on the contrary, 'in this world you will have tribulation' (John 16:33 KJV). Nor is it thinkable that Messianic Jews are to be faced with the decision of whether to identify with their own people the Jews and stay to suffer, or with their own people the believers (the Messianic Community, the Church) and escape.

　　Pre-Tribulationists must answer this question: when the rapture takes place, do Jewish believers in Yeshua stay behind with the rest of physical Israel, or do they join the rest of the Messianic community with Yeshua in the air? They can't be in both places at once. Is it a matter of personal choice? Do we have to choose whether to be more loyal to the Jewish people or to our brothers in the Messiah? This is an absurd question, absurd because the situation proposed will never arise. The Jewish believer does not abandon his people. He never has to choose between loyalty to the Jews and loyalty to the Messianic community, except in worldly relationships – that is, in order to follow the Jewish Messiah, he may have to choose rejection by the Jewish community as presently constituted in the world.[53]

---

[51] David H. Stern, *Jewish New Testament Commentary* (Jerusalem: Jewish New Testament Publications, 1992), 622–23.

[52] It appears that Stern has also misread Ladd, who argues that the 144,000 of Rev. 7 who go through the tribulation are in fact not Jews or Jewish believers in Jesus. 'The twelve tribes listed are simply not the twelve tribes of Israel' (George Elton Ladd, *The Last Things: An Eschatology for the Layman* (Grand Rapids MI: Eerdmans, 1974), 70.

[53] Stern, *JNTC*, 623.

By focusing on the identity issues that Jewish believers face Stern shows one inadequacy of Dispensational eschatology, but his argument is primarily about a projection into the future of present social realities, rather than a thoroughgoing critique of a theological system by challenging its methods and assumptions, which he accepts up to a point, then finds the conclusion (as he sees it) unacceptable, and responds with agnosticism.

There is some confusion in Stern's position. Whilst wanting to avoid the uncomfortable choice facing Jewish believers in Jesus at the time of the Tribulation – whether to be raptured with the Church or stay on earth with the Jewish people – Stern still affirms a literal Israel and Messianic Jews as the remnant, and adopts a modified and less spiritualising Historic Premillennialism. He admits to agnosticism on the question.

> Messianic Jews seem to hold especially strong opinions about these things – perhaps because there is no certain way of determining who is right until events eliminate all but one possibility! For the *Jewish New Testament Commentary* it seems less important for me to stand unyieldingly for my own viewpoint than to observe that there are several options, and any of them can be expressed in a way that honours the Jewishness of the New Testament.[54]
>
> Premillennialism alone expects a future Millennium in which the Messiah himself will reign on earth, and I share this opinion. But I also agree with Lance Lambert, a Messianic Jew living in Jerusalem, who writes: 'It is my belief that there will be a millennium. It would not alter my faith or joy in the Lord if there were no such proof. I find myself unable to hold such a conviction in argument or hotly dogmatic spirit. If we are honest, both views present us with problems which are not easily answered. The vital need is to be ready for the Lord's coming and for all that will follow it'.[55]

Stern expresses correctly the breadth of opinion amongst Messianic Jews, but also adds theological depth to the topic by considering the context of Jewish apocalyptic eschatology which the New Testament reflects, giving a brief survey of views of the millennium in inter-testamental[56] and rabbinic thought.[57] He finds a 'millennium of sorts' in Sanhedrin 97a,[58] quotes some Talmudic and Zohar passages on the *Olam haba'ah*, and considers the passage in 4 Ezra 7:25–44 on the Day of Judgement. Little attempt is made to integrate these Jewish insights into a Messianic Jewish perspective, and

---

[54] Ibid.

[55] Ibid., 842, quoting Lance Lambert, *Till the Day Dawns* (Eastbourne: Kingsway Publications, 1982), 160. Lambert himself would be closer to the classic Dispensationalist position.

[56] Ibid., 843–44.

[57] Ibid., 763–64, 842–44.

[58] Ibid., 842.

the fact that they are quoted in Stern's commentary in Rev. 20, the one place in the New Testament where the millennium is mentioned, raises important questions of method and approach for the development of a Messianic Jewish eschatological perspective that is not entirely derivative of Christian systems.

Stern is a most active advocate of *Aliyah* for Messianic Jews,[59] and whilst he does not rely on his eschatological views to argue his case, elements of his eschatology are used to show that it is right for Messianic Jews to return to the Land.[60] 'If these "redeemed of the Lord" who have "come with singing unto Zion" are not the Messianic Jews now living in the land, then who are they? In sum, even if there were not other reasons, God's promise of the land to the Jewish people would remain literally valid today for the sake of the faithful remnant, the Messianic Jews.'[61]

For Stern the main enemy is 'replacement theology' which denies the right to the Land to the Jewish people today or in the future. 'To say that the New Covenant transforms this plain sense into an assertion that those who believe in Yeshua come into some vague spiritual 'possession' of a "spiritual territory" is intellectual sleight-of-hand aimed at denying, cancelling and reducing to nought a real promise given to real people in the real world. This is an intellectually unacceptable way of dealing with a text or with ideas.'[62]

Restorationist Historic Premillennialism (Juster)

Daniel Juster critiques Dispensationalism from a historic premillennialist perspective.[63] He combines the eschatology of George Eldon Ladd with the restorationist teaching found in the charismatic movement of North American Evangelical Protestantism. This strand of teaching is part of the 'Kingdom Now' movement of Reformed amillennialists in the charismatic movement, but there is no reason why this historic premillennial position should be problematic for fellow charismatics, as 'our teaching, for the most part, transcends this distinction'.[64]

---

[59] David H. Stern, 'Messianic Jews Should Make *Aliyah*' in *Voices of Messianic Judaism: Confronting Critical Issues Facing a Maturing Movement*, ed. Dan Cohn-Sherbok (Baltimore MA: Lederer, 2001), 193–201.

[60] Ibid., 194.

[61] David H. Stern, 'Making the Issues Clear: The Land from a Messianic Jewish Perspective' in Lisa Loden, Peter Walker, and Michael Wood (eds.), *The Bible and the Land: An Encounter* (Jerusalem: Musalaha, 2000), 42–43.

[62] Ibid., 42.

[63] Daniel C. Juster and Keith Intrater, *Israel, the Church and the Last Days*, (Shippensburg, PA: Destiny Image, 2003). Cf. Daniel C. Juster, *The Irrevocable Calling: Israel's Role as a Light to the Nations* (Clarksville: Lederer Books, 1996, 2007).

[64] Juster and Intrater, *Israel, the Church and the Last Days*, 12.

First of all, **this book is restorationist**. We believe in the restoration of the Body of Christ in the Last Days, a restoration of unity, power, gifts of the Spirit, and fivefold ministry.

Secondly, **we believe in a key role for Israel** in the Last Days events and her re-engrafting into the olive tree (see Rom. 11). This role includes the importance of establishing a saved remnant of Israel.

Thirdly, **we are Kingdom of God oriented**. We believe the Kingdom of God has broken into this world through Jesus and His people. Signs, wonders, deliverance, healing, and living by Kingdom principles, as applied to all realms of life, are all part of our witness – although the Kingdom will not come in fullness until Jesus returns.

Lastly, **we are premillennial** in its historic pre–1830 form, as taught by George Ladd … Our Last Days view combines tribulation, glory, and victory for God's people.[65]

The dispensationalist focus on the kingdom of God separates the 'Church age' where the 'gospel of Grace' is preached too rigidly from the 'kingdom age' where the 'Gospel of the Kingdom is preached, and unhelpfully keeps Israel separate from the Church'.[66]

The dispensational movement holds that the Kingdom of God refers mostly to the earthly rule of the Messiah in an age of peace. Their teaching roughly follows these lines: When Jesus came he offered the Kingdom to Israel, but Israel rejected the Kingdom. Therefore, the Kingdom was postponed, and God inserted a 'Parenthetical Church Age' that was not foreseen by the prophets. This church age will end when the Rapture takes place. At that time the Kingdom of God will be preached again.[67]

The 'gospel of the Kingdom' preached by Jesus and his disciples, is not, according to dispensationalists, the same gospel that is preached by believers today. Now it is the 'gospel of grace' that conveys personal salvation to the individual believer. Dispensationalists believe that it is only when the Church is taken up in the rapture that the 144,000 Jews of Rev. 7 will renew the preaching of the 'gospel of the kingdom', when the Messiah reigns for a thousand years in the millennial kingdom. Juster sees this understanding of the kingdom as relegating everything to the future, and 'our own view lies in great contrast to this'.[68]

Juster affirms some aspects of Dispensationalism, but is critical of others.

---

[65] Ibid.
[66] Ibid., 14.
[67] Ibid.
[68] Ibid., 15.

The dispensationalist is correct in stating that there are two chosen peoples. Israel is chosen as a nation, and the Church is chosen as a universal people from all nations. On the other hand, there is no reason why a person cannot be part of both. Personally, I have not been able to find the dispensationalist distinctions between an earthly and a heavenly people and earthly and heavenly programme in Scripture. There is rather one purpose of world salvation worked out in history through both a chosen nation and a universal pilgrim people.[69]

Dispensationalist hermeneutics fails to take seriously the meaning intended by the original authors of scripture, and builds its own doctrinal system onto texts taken out of context.[70]

Most people would rather not grapple in the Spirit with the intended meaning of a particular text. If you ignore author-intended meaning, however, you can say that you believe the Bible is the test of doctrine all you want, but it will be meaningless because you will be allowing yourself the freedom to go to the Bible and find anything you want to find. The Bible could then say whatever you want it to say.[71]

Juster exegetes key passages used as the basis for Dispensationalism, correcting misunderstandings.[72] For example, Is. 45:22–25 cannot be used to describe the 'Great White Throne Judgment' of Rev. 20.

I was taught that this verse [Is. 45:22–25] describes the Great White Throne Judgment of Revelation 20. When all unsaved humanity stands before God before being cast into hell, each one would be forced to bow the knee and acknowledge the lordship of Yeshua. However, when taken in context, this is not the true meaning. The meaning is that an age is coming in which the whole world will acknowledge God and in which the knowledge of God will cover the earth as the waters cover the sea.[73]

---

[69] Daniel C. Juster, 'Covenant and Dispensation' in *Torah and Other Essays: A Symposium in Honour of the 80th Birthday of H.L. Ellison*, ed. Ronald Lewis (Ramsgate, IHCA, 1983), 51.

[70] For critiques of Dispensationalism by non-Messianic Jewish authors, see Stephen R. Sizer, 'Dispensational Approaches to the Land' in *The Land of Promise: Biblical, Contemporary and Theological Approaches*, eds. Philip Johnston and Peter Walker (Leicester: Apollos, 2000) 142–171. The rigour of this approach has yet to be factored into Messianic Judaism.

[71] Dan Juster and Keith Intrater, *Israel, the Church and the Last Days* (Shippensburg, PA: Destiny Image, 2003), 16.

[72] Dispensationalists such as Ryrie and Fruchtenbaum assert that Ladd's critique (which Juster follows) misunderstood their position on a number of issues. For examples see Fruchtenbaum, *Israelology*, 296.

[73] Juster, *Israel, the Church and the Last Days*, 23.

Juster envisages a different and opposite outcome to the dispensationalist – one of universal salvation and the 'redemption of the whole world'. 'What an optimistic hope about the ultimate destiny of humanity! All of humanity is to be saved, not lost. Is this heresy? Or is this what God's word proclaims?'[74] It is with this more optimistic scenario in mind that Juster expects the people of God will 'so fulfil their destiny that the knowledge of the Lord would cover the earth as the waters cover the sea'.[75]

Jesus, according to Juster, inaugurated the kingdom, and whilst it awaits fulfilment, it is the task of the Church to proclaim the kingdom, which 'breaks through in the Spirit' in fulfilment of the prophecy of Joel 2 that is realised in the book of Acts.[76] The restoration of all things has begun.

> What is important is that the New Testament perspective on the Kingdom of God is that the Kingdom really did come in the life and ministry of Jesus and in the reception of the Spirit by his disciples. The age to come did dawn, but it did not come in fullness. The Kingdom of God is already here, but it is not yet here in fullness. *It is already, but not yet.* It is a reality. The Kingdom has come, but it has not come in totality.[77]

Juster's critique of Dispensationalism is that it inserts a 'parenthetical Church age'[78] between the preaching of the kingdom of God previously offered to Israel by Jesus, but refused, and the renewed preaching of the kingdom of God. This, say dispensationalists, will be offered again at the end of the Church age, after the Church is raptured and just before the tribulation. The 144,000 of Israel will be on earth to renew this preaching of the gospel of the kingdom. 'It will be preached again because we will be at the stage, as in the first century, when the Kingdom can come in fullness.'[79]

Juster admits 'there is a grain of truth in all this, maybe more than a grain,' yet expresses 'major problems with the thrust of the teaching'. These are that the dispensationalists' 'selective use of texts' does not recognise the gifts of the Spirit that are signs accompanying the preaching of the gospel of the kingdom. As a Restorationist committed to the ministry and gifts of the Holy Spirit, Juster is not content to see these sidelined by the generally anti-charismatic emphasis of dispensationalist teaching. Therefore he maintains the connection between the Church and kingdom, both in the connection between the present age and the age to come, and in the preaching of the kingdom as the message of the Church.

---

[74] Ibid., 24.

[75] Ibid., 35.

[76] Ibid., 44.

[77] Ibid., 45–46.

[78] Ibid., 47.

[79] Ibid., 48.

Juster's and Intrater's exposition of the last days' events differs from the dispensationalist position in placing the rapture at the end of the tribulation period,[80] but in other respects remains similar. Intrater includes reference to the kabbalistic *shevirat hakelim* ('shattering of vessels') as a description of the destruction of Jerusalem and the dispersion of the Jewish people, and the *tikkun* as the 'repairing' or 'restoration' taking place in the re-establishment of Israel as a nation. Jewish mystical understanding is linked to the Christian premillennial scheme without explanation of how the two traditions are to be more rigorously attuned.[81]

Juster has difficulties with the rigid separation between the Church and Israel, between the preaching of the 'gospel of grace' and the 'gospel of the kingdom'. But it is not clear how much his own views are different from those forms of Dispensationalism which are more nuanced in the description of the relationship between the Church and Israel. Many of the features of Juster's eschatology resemble those of Dispensationalism, and his prophetic timetable of events places him within the mainstream of premillennial thinking, of which the historic premillennial position remains a dwarf beside the giant of Dispensationalism, both opposed to the very different amillennial and postmillennial positions.

Messianic Amillennialism

Studied Agnosticism (Maoz)

Baruch Maoz's eschatological position may be inferred from the substance of his major review of Premillennialism.[82] Maoz's concern begins at the pastoral level. Premillennialist teaching splits churches and threatens unity.

> Whatever importance we might attribute to this unquestionably important subject, it is not of the kind that should be allowed to rupture churches or threaten meaningful, whole-hearted cooperation in other areas. When it is allowed to do

---

[80] Keith Intrater, 'Last Days Tribulation' in Dan Juster and Keith Intrater, *Israel, the Church and the Last Days* (Shippensburg, PA: Destiny Image, 2003), ch. 5, 139–61.

[81] Keith Intrater, 'The Millennium' in Dan Juster and Keith Intrater, *Israel, the Church and the Last Days*, (Shippensburg, PA: Destiny Image, 2003), ch.6, 163–201, 164.

[82] Baruch Maoz, 'Israel – People, Land, State and Torah' in *Mishkan* no. 2 (1986), 59–69; revised as 'People, Land and Torah: a Jewish Christian Perspective' in *The Land of Promise: Biblical, Theological and Contemporary Perspectives*, eds. Philip Johnston and Peter Walker (Downers Grove, IL: Apollos, 2000), 188–200; 'A Review of Premillennialism' (paper presented to the Elders of Grace and Truth Christian Congregation, Rehovot, December 2003), 1–64.

so, it obscures the far more important issues of the Faith, relegating them to a secondary position because they are not deemed sufficient to ensure congregational unity.[83]

Maoz calls for a less dogmatic and more agnostic approach. Premillenialism assumes there is sufficient biblical data to be properly systematised into a coherent account.

> I question the validity of this assumption. It seems to me that, beyond the broad sweep of events, scripture does not provide a detailed chronology … We would do best not to affirm a system and then approach the scriptures in an effort to understand them. It would be better for us to accept apparent contradictions as one of the important features of biblical eschatology, even if this means that we eschew the formation of a chronological system beyond the general events on which all evangelical believers are agreed because the Bible is unequivocal about them.[84]

Maoz reviews the exegetical and theological basis for Premillennialism, explores the system's implications for mission and the life of the believer and proposes his own 'priorities in eschatology'.[85] In addition to the main types of millennialism (Amillennialism, Postmillennialism and Premillennialism) Maoz presents an unnamed fourth view that 'affirms that scripture sketches a very minimal chronology of End Time events and that an effort to formulate a more detailed chronology is misplaced. All one needs to do is to hold to those truths that the Bible clearly teaches concerning the End Time, and to avoid the formation of chronological schemes.'[86]

Premillennialism fails on hermeneutical grounds because it 'claims to adhere to what it describes as the literal interpretation of scripture,' dismissing other views as 'spiritualising.' 'The fact is that Premillennialism inclines toward a literalism that does not sufficiently take the metaphors of scripture into account, tends to ignore the nature of various genres and styles of writing and often disregards the historical and cultural contexts. As a result, it restricts its own ability to understand and apply the scriptures.'[87] It also shows a 'lack of interest in the moral aspects of the prophetic message', displaying its 'almost total lack of interest in issues of holiness, morality and the fear of God'.[88] Many books on eschatology are written with 'at best, a

---

[83] Maoz, 'A Review of Premillennialism,' 1.

[84] Ibid.

[85] Ibid., 2.

[86] Ibid., 3. David Pawson named this view 'Pan-millennialism' – It will all "pan out right" in the end' (apocryphal).

[87] Ibid., 5.

[88] Ibid., 7.

passing reference to an issue that is central to biblical eschatology: the importance and achievement of holiness'.[89]

The handling of texts on the last days, the separation of Israel and the Church into two peoples of God, offends Maoz's Reformed and Calvinist hermeneutics.

> Premillennialism's tendency to divorce texts from their contexts, to isolate portions from their preceding and succeeding verses, and to claim that they speak of some future event is disturbing. This atomization of scripture tends to transform scripture into a promise-box of isolated texts which can be made to mean whatever the purported interpreter wants them to mean. It is a system widely practiced to this very day by Orthodox Judaism for the same purpose.[90]

The Dispensationalist principle of 'dual fulfillment' imposes on scripture an unnatural reading.

> Prophecies are said to be fulfilled, first in their own time, and then sometime in the future. No such principle is enunciated in scripture. Moreover, if a dual fulfillment is asserted, why not triple, quadruple or who knows how many? Why only dual? This invention is a relatively modern idea that was formulated to defend the system it serves and is but another example of how a theological grid (in this case, an eschatology) is allowed to determine how scripture is to be understood. The scripture alone must determine how it is to be understood.[91]

Unnecessary division is caused within the Church and the Messianic movement by the distinction between Israel and the Church as two peoples of God.

> Modern versions of Premillennialism have paved the way for the errors of Messianic Judaism by teaching that there is a clear distinction between Israel and the Church. Jewish believers until the coming of Christ are part of the Church. Jewish believers who live after the coming of Christ are to be part of Israel. Such a view, coupled with the expectation of a restored Levitical system and of the temple services, all tend toward a Messianic division of the Church.
>
> The unity of the Church and of believing Israel is not a matter for this age only. It is the intended product of the purposes of God. The church does not replace Israel. It joins the remnant of Israel in enjoying the blessing of eternal life through the sacrifice of the Son of God. Israel is yet to be blessed as a nation. The land will one day be given to the nation in peace and in tranquillity. But this is in order for the Gospel and by far subservient to it.[92]

---

[89] Ibid., 8.
[90] Ibid., 14.
[91] Ibid., 14. However, Maoz would acknowledge a *sensus plenior* for texts like Is. 7:14.
[92] Ibid., 15.

Premillennialism unduly emphasises the physical promises of the Land rather than the spiritual blessings of the presence of God. It prophesies the 'carnal worship of the millennial temple' and the 'rebuilding of the middle wall of partition' between Jewish and Gentile believers in the millennium. According to Maoz these promises are primarily spiritual. 'Hence, the promises have more to do with the spiritual life than they have to do with the issue of physical life on earth as we now know it. In that sense the writer to the Hebrews speaks of "a better hope", "better promises", "a better covenant" and of an expectation that looked beyond the realities of life in Canaan.'[93]

The multiple future comings of the Messiah, the rapture, the literal millennium, a series of three resurrections and three different judgments are demanded if the complex and uncertain material of scripture is to be systematised. But such systematisation stretches the reader beyond credulity and does an injustice to scripture itself. Maoz quotes Berkouwer:

> We must learn to live within the tension of truths provided for us by the word of God, between fulfillment and promise, between hope and satisfaction. 'The process of history is too complicated, too forbidding, too incalculable, and subject to too many varied factors to allow us confidence in what we may deduce about it. Already in the Old Testament we find pointed warnings against trying to penetrate the secret of the future. Significantly, these warnings are not based primarily on the impossibility and uncertainty of such speculation; they are rather admonitions not to become engrossed in such activity or to place trust in its findings' [Berkouwer, pg. 10–11].
>
> If God wanted us to have a scheme of future events, he could have easily provided us with one such, thereby sparing us the endless discussions that are often held with regard to eschatology. He preferred not to divulge the blueprint of the future and to teach us the kind of faith that does not claim to have a handle on all that will be.[94]

Although Maoz does not state his own position, and has yet to do so, his focus is clearly on the meaning of the Messiah today. 'The focus of eschatology is Christ rather than chronology. Our eschatology should take its shape from the central thrust of scripture rather than from a supposed chronological order … In other words, rather than seeking to sort out the details of eschatology, we should be busy trying to discover the meaning of it all.'[95] Maoz's eschatology is Christocentric.

---

[93] Ibid., 15–16.

[94] Maoz, 26–27, quoting G.C. Berkouwer, *The Return of Christ: Studies in Dogmatics* (Grand Rapids: William B. Eerdmans, 1972), 10–11.

[95] Maoz, 'A Review of Premillennialism,' 27.

Jesus is the focus of biblical eschatology. We should never allow any event or series of events to eclipse that fact. The political restoration of Israel in its own land, the blossoming deserts, the young nation's military prowess, the ingathering of remote segments of the nation, these all pale into insignificance in comparison with the ultimate eschatological sign which is the coming of the Son of Man and his supernatural ministry ever since.[96]

The future is already realised in the present. 'In Christ, the future has invaded our present, powerfully and increasingly transforming it into his own image. Because he lives, we also live and the future is unquestionably ours because it is his. Nothing in heaven, on earth or under the earth can undo his wonderful work. All things are ours, and we are Christ's, and Christ is God's.'[97]

Following the classic amillennial position developed by Augustine and Calvin, and bringing the insights of the English Puritans about a future for the Jewish people and their restoration to the Land, Maoz avoids the literalism of Dispensationalism, and the speculative conjecture of Historic Premillennialism. Without requiring an intermediate millennial kingdom or the complications of the rapture and tribulation, he maintains the continuing theological significance of the Jewish people and a role for them in the Land of their inheritance. Whilst agnostic about details he still expects the return of Yeshua in fulfilment of his promises for the salvation of Israel and the inauguration of the age to come. Maoz's 'studied agnosticism' and christocentric focus firmly prioritises the need for responsible hermeneutics, the pursuit of holiness, engagement with the world as it is, and the fulfilment of the great commission in this present age.

Present and Future in Tension (Nichol)

Rich Nichol critiques the common premillennial position of the Messianic movement, noting that it arose from the soil of Protestant Evangelicalism in which the movement itself was nurtured.

> Messianic Judaism has its recent origins, not primarily in traditional Judaism, but in Protestant evangelical Christianity, particularly the dispensational variety. This vibrant form of Christian faith provided the soil in which the remnant of Israel could take root in modern times … Its effects on nascent Messianic Judaism have been profound.

---

[96] Ibid., 53.
[97] Ibid., 53–54.

Our interest lies in one particular aspect of evangelical Christianity's theological outlook – the conviction held by many, but not all, that we are now living in the end of the End Times. Messianic Judaism, as it took root in the early 1970s, drank deeply of this tenet of the dispensational outlook. I know. I was there.[98]

Nichol notes the influence of Hal Lindsey's dispensationalist-influenced bestseller *The Late Great Planet Earth*.[99] '*Messianic Judaism* [emphasis his] *has been more than influenced* – it has actually defined itself in terms of the End Times. Almost a fundamental axiom of our faith is the conviction that God raised up Messianic Judaism at this very period of human history because we figure prominently in his plans to rescue the world from itself.'[100]

Whilst not disassociating himself from this view, Nichol continues: 'Though this conviction may be justified, some disengagement with the motif of the End Times would be very helpful for Messianic Judaism at this time.'[101] For Nichol there are several problems with this position. The timing of the 'End of Days' cannot be predicted and those who attempt it are uniformly mistaken. The world is not going from 'bad to worse' but shows signs of improvement which should not be ignored but produce a positive outlook towards creation. An over-identification with the end of the age 'causes us to loose sight of the Biblical/Jewish emphasis on the goodness of creation and thus, our role in the Created order'.[102] Overemphasis on the end times produces a mentality that opts out of improving society and the environment. It becomes 'an excuse for not making life's hard choices'.

Nichol awaits the Messiah's return, but embraces the 'dynamic tension of living in the good world that the God of Israel has made, while at the same time, looking forward to the eventual and assured fulfilment of that promise'.[103] Important challenges to Dispensationalism arise from his practical, personal and pastoral perspective, but Nichol refrains from a direct hermeneutical or theological critique.

---

[98] Richard C. Nichol, 'Are We Really at the End of the End Times? A Reappraisal' in *Voices of Messianic Judaism*, ed. Dan Cohn-Sherbok (Baltimore, MA: Lederer, 2001), 203.

[99] Hal Lindsey and C.C. Carson, *The Late Great Planet Earth* (Grand Rapids: Zondervan, 1970).

[100] Nichol, 'Are We Really at the End of the End Times?', 204.

[101] Ibid.

[102] Ibid., 207.

[103] Ibid., 209.

Re-Ordering the Messianic Jewish Canonical Narrative (Kinzer)

Building on the work of R. Kendall Soulen, David Novak, Wolfhart Pannenburg and others, Mark Kinzer locates eschatology as part of the 'Messianic Jewish canonical narrative'.[104] Rather than discuss in detail the traditional millennial controversies, end-time scenarios and the dating of the second coming, Kinzer attempts a different approach, exploring various Christian and Jewish eschatological understandings as they impinge upon the construction of Messianic Jewish world-view, identity and practice.

A 'canonical narrative' is an 'interpretive instrument' which orders the Bible's complex story and gives a theological and narrative unity that brings understanding of the past and sheds light on the future. A new shaping of the biblical story shows how eschatology informs the biblical material, and is informed by it. The description of creation is infused with eschatological overtones. The election of Israel, the covenant at Sinai and Israel's institutions of Sabbath, *kashrut* and Temple are replete with eschatological significance. The incarnation of Yeshua, the 'enfleshment of the primordial human', his death and resurrection, are 'previews of the *eschaton*'. 'The gift of the *Ruach*, the exile of the *Shekinah*, and the intertwined histories of the Christian church and the Jewish people point to that final breakthrough that will simultaneously renew, transform and transcend history.'[105]

A new Messianic Jewish canonical narrative is needed to incorporate post-biblical Judaism within the framework of salvation history, providing a hermeneutical tool both for reading the Bible and interpreting history. Messianic Jews consider these issues from a unique perspective. They are 'rooted in the Jewish soil of Israel's continuous covenant existence' with its literature, liturgy and institutions embodying that experience. They are also disciples of Yeshua, who accept his authority and that of the New Testament. They recognise Yeshua's inauguration of a 'decisive new phase in the outworking of the divine plan' that includes drawing of the nations 'into Israel's orbit with its covenantal centre'. A Messianic Jewish covenantal narrative must both reflect and reinforce the identity of Messianic Jews.

Kinzer employs David Novak's concept of 'eschatological horizon',[106] the way a theology sees the relationship between this world (*olam hazzeh*) and the world to come (*olam haba'ah*), to analyse the eschatologies found in Jewish and Christian readings of the biblical narrative. A 'low'

---

[104] Mark Kinzer, 'Beginning with the End: The Place of Eschatology in the MJ Canonical Narrative' (paper presented at the 4th Hashivenu Forum, Los Angeles, February 2002).

[105] Ibid., 1.

[106] David Novak, 'Beyond Supersessionism,' *First Things* 81 (March 1998), 58–60.

eschatological horizon minimises the difference between this world and the next, and is found in the traditional, Maimonidean anti-supernaturalist and rationalist understanding of the Messiah. It is also present in the modern utopian vision of human progress in Reform Jewish eschatologies. Both see the Messianic Age as a restored Davidic kingdom and reign of peace, brought about through human means rather than through a dramatic change in the world's 'fundamental ontological structure'. This approach Kinzer understands as an 'excessively low eschatological horizon (Jewish)'.[107] The Christian equivalent of a 'low eschatological horizon' exaggerates the transformation of the world's 'ontological structure' that has *already* taken place in the death and resurrection of Yeshua. It then 'spiritualises' the future world and sees it present in the life of the Church in this age. Johannine eschatology in particular does not consider the 'world to come' to be significant in its material restoration and consummation of the present world, as that has already taken place in the life of the believer, who has entered into the kingdom of God by faith.

A third approach is the Jewish 'excessively high eschatological horizon' which 'maximises the distance between Jewish life under the Torah of this age' (Jewish life today) and life in the world to come. It emphasises the transformed character of the future world and denies the eschatological nature of Jewish life in this world. Christians who have a 'low eschatological horizon' share this perspective. They see themselves already living in the Messianic age, but do not recognise this as a possibility for Jewish people who do not accept Yeshua as Messiah.

Kinzer aims to raise the 'excessively low horizons' by stressing a 'realised eschatology' that allows the 'presence of the future' in the present age. He opts for a sufficiently 'high' eschatological horizon that recognises the radical newness of the Messiah's death and resurrection as the inauguration of the Messianic age. This allows sufficient room for expectation of the final consummation of which the 'Christ event' is a proleptic foretaste.

According to Kinzer, whilst there are a variety of eschatological approaches in Judaism, polemics between Jews and Christians have polarised and distorted the Jewish position. They have prevented expression of an eschatological horizon sufficiently low to be attainable, and sufficiently high to allow for Jewish life in this world to evidence a foretaste of the world to come. Yet traditionally the concept of *kedushah,* as articulated in the creation narratives and expressed in Sabbath, *kashrut* and the observance of the festivals, has always had an eschatological dimension. There the future is proleptically realised without denying the 'thisness' of this world and the 'otherness' of the 'world to come'. Israel's existence as a 'holy people,' embodying the *Shekinah* as did the Tabernacle and Temple, is also a foretaste and anticipation of the life of the world to come. Israel, the Sabbath and the

---

[107] Kinzer, 'Beginning with the End,' 2.

Land all evidence a 'proleptic eschatological character', as do daily prayers and grace after meals. [108]

Following rabbinic tradition and the writings of Michael Wyschogrod, Kinzer affirms the nature of Israel in exile as incarnating the *Shekinah*.[109] This relates to the Hasidism of Martin Buber. 'Israel participates in the divine drama leading to redemption by living within the profane world in such a way as to lift it to the level of holiness. *Kedushah* is an eschatological reality, and Israel shares in that reality in anticipation and also extends that reality as part of the process of preparing for final redemption.'[110] Kinzer's eschatology thus mirrors closely a major eschatological position within Jewish thought, that Israel both awaits redemption and is the means to it. This 'Jewish proleptic eschatology' is then considered in the light of the mission of Yeshua.

For Kinzer the 'usual strategy' of Christian theology is inadequate in ignoring the eschatological character of Israel's *kedushah*. It accents the 'discontinuity between Israel's covenant existence before Yeshua's coming and the eschatological newness that Yeshua brings'.[111] It follows the supersessionist agenda of downgrading the importance of Moses and Israel and does not do justice to the biblical text and the traditional Jewish way of understanding it. Kinzer therefore constructs a new Messianic Jewish canonical narrative on the grounds of Yeshua's identity as the 'individual embodiment of Israel' in his life, death and resurrection, showing how these both reflect and intertwine with the Jewish tradition of *kedushah* and eschatological expectation rather than negate them.

Kinzer appreciates the full implications of Yeshua's embodiment and representation of Israel that have been previously noted by Hertzberg, Stern and Juster, and highlighted by the recent scholarship of N.T. Wright.[112] Just

---

[108] Ibid., 4.

[109] Michael Wyschogrod, *The Body of Faith* (Northvale, N.J.: Aronson, 1996), 212–14, 256. 'Salvation is of the Jews because the flesh of Israel is the abode of the divine presence in the world. It is the carnal anchor that God has sunk into the soil of creation.'

[110] Kinzer, 'Beginning with the End,' 8.

[111] Ibid.

[112] N.T. Wright, *The Climax of the Covenant* (Minneapolis: Fortress, 1992), 18–40; *The New Testament and the People of God* (Minneapolis: Fortress, 1992), 402, 407, 416–17; and *What Saint Paul Really Said* (Grand Rapids: Eerdmans, 1997), 106. Kinzer points out that Wright takes the extreme opposite position from Herberg: for him Yeshua in effect *replaces* Israel. Cf. David Stern, *MJM* (Clarksville, MD: Jewish New Testament Publications, 1988) 105, 107; Daniel Juster, *Jewish Roots* (Rockville, MD: Davar, 1986), 47–48. For a critique of Wright's supersessionism see Douglas Harink, *Paul Among the Postliberals: Pauline Theology Beyond Christendom and Modernity* (Grand Rapids: Brazos, 2003), ch. 4.

as Israel is called to be a holy people, with the divine presence (the *kavod* or *Shekinah*) present in the midst of the people, so the experience of the 'abiding presence of *Hashem*,' anticipated in the *Mishkan* and Temple, 'is brought to a new height in the coming of Yeshua, the one-man Israel, in whom the Divine Word becomes flesh'.[113] Whilst this is a 'new and unique event', it should

> Nonetheless be viewed in continuity with what precedes it – as a concentrated and intensified form of the Divine Presence that accompanies Israel through its historical journey. Thus, contrary to the common Christian canonical narrative, the Divinity of Yeshua can be seen not as a radical rupture and disjunction in the story but as a continuation and elevation of a process initiated long before.[114]

Kinzer here balances continuity and discontinuity, keeping a high enough eschatological horizon to recognise the radical newness of Yeshua's incarnation, whilst keeping it low enough to recognise the continuity between Jewish and 'Christian' dispensations. For Kinzer this means a two-fold, or even manifold manifestations of the Divine Presence, both in the life, traditions and institutions of Israel, and in the incarnation of Yeshua and the new covenant community formed of those from Israel and the Nations who come to faith in Him. Whilst echoing the views of Michael Wyschogrod and R.K. Soulen here, Kinzer's proposal is difficult to reconcile with the uniqueness of the Messiah and his soteriological role, and has met with limited acceptance within the Messianic movement to date.

Kinzer's echoes Karl Barth's view of the double predestination of the Church and the Jewish people, although Kinzer would stress more the redemptive efficacy of God's election of Israel, which for Barth is subsumed in the universalist implications of his eschatology.[115]

> If we view the ongoing life of the Jewish people as a providential blessing for the world, and if we believe that Israel maintains a distinctive national holiness despite its refusal to accept Yeshua as the Messiah (Rom 11:16), and if we believe that there is even a mysterious Divine purpose behind that refusal (Rom. 11:25–36), then we should seek an explanation that is as favourable as possible to these parallel trajectories. I propose that we see Yeshua at work not only in the *ekklesia* but also among the very Rabbis who reject his claims. The power of Yeshua's death and resurrection extends beyond the boundaries of the *ekklesia*.[116]

---

[113] Kinzer, 'Beginning with the End,' 9.

[114] Ibid., 10.

[115] Robert Lindsay, *Barth, Israel and Jesus: Karl Barth's Theology of Israel* (Aldershot: Ashgate, 2007). Kinzer is indebted to Barth in several areas of his thought (cf. *PMJ*) but a full study of the influence of Barth on MJT is beyond the purposes of the present study.

[116] Kinzer, 'Beginning with the End,' 15.

Kinzer quotes David Stern's understanding of Yeshua's embodiment of the Jewish people, even in their unbelief. 'This concept, that the Messiah embodies the Jewish people, should not seem strange to believers, who learn precisely that about Yeshua and the Church ... But the Church has not clearly grasped that the Holy One of Israel, Yeshua, is in union not only with the Church, but also with the Jewish people.'[117]

That the Jewish people are included in the Body of the Messiah without their conscious confession of faith in Yeshua's Messiahship is one of the paradoxes of Kinzer's position, which he draws from Stern's argument. 'Stern draws upon the notion that Yeshua is the one-man Israel, and comes to this radical but sensible conclusion. Try though it may, Israel cannot escape its Messiah. Wanted or unwanted, noticed or unnoticed, acknowledged or unacknowledged, he still rules over his people. Therefore, we should not be surprised to find signs of his presence and activity within the people and tradition of Israel.'[118]

Messianic Jews, recognising the continuity between the *kedushah* of Israel which proleptically manifests the *eschaton* in the Torah and rabbinic tradition, should thus lower the eschatological horizon to sufficiently allow enjoyment of the 'not yet' present in the 'now', and 'allow for the foretaste of redemption and consummation given in Israel's life of *kedushah*'. But they should also raise the low Christian eschatological horizon that 'overstates the continuity between life in the Messiah in this age and life in the Messiah in the age to come'.[119] This tends to so accentuate the 'redemptive power of Yeshua's incarnation, death and resurrection, and the richness of life in the Spirit and in the Church, that the future redemption drops out of the picture completely or survives merely as an anticlimactic wrap-up of an already completed story'.[120]

This lowering of the Christian eschatological horizon has led to a false dichotomy between the Jewish and Christian views, as emphasised by Leo Baeck who inaccurately contrasted the 'romantic faith in salvation' of Paul and the early Church with the 'ancient messianic idea that was still the ideal of Jesus'.[121] According to Baeck, Paul's sense of the fulfilment of Messianic expectation in the coming of Jesus 'was something which had already been fulfilled, was already an actual possession of the present' and so the 'idea of the great future hope had consequently lost its significance'.

---

[117] Stern, *MJM*, 108.

[118] Kinzer, 'Beginning with the End,' 15.

[119] Ibid.

[120] Ibid.

[121] Ibid., quoting Leo Baeck, 'Romantic Religion,' in *Jewish Perspectives on Christianity: Leo Baeck, Martin Buber, Franz Rosenzweig, Will Herberg, and Abraham J. Heschel*, ed. Fritz A. Rothschild (New York: Crossroad Publishing, 1990), 86–87.

Likewise Kinzer quotes Michael Wyschogrod and David Novak to show how the low Christian horizon is used 'as a foil' to contrast the raised horizon of Jewish eschatological expectation, where full redemption has yet to be realised, is 'shrouded in darkness' and is incomplete. 'Against the hidden horizon of the final redeemed future, everything past and present is ultimately provisional. God has not yet fulfilled his own purposes in history.'[122]

Kinzer also shows how Franz Rosenzweig contrasts the Jewish orientation to a future redemption with the assumed Christian orientation to a past redemption that has already been accomplished.

> The [Jewish] people ... lives in its own redemption. It has anticipated eternity. The future is the driving power in the circuit of its year. Its rotation originates, so to speak, not in a thrust but in a pull.
>
> In Christianity, correspondingly, the idea of redemption is swallowed back into creation, into revelation; as often as it erupts as something independent, just so often it loses its independence again. The retrospect to cross and manger, the eventuation of the events of Bethlehem and Golgotha into one's own heart, there become more important than the prospect of the future of the Lord. The advent of the kingdom becomes a matter of secular and ecclesiastical history. But it has no place in the heart of Christendom.[123]

Kinzer notes how Jewish authors see the 'subordination of the final redemption to the finished work of Messiah as a problematic feature of the Christian canonical narrative', and proceeds to outline Soulen's attempt to craft a 'new canonical narrative' which 'overcomes supersessionism and facilitates constructive dialogue with contemporary Judaism'. If Christian thinkers could reconceptualise the canonical narrative, stressing the creation and consummation aspects more than the traditional focus on Christ's first coming, this would allow a 'more fruitful theological relationship with Judaism and the Jewish people'.[124]

Soulen, according to Kinzer, 'takes the traditional Christian canonical narrative, centred in the incarnation, and reorders it so that it is closer to the traditional Jewish narrative, oriented to the final redemption'.[125]

---

[122] Ibid., 16, quoting David Novak, *The Election of Israel* (Cambridge: Cambridge University Press, 1995), 255.

[123] Ibid., quoting F. Rosenzweig, *The Star of Redemption* (Notre Dame: University of Notre Dame Press, 1985) 328, 368.

[124] Novak, *The Election of Israel*, 57, quoted in Kinzer, 'Beginning with the End,' 17.

[125] Ibid.

The gospel is good news about the God of Israel's coming reign, which proclaims in Jesus' life, death, and resurrection the victorious guarantee of God's fidelity to the work of consummation, that is, to fullness of mutual blessing as the outcome of God's economy with Israel, the nations, and all creation.[126]

The necessary correction … is a frank reorientation of the hermeneutical centre of the Scriptures from the incarnation to the reign of God, where God's reign is understood as the eschatological outcome of human history at the end of time.[127]

Kinzer reports Novak's observation that Soulen has effectively raised the eschatological horizon to bring Jewish and Christian views into alignment.

Soulen seems to be constituting what I would call 'the highest possible eschatological horizon.' This comes out when he says, 'The Church is not a community that issues directly into God's reign … A hiatus separates the Church and God's eschatological reign' … Clearly, when Christian theologians constitute a 'lower' eschatological horizon, which usually has meant seeing the *Eschaton* as the extension of the Church's reign on earth, it has been most susceptible to the types of supersessionism so opposed by Soulen … Conversely, when Christians regard themselves within history but not its masters, they become most like the Jews.[128]

Kinzer is anxious to follow Soulen in this direction, and adduces in support of this the work of Wolfhart Pannenburg and Jürgen Moltmann in their restructuring of Christian theology to give greater prominence to the place of eschatology. Pannenburg emphasises the proleptic eschatological nature of the *ekklesia* and of Israel, refusing to blur the distinction between the *ekklesia* and the coming kingdom.[129] For Pannenburg the Church failed to realise its provisional nature, because it misunderstood the nature of its continuing relationship with Israel. Kinzer quotes from Pannenburg:

In its relations with the Jewish people the church had to decide for the first time whether it would view its own place in God's history with the human race along the lines of a provisional sign of a still awaited consummation, or view itself as the place of the at least initially actualised eschatological consummation itself. The decision went in favour of the second alternative and it came to expression in the church's claim to be exclusively identical with the eschatologically 'new' people of God. The dangerous and destructive consequences of this choice mark the further history of Christianity. They take the form of dogmatic intolerance,

---

[126] R. Kendall Soulen, *The God of Israel and Christian Theology* (Minneapolis: Fortress Press, 1996), 166.

[127] Ibid., 138.

[128] Novak, *The Election of Israel,* 58, 60, quoted in Kinzer, 'Beginning with the End,' 18.

[129] Ibid.

the result of a false sense of eschatological finality that fails to see the church's provisional nature, and an endless series of divisions that follow from dogmatic exclusiveness. It is important to realize that this painful false development began with a primary mistake in the church's relation to the Jewish people.[130]

Kinzer is not impressed with the traditional Christian lowering of the eschatological horizon, seeing it responsible for a multitude of negative factors. It exaggerated the finished nature of the work of Yeshua, and the 'eschatological powers inherent in the church'. Individualising and spiritualising the *eschaton* rendered it 'virtually indistinguishable from the destiny of the soul after death'.

> The Christian Church thus suffered a diminished vision of its true hope – to be resurrected as a community and to inhabit a renewed creation. As the 'last things' were individualized and spiritualized, the eschatological horizon was lowered once again – now not through the inordinate exaltation of the eschatological potential of life in this age, but through the downgrading of the nature of the future hope. In this scheme, if one turns from earthly concerns and cultivates the life of the soul in this world, one already partakes of the life of the world to come. As we seek to develop a Messianic Jewish canonical narrative, we should follow the lead of Soulen and Pannenberg. Without detracting from the significance of Yeshua's incarnation, death, and resurrection, we should raise our eschatological horizon so that life in this age, while anticipating life in the world to come, is never confused with it.[131]

Kinzer argues for a rediscovery of the proleptic eschatology that exists in Jewish life today, a renewed focus on the continuity between the *kedushah* of Israel and the incarnation and resurrection of Yeshua as proleptic eschatological events, and an 'increased awareness of the preliminary and provisional nature of life in Messiah in this age in relation to the eschatological fullness of life in the world to come'.[132] The recognition of Yeshua as the 'true Israelite' who sums up all that Israel was intended to be is demonstrated by his sacrificial death and martyrdom to prepare the way for the coming of the *olam haba'ah*. 'That new world is anticipated and proleptically realized in the resurrection of Israel's perfect martyr, and the gift of the *Ruach* and the founding of a two-fold *ekklesia* that extends Israel's heritage among the nations likewise represent anticipations of the renewed world to come.'[133]

---

[130] Ibid., 19., quoting W. Pannenberg, *Systematic Theology*, Vol. 3 (Grand Rapids: Eerdmans, 1998), 476.

[131] Ibid., 20.

[132] Ibid., 21.

[133] Ibid., 22.

For Kinzer the 'two-fold *ekklesia*' is a crucial tool for the coherence of his re-ordered canonical narrative. It suffers a 'profound disruption' early in its history, and one of its components, the Jewish people, is 'lost or at least hidden from view'.

> This disruption brings the brokenness of the present world into the very heart of the preliminary realization of the world to come, and serves as a continual reminder of the provisional nature of that realization. Nevertheless, the two-fold ekklesia never completely loses its two-fold nature, for it always includes Jews and is always headed by a Resurrected Jew. Similarly, the Jewish people never succeeds in eluding the grasp of its Resurrected brother.[134]

Kinzer points out the implications for Messianic Jews in the light of this re-ordered canonical narrative. The highlighting of Israel's *kedushah* will lead to an increased appreciation and observance of the *mitzvot*. An increased eschatological awareness will result in a more sensitive appreciation of all that is good within the creation. The proleptic features of the age to come such as the *charismata*, baptism and table-fellowship in the Church will, like *kashrut* and *Shabbat*, observance of the festivals and the saying of grace after meals, take a more significant place in the life of Messianic Jews. Such observances point forward to a greater consummation yet to come.

Kinzer's new Messianic Jewish canonical narrative does not explicitly address the questions of the millennium, rapture, and the timetabling of events that are usually present in discussion of eschatology. He attempts to both 'raise' and 'lower' the 'eschatological horizon.' A lower horizon recognises that the proleptic *eschaton* found in the life of Israel and her observance of *kedushah* is a valid realisation of the world to come. Messianic Jews should adopt this as part of their continuing membership of the Israel, which is already part of the two-fold *ekklesia*. A raised eschatological horizon means that Christians and Messianic Jews still have more to look forward to, in that even the incarnation and resurrection of Yeshua, whilst inaugurating the *olam haba'ah*, should itself expect radical transformation and restoration at the *parousia*.

Conclusion

Dan Cohn-Sherbok summarises the eschatology of Messianic Judaism along the lines of Christian Zionism.

---

[134] Ibid.

Because of the centrality of Israel in God's plan ... Messianic Jews are ardent Zionists. They support Israel because the Jewish State is viewed as a direct fulfilment of biblical prophecy. Although Israel is far from perfect, Messianic Jews believe that God is active in the history of the nation and that the Jews will never be driven out of their land again. While God loves the Arabs, he gave the Holy land to his chosen people.[135]

Whilst this is a fair assessment of those streams of the movement influenced by Dispensational Premillennialism and Historic Premillennialism, there are alternative voices within the Messianic movement that articulate less dogmatic and more speculative proposals. Rich Nichol's amillennialist position, Baruch Maoz's studied agnosticism, and Mark Kinzer's reconceptualising of eschatology in line with the Jewish covenantal theology of David Novak are illustrations of dissatisfaction with the dominant influence of dispensationalist thought.

Fruchtenbaum's system pays due attention to the continuing place of Israel and the role of Jewish believers. It preserves the distinction between the Church and Israel rather than concede to supersessionism or a bilateral ecclesiology. Such a view holds attractions to the Messianic movement, preserving its own distinctive place and identity as belonging to both Israel and the Church. Messianic Judaism has a special role to play as an expression of the believing remnant. The Land of Israel, both as the original evidence of God's covenantal promises with the patriarchs, and as the place of dénouement for the final outcome of God's purposes, still has significance.

Baruch Maoz challenges the assumptions and methods of such a hermeneutic, retaining the complexities of the biblical material, which Fruchtenbaum carefully systematises. What is needed is an authentic and coherent eschatology to emerge within the MJM that does not rely wholly on the Christian (or Jewish) thinking that preponderates the discussion. To achieve this a more robust engagement with the biblical material is needed, with greater awareness of the assumptions that are brought to the texts by the various schools of thought.[136] Maoz recognises and critiques the hermeneutic of Dispensationalism that emerged within the particular set of historical conditions of rationalism, romanticism and 19th century positivism.[137] If

---

[135] Dan Cohn-Sherbok, 'Introduction', in Dan Cohn-Sherbok (ed.), *Voices of Messianic Judaism: Confronting Critical Issues Facing a Maturing Movement* (Baltimore MA: Lederer, 2001), xi.

[136] Cf. Robert C. Doyle, *Eschatology and the Shape of Christian Belief* (Carlisle: Paternoster, 1999) for a historical survey of the doctrine of eschatology in Christianity.

[137] Cf. David Rausch, *Zionism Within Early American Fundamentalism, 1878–1918: A Convergence of Two Traditions* (Lewiston, NY: Edwin Mellen Press, 1979); Dan Cohn-Sherbok, *The Politics of Apocalypse: The History and Influence of Christian Zionism* (Oxford: Oneworld, 2006).

Messianic Judaism disassociates itself from Dispensationalism it would render less dogmatic some of the assertions of the movement, and would open it to a broader range of theological influences within Judaism and Christianity.

Both Dispensational and Historic Premillennialism emphasise the Land of Israel as the locus for the fulfilment of prophecy, and recognise God's continuing purposes for the people of Israel. Her regathering in unbelief, eventual salvation, and future role in the millennial kingdom, are affirmed by both systems, which are more closely linked than their various advocates might suppose. It is likely that the consensus in the Messianic movement will remain amongst the two types of Premillennialism. Despite the exegetical, hermeneutical and theological limitations of the dispensationalist position, it continues to be held as the majority view. The radical reconceptualisation of Kinzer and Nichol, and the studied agnosticism of Maoz, are theologically venturesome but at present lack popular appeal. Daniel Juster's historic premillennial position, with its more nuanced exegetical base and hermeneutical framework, provides an alternative option for those arguing for God's continuing purposes for Israel without dispensationalist features.

Nichol critiques the negative otherworldly tendencies of Dispensationalism, and Kinzer explores the proleptic eschatological aspects of traditional Jewish life to give an understanding of this-worldly life as indicative of the days to come. Kinzer and Nichol explore dimensions of Jewish eschatological thinking that are new to the MJM. The Messianic movement has yet to engage with the Jewish mystical tradition of which the signs of the Messiah's coming to inaugurate the redemption of Israel are so strong a theme.[138]

The future of Israel, as part of the eschatological map, relates to the broader issues of a theology of land and the Land of Israel in particular. Other urgent issues linked to eschatology include a practical theology of reconciliation with Arab Christians and the Arab population in the light of the Israel-Palestine conflict.[139] Those who see the State of Israel as a fulfilment of prophecy must still give opportunity for self-critical reflection on present issues of justice, peace and reconciliation whatever their understanding of the future.

---

[138] E.g. Arthur Cohen 'Eschatology' in *Contemporary Jewish Religious Thought*, eds. Arthur Cohen and Paul Mendes Flohr (New York: MacMillan, 1987), 183–88; Dan Cohn-Sherbok, 'The Afterlife' in *Judaism: History, Belief and Practice* (London: Routledge, 2003), 456–60; *The Jewish Messiah* (Edinburgh: T.&T. Clark, 1997); Gershom Scholem, *The Messianic Idea in Judaism* (New York: Schocken Books, 1971).

[139] Judy Houston, 'Towards Interdependence, Remembrance and Justice: Reconciliation Ministry in the Israeli/Palestinian Context' (MA diss., All Nations Christian College, 2006).

It is so; God chose the Jews; the land is theirs by divine gift. These dicta cannot be questioned or resisted. They are final. Such verdicts come infallibly from Christian biblicists for whom Israel can do no wrong – thus fortified [*sic*]. But can such positivism, this unquestioning finality, be compatible with the integrity of the prophets themselves? It certainly cannot square with the open peoplehood under God which is the crux of New Testament faith. Nor can it well be reconciled with the ethical demands central to law and election alike ... Chosenness cannot properly be either an ethical exclusivism or a political facility.[140]

MJT will need to develop its understanding of Israel in the present, as the people of God and as a people like others, if it is to effectively integrate faith, identity and daily life in political and eschatological context. It remains to be seen whether Messianic thought will cohere around one main view, or continue to develop into separate streams reflecting, as one would expect from the variation and diversity within both Judaism and Christianity on the topic, a confusion of voices which will only be finally resolved at the return of the Messiah himself.

---

[140] Kenneth Cragg, *The Arab Christian: A History in the Middle East* (London: Mowbray, 1992), 237–38.

Chapter 9

Conclusion: The Future of Messianic Jewish Theology

Introduction

The aim of this book has been to clarify the nature of contemporary MJT. Having surveyed a wide range of Messianic Jewish reflections on a number of issues we are now in a position to propose a typology of eight major streams of thought within MJT. Having done that, we need to look to the future and consider some proposals on methods and issues to be addressed in the development of MJT.

Summary of Findings

Approaching Messianic Jewish Theology

Chapters 1–3 defined MJT as a theology constructed in dialogue with Judaism and Christianity, refined in discussion between reflective practitioners engaged with Messianic Judaism, and developed into a new theological tradition based on the twin epistemic priorities of the continuing election of Israel and the Messiahship of Jesus. It reviewed previous studies of Messianic Judaism and its theology, and identified the need for a theological study of MJT.

The Doctrine of God

Chapter 4 observed that MJT has accepted the understandings of monotheism found in the scriptures and developed in Jewish and Christian tradition. It has not made new proposals, but clarified areas of discussion. Christian Trinitarian doctrine is generally accepted by Messianic Jews but expressed in ways more relevant to and consistent with Jewish thought. Further work is needed to articulate a doctrine of Revelation in the light of Jewish and Christian understandings, and to find appropriate ways of expressing the doctrine of the Trinity. Whilst some postmodern Jewish theological reflection allows for the plural nature of the one God of Israel, MJT has yet to articulate the Triune nature of God effectively.

Yeshua the Messiah

Chapter 5 identified five emerging Christologies within MJT, each proposing new ways of understanding the uniqueness and divinity of Jesus within Jewish frameworks of thought. MJT needs to provide a more detailed understanding of hermeneutics and biblical interpretation in the light of its theological interpretation of scripture, and its engagement with Jewish monotheistic and Christian Trinitarian thought. MJT is not united in its belief on the divine nature of Yeshua, and this will continue to cause controversy within the movement. Soteriology and Ecclesiology are closely connected to Christology, and more work is needed in these two areas for a comprehensive theological system.

Torah in Theory

In chapter 6 several approaches to the Torah were examined. Messianic Jews adopt, adapt, or abandon the rabbinic notion of the dual Torah and modify their understanding of *halacha* in the light of Jesus and the New Testament. Some argue that all Jewish believers in Jesus should remain, or become, Torah-observant, or they will be lost to their people. However, this view has not been accepted by the majority of Messianic Jews who are content with a selective approach to the Torah, motivated by the desire for appropriate cultural expressions rather than by any explicit theological rationale.

Messianic Jews negotiate between two major emphases, of liberty and Law. On the one hand, they affirm that salvation is only found in the Messiah, and nothing can be added to their righteousness by keeping the works of the Law. On the other, they embrace the concept of Torah as a means of fruitful living in the covenant relationship God intended for Israel. They negotiate between Jewish understandings of Torah found in Orthodox, Conservative or Reform Judaism, and different Christian understandings of the Law in its relation to grace. They want to affirm and adopt Torah practices alongside their faith in the Messiah, without seeing these two as contradictory.

Further study is needed on the significance of the Torah in MJT. More work is needed on: the nature of biblical Law; the development of the doctrine of the Torah in Judaism; the theology of Law in Judaism and Christianity; the forms of Torah observance practiced by Yeshua and the early believers; the effect of Yeshua's Messiahship, death and resurrection on the nature of Torah; and the authority and observance of Messianic *halacha* today. Torah remains a key issue for Messianic Jews.

Torah in Practice

The survey of Sabbath, *kashrut* and Passover explored different understandings of the practice of Torah. On one hand, Messianic Jewish *halacha* mirrors Conservative and Reform practice, or is modelled on Orthodox Judaism. Alternatively, a distinctively 'non-religious' cultural approach is advocated by some, whose social identification with the wider community takes precedence over the need for a particular theology of Torah. In this the Messianic community follows the trends that affect the wider Jewish community. Further discussion is needed on an MJ approach to Torah and *halacha*. A uniformity of practice is unlikely to emerge, given the variations of belief, context and concerns that affect the Messianic Jewish community worldwide. A theology of Torah in practice that accepts catholicity and plurality within the Messianic Jewish community is needed.

The Future of Israel

The survey of the eschatology of the Messianic movement observed the influence of Christian hermeneutical systems, and also a concern to address eschatological questions with Jewish frameworks of thought. This resulted in a diversity of views, ranging from Dispensational and Historic Premillennial schemes, to more Amillennial, agnostic and speculative views. There were different understandings of the linkage of eschatology to the present realities of Israel and the call for Messianic Jews to make *Aliyah*.

It is clear that a consensus on eschatology will not quickly emerge in MJT. The influence of Dispensational Premillenialism is strong. Alternative but less strident voices are heard which critique and challenge such an approach. There are growing concerns for a more reflective approach to biblical interpretation that critiques the assumptions behind the traditional schemes. There is also growing concern that issues of justice and reconciliation with Palestinian Arab Christians and the Palestinian people should be addressed. MJT will need to develop such discussion if it is to result in a more nuanced understanding of the prophetic and political significance of the Land.

Identifying Messianic Jewish Theology

This summary of conclusions demonstrates that MJT is an emerging theology. Byron Sherwin's categories of authenticity, coherence, contemporaneity and communal acceptance that 'characterise a valid Jewish theology,' are applicable to it and serve as guidelines for its development.[1] The *authenticity*

---

[1] Byron L. Sherwin, *Toward a Jewish Theology: Methods, Problems and Possibilities*, (Lampeter: Edwin Mellen Press, 1991), 9.

of MJT is evident in that whilst it draws from both Jewish and Christian theological traditions, it is in the process of articulating its own position. It is beginning to speak with its own 'inner voice'. Its claim to authenticity will only be recognised as it responds effectively to the louder voices of the two larger theological traditions amongst which it clamours for a hearing. By finding and articulating its own authentic 'theological voice' it will challenge the boundary lines that have traditionally separated Judaism from Christianity.

The *coherence* of MJT around the two epistemic priorities of the Messiahship of Jesus and the election of Israel (the Jewish people) has yet to be stated systematically and comprehensively. These two key affirmations, if held together in creative tension, provide fruitful ground for the elaboration of a coherent theology. The methodological issues to be addressed pose a considerable challenge to such a project. Questions of the nature of the sources, norms, methods, content and results of such a systematic MJT await the production of a comprehensive work at a level that has thus far been beyond any one individual within the Messianic movement. This book aims to make a small contribution to that endeavour, by summarising and assessing existing work in progress.

The *contemporaneity* of MJT is also a concern. The writings of the formative period in the 1970s and 1980s, when they expressed the thinking of those pioneering the movement, are not as relevant in the new millennium. The post-formative positions proposed by Mark Kinzer and the Hashivenu group have yet to gain general support. The issues that concern the contemporary Jewish community and its Messianic contingent are as pressing as ever. Jewish identity, the survival of the Jewish people, the question of Israel and the coming of the Messiah are issues that MJT must address appropriately, constructively and persuasively in a contemporary context.

The *communal acceptance* of MJT is vital, as the growth and maturity of the Messianic movement is dependent on its acceptance of MJT in the light of changing needs and contexts. For MJT to be accepted by the Messianic community and the wider Jewish and Christian communities with which it interacts, it must provide answers that are satisfying, relevant and applicable to future generations. Bearing in mind such concerns for authenticity, coherence, contemporaneity and communal acceptance, we shall now examine the present state of MJT through a characterisation of the various theological streams within the Messianic movement.

A Typology of Messianic Jewish Theologies

At present there is no consensus or unitary theology of Messianic Judaism. The purpose of this book has been to map not only the theological concerns of MJT, but also how these are addressed by various practitioners. We are now in a position to propose a new typology to describe the plurality of MJT on the basis of our findings so far.

Previous typologies have observed different strands within the Messianic movement. David Stern described a series of future options for Messianic Jews, based on 'ideal types' of Messianic Judaism and Hebrew Christianity.[2] His options are 'Ultimate Messianic Jew' (UMJ), 'Ultimate Hebrew Christian' (UHC), and a range of more limited possibilities within these two main categories; 'Ultimately Jewish but Limited Messianic possibilities' (UJLM); 'Ultimate Hebrew Christianity of Today' (UHCT); 'Present Limit of Hebrew Christianity' (PLHC); 'Present Limit of Messianic Judaism' (PLMJ). He poses the question 'if you are a Messianic Jew, in which direction are you headed?' His discussion is unsatisfactory, limited as it was by the then incipient nature of the Messianic Movement and its lack of theological development at the time. Stern's grid constructs a dualistic and antithetical relationship between 'Hebrew Christianity' and 'Messianic Judaism'. As one of the leaders of Messianic Judaism in the 1970s, he is at pains to distance Messianic Judaism from Hebrew Christianity, and his use of the metaphor of parent and child oversimplifies the questions and polarises the alternatives, without articulating the nature of the theological questions involved.

Mark Kinzer distinguishes between 'Missionary' and 'Postmissionary' Messianic Judaism.[3] 'Missionary Messianic Judaism' developed from Hebrew Christianity and the Jewish Missions. It was formulated by individuals like Joseph Rabinowitz and organisations such as 'Jews for Jesus'. It was then expressed in the 1970s and 1980s by the MJAA and the UMJC. Kinzer articulates five principles that Postmissionary Messianic Judaism affirms, and assesses to what degree they are held by others.[4] These are: Israel's irrevocable election and covenant; the normative force of basic Jewish practice (Torah observance); the validity of rabbinic tradition; a 'bilateral ecclesiology' that accepts the continuing position of the Jewish people as the people of God in partnership with the *ekklesia* of the nations; and national solidarity with Israel. This enables Kinzer to distinguish between the new 'Postmissionary' paradigm he proposes, and other previous forms.

Both Stern and Kinzer use dualist conceptual schemes, of Hebrew Christianity and Messianic Judaism (Stern) and more recently of 'Missionary' and 'Postmissionary' Messianic Judaism (Kinzer). Stern's aim is to argue for 'Messianic Judaism' over against 'Hebrew Christianity', and Kinzer favours 'Postmissionary Messianic Judaism' against 'Missionary Messianic Judaism.' Both oversimplify the complexity of MJT for their own

---

[2] David Stern, *Messianic Jewish Manifesto*, 234–38.
[3] Mark S. Kinzer, *Postmissionary Messianic Judaism: Redefining Christian Engagement with the Jewish People* (Grand Rapids: Brazos Press, 2005).
[4] Ibid., 293.

purposes, and without further detailing of the considerable theological variation found within MJT. Therefore a new typology is needed.

Eight Types of Messianic Jewish Theology

The present typology is more tentative and less dualist than those of Stern and Kinzer, tracing developing 'streams' rather than clearly defined 'schools' of theology within Messianic Judaism. The groupings are somewhat arbitrary and there are some overlaps, but leading voices are identified that speak representatively for each stream. The methods, criteria and assumptions used are characterised; the structure and organisation of their thought; their key concerns and emphases; the influences and the resources they draw from in Jewish and Christian theology; the degree to which they are reflective and self-aware of the process of theologising; the contexts and constituencies to which they are linked; and a possible future for their thought.

The views of each stream on the nature of God, the Messiah, the Torah in theory and in practice and the future of Israel will be summarised where they have been addressed. The types of MJT begin with those closest to the Protestant Evangelicalism from which the Messianic movement has emerged, at the one end of the spectrum, to those who locate their core identity within 'Jewish social space' and Jewish religious and theological norms.

Type 1 – Jewish Christianity, Christocentric and Reformed (Maoz)

This type of MJT may be characterised as Christian proclamation, with limited cultural and linguistic translation into a Jewish frame of reference. Baruch Maoz identifies himself as an ethno-cultural 'Jewish' Christian in dialogue with those in the Messianic movement who advocate a return to a religious 'Judaism'.[5] Maoz works with the presuppositions of Reformed Protestantism and is highly critical of rabbinic Judaism. His theology is shaped to correct what he sees as the error of Messianic Judaism of compromise on Christian essentials by acceptance of rabbinic Judaism.

Maoz's doctrine of God reflects Christian orthodoxy with little engagement with Jewish theological concerns. His Christology is expressed in the Creeds, and expounded as Reformed Dogmatics. The Law is fulfilled in Christ, with Jewish observance permitted only when in conformity with New Testament practice. The key theological concern is the elevation of Jesus as Messiah, the uniqueness of his saving work, and the challenge to

---

[5] Baruch Maoz, *Judaism is not Jewish: A Friendly Critique of the Messianic Movement* (Fearn, UK: Mentor/Christian Focus Publications, 2003). Others include Stan Telchin, *Messianic Judaism is not Christianity: A Loving Call to Unity* (Grand Rapids: Baker/Chosen Books, 2004).

Rabbinic Judaism that this poses. Judaism and Jewish identity cannot be allowed to diminish the authority of Christ as revealed in scripture. The hermeneutical system is that of the Protestant Reformation and conservative Evangelicalism.

Maoz has a strong political loyalty to the State of Israel, but justifies this on the grounds of national and cultural identity. He is critical of Premillennialism and studiedly agnostic on eschatology. Maoz's thought, with its Christian Reformed theological emphasis, its non-charismatic and anti-rabbinic attitude, appeals to those with a focus on scripture as interpreted through the Reformation tradition. Within the Land of Israel such views are popular with those disaffected with the more superficial elements of the Messianic movement and unimpressed with more engaged forms of Torah-observance. The challenge for Maoz's approach will be to develop an appropriate, coherent doctrine of Israel, and a theology of culture that does not artificially separate an ethno-cultural 'Jewishness' from religious 'Judaism'. Maoz's arbitrary distinction between the two is problematic, and has not met with general acceptance.[6]

Type 2 – Dispensationalist Hebrew Christianity (Fruchtenbaum)

Arnold Fruchtenbaum is the leading theologian in this group, whose expression of Jewishness and Jewish identity are defined within the parameters of Dispensationalism.[7] The shape of Fruchtenbaum's theology is determined by a systematic and programmatic application of dispensationalist teaching and method to existential questions of Jewish identity and faith in Jesus.

Fruchtenbaum's God is the God of Protestant evangelicalism, articulated in the mode of revised Dispensationalism, with little room for speculative thought or contextualisation.[8] There is no use for rabbinic or Jewish tradition unless it confirms and illustrates biblical revelation as reflected through a dispensationalist hermeneutic. Orthodox Christology is viewed through a conservative evangelical lens. There are some attempts at translation into Jewish cultural contexts, but a literal rather than dynamic equivalence is sought. The Abrahamic covenant is fulfilled in the Messiah, and the Torah – seen as the dispensation of the Mosaic Law – has come to an end. Practice of those national and cultural Jewish elements that do not go against the NT is permitted, but the rabbinic reinterpretation of the Torah and its claims to authority are false.

---

[6] Richard Harvey, 'Judaism is Not Jewish [by Baruch Maoz]: A Review,' CWI Herald (Summer 2003), http://www.banneroftruth.org/pages/articles/article_detail.php?490 (accessed October 6, 2007).

[7] Others include Barry Leventhal, Louis Goldberg and Louis Lapides.

[8] For distinctions between classical, revised and progressive dispensational see Craig A. Blaising and Darrell L. Bock, *Progressive Dispensationalism* (Grand Rapids: Baker, 1993, 2000).

Fruchtenbaum's concern is an effective rooting of gospel proclamation within a Jewish context, and with a strong eschatological agenda of Dispensationalism, which looks forward with certainty to the imminent return of Christ, the rapture, tribulation and millennial kingdom. This is the focus and centre of his system.

With this clearly defined theological base, hermeneutical method and eschatological scheme, Fruchtenbaum's articulate exposition appeals to those looking for a clear theological system. The combination of political support for Israel and a strong eschatological emphasis will continue to influence the Messianic movement. However, it also contains the weaknesses of Dispensationalism: its hermeneutical methods; its 19th century amalgam of rationalism, romanticism and historical consciousness; and the problem of Israel and the Church as two peoples of God. These will not gain acceptance with the majority of Messianic Jews, and they will look for alternatives.

Type 3 – Israeli National and Restorationist (Nerel)

Gershon Nerel's theology is observable in his historical studies of Jewish believers in the early church, and in the 19th and early 20th centuries. His theological system is implicit rather than explicit in his narrative of the histories of Jewish believers in Yeshua (JBYs). He has yet to produce a systematic exposition of his theology. Nevertheless he is representative of many Israeli Messianic Jews, who express their proximity to Christianity in solid creedal affirmations, and practice a form of Messianic Judaism which is Hebrew-speaking, rooted in modern Israeli society and culture, but with little regard for rabbinic orthodoxy as a religious system. Culturally, ethnically and nationally, like the majority of secular Israelis, they identify with Israel and its aspirations as a State, serving in the army, living in kibbutz and moshav, and putting their children through the Israeli school system.

The heart of Nerel's theology is the eschatological significance not just of the modern Zionist movement and the return to the Land, but also the re-establishment of Jewish believers in Jesus in Israel to renew the original apostolic church of Peter and James. For Nerel this has significant implications for the shape and unity of the Church, challenging it to repent of supersessionism and anti-Judaism. JBYs bear a special 'eschatological spiritual authority'. This challenges Israel to recognise the imminent return of her Messiah, and calls Jewish people world-wide to make *Aliyah*, in preparation for the end times. In the light of anti-Semitism and supersessionism, Nerel's Messianic Judaism is a powerful prophetic call to Israel and the nations to see what God is doing today. His theological system is not concerned with *minutiae* of doctrinal formulas, but with a clear pragmatic involvement in a restorationist programme. The fact that Messianic Judaism does not have twenty centuries of tradition to look to is a distinct advantage as it develops its theology. 'The very fact that *congregations of JBY lack a two-millennia tradition* [italics his] helps them to easily find the bridge between themselves and the first-century model of JBY as portrayed in the New Testament.'[9]

> There exists a clear resemblance between the messianic movement of Jewish believers in Jesus and the modern Zionist movement. Basically, both movements highlight the idea of bridging a historical gap between modern times and biblical times. Namely, they consciously reject allegations that they maintain anachronistic approaches. On the contrary, contemporary Jewish Jesus-believers and mainstream Zionists raise the opposite argument that they still possess a natural right to bypass the last two millennia and directly relate to the pre-exilic period in Israel's history.[10]

Nerel's theological method and shape blends the independent evangelical stream of the previous generation of Messianic Jews who made *Aliyah* in the 1950s with the establishment of the State of Israel and the Zionist movement, combining Jewish political action and Christian eschatology. His eschatology is premillennial, but he avoids the systematisation of Dispensationalism. His realised eschatology stresses the significance of the re-emergence of Messianic Jews in the Land. This could become an important factor in the future, as the Messianic movement grows in Israel, and takes on greater political and prophetic relevance.

Type 4 – New Testament Halacha, Charismatic and Evangelical (Juster, Stern)

The most popular type of MJT found within the Messianic movement is that of David Stern and Daniel Juster, who advocate 'New Testament *halacha*' within a Jewish expression of faith that is evangelical and charismatic.[11] It is the dominant influence within the UMJC and integrates belief in Jesus as Messiah with Jewish tradition. It expresses Christian orthodoxy within a Jewish cultural and religious matrix, seeing a prophetic and restorative role for Messianic Judaism in the renewal of both Judaism and Christianity. Its

---

[9] Gershon Nerel, 'Modern Assemblies of Jewish Yeshua-Believers between Church and Synagogue,' in *How Jewish is Christianity? Two Views on the Messianic Movement*, edited by Stanley N. Gundry and Louis Goldberg (Grand Rapids: Zondervan, 2003), 106.

[10] Gershon Nerel, 'Primitive Jewish Christians in the Modern thought of Messianic Jews.' In *Le Judéo-Christianisme Dans Tous Ses États: Actes Du Colloque De Jérusalem 6–10 Juillet 1998*, edited by Simon C. Mimouni and F. Stanley Jones (Paris: Cerf, 2001), 399–425.

[11] Other key practitioners are Burt Yellin, Barney Kasdan and the majority of UMJC and MJAA leaders.

theological system is an eclectic combination of evangelical innovation and traditional Jewish observance.

Belief in God and the Trinity follows Christian orthodoxy, but this is translated into Jewish forms of thought and expression. Nicene Christology is recontextualised and expressed in Jewish terms. The doctrine of the Incarnation is expressed apologetically and in dynamically equivalent Jewish terms. The Torah is re-defined in the light of Yeshua, and the Oral Torah is critically evaluated in the light of the New Testament. The Messianic Movement belongs to the movement of restoration of the whole Church, and is part of Israel. Historic Premillennialist eschatology brings urgent expectation of what God is doing in the Land and among the people of Israel.

Salvation is only by faith in Yeshua. Yet Israel is still the people of God, and her future salvation is assured. Until this happens evangelistic witness is imperative, but must be done in ways that are culturally sensitive, showing how the Messianic movement is part of the Jewish community, not separate from it or outside it. Scripture is the supreme authority, but must be interpreted and applied contextually, following the 'Fuller School of World Mission' approach developed by Glasser, Goble and Hutchens. The Oral Torah can help understand and interpret NT *halacha*. The Torah to be observed is that of Yeshua and his followers, with some appropriate adjustments for today.

The future of this stream within the movement is bright, as it occupies the middle ground between Jewish and Christian spheres of influence. It has found popular expression in many Messianic congregations, especially in the USA, combining a vibrant charismatic expression of faith with a 'Torah positive' attitude to Jewish tradition. However, its theological integrity and authenticity has yet to be made explicit, and the tension between tradition and innovation reconciled. The pioneering statements made by Juster and Stern in the formative period of the 1970s and 1980s have yet to be consolidated. It remains to be seen how the combination of charismatic evangelicalism and 'New Covenant Torah observance' will be accepted by the next generation in Israel and the USA.

Type 5 – Traditional Judaism and the Messiah (Schiffman, Fischer, Berkowitz)

Several independent thinkers can be situated between Stern and Juster on one side and Kinzer and Hashivenu on the other. They cannot be easily aligned, as their thinking has not fully emerged and it is difficult to locate their contribution precisely. Nevertheless in the USA John Fischer and Michael Schiffman and in Israel Ariel Berkowitz, David Freedman and Arieh Powlison bring perspectives which are both 'Torah positive' and appreciative of Rabbinic tradition without the full affirmation given them by Kinzer and the Hashivenu group. The systematisation of their views is incomplete, and their theological reflection has yet to be abstracted. They practice a halachic orthopraxy informed by faith in Jesus. It is possible that new streams of MJT may emerge more fully from this as yet disparate group. Whilst they remain close to Jewish orthodoxy their doctrine of Revelation does not see rabbinic tradition as the inspired, God-given means for the preservation of the Jewish people (as does Kinzer), but their observance of rabbinic *halacha* is stronger than that of Juster and Stern.

Powlison brings a new spirituality to his thinking, and Freedman and Berkowitz bring a new orientation to the Torah making it available, in principle if not in practice, to the Nations. Fischer approaches Torah from his own orthodox Jewish background, but with the eyes of a New Testament follower of Yeshua. This group have maintained orthodox Christian beliefs, whilst interacting with Jewish traditional views and objections, on the nature of God, the Messiah, and the Torah. Their eschatology is premillennial. Their observance of Torah follows orthodoxy, whilst allowing for re-statement where appropriate. Scripture is read in the light of rabbinic tradition, but is still supreme as authoritative revelation. The emerging shape of this theology is not clear, but could result in 'Messianic Hasidism' with a possibly more Orthodox Jewish expression.

Type 6 – 'Postmissionary Messianic Judaism' (Kinzer, Nichol, Sadan)

Mark Kinzer's 'Postmissionary Messianic Judaism' presents the potential for a programmatic theological system. Combating supersessionist readings of scripture to argue for the ongoing election of Israel and the legitimacy of a Torah-observant Messianic Judaism, Kinzer employs postliberal[12] and postcritical Jewish and Christian theological resources. His understanding of the revelation of God through the scriptures and Jewish tradition acknowledges the significance of the Jewish and Christian faith communities through which such revelation is mediated. Ecclesiology and soteriology cohere around his bilateral understanding (reflecting Karl Barth) of the community of God made up of both 'unbelieving' Israel, and the Church, with

---

[12] Postliberalism began as a reaction to theological liberalism. Karl Barth's reaction against Protestant liberal theology of the 19th and early 20th centuries was taken up by some of his followers in the USA to produce a new engagement with the Bible, Church tradition and contemporary culture. This sat in between the 'liberal' and 'conservative' labels. Key postliberal theologians include George Lindbeck, Hans Frei and Stanley Hauerwas, and the academic journals *First Things* and *Pro Ecclesia* are representative of postliberal thought. Postliberalism reacts against the relativism and rationalism of theological liberalism, with a more sympathetic reading of the Bible and Church tradition, but with an openness to theological ecumenism, the existence and impact of other faiths, and engagement with contemporary culture. Cf. Richard Harvey, 'Shaping the Aims and Aspirations of Jewish Believers (Review of Mark Kinzer's *Postmissionary Messianic Judaism*)' *Mishkan* 48 (2006): 18–21.

Jesus present in both, visible to the *ekklesia* but only partially recognised by Israel. This 'mature Messianic Judaism' is summarised by the Hashivenu statement of purpose:

> Our goal is a mature Messianic Judaism. We seek an authentic expression of Jewish life maintaining substantial continuity with Jewish tradition. However, Messianic Judaism is energized by the belief that Yeshua of Nazareth is the promised Messiah, the fullness of Torah. Mature Messianic Judaism is not simply Judaism plus Yeshua, but is instead an integrated following of Yeshua through traditional Jewish forms and the modern day practice of Judaism in and through Yeshua.[13]

It is clear that Kinzer's influences and assumptions place him outside the mainstream of Protestant evangelicalism, especially the conservative variety often found within previous forms of Messianic Judaism. His view of the authority and inspiration of scripture is tempered by respect for Jewish traditions of interpretation, the influence of critical and postcritical biblical scholarship and postliberal theology.

Kinzer advocates solidarity with the Jewish community.[14] He encourages sympathetic identification with the religious and cultural concerns of Judaism, as found in the North American context. The primary location of identity is 'within the Jewish community' in order that Messianic Jews will 'have Jewish grandchildren'. One purpose is to refute the accusation of assimilation that is levelled at Jewish believers in Jesus by the Jewish community.

'Postmissionary Messianic Judaism' arises as one way of negotiating the tension between proclamation of Jesus as Messiah, and the preservation of Jewish belief, practice and identity. Such concerns reflect the challenges facing the Messianic movement worldwide as it grows in theological, spiritual, communal and personal maturity. Kinzer's response is a Messianic Judaism that echoes Conservative Judaism in its liturgy and practice, and integrates belief in Yeshua in the context of loyalties and identity to 'Jewish space.'

Kinzer sees Jesus as divine, but within a Judaism not inhospitable to the possibility of the divinity and incarnation of the Son of God. The historic Christian formulations of the Trinity are inadequate in Jewish contexts because they are steeped in Hellenism. New postcritical formulations are required that emerge from Jewish tradition and are recognised as possible understandings of the nature of God. The scriptures of Judaism and Christianity are both inspired, and to be interpreted within a non-

---

[13] http://www.hashivenu.org/what_is.htm (accessed 17 March 2006).

[14] Others in this group include Stuart Dauermann, Paul Saal, Rich Nichol, Jason Sobel, and the New England Halachic Council.

supersessionist appreciation of the canonical and communal contexts in which they arose.

Torah is observed in the light of Orthodox and Conservative *halacha*, with some modifications. Jewish believers thus integrate Messianic beliefs within traditional synagogal life, and witness to the Messiah through the presence of a community within the Jewish community rather than through overt appeal to individuals from without.

Kinzer's approach is the most theologically creative proposal to have emerged within Messianic Judaism in recent years, but it remains to be seen how much communal acceptance it will receive. It builds on North American Conservative Judaism in its method and expression, and departs significantly from the evangelical foundations to which much of Messianic Judaism still adheres. Its theological articulation, whilst profound, may not find popular appeal.[15]

Type 7 – Rabbinic Halacha in the Light of the NT (Shulam)

Joseph Shulam expresses an Israeli form of Messianic Judaism using the resources of Orthodox Judaism. Shulam makes the call to 'do Messianic Jewish *halacha*' and to cut the 'umbilical cord' that connects Messianic Judaism to Christian denominations. He reads the scriptures within the controlling hermeneutical framework of the Jewish tradition. His aim is to teach the Church the Jewish roots of its faith by a series of commentaries on the Jewish sources of the New Testament writings.[16]

The project is incomplete, and it is not clear how such a theology will be formulated. Shulam's main concern is to clear away the preliminary barriers of twenty centuries of non-Jewish reading of the scriptures. His call for Messianic *halacha* is in reaction to the 'Gentilisation' of Messianic Judaism. Whilst he advocates a return to *halacha*, it is not clear in what form this will emerge. However, his is a genuine and Israeli-based expression of a Jewish orthodoxy linked to orthodox Christian beliefs about Jesus. His perspective is one that should be recognised within the spectrum of MJT, and it is possible that others will follow in his emphases.[17]

---

[15] Kinzer's work *Postmissionary Messianic Judaism* (Grand Rapids: Baker Academic/ Brazos, 2005) has been the subject of major discussions and reviews in *Mishkan* 48 (2006) 'Reactions to Postmissionary Messianic Judaism' and *Kesher* 20 (Winter/ Spring 2006).

[16] Joseph Shulam, with Hilary Le Cornu, *A Commentary of the Jewish Roots of Romans* (Baltimore: Lederer Books, 1997).

[17] Shulam's position is further complicated by repeated concerns that his Christology is not fully orthodox. Reference has been made to his written work, and not to unconfirmed verbal remarks attributed to him.

Shulam disassociates himself from mainstream (and 'Gentilised') Christianity, situating himself within Jewish social and religious space. He combines Messianic Judaism with mystical traditions in Judaism that lead to affirmations of his faith. Rabbinic, and even mystical traditions are part of the revelatory process, and are to be held in balance with scripture. Shulam's theological system is based on a midrashic approach to scripture, a reading of the New Testament influenced by David Flusser, and some expression of the Jewish mystical tradition (Kabbalah) factored into his overall approach.

Type 8 – Messianic Rabbinic Orthodoxy (Brandt, Marcus)

Elazar Brandt advocates a form of Messianic Judaism that is close to rabbinic orthodoxy, but is a minority position within the Messianic movement. He is convinced that Messianic Jews must: 'make every effort to remain committed to the 4 pillars of Jewish existence that have always held us together – G-d[18], land, people and Torah. History repeatedly shows that groups who have abandoned any of these commitments have quickly disappeared from the scene.'[19] His advocacy of Torah observance is so strong that: 'I dare say that it is less dangerous to follow the wrong Messiah than to follow the wrong Torah.'[20]

The authority of Torah, which for him is interpreted through rabbinic tradition, influences his Christology: 'The rightful Messiah will come to Jerusalem where his throne will be established and where he will rule Israel and the nations with justice according to the Torah. There is no such thing as a Messiah who does not keep Torah and teach his people to do so. If Yeshua does not do and teach Torah, then he is not the Messiah – not for Israel, and not for anybody else.'[21] This leads him to oppose all forms of supersessionism. 'There is no such thing as a Messiah who is not the Messiah of Israel. A Messiah who rejects Israel and chooses another people group is not the Messiah promised in the Bible.'[22]

Messianic Jews have no special status among their people as the 'faithful remnant' of Romans 9–11, but rather take their stand within the faithful found within all Israel. They cannot claim special status as the 'remnant' because of their belief in Yeshua, as this would disenfranchise others who do not believe in him. 'Jews who claim to follow Yeshua and to know and do his

---

[18] Brandt follows an Orthodox Jewish custom of not writing the word 'God' in full.

[19] Elazar Brandt, e-mail message to author, February 26, 2007. This has been referred to at length to ensure accurate representation of Brandt's views, and because he has published few statements of his position on these questions.

[20] Ibid.

[21] Ibid.

[22] Ibid.

Torah more perfectly than other Jews, and on such a basis claim to be the "true Israel", or the "true remnant of Israel", or other such language, are no less in the replacement camp than Christians who believe G-d has rejected Israel and chosen them instead.'[23] Brandt's soteriology includes all Israel.

> The 'Israel' who today walks the streets of Jerusalem and the cities throughout the land, and the Jews who are identifiable outside of the land, are the Israel that G-d is going to see through to redemption. He staked his name on this by an oath. This includes Haredis and secular, Conservative and Reform as well as Zionist and uncommitted. 'All Israel shall be saved,' said Paul. If G-d does not keep this promise, then he is not G-d. He said so Himself.[24]

Brandt's hermeneutics call for a return to halachic orthodoxy. To Brandt this means abandoning a 'spiritualising and fantasising' approach to the Bible, and returning to 'literal interpretation and obedience'. Jews who believe in Yeshua remain Jews. They are called to repent, not by being 'sorry for personal sins', but by returning to the covenant, and remaining 'faithful to our G-d, land, people and Torah'. As regards the witness of Messianic Jews to their people: 'Our best testimony to our own people will be if we can show that we are doing this because we met Yeshua. Instead, we have been doing our best to show that we have broken our covenant with the four pillars [God, Land, People and Torah] since we have met Yeshua. What reason is there today or in the past for our people to see us otherwise?'[25]

This type is at the far end of the continuum, and expresses a tendency to move back into Judaism at the expense of Christian affirmations and distinctives. Uri Marcus puts forward a revised adoptionist Christology, Elazar Brandt is more comfortable within Jewish Orthodoxy, and ultra-orthodox Hasidim who come to believe in Jesus and remain in their communities, practising as 'secret believers', invisible to outsiders, as part of an 'insider movement.'

Like Brandt, Marcus distances himself from 'Hellenistic' and 'Gentile' Christianity. Marcus subscribes to Orthodox Jewish views on the indivisibility and singularity of the Divine nature which rules out the possibility of the Trinity. However, his dispensational premillennial eschatology and its charismatic expression relate closely to Christian Zionism, and his denial of the Trinity and Incarnation has caused controversy in Christian Zionist and Messianic Jewish circles.

For Marcus, Jesus is the human Messiah, who did not claim deity and is not divine. Scripture is read in context of rabbinic tradition, which informs and controls the results of such reading. Rabbinic *halacha* is accepted, and

---

[23] Ibid.

[24] Ibid.

[25] Ibid.

there is little overt proclamation. Whilst the theology of this stream has yet to be comprehensively or systematically articulated, it is an influential if heterodox group within the Messianic movement. Without clearer definition of the significance of Yeshua, it is likely that for some it will be a means back into Jewish orthodoxy, and that an increasing number of Messianic Jews will take up the label of 'Orthodox' or 'Just Jewish'.

The Future of Messianic Jewish Theology

The above typology leaves many questions unanswered, but suggests several ways forward for MJT. The following section makes proposals for the development of MJT and highlights the theological concerns it needs to address.

The Task of Messianic Jewish Theology

The methodology followed in this book has been primarily descriptive and evaluative, but has considered requirements for the development and construction of MJT. A fully detailed articulation of MJT would of necessity be far more rigorous in its engagement with the primary and secondary sources of Jewish, Christian and Messianic Jewish thought. It would need to engage directly with, for example, the Hebrew Bible, Mishnaic, Midrashic and Talmudic literature, the Codes, Responsa, mystical traditions, and contemporary Jewish thought. The Christian tradition from the Church Fathers, Scholastics, and Reformers, through to modern and postmodern theological authors would also need to be fully discussed. The medieval and modern Hebrew Christian tradition would also be included. Such work on the primary sources has been beyond the remit of the present undertaking. My aim has been more modest, and has situated contemporary practitioners in the context of these traditions, examining and commenting on their own proposals. But such a treatment would be necessary for a future comprehensive statement of MJT.

There is as yet no standard work of MJT. This is a priority for the movement, and this study forms part of the prolegomena to such a contribution. Therefore proposals made for the future development of MJT must be appropriately modest at this stage. Nevertheless I tentatively offer three proposals on method and eight on content.

Recognition of the Need for MJT

If MJT is to develop, one important need is the production of theological works. Whilst there are significant materials from which to construct MJT, they have yet to be organised, consolidated and processed reflectively. There exists no *Dictionary of Messianic Judaism* or *Dictionary of Messianic*

Jewish Theology. There is no *Encyclopaedia Judaica Messianica* at present, and no attempt has been made to compose a one-volume work of *Messianic Jewish Theology* or multi-volume *Messianic Jewish Dogmatics* or *Talmud*. Individuals or groups of Messianic Jews willing to co-operate in this activity could undertake such projects.[26]

The shape and structure of such projects requires further discussion. There are at present no systematic presentations of Messianic Jewish Theology, in any form. Several possible organising frameworks can be suggested for a systematic MJT. These include: a systematic/dogmatic presentation organised on the lines of Jewish and Christian systematic theologies; a dialectical theology working 'in terms of complementary polar opposites rather than in definitional and systematic categories characteristic of Western philosophy;'[27] in a Talmudic argument or record of discussions; theology organised as biblical commentary or halachic compendium; a pedagogical primer or catechetical manual.

Interdependency within MJT

MJT lacks a theological tradition, and is in the early stages of forming one. To do this its practitioners will need to interact more effectively, both affirming their own distinctives whilst engaging with one another in critical but respectful expression of differences. At present there are few forums where such interaction takes place.[28] A growing interdependence needs to emerge for the successful development of a theological tradition. Whilst a universal or 'catholic MJT' is unlikely to emerge, the present need is for those already doing such theology to constructively interact with one another in the formation of a developing tradition and ongoing theological conversation. The first *Borough Park Symposium* represents such an attempt. Its guiding principles for discussion brought a wide range of Messianic Jewish participants together to encourage such interdependency:

> The purpose of the symposium is to provide a forum for members of the broader Messianic Jewish community to articulate their beliefs with an expectation that they will receive a respectful hearing, but without the expectation that agreement concerning these beliefs will be achieved. The Symposium is designed to provide

---

[26] One notable exception to this lack is the co-operative effort edited by Dan Cohn-Sherbok, *Voices of Messianic Judaism: Confronting Critical Issues Facing a Maturing Movement* (Baltimore: Lederer Books, 2001).

[27] Sherwin, *Towards a Jewish Theology*, 3.

[28] Those forums that take place regularly are the Hashivenu Forum (Pasadena), the Lausanne Consultation on Jewish Evangelism (LCJE) national and international conferences. Journals devoted to Messianic Judaism include *Kesher* and *Mishkan*.

an internal platform for leaders to better understand each another and the various positions held within the Messianic movement.[29]

Discussion of Methodology

With the exceptions of Mark Kinzer, David Stern and Arnold Fruchtenbaum there has been little reflection on the methods to be employed in the construction of MJT. Yet it will be vital for the development of MJT and the growth of Messianic Judaism that discussion of such necessary prolegomena should be held, as the implicit assumptions of Messianic Jews need to be recognised and evaluated in the light of Jewish, Christian and Messianic Jewish tradition.

There are at present no agreed statements of theological method in MJT, nor proposals for hermeneutics, engagement with Jewish and Christian traditions, or the formulation of doctrine. The validity of the project of MJT has yet to be recognised and affirmed, in the light of more pressing pastoral and governantal concerns.

Future Topics for Consideration in Messianic Jewish Theology

As regards the content of MJT, proposals for the development of the topics discussed in previous chapters have been made. Here further topics on which important work needs to be done are identified, and the directions in which such reflection might proceed.

Revelation and Tradition

Consideration needs given to be nature of revelation and its relationship to scripture, and to the dual traditions and canonical communities of Judaism and Christianity. How revelation is mediated, and the role of tradition in this process, needs clarification in the light of the faith communities with which Messianic Judaism is engaged.

---

[29] David J. Rudolph, 'About the Symposium,' http://www.chosenpeople.com/symposium (accessed December 10, 2007). The first Borough Park Symposium (held in Borough Park, New York, October 8–10, 2007) brought together several streams of the Messianic movement. See especially David J. Rudolph, 'Guidelines for Healthy Theological Discussion. (A Paper Presented at the Borough Park Symposium on the Gospel, October 8, 2007),' http://www.chosenpeople.com/symposium/papers/ RudolphFinal.pdf (accessed December 10, 2007).

Ecclesiology and Israelology

Major discussion will also be needed on the understanding of the relationship between Israel and the Church, and the place of Messianic Jews. Mark
Kinzer suggests:

> I think the first issue that Messianic Jewish thought must address in order to
> develop at a higher level of reflection is that of ecclesiology. Before we can under-
> stand ourselves, we need to understand the Church and the Jewish people, and the
> relationship between them. Before we can determine our own distinctive place (as
> Messianic Jews) in relation to these two historic communities and traditions, we
> need to assess their respective theological status – where they stand before God and
> in Messiah – and the mysterious way they are both united and divided.[30]

Kinzer's proposals will not appeal to the majority of Messianic Jews, as his
ecclesiology holds the Jewish 'no' and the Church's 'yes' to Jesus in an
uneasy tension. Messianic Jews need to assess their own significance as 'the
remnant', as much as that of the Church and Israel. The criteria and methodology for such an investigation has not been addressed. The 'epistemic
priority' of Israel needs to be understood in the light of the Messiahship of
Yeshua, and the relationship between the Church and Israel needs to be
understood in a post-supersessionist way that still sees a place for Messianic
Jews.[31] For MJT, this affirmation needs to be properly aligned with an adequate soteriology in order to correctly conceive the relationship between
Israel and the Church.

Christology and Election

A subsequent topic that needs further investigation is the relationship
between Christology and Election, both of the individual, the Church, and
Israel. Mark Kinzer asks:

> Is the Church's relationship to the Messiah severely compromised when its rela-
> tionship to the Jewish people and tradition are hostile or tenuous? Is the Jewish
> people's relationship with the crucified and risen Yeshua determined definitively

---

[30] Mark Kinzer, e-mail to author, January 6, 2005.
[31] Bruce D. Marshall, *Trinity and Truth* (Cambridge: CUP, 2000), 171–72. Marshall
states: 'When it comes to deciding about truth, God's unshakeable electing love for
Israel forms that conviction within the open field of possible beliefs which the faithful Jew is most unwilling to give up or reinterpret, and correlatively that with
which all other belief and practice must at least be consistent in order to be held true
or regarded as right.'

and negatively by its communal decision that he is not Israel's Messiah? You still presume that historical Judaism has been without Messiah Yeshua these past two thousand years. That is both a Christological and ecclesiological conclusion that is not self-evident (at least to me).[32]

A fuller exploration is needed of the mystery of Israel's election, and the significance of the Messiah in the light of that election.

Holocaust Theology

Whilst several Messianic Jews have written on the Holocaust,[33] there exists no systematic survey of their views, or a compilation of Messianic Jewish Holocaust Theology. As a key question relating to theodicy and apologetics in the light of Christian Anti-Semitism, the need for such a treatment is clear.

Pneumatology

Whilst the influence of the Charismatic movement is strong in Messianic Judaism, no developed Pneumatology exists in the movement, which is divided on the question of the activity and role of the Holy Spirit. The place of liturgy, and especially Messianic Jewish Synagogal liturgy, in the light of the work of the Holy Spirit, needs further investigation. Also the role of the Holy Spirit in inspiring scripture and guiding the Church and the Jewish community in the development of an inspired and authoritative tradition needs exploration. How the Holy Spirit inspires the Jewish tradition, and how Messianic Jews claim significant prophetic inspiration and authority has also to be addressed.

Messianic Jewish Identity

A deeper theological understanding of Jewish and Messianic Jewish identity is needed. How identity is constructed, and how a theology of identity is developed, are questions Messianic Jews have frequently discussed, but without organised reflection. Questions of identity are directly relevant to the construction of MJT, and the issues raised by the location of identity primarily within 'Jewish space' are driven by theological as well as anthropological concerns. How Messianic Jews define their 'Jewish identity' as primary and their membership of the Body of the Messiah as secondary – a particular concern of the Hashivenu forum – will need explanation. Further theological investigation of the construction of various Messianic Jewish

---

[32] Mark Kinzer, e-mail to author, January 6, 2005.
[33] Barry Leventhal, Tsvi Sadan, Arthur Katz.

identities found in Israel and Diaspora is also needed. This should include the differences between older and younger generations, and between the varieties of Orthodox, Conservative and Reform expressions as they link to different forms of Christian tradition.

Study of the nature of Israel as the people of God will discuss several areas. The vexed questions of 'Who is a Jew?' and 'What shapes Jewish identity?' will need investigation in the light of historical, anthropological and theological factors. Also needing consideration are: conversion to Judaism and Messianic Judaism; intermarriage; and the nature of mission to Israel, the Church and the world.

Jewish-Christian Relations, Ecumenism and Inter-faith Activity

With few exceptions, Messianic Jewish theology has not addressed the wider circles of Jewish and Christian theological reflection. Yet MJT claims to make a distinctive and significant contribution to the theological thinking of both traditions. It also raises important questions for Jewish-Christian relations. Messianic Jews will need to assess their own significance in the light of changing paradigms of practical interaction and theological engagement between Christians and Jews.

The existence of Messianic Judaism and its theological implications have yet to be recognised in Jewish-Christian dialogue, and Messianic Jews are seldom invited to contribute to such discussions.[34] Whether the presence of Messianic Jews is an unhelpful distraction to the work of Jewish-Christian relations, or the catalyst for a new paradigm, has yet to be seen, and MJT can make a significant contribution to such a discussion.

In terms of ecumenism within both Judaism and Christianity, MJT must address itself to the issues and concerns of ecumenical encounter at several levels, entering into dialogue with both Orthodox, Conservative and Reform Judaism, and with the historic and new churches within Christianity.

As regards wider interfaith activity, MJT has yet to address itself to world religions and others faiths. Particularly in relation to Islam and Buddhism the movement has much to learn and contribute. Such activity is particularly relevant in the light of the Israel-Palestine conflict and the growing number of Jewish Buddhists.

---

[34] Cf. David Rudolph, 'Messianic Jews and Christian Theology: Restoring an Historical Voice to the Contemporary Discussion,' *Pro Ecclesia* 14, no. 1 (March 2005): 65–86. See also Mark Kinzer and Matthew Levering, "Messianic Gentiles and Messianic Jews" in *First Things* (January 2009), 43–49.

Other Issues

Other issues to be considered more fully include the role of women in Messianic Judaism, the relationship between Israel and the Diaspora in MJT, and the politics and theology of peace and reconciliation in the Israel/Palestine context.

Questions for Future Research

There remain several questions that should be pursued in future research on MJT. These include the following.

Models For Messianic Jewish Theology as Theology and Contextual Theology

Whilst a description has been given of the emerging types of theology within the Messianic movement, more detailed and reflective consideration of these theologies would be achieved by applying appropriate models for their understanding. George Lindbeck and Hans Frei have proposed models for types of theology.[35] Stephen Bevans and Robert Schreiter have considered models of contextual theology.[36] The appropriate application of such models has been beyond the purpose of the present study, but may be important in understanding further the nature of MJT.

Detailed Studies of Messianic Jewish Theologians

There are at present no detailed studies of any contemporary Messianic Jewish theologian.[37] It would be of value to have a theological biography of one or more of the practitioners discussed in the present study, showing their own theological development, the contexts in which they function, and the key concerns they address.

---

[35] George Lindbeck, *The Nature of Doctrine: Religions and Theology in a Postliberal Age* (Westminster: John Knox Press, 1984); Hans W. Frei, *Types of Christian Theology*, edited by George Hunsinger and William C. Placher (New Haven: Yale University Press, 1992).

[36] Stephen B. Bevans and Robert J. Schreiter, *Models of Contextual Theology* Rev. ed. (Maryknoll: Orbis Books, 2002).

[37] Cf. Kai Kjær-Hansen, *Joseph Rabinowitz and the Messianic Movement*, trans. Birger Petterson (Grand Rapids: Eerdmans, 1995).

Theological Methodology and Interface with Cultural Studies

The present study has demonstrated the need for a theological study of MJT, but further exposition of theological method in the light of cultural studies and other academic disciplines is needed.[38]

Concluding Summary

This book is the first account of MJT from a theological perspective by an engaged practitioner. It has focused on the theological nature of Messianic Judaism, providing a theological reading of MJT and clarifying the main issues of theological concern. Whilst MJT is still at an embryonic and developmental stage, the study has shown that it does exist and must continue to develop if it is to meet the challenges facing Messianic Judaism. 'It is not incumbent on you to finish the task; yet, you are not free to desist from it.'[39]

---

[38] Cf. Katherine Tanner, *Theories of Culture: A New Agenda for Theology*, (Minneapolis: Augsburg, 1997).

[39] Pirkei Avot [Sayings of the Fathers], 2:21 in Nosson Scherman (ed.), *The Complete Artscroll Siddur*, 2nd ed. (Brooklyn: Mesorah Publications, 1986), 568.

Appendix

Materials

Primary Sources

Rationale for the Use of Quotations

The primary sources for the study of MJT are the written materials of its practitioners.[1] Wherever possible reference is made to published works. Online resources such as the websites of different organisations have been used where appropriate. Unpublished materials include lecture notes, unpublished papers and correspondence.[2] Considerable use of quotation from the sources is found throughout the book, for the following reasons. Many of the materials referred to have not been previously published. This is the first documentation of many primary sources that are not easily accessible, or available elsewhere. Significant quotation also enables the voices of MJT to be heard clearly as they speak for themselves. It avoids the imposition of the author's theological framework upon them.

Choice of Contributors

The present study thus provides the first airing and consideration of theological material by a range of Messianic Jewish theologians in the context of the key themes under discussion. Materials are limited to those written by Jewish believers in Jesus who have been active in the modern Messianic

---

[1] The literature in Hebrew on MJT will not be considered in the present work. Attention is drawn to *Kivun* (published by Tsvi Sadan, Jerusalem, kivun@netvision.net.il) and *Zot Habrit* (The Magazine of the Messianic Jewish Alliance of Israel, http://www.mjai.org) for Hebrew material on Messianic Judaism.

[2] Permissions have been give for the use of published and unpublished material, and clearance of copyright has been acknowledged by Arnold Fruchtenbaum, Daniel Juster, Mark Kinzer, Baruch Maoz, Uri Marcus, Rich Nichol, David Rudolph, Tsvi Sadan and David Stern.

movement and have made original contributions to the topics under investigation.[3]

Not all those included in the present study are recognised as 'Messianic Jewish theologians' by all streams of the movement, or identify themselves as such. Arnold Fruchtenbaum identifies himself as both a Messianic Jew and a Hebrew Christian. Yet he writes as an advocate for a particular type of Messianic Judaism and as a member of a Messianic Jewish congregation.[4] The editorial decision to include his material in *Voices of Messianic Judaism* indicates recognition of his influence as a theologian within the movement, despite his early work under the title of *Hebrew Christianity*.[5] Similarly Baruch Maoz distinguishes strongly between his own 'Jewish Christianity' and 'Messianic Judaism' in his book *Judaism is not Jewish: A Friendly Critique of the Messianic Movement*. Yet he represents the views of many Messianic Jews in Israel, and is deeply engaged with theological issues in the movement. As pastor of one of the largest Hebrew-speaking Congregations in Israel, his views have significant influence.[6]

---

[3] Thus excluding from consideration important pre-formative theologians, such as John Toland, Joseph Rabinowitz, Paul Levertoff, Jacob Jocz, Abraham Poljak. Hebrew Catholic contributions have not been included, although they address many of the same questions within the Roman Catholic Church. Cf. Leon Menzies Racionzer, 'Hebrew Catholicism: Theology and Politics in Modern Israel,' *Heythrop Journal* 45 (2004): 405–15. Whilst there have been significant contributions to MJT by those who are not Jewish themselves (e.g. Philip Goble), for the purposes of this study those writers are not included.

[4] Arnold Fruchtenbaum, 'Messianic Congregations May Exist Within the Body of Messiah, as Long As They Don't Function Contrary to the New Testament' in *How Jewish is Christianity? Two Views on the Messianic Movement* edited by Stanley N. Gundry and Louis Goldberg (Grand Rapids: Zondervan, 2003), 112. 'As I write this chapter, the reader should be aware that I am in favour of Messianic Congregations and am a member of one but I do not necessarily see Messianic Congregations being the final answer or the best solution for all Jewish believers everywhere.' Fruchtenbaum affirms his support for MJCs but challenges the UMJC definition that makes membership normative. Daniel Juster comments 'Arnold Fruchtenbaum is a Messianic Jewish theologian of sorts' (e-mail message to author, February 25, 2006).

[5] Cf. Arnold Fruchtenbaum, 'Eschatology and Messianic Jews: A Theological Perspective' in *Voices of Messianic Judaism: Confronting Critical Issues Facing a Maturing Movement* edited by Dan Cohn-Sherbok (Baltimore: Lederer Books, 2001): 211–20.

[6] Maoz is Pastor of the Grace and Truth Assembly in Rehovot, Israel. The dedication of his book *Judaism is not Jewish: A Friendly Critique of the Messianic Movement*, (Christian Focus Publications and CWI, 2003) is to Paul Lieberman, the Executive Director of the IMJA and author of *The Fig Tree Blossoms: Messianic Judaism Emerges*, (Indianola, Iowa: Fountain Press Inc., 1976, 1977, 1980). He is willing to be identified as a Messianic Jewish theologian (email correspondence with author, May 2003.)

Official Documents of Messianic Jewish Organisations

References to conference proceedings, official statements, creeds and doctrinal bases of messianic organisations will be given as appropriate. Whilst Messianic Jews have discussed how creeds have been formulated in Judaism, there has been little discussion in the modern movement on the *authority* of creeds.[7] Messianic Jews have yet to recognise any one creed as authoritative, although those joining congregations and messianic organisations are often asked to subscribe to a doctrinal basis in order to become members.

Secondary Sources

There are few secondary sources for MJT. In additions to the research referred to above, other secondary materials that contribute to the discussion of MJT are used as appropriate. These include reviews and studies published in the journals *Mishkan* and *Kesher*, and the LCJE Bulletin.

---

[7] Kai Kjær-Hansen and Bodil Skjøtt, eds., *Mishkan* 34 (The Development of Creeds) (2001) contains articles on the 'Making of Creeds', 'Creeds in Judaism', and 'Creeds in the Early Hebrew Christian Movement', but no survey of contemporary Messianic Jewish Creeds. Kai Kjær-Hansen and Bodil Skjøtt, *Facts and Myths about the Messianic Congregations in Israel* (Israel: UCCI, 1999) note those Messianic Congregations in Israel that have a doctrinal statement, but do not reproduce them.

Bibliography

Abramson, Barry. 'The Differences between Israeli and American Messianic Jewish Believers and the Implications for the Future.' MA diss., All Nations Christian College, 2005.

Adams, Gillian. 'Issues that Face Jewish Believers.' Advanced Diploma in Pastoral Studies diss., Trinity College, Bristol, 1985.

Ariel, Yacov. *Evangelising the Chosen People: Missions to the Jews in America 1880–2000*. Chapel Hill: University of North Carolina Press, 2000.

Bacciochi, Samuele. *From Saturday to Sunday: A Historical Investigation of the Rise of Sunday Observance in Early Christianity*. Rome: Pontifical Gregorian University Press, 1977.

Baeck, Leo. 'Romantic Religion,' in *Jewish Perspectives on Christianity: Leo Baeck, Martin Buber, Franz Rosenzweig, Will Herberg, and Abraham J. Heschel*. Ed. Fritz A. Rothschild. New York: Crossroad Publishing, 1990.

Barth, Karl. *The Epistle to the Romans*. 6th ed. Translated by Edwyn C. Hoskins. Oxford: Oxford University Press, 1933.

Bauckham, Richard. *God Crucified*. Carlisle: Paternoster, 1998.

———. 'Must Christian Eschatology Be Millenarian? A Response to Jürgen Moltmann.' In *'The Reader Must Understand': Eschatology in Bible and Theology*, edited by K.E. Brewer and M.W. Elliott, 263–78. Leicester: Apollos, 1997.

———. *Jesus and the God of Israel: 'God Crucified' and Other Studies on the New Testament's Christology of Divine Identity*. Milton Keynes: Paternoster, 2008.

Benhayim, Menachem. *Jews, Gentiles and the New Testament: Alleged Anti-semitism in the New Testament*. Jerusalem: Yanetz Press, 1985.

Becker, Adam H. and Annette Yoshiko Reed, eds. *The Ways That Never Parted: Jews and Christians in Late Antiquity and the Early Middle Ages*. Minneapolis: Fortress Press, 2007.

Berger, David. *The Rebbe, The Messiah, and the Scandal of Orthodox Indifference*. London: Littman Library of Jewish Civilisation, 2001.

Berger, David and Michael Wyschogrod. *Jews and 'Jewish Christianity'*. New York: Ktav, 1978.

Berger, Leigh Paula. 'Messianic Judaism: Searching the Spirit.' PhD diss., University of South Florida, 2000.

Berkouwer, G.C. *The Return of Christ: Studies in Dogmatics.* Grand Rapids: William B. Eerdmans, 1972.

Berkowitz, Ariel. *According to God's Heart: A Biblical Case for a Torah Lifestyle.* Portland: Torah Resources International, 2003.

———. 'Torah Study.' *Tishrei* 3, no. 2 (Summer 1995): 31–44.

Berkowitz, Ariel and Devorah Berkowitz. *Torah Rediscovered: Challenging Centuries of Misinterpretation and Neglect.* 3rd ed. Littleton: First Fruits of Zion, 1998.

Berner, Astrid. 'Messianic Jews in Israel: Seen from Within and Without.' MA diss., Queen's University, Belfast, 1989.

Bernstein, A. *Some Jewish Witnesses for Christ.* London: Operative Jewish Converts Institution, 1909.

Bernstein, Jacob. 'Torah and Messianic Judaism.' *Gates of Zion* 4 (1992): 11.

Bevans, Stephen B. and Robert J. Schreiter. *Models of Contextual Theology.* Rev. ed. New York: Orbis, 2002.

Bhabha, Homi K. *The Location of Culture.* New York: Routledge, 1994.

Blaising, Craig A., and Darrell L. Bock. *Progressive Dispensationalism.* Grand Rapids: Baker, 1993, 2000.

Blum, Julia. *If You Be the Son of God, Come Down from the Cross.* Translated by Rebecca Mildren. Chichester: New Wine Press, 2006.

Borowitz, Eugene. 'The Way to a Postmodern Theology.' In *Judaism After Modernity: Papers from a Decade of Fruition.* Lanham: University Press of America, 1999.

———. *Renewing the Covenant: A Theology for the Postmodern Jew.* Philadelphia: Jewish Publication Society of America, 1991.

Boyarin, Daniel. *Border Lines: The Partition of Judaeo-Christianity.* Philadelphia: University of Pennsylvania Press, 2004.

Brandt, Elazar. 'Response to "The Value of Tradition" by Daniel C. Juster.' Paper given at Hashivenu Forum, Messianic Judaism and Jewish Tradition in the 21st Century, Pasadena, February 2003.

Brickner, David. *Misphochah Matters: Speaking Frankly to God's Family.* San Francisco: Purple Pomegranate Productions, 1996.

Bronstein, David. *The Living Scriptures Paraphrased: Messianic Edition of the Living Bible.* Wheaton: Tyndale House, 1982.

Bronstein, David and John Fischer. *Siddur for Messianic Jews.* St. Petersburg: Menorah Ministries, 1988.

Brown, Michael L. *Answering Jewish Objections to Jesus.* Vol. 1. Grand Rapids: Baker, 2000.

Buzzard, Anthony, and Charles Hunting. *The Doctrine of the Trinity: Christianity's Self-Inflicted Wound.* New York: International Scholars Publications, 1998.

Chazan, Robert. *Daggers of Faith.* Berkeley: University of California Press, 1989.

Chernoff, David. *Introduction to Messianic Judaism.* Havertown: MMI Publishing, 1990.

———. *Yeshua the Messiah.* Havertown: MMI Publishing, 1989.

Clouse, Robert, ed. *The Meaning of the Millennium: Four Views.* Downers Grove, IL: InterVarsity Press, 1977.

Cohen, Arthur A. 'Eschatology.' In *Contemporary Jewish Religious Thought,* edited by Arthur A. Cohen and Paul Mendes Flohr, 183–88. New York: The Free Press/ MacMillan, 1987.

———. 'Theology.' In *Contemporary Jewish Religious Thought,* edited by Arthur A. Cohen and Paul Mendes Flohr, 971–81. New York: The Free Press/ MacMillan, 1987.

Cohen, Elliot Marc. 'Brother or Other: Jews for Jesus.' PhD diss., Manchester Metropolitan University, 2004.

Cohn-Sherbok, Dan. 'Introduction.' In *Voices of Messianic Judaism: Confronting Critical Issues Facing a Maturing Movement,* ix–xx. Edited by Dan Cohn-Sherbok. Baltimore: Lederer Books, 2001.

———. *The Jewish Faith.* London, SPCK: 1993.

———. *The Jewish Messiah.* Edinburgh: T&T Clark, 1997.

———. *Judaism: History, Belief and Practice.* London: Routledge, 2003.

———. *Messianic Judaism.* London: Continuum, 2000.

———. *The Politics of Apocalypse: The History and Influence of Christian Zionism.* Oxford: Oneworld, 2006.

———, ed. *Voices of Messianic Judaism: Confronting Critical Issues Facing a Maturing Movement.* Baltimore: Lederer Books, 2001.

Conn, Harvie. 'Ethnotheologies.' In *Evangelical Dictionary of World Missions,* edited by A. Scott Moreau, 328–30. Grand Rapids, MI: Baker, 2000.

Cragg, Kenneth. *The Arab Christian: A History in the Middle East.* London: Mowbray, 1992.

D'Andrade, Roy G. *The Development of Cognitive Anthropology.* Cambridge: Cambridge University Press, 1995.

Daniélou, Jean. *The Theology of Jewish Christianity.* London: Darton, Longman and Todd, 1974.

Daube, David. *He That Cometh.* London: Council for Jewish-Christian Understanding, 1966.

Dauermann, Stuart. 'Making Israel's Story Our Own: Towards a Messianic Jewish Canonical Narrative.' Paper presented at the 4th annual meeting of the *Hashivenu* Forum, Pasadena, January, 2001.

———. 'Selected Aspects of My Hermeneutical Journey – Telling My Story.' Paper presented at the 4th annual meeting of the *Hashivenu* Forum, Pasadena, January, 2001.

Dauermann, Stuart, and Fana Spielberg. 'Contextualisation: Witness and Reflection, Messianic Jews as a Case.' *Missiology: An International Review* 25, no. 1 (January 1997): 15–35.

DellaPergola, Sergio. *World Jewish Population 2000.* Vol. 100. New York: Division of Jewish Demography and Statistics, American Jewish Year Book, 2000. http://ajcarchives.org/AJC_DATA/FILES/2000_13_WJP.pdf.

Dennison, James T. 'Amillennialism.' http://blueletterbible.org/faq/nunc. html (accessed October 20, 2007).

———. 'Dispensational Premillennialism.' http://blueletterbible.org/faq/ dispre.html (accessed October 20, 2007).

———. 'Historic Premillennialism.' http://blueletterbible.org/faq/ hispre.html (accessed October 20, 2007).

———. 'Postmillennialism.' http://blueletterbible.org/faq/post.html (accessed October 20, 2007).

Dorff, Eliot N. and Louis E. Newman, eds. *Contemporary Jewish Theology: A Reader.* Oxford: Oxford University Press, 1999.

Doyle, Robert C. *Eschatology and the Shape of Christian Belief.* Carlisle: Paternoster, 1998.

Dunn, James D.G. *Unity and Diversity in the New Testament.* London, SCM Press, 1977.

Eichorn, D.M. *Evangelising the American Jew.* Middle Village, NY: Jonathan David Publishers, 1978.

Elgvin, Torleif, ed. *Israel and Yeshua.* Jerusalem: Caspari Centre for Biblical and Jewish Studies, 1993.

Ellis, Carolyn. *The Ethnographic I: A Methodological Novel About Ethnography.* Ethnographic Alternatives Book Series 13. Lanham, MD: Rowman and Littlefield, 2004.

Endelman, Todd, ed. *Jewish Apostasy in the Modern World.* New York: Holmes and Meier, 1987.

Epstein, Isadore. *Babylonian Talmud: Tractate Sanhedrin.* London: Soncino Press, 1933.

Feher, Shoshana. 'Challenges to Messianic Judaism.' In *Voices of Messianic Judaism: Confronting Critical Issues Facing a Maturing Movement,* edited by Dan Cohn-Sherbok, 221–28. Baltimore: Lederer Books, 2001.

———. *Passing Over Easter: Constructing the Boundaries of Messianic Judaism.* Walnut Creek: Alta Mira Press, 1998.

Fieldsend, John. *Messianic Jews: Challenging Church and Synagogue.* Tunbridge Wells: Monarch Publications, 1993.

Fisher, Eugene. 'Divided Peoples of the Covenant: Book Review of *After the Evil: Christianity and Judaism in the shadow of the Holocaust* by Richard Harries.' *The Tablet* (23rd August 2003), 16.

Fischer, John, ed. *The Enduring Paradox: Exploratory Essays in Messianic Judaism.* Baltimore: Lederer, 2000.

———. 'Foundations of Messianic Theology: Following in Jesus' Footsteps?' *Mishkan* 23, no. 2 (1995): 65–89.

———. 'Messianic Congregations Should Exist and Should Be Very Jewish: A Response to Arnold Fruchtenbaum.' In *How Jewish is Christianity? Two*

Views on the Messianic Movement, edited by Stanley N. Gundry and Louis Goldberg, 129–39. Grand Rapids: Zondervan, 2003.

——. *Messianic Services for the Festivals and Holy Days*. Palm Harbor, FL: Menorah Ministries, 1992.

——. *The Olive Tree Connection: Sharing Messiah with Israel*. Downers Grove, IL: InterVarsity Press, 1983.

——. 'The Place of Rabbinic Tradition in a Messianic Jewish Lifestyle.' In *The Enduring Paradox: Exploratory Essays in Messianic Judaism*. Edited by John Fischer, 145–70. Baltimore: Lederer, 2000.

——. 'Would Yeshua Support Halacha?' In *Kesher: A Journal of Messianic Judaism* 5 (Summer 1997): 51–81.

——. 'Yeshua – The Deity Debate.' In *Mishkan* 39 (2003): 20–28.

Fischer, Robert Raymond. *Full Circle*. Galilee: Olim Publications, 2002.

Fleischer-Snow, Ruth Irene. *The Emergence of a Distinctively Jewish Faith in Jesus 1925–1993*. PhD diss., Kings College, University of London, 1993. Printed privately as *So Great a Cloud of Witnesses*. Boreham Wood, Ruth Fleischer, 1994.

Flusser, David. *Jesus*. New York: Herder, 1969.

——. *Jewish Sources in Early Christianity*. Tel Aviv: MOD Books, 1989.

Foreman, Esther. 'Messianic Judaism in London: A Study of a Continuum Between Judaism and Christianity.' MA diss., King's College, London, 2002.

Frei, Hans W. *Types of Christian Theology*. Edited by George Hunsinger and William C. Placher. New Haven: Yale University Press, 1992.

Frey, Joseph Christian. *Joseph and Benjamin: A Series of Letters on the Controversy Between Jews and Christians*. New York: Daniel Fanshaw, 1840. Reprinted as *The Divinity of the Messiah*. Israel: Keren Ahavah Meshichit, 2002.

Friedman, David. *The Relationship of Yeshua and the First Century CE Messianic Jewish Community to the Mitzvot of the Mosaic Covenant*. PhD diss., California Graduate School of Theology, 1992.

Friedman, Elias. *Jewish Identity*. New York: Miriam Press, 1987.

Fruchtenbaum, Arnold G. *The Bible and Divine Revelation*. Tustin: Ariel Ministries, 1983.

——. 'Creeds in Judaism.' *Mishkan* 34 (2001): 40–46.

——. 'Eschatology and Messianic Jews: A Theological Perspective.' In *Voices of Messianic Judaism*, edited by Dan Cohn-Sherbok, 211–19. Baltimore: Lederer, 2001.

——. *Footsteps of the Messiah: A Study of the Sequence of Prophetic Events*. Tustin, CA: Ariel Ministries, 1982.

——. *God the Father*. Tustin: Ariel Ministries, 1985.

——. *The Grace of God*. Tustin: Ariel Ministries, 1985.

——. *Hebrew Christianity: Its Theology, History and Philosophy*. Tustin: Ariel Ministries, 1983.

———. *The Inspiration of the Scriptures*. Tustin: Ariel Ministries, 1983.

———. *Israelology: The Missing Link in Systematic Theology*. Tustin: Ariel Ministries, 1992.

———. *Jewishness and the Trinity*. Tustin: Ariel Ministries, 1985.

———. *Messianic Christology*. Tustin: Ariel Ministries, 1998.

———. 'Messianic Congregations May Exist Within the Body of Messiah, as Long As They Don't Function Contrary to the New Testament.' In *How Jewish is Christianity? Two Views on the Messianic Movement*. Edited by Stanley N. Gundry and Louis Goldberg, 109–28. Grand Rapids: Zondervan, 2003.

———. *A Passover Haggadah for Jewish Believers*. 5th ed. Tustin: Ariel Ministries, 1991.

———. 'The Quest for a Messianic Theology.' *Mishkan* 2 (Winter 1985): 1–17.

———.*The Seven Days of Creation: Genesis 1:1–2:3*. Tustin: Ariel Ministries, 2005.

———. *The Trinity*. Tustin, Ariel Ministries, 1985.

———. 'The Use of the Siddur by Messianic Jews.' *Mishkan* 25, no. 2 (1996): 43–49.

Frydland, Rachmiel. *What the Rabbis Know about the Messiah*. Edited by Elliott Klayman. Columbus, OH: Messianic Literature Outreach, 1993.

Funkenstein, Amos. 'Basic Types of Christian Anti-Jewish Polemic in the Middle Ages.' *Viator* 2 (1971): 373–82.

Gidney, William Thomas. *The History of the London Society For Promoting Christianity Amongst the Jews: From 1809–1908*. London: London Society for Promoting Christianity Amongst the Jews, 1908.

Gillet, Lev. *Communion in the Messiah: Studies in the Relationship Between Judaism and Christianity*. London: Lutterworth Press, 1942.

Gillman, Neil. *Sacred Fragments: Recovering Theology for the Modern Jew*. Philadelphia: Jewish Publication Society of America, 1990.

Glaser, Mitchell Leslie. 'An Outsider Looking In: A Review of David A. Rausch's *Messianic Judaism: Its History, Theology and Policy*.' *LCJE Bulletin* (August 1984), 6–7.

———. *A Survey of Missions to the Jews in Continental Europe 1900–1950*. PhD diss., Fuller Theological Seminary, 1998.

Glasser, Arthur F. 'More Issues in Jewish Evangelization' ('LCJE Gatherings in North America (1985–1997) – Part 2'). *Missionary Monthly* (March 1998): 20–21.

———. 'Thoughts from a Longtime Friend.' In *Voices of Messianic Judaism*, edited by Dan Cohn-Sherbok, 229–234. Baltimore, Lederer, 2001.

Glick, I. 'The Hebrew Christians: A Marginal Religious Group.' In *The Jews*, edited by M. Sklare, 415–31. Glencoe, IL: The Free Press, 1958.

Goble, Philip E. *Everything You Need to Know to Grow a Messianic Synagogue*. South Pasadena, CA: William Carey Library, 1974.

———. *Everything You Need to Know to Grow a Messianic Yeshiva*. South Pasadena, CA: William Carey Library, 1981.

——. 'Messianic Judaism: A Biblical Apologetic with a View to Liturgical Reform.' D. Min. diss., Fuller Theological Seminary, 1975.

Goldberg, Louis. 'The Borders of Israel according to Ezekiel.' *Mishkan* 26, no. 1 (1997): 44–48.

——. 'Israel and Prophecy.' In *The Enduring Paradox: Exploratory Essays in Messianic Judaism,* edited by John Fischer, 105–121. Baltimore MA: Lederer, 2000.

——. 'Living the Messianic Jewish Lifestyle: A Response to William Varner.' In *How Jewish is Christianity? Two Views on the Messianic Movement,* edited by Stanley N. Gundry and Louis Goldberg, 79–91. Grand Rapids: Zondervan, 2003.

——. 'A Messianic Jewish Theology.' Manuscript, Jews for Jesus Memorial Research Library. San Francisco, 2003. To be published as *God, Torah, Messiah: The Messianic Theology of Dr. Louis Goldberg.* Ed. Richard A. Robinson. San Fransisco: Purple Pomegranate Productions, forthcoming.

——. 'Recontextualising the Doctrine of the Trinity as Formulated by the Council of Nicaea.' LCJE-NA Regional Conference, Chicago, 1996.

——. 'Testing In How Jewish We Should Be.' In *How Jewish is Christianity? Two Views on the Messianic Movement,* edited by Stanley N. Gundry and Louis Goldberg, 140–51. Grand Rapids: Zondervan, 2003.

Goodman, Martin, Adam H. Becker and Peter Schafer, eds. *The Ways That Never Parted: Jews and Christians in Late Antiquity and the Early Middle Ages.* Minneapolis: Fortress, 2007.

Gruenler, R. G. 'Constructive Theology.' In *Evangelical Dictionary of Theology,* edited by Walter A. Elwell, 269–71. Basingstoke: Marshall Pickering, 1985.

Gundry, Stanley N. and Louis Goldberg, eds. *How Jewish is Christianity? Two Views on the Messianic Movement.* Grand Rapids: Zondervan, 2003.

Gutwirth, Jacques. *Les Judéo-Chrétiens d'aujourd'hui.* Paris: Les Éditions du Cerf, 1987.

Hagner, Donald. *The Jewish Reclamation of Jesus.* Grand Rapids, MI: Zondervan, 1984.

Halivni, David Weiss. *Revelation Restored.* Boulder: Westview, 1997.

Harink, Douglas. *Paul Among the Postliberals: Pauline Theology Beyond Christendom and Modernity.* Grand Rapids: Brazos, 2003.

Harley, C. David, ed. *Christian Witness to the Jewish People.* Lausanne Occasional Paper 7. Thailand: Lausanne Consultation on World Evangelization (COWE), 1980.

Harris-Shapiro, Carol A. 'Syncretism or Struggle: The Case of Messianic Judaism.' PhD diss., Temple University, 1992. Published as *Messianic Judaism: A Rabbi's Journey through Religious Change in America.* Boston: Beacon Press, 1999.

Harvey, Richard S. 'The Hidden Messiah in Judaism and Messianic Judaism.' Paper presented at the Ninth International Conference of the

Lausanne Consultation on Jewish Evangelism, Lake Balaton, Hungary, 2007.

——. *'Judaism is Not Jewish* [by Baruch Maoz]: A Review.' In *CWI Herald* (Summer 2003). http://www.banneroftruth.org/pages/articles/article_detail.php?490 (accessed 6th October 2007).

——. 'Passing over the Plot? The Life and Work of Hugh Schonfield.' *Mishkan* 37 (2002): 35–48.

——. 'Raymundus Martini and the Pugio Fidei: A Survey of the Life and Works of a Medieval Controversialist.' MA diss., University College, London, 1991.

——. 'Shaping the Aims and Aspirations of Jewish Believers (Review of Mark Kinzer's *Postmissionary Messianic Judaism*).' *Mishkan* 48 (2006): 18–21.

——. 'Who Is A Messianic Jew?' Paper presented at the IHCA Theological Commission, Ramsgate, 1983.

Hashivenu. 'Towards a Mature Messianic Judaism.' http://Hashivenu.org/core_values.htm#top (accessed June 1, 2003).

——. 'What is Hashivenu?' http://Hashivenu.org/what_is.htm (accessed June 1, 2003).

——. 'Who is Hashivenu?' http://Hashivenu.org/who_is.htm (accessed June 1, 2003).

Hegstad, Harald. 'The Development of a Messianic Jewish Theology – Affirmations and Questions.' *Mishkan* 25 (1996): 60–64.

Heschel, Abraham J. 'God, Torah and Israel.' In *Theology and Church in Times of Change*, edited by E.L. Long and R. Handy, 71–90. Philadelphia: Westminster, 1970.

Hinchliff, Peter. *History, Tradition and Change: Church History and the Development of Doctrine*. London: Affirming Catholicism, 1993.

Hocken, Peter. *The Challenges of the Pentecostal, Charismatic and Messianic Jewish Movements: The Tensions of the Spirit*. New Critical Thinking in Religion, Theology and Biblical Studies. Ashgate: Oxford, 2009.

Hoedendijk, Ben. *Twelve Jews Discover Messiah*. Eastbourne: Kingsway, 1992.

Hoffman, Lawrence A., ed. *The Land of Israel: Jewish Perspectives*. Notre Dame: University of Notre Dame Press, 1986.

Hodgson, Peter and Robert King, eds. *Christian Theology: An Introduction to its Traditions and Tasks*. UK edition. London: SPCK, 1983.

Horbury, William. *Jews and Christians: In Contact and Controversy*. Edinburgh: T.&T. Clark, 1998.

Houston, Judy. 'Towards Interdependence, Remembrance and Justice: Reconciliation Ministry in the Israeli/Palestinian Context.' MA diss., All Nations Christian College, 2006.

Hurtado, Larry W. *One God, One Lord: Early Christian Devotion and Ancient Jewish Monotheism*. London: SCM, 1988.

Husik, Isaak. *A History of Medieval Jewish Philosophy*. New York: Temple, 1916, reprint 1969.

Hutchens, James. 'Messianic Judaism: A Progress Report.' *Missiology* 5, no. 3 (July 1977): 279–85.

——. 'A Case for Messianic Judaism.' D. Miss. diss., Fuller Theological Seminary, 1974.

Hynd, Fiona. *Messianic Jewish Religious Practice and the Question of Jewish Authenticity*. MA diss., University of Manchester, 2003.

Intrater, Keith 'Last Days Tribulation.' In *Israel, the Church and the Last Days*, by Dan Juster and Keith Intrater, 139–161. Shippensburg, PA: Destiny Image, 2003.

——. 'The Millennium.' In *Israel, the Church and the Last Days*, by Dan Juster and Keith Intrater, 163–201. Shippensburg, PA: Destiny Image, 2003.

Jacobs, Louis. 'God.' In *Contemporary Jewish Religious Thought*, edited by Arthur A. Cohen and Paul Mendes-Flohr, 290–98. New York: Macmillan/Free Press, 1988.

——. *God, Torah, Israel: Traditionalism Without Fundamentalism*. Cincinnati: Hebrew Union College Press, 1990.

——. *A Jewish Theology*. London: Darton, Longman and Todd, 1973.

——. *Principles of the Jewish Faith: An Analytical Study*. New York: Basic Books, 1964.

Jaffe, Devra Gillet. 'Straddling the Boundary: Messianic Judaism and the Construction of Culture.' MA diss., Rice University, Houston, 2000.

Jenson, Robert W. 'Towards a Christian Theology of Judaism.' In *Jews and Christians*, edited by Carl E. Braaten and Robert W. Jenson, 9–11. Grand Rapids: Eerdmans, 2003.

Jocz, Jacob. 'The Invisibility of God and the Incarnation.' In *The Messiahship of Jesus*, edited by Arthur Kac, 189–196. Rev. ed., Grand Rapids, Baker: 1986. Reprinted from *Canadian Journal of Theology* 4, no. 3 (1958).

——. *The Jewish People and Jesus Christ: A Study in the Controversy Between Church and Synagogue*. London: SPCK, 1949.

Jones, Serene and Paul Lakeland, eds. *Constructive Theology: A Contemporary Approach to Classical Themes*. Minneapolis: Fortress Press, 2005.

Joseph, Morris. *Judaism as Creed and Life*. New York: Bloch, 1920.

Juster, Daniel C. 'The Christological Dogma of Nicaea — Greek or Jewish?' *Mishkan* 1, no.1 (1984): 54–56.

——. 'Covenant and Dispensation.' In *Torah and Other Essays: A Symposium in Honour of the 80th Birthday of H. L. Ellison*, edited by Ronald H. Lewis, 42–58. Ramsgate, IHCA, 1983.

——. *Growing To Maturity: A Messianic Jewish Guide*. 2nd ed. Denver CO: UMJC Press, 1985. 4th ed., 1996.

——. *The Irrevocable Calling: Israel's Role as a Light to the Nations*. Clarksville: Lederer Books, 1996, 2007.

——. *Jewish Roots: A Foundation of Biblical Theology for Messianic Judaism.* Rockville: Davar Publishing, 1986.

——. 'Messianic Judaism and the Torah.' In *Jewish Identity and Faith in Jesus,* edited by Kai Kjær-Hansen, 113–21. Jerusalem: Caspari Centre for Biblical and Jewish Studies, 1966.

——. 'Torah and Messianic Jewish Practice.' Paper presented at the Third International Conference of the Lausanne Consultation on Jewish Evangelism, Easneye, 1986. In Arnold G. Fruchtenbaum, *Israelology: The Missing Link in Systematic Theology,* 896–905. Tustin: Ariel Ministries, 1992.

——. 'Towards a Messianic Jewish Theology.' In *Jewish Identity and Faith in Jesus,* edited by Kai Kjær-Hansen, 57–62. Jerusalem: Caspari Centre for Biblical and Jewish Studies, 1966.

Juster, Daniel and Keith Intrater. *Israel, the Church and the Last Days.* Shippensburg: Destiny Image, 2003.

Kac, Arthur W., ed. *The Messiahship of Jesus: Are Jews Changing Their Attitude Toward Jesus?* Rev. ed. Grand Rapids, MI: Baker Book House, 1986.

Kasdan, Barney. *God's Appointed Customs.* Baltimore: Lederer Publications, 1996.

——. *God's Appointed Times.* Baltimore: Lederer Publications, 1993.

Kashdan, Michael A. 'The Place of Talmud: A Response To Walter Leiber's "The Oral Torah According to Moses".' *The Messianic Outreach* 13, no. 3 (Spring 1994): 20–22.

Katz, Arthur. 'Ezekiel 37: The Necessary Death and Resurrection of Israel: A Prophetic Scenario for the Last Days.' http://www.hearnow.org/ezek37.html (accessed 6th October 2007).

——. 'The Holocaust As Judgement.' Paper presented at the Lausanne Consultation on Jewish Evangelism – North American Regional Conference, 1995.

——. *The Holocaust: Where Was God?* Pensacola, Fl: Mt. Zion Publications, 1998.

Kaufman, Gordon. *An Essay on Theological Method.* 3rd ed. Atlanta: Scholars Press, 1995.

Kinzer, Mark S. 'Beginning with the End: The Place of Eschatology in the Messianic Jewish Canonical Narrative.' Paper presented at the 4th Annual Hashivenu Forum, Pasadena, February 2002.

——. 'Creation, Covenant, & Consummation: Part III: Differentiation & Blessing. Session #9.' Paper presented at Messianic Jewish Theological Institute, Fuller Theological Seminary, 2005.

——. 'God and the Messiah: Course Outline, MJ518.' Paper presented at Messianic Jewish Theological Institute, Fuller Theological Seminary, 2002.

——. 'Jewish Models of the Differentiated Godhead. Session #17.' Paper presented at Messianic Jewish Theological Institute, Fuller Theological Seminary, 2002.

——. 'The Messianic Fulfilment of the Jewish Faith.' In *The Witness of the Jews to God*, edited by David W. Torrance, 115–25. Edinburgh, Handsel Press, 1982.

——. 'Messianic Jewish Theological Institute Syllabus.' http://www.mjti.org/docs/mjticatalog.pdf (accessed June 29, 2007).

——. 'Messianic Judaism and Jewish Tradition in the 21st Century: A Biblical Defense of "Oral Torah".' Paper presented at the 2003 Hashivenu Forum, Pasadena, January 2003.

——. *The Nature of Messianic Judaism: Judaism as Genus, Messianic as Species.* West Hartford, CT: Hashivenu Archives, 2000.

——. *Postmissionary Messianic Judaism: Redefining Christian Engagement with the Jewish People.* Grand Rapids: Baker Academic/Brazos, 2005.

——. 'The Shape of Messianic Jewish Theology (Session 1): What Is Messianic Jewish Theology?' Paper presented at Messianic Jewish Theological Institute, Fuller Theological Seminary, 2005.

Kircheiner, Hanne. 'Arthur Glasser and Jewish Evangelism.' MA diss., All Nations Christian College, 2006.

Kjær-Hansen, Kai, ed. *The Death of the Messiah*, Baltimore, MO: Lederer Publications, 1994.

——. ed. *Jewish Identity and Faith in Jesus.* Jerusalem: Caspari Centre for Biblical and Jewish Studies, 1996.

——. *Joseph Rabinowitz and the Messianic Movement.* Translated by Birger Petterson. Edinburgh: Handsel Press, 1995.

——. ed. *Mishkan: A Forum on the Gospel and the Jewish People.* Jerusalem: United Christian Council in Israel/Caspari Centre for Biblical and Jewish Studies, 1984–2007.

——. 'Upside-down for the sake of Yeshua: Challenges and pressures on Israeli Jewish believers in Jesus.' Paper presented at the Seventeenth North American Coordinating Committee of the LCJE, Atlanta, March 13–15, 2000. http://www.lcje.net/papers/2000/LCJE-kai.pdf (accessed June 7, 2004).

Kjær-Hansen, Kai and Bodil F. Skjøtt. *Facts and Myths about the Messianic Congregations in Israel 1998–1999* (*Mishkan* Double Issue 30–31). Jerusalem: United Christian Council in Israel/Caspari Centre for Biblical and Jewish Studies, 1999.

Kohler, Kaufman. *Jewish Theology Systematically and Historically Considered.* New York: Macmillan, 1918.

Kohn, Rachael L.E. 'Ethnic Judaism and the Messianic Movement.' *Journal of Jewish Studies* 29, no. 2 (1987): 85–96.

——. 'Hebrew Christianity and Messianic Judaism on the Church-Sect Continuum.' PhD. diss., McMaster University, 1985.

Kollontai, Pauline. 'Between Judaism and Christianity: The Case of Messianic Jews.' *Journal of Religion and Society* (2006): 1–9.

——. 'Messianic Jews and Jewish Identity.' *Journal of Modern Jewish Studies* 3, vol. 2 (July 2004): 195–205.

Krell, Marc A. *Intersecting Pathways: Modern Jewish Theologians in Conversation with Christianity.* Oxford: OUP, 2003.

Kvarme, Ole Chr. M. 'Torah and Christ.' *Evangelical Review of Theology,* 8, no. 2 (October 1984): 183–201.

Ladd, George Elton. *The Gospel of the Kingdom.* Grand Rapids: William B. Eerdmans, 1981.

——. *The Last Things: An Eschatology for the Layman.* Rev. ed. Grand Rapids: William B. Eerdmans, 1982.

Lambert, Lance. *Till the Day Dawns.* Eastbourne: Kingsway Publications, 1974, 2nd ed. 1982.

Lapide, Pinchas E. *Hebrew in the Church.* Grand Rapids: Eerdmans, 1984.

Leiber, Walter. 'The Oral Torah According to Moses.' *The Messianic Outreach* 13, no. 1 (Autumn 1993): 3–8.

Leventhal, Barry. 'Holocaust Apologetics: Toward a Case for the Existence of God.' Paper presented at the Lausanne Consultation on Jewish Evangelism – North American Regional Conference, 1997.

Lieberman, Paul. *The Fig Tree Blossoms: Messianic Judaism Emerges.* Indianola, Iowa: Fountain Press, 1976, 3rd ed. 1980.

Lindbeck, George. *The Nature of Doctrine: Religions and Theology in a Post-liberal Age.* Westminster: John Knox Press, 1984.

Lindsay, Mark R. *Barth, Israel and Jesus: Karl Barth's Theology of Israel.* Aldershot: Ashgate, 2007.

Lindsey, Hal and C.C. Carson. *The Late Great Planet Earth.* Grand Rapids: Zondervan, 1970.

Lipson, Eric P.E. *Messianic Passover Haggadah.* San Francisco: Purple Pomegranate Productions, 1992.

Lipson, Julienne L. *Jews for Jesus: an Anthropological Study.* New York: AMS Press, 1990.

Loden, Lisa, Peter Walker and Michael Wood, eds. *The Bible and the Land: An Encounter.* Jerusalem: Musalaha, 2000.

——. 'Messianic Jewish Views of Israel's Rebirth and Survival in the Light of Scripture.' Paper presented at Director's Conference: Christian Perspectives on the Israeli-Palestinian Conflict, International Baptist Theological Seminary, Prague, Czech Republic, November 14, 2006.

Longenecker, Richard N. *The Christology of Early Jewish Christianity.* Rev. ed. Vancouver: Regent College Pub., 2001.

Lukyn Williams, A. *The Hebrew-Christian Messiah.* London: SPCK, 1916.

MacGregor, Geddes, *Philosophical Issues in Religious Thought.* Boston: Houghton Mifflin, 1973.

Maoz, Baruch. *Judaism is not Jewish: A Friendly Critique of the Messianic Movement.* Fearn, UK: Mentor/Christian Focus Publications, 2003.

——. 'Israel – People, Land, State and Torah.' *Mishkan* 2 (1986): 59–69. Revised as 'People, Land and Torah: a Jewish Christian Perspective.' In *The Land of Promise: Biblical, Theological and Contemporary Perspectives* eds. Philip Johnston and Peter Walker. Downers Grove, IL: Apollos, 2000.

———. 'Lectures on The Person of Christ.' Paper presented at Grace and Truth Christian Congregation, Rehovot (2003).

———. 'Lessons on the Doctrine of God: A Tutorial on the Biblical Doctrine of God.' Paper presented at Grace and Truth Christian Congregation, Rehovot (1997).

———. 'The Person of Christ.' Annual Lecture of the Israel College of the Bible in Jerusalem, March 2002. Reprinted in abbreviated form in *Maoz News* 4, no. 69 (May 10, 2002).

———. 'A Review of Premillennialism.' Paper presented to the Elders of Grace and Truth Christian Congregation, Rehovot, (2003).

Marcus, Uri. 'Adonai Echad: Deity of Yeshua Debate: Why Yeshua is NOT G-d: An Internet Course from a Jewish Perspective.' http://groups.yahoo.com/group/AdonaiEchad/ (accessed September 6, 2002).

———. 'Lesson 3 I'll take ONE please.' http://groups.yahoo.com/group/AdonaiEchad/message/16 (accessed September 6, 2002).

———. 'Lesson 6 – 'And the Word was G-d?' Yochanan 1:1–3', http://groups.yahoo.com/group/AdonaiEchad/message/23 (accessed September 6, 2002)

Marshall, Bruce D. *Trinity and Truth.* Cambridge: Cambridge University Press, 2000.

McGrath, Alistair E. *Christian Theology: An Introduction.* 3rd ed. Oxford: Blackwell, 2001.

———. 'The Need for a Scientific Theology' in *Shaping a Theological Mind: Theological Context and Methodology,* edited by Darren C. Marks, 37–44. Aldershot: Ashgate, 2002.

Messianic Jewish Rabbinical Council (New England Halakhic Council). 'Collected Halakhic Decisions (May 2006).' Boston: New England Halakhic Council, 2007. http://www.ourrabbis.org/main/ (accessed December 10, 2007).

Messianic Jewish Alliance of America. 'MJAA Doctrinal Basis, Article 2.' http://mjaa.org/StatementofFaith.html (accessed August 8, 2005).

Miller, David. 'Messianic Judaism and the Theology of the Land.' *Mishkan* 26, no. 1 (1997): 31–38.

Moltmann, Jürgen. *The Coming of God: Christian Eschatology.* Translated by Margaret Kohl. London: SCM Press, 1996.

———. *History and the Triune God: Contributions to Trinitarian Theology.* Translated by John Bowden. London: SCM Press, 1991. ET of *In der Geschichte des dreieinigen Gottes. Beiträge zur trinitarischen Theologie* (Munich: Christian Kaiser Verlag, 1991).

Nadler, Sam. 'What is Legalism? What is Liberty?' Quoted in Louis Goldberg, 'Testing In How Jewish We Should Be,' in *How Jewish Is Christianity? Two*

Views of the Messianic Movement, edited by Stanley N. Gundry and L. Goldberg, 148. Grand Rapids: Zondervan, 2003.

Nerel, Gershon. 'Creeds among Jewish Believers in Yeshua.' *Mishkan* 34 (2001), 61–79.

——. 'Eusebius' *Ecclesiastical History* and the Modern Yeshua Movement: Some Comparisons.' *Mishkan* 39 (2003), 65–86.

——. 'Haim (Haimoff) Bar-David: Restoring Apostolic Authority among Jewish Yeshua-Believers.' *Mishkan*, 37 (2002), 59–78.

——. 'Messianic Jews in Eretz Israel, 1917–1967: Trends and Changes in Shaping Self-Identity' (Hebrew). PhD diss., Hebrew University, 1996.

——. 'Modern Assemblies of Jewish Yeshua-Believers between Church and Synagogue.' In *How Jewish is Christianity? Two Views on the Messianic Movement*. Edited by Stanley N. Gundry and L. Goldberg, 92–107. Grand Rapids: Zondervan, 2003.

——. 'Observing the Torah according to Yeshua.' In *CHAI: The Quarterly Magazine of the British Messianic Jewish Alliance* 212 (2001): 5–8. http://www.bmja.il12.com/chai_page_5/htm (accessed May 5, 2003).

——. 'Primitive Jewish Christians in the Modern Thought of Messianic Jews.' In *Le Judéo-Christianisme Dans Tous Ses États: Actes Du Colloque De Jérusalem 6–10 Juillet 1998*. Edited by Simon C. Mimouni and F. Stanley Jones. Paris: Cerf, 2001. 399–425.

——. 'Torah and *Halakhah* among Modern Assemblies of Jewish Yeshua-Believers.' In *How Jewish is Christianity? Two Views on the Messianic Movement*. Edited by Stanley N. Gundry and L. Goldberg, 152–65. Grand Rapids: Zondervan, 2003.

——. 'The Trinity and the Contemporary Jewish Believers in Yeshua.' *Nachrichten Aus Israel (Beth-Shalom)* no. 5, (May 2003): 1.

——. 'Zion in the Theology of L. Averbuch and S. Rohold.' *Mishkan* 26, no. 1 (1997): 64–71.

Nichol, Richard C. 'Are We Really at the End of the End Times? A Reappraisal.' In *Voices of Messianic Judaism*, edited by Dan Cohn-Sherbok, 203–210. Baltimore, MA: Lederer, 2001.

Novak, David. 'Beyond Supersessionism.' *First Things* 81 (March 1998): 58–60.

——. *The Election of Israel*. Cambridge: Cambridge University Press, 1995.

——. *Talking With Christians: Musings of a Jewish Theologian*. Grand Rapids: Eerdmans, 2005.

Ochs, Peter. 'The God of Jews and Christians.' In *Christianity in Jewish Terms*, edited by Tikva Frymer-Kensky, David Novak, Peter Ochs, David Fox Sandmel and Michael A Signer, 49–68. Boulder: Westview Press, 2000.

Packer, J.I. 'God. ' In *New Dictionary of Theology*, edited by Sinclair B. Ferguson, David F. Wright and J. I. Packer, 274–77. Leicester: IVP, 1988.

Pannenberg, W. *Systematic Theology*. Vol. 3. Grand Rapids: Eerdmans, 1998.

Pardo-Kaplan, Deborah. 'Jacob vs. Jacob: Jewish believers in Jesus quarrel over both style and substance.' *Christianity Today* 49, no. 2 (February 2005). http://www.ctlibrary.com/34339 (accessed June 26, 2007).

Parkes, James. 'The Concept of a Chosen People in Judaism and Christianity.' *Inward Light* 49 (1955). http://fcrp.quaker.org/InwardLight049/049Parkes.html (accessed May 3, 2007).

Poll, Evert W. van de. *Sacred Times For Chosen People: Development of the Messianic Jewish Movement and its Holiday Practice.* Zoetermeer: Boekencentrum, 2008.

Powlison, Arye. 'Rabbinic Judaism as a Background to Scripture.' In *Tishrei* 32, no. 2 (May 2003). Under 'Yeshua and Limits of Rabbinic Authority,' http://www.familyrestorationmagazine.org/tishrei032.htm (accessed June 7, 2007).

Prinz, Hirsch (=Tzvi Nassi/Rev. C.W.H. Pauli). *The Great Mystery: How Can Three Be One?* Jerusalem: Yanetz, 1974.

Pritz, Ray. 'The Divinity of Jesus.' *LCJE Bulletin* 69 (August 2002): 3.

———. *Nazarene Jewish Christianity: From the End of the New Testament Period.* Leiden: E.J. Brill, 1988.

Pruter, Karl. *Jewish Christians in the United States: A Bibliography.* New York: Garland Publishing, 1987.

Quiñónez, Jorge. 'Paul Phillip Levertoff: Hebrew-Christian Scholar and Leader.' *Mishkan* 37 (2002): 21–34.

Racionzer, Leon Menzies. 'Hebrew Catholicism: Theology and Politics in Modern Israel.' *Heythrop Journal* 45 (2004): 405–15.

Rausch, David A. *Messianic Judaism: Its History, Theology and Polity.* Lewiston, NY: Edwin Mellen Press, 1982.

Ravitzky, Aviezer. *Messianism, Zionism and Jewish Religious Radicalism.* Translated by Michael Swirsky and Jonathan Chipman. Chicago: University of Chicago Press, 1996.

Rayner, John D. 'Christianity in Jewish Clothing: Review of *Messianic Judaism* by Dan Cohn-Sherbok.' *Manna: The Quarterly Journal of the Sternberg Centre for Judaism* (Autumn 2000): 1–3.

———. *Jewish Religious Law: A Progressive Perspective.* New York: Berghahn Books, 1998.

Reason (née Karabelnik), Gabriela. 'Competing Trends In Messianic Judaism: The Debate Over Evangelicalism.' Senior Diss., Yale University, 2002.

Reichardt, J.C., *Proofs that the Messiah, the Son of David, is also the Son of God.* London: Operative Jewish Converts' Institution, 1900.

Resnick, Russ. 'Defining Messianic Judaism.' UMJC Theology Committee, Summer 2002, Commentary. http://www.umjc.org/main/faq/definition/ResnickCommentary (accessed June 28, 2007).

Riggans, Walter. *Messianic Judaism and Jewish-Christian Relations: A Case Study in the Field of Religious Identity.* PhD diss., University of Birmingham, 1991.

——. *Yeshua Ben David.* Crowborough: MARC/Olive Press, 1995.

Robinson, Richard A., ed. *The Messianic Movement: A Field Guide for Evangelical Christians from Jews for Jesus.* San Francisco: Purple Pomegranate Productions, 2005.

Rosen, Moishe. *Y'shua: The Jewish Way to Say Jesus.* Chicago: Moody Press, 1995.

Rosenbaum, M. and A.M. Silbermann, translators. *Pentateuch with Rashi's Commentary.* London: Vallentine Shapiro, 1930.

Rosenfarb, Joseph. 'Eschatology: Views Which Effect/Affect Messianic Jewish Philosophy of Ministry.' In *Israel and the People of G-d*, 245–262. Rev. ed. Virginia Beach, VA: Kochav Publishing, 1989.

——. *Talmud, Torah and Messianic Jews.* Virginia Beach, VA: Kochav Publishing, 1989.

Rosenthal, Gilbert S. *The Many Faces of Judaism: Orthodox, Conservative, Reconstructionist and Reform.* New York: Behrman House, 1978.

Rosenthal, Stanley. *One God or Three? Exploring the Tri-Unity of God in the Old Testament.* West Collingswood, NJ: Spearhead Press, Friends of Israel Gospel Ministry, 1978.

Rosenzweig, Franz. *The Star of Redemption.* Notre Dame: University of Notre Dame Press, 1985.

Roth, Cecil and Geoffrey Wigoder, eds. *Encyclopaedia Judaica.* 16 vols. Keter: Israel, 1974.

Rubenstein, Richard E. *When Jesus Became God.* New York: Harvest Books, 2000.

Rubin, Barry and Steffi Rubin, *The Messianic Passover Haggadah.* Baltimore: Lederer Messianic Publication, 1990.

Rudolph, David J. 'Guidelines for Healthy Theological Discussion. (A Paper Presented at the Borough Park Symposium on the Gospel, October 8, 2007).' http://www.chosenpeople.com/symposium/papers/Rudolph Final.pdf. (accessed December 10, 2007).

——. 'Jesus and the Food Laws: A Reassessment of Mark 7:19b.' In *Evangelical Quarterly* 74, no. 4 (October 2002): 291–311.

——. 'Messianic Jews and Christian Theology: Restoring an Historical Voice to the Contemporary Discussion.' *Pro Ecclesia* 14, no. 1. (March 2005): 65–86.

——. 'Raising the Bar of Our Devotion to Yeshua.' Sermon Preached at Congregation Ruach Israel, Boston, MA, April 27, 2002.

Rudolph, Michael. 'The Law of the Messiah.' Unpublished paper, 2001.

Ruether, Rosemary R. *Faith and Fratricide.* New York: Search Press, 1974.

Ryrie, Charles. *Dispensationalism Today.* Chicago: Moody Press, 1965.

Sadan, Tsvi. 'The Jewishness I Reject and the Jewishness I Embrace or: From Yavneh to Golgotha.' Proceedings of the LCJE International Conference, New York, 12–17 August, 1999.

———. 'The Torah: what do we do with it?' *Teaching from Zion* 5, no. 2 (May-June 1994): 17–44.

———. *The Trinity – Midrash or Dogma?* Unpublished paper, 2002.

———. 'One Hundred Names of the Messiah.' In *Israel Today* (January 2003). http://israeltoday/co/il/archives (accessed March 10, 2003).

Sandmel, David F., Rosann M. Catalono, and Christopher M. Leighton (eds.). *Irreconcilable Differences? A Learning Resource for Jews and Christians.* Westview Press: Oxford, 2001.

Samuelson, Francine. 'Messianic Judaism: Church, Denomination, Sect or Cult?' *Journal of Ecumenical Studies* 37, no. 2 (2000): 161–86.

Sanders, E.P. *Paul and Palestinian Judaism.* London: SCM Press, 1979.

Schechter, Solomon. *Aspects of Rabbinic Theology.* New York: Schocken Books, 1969.

Scherman, Nosson, ed. *The Complete Artscroll Siddur.* 2nd ed. Brooklyn: Mesorah Publications, 1986.

Schiffman, Michael. 'Messianic Jews and the Tri-Unity of God.' In *The Enduring Paradox: Exploratory Essays in Messianic Judaism*, edited by John Fischer, 93–104. Baltimore: Lederer, 2000.

———. *Return from Exile: The Re-emergence of the Messianic Congregational Movement.* Rev. ed. New York: Teshuvah Publishing Co., 1991. Rev. ed. *The Return of the Remnant: The Rebirth of Messianic Judaism.* Baltimore, Lederer, 1992, 1996.

Schneider, A., ed. 'Messianic Jews Debate the Deity of Jesus.' *Israel Today* 22 (November 2001): 21.

Scholem, Gershom. *Kabbalah.* Israel: Keter, 1974. Reprint, New York: Meridian, 1978.

———. *The Messianic Idea in Judaism.* New York: Schocken Books, 1971.

———. 'Metatron.' In *Encyclopedia Judaica* 11: 1443–46. Jerusalem: Keter, 1971.

———. 'Reflections on Jewish Theology.' In *On Jews and Judaism in Crisis: Selected Essays*, 261–297. New York: Schocken Books, 1976.

Schonfield, Hugh J. *The History of Jewish Christianity: From the First to the Twentieth Century.* London: Duckworth, 1936. Reprint, Ashford, Kent: Manna Books, 1995.

———. *The Jew of Tarsus: An Unorthodox Portrait of Paul.* London: Macdonald, 1946.

———. *The Passover Plot.* London: Hutchinson, 1965.

Secret, François. *Les Kabbalistes Chrétiens de la Renaissance.* Rev. ed. Milan: Arché, 1985.

Senay, Bulent. 'The Making of Jewish Christianity in Britain: Hybridity, Identity and Tradition.' PhD diss., University of Lancaster, 2000.

——. 'The Making of a Tradition – Jewish Christianity.' *Mishkan* 27 (1997): 36–42.

Sevener, Harold A., ed. *Messianic Passover Haggadah*. Charlotte, NC: Chosen People Ministries, n.d.

Sherwin, Byron L. 'An Incessantly Gushing Fountain: The Nature of Jewish Theology.' In Elliot N. Dorff and Louis E. Newman, eds., 7–22. *Contemporary Jewish Theology: A Reader*. Oxford/New York: OUP, 1999.

——. *Toward a Jewish Theology: Methods, Problems and Possibilities*. Lewiston: Edwin Mellen Press, 1991.

Shulam, Joseph. 'Covenant and Dispensation: Towards a Messianic Jewish Perspective: Response by Joseph Shulam. ' *Mishkan* 2 (1985): 35–37.

——. 'The Halachic Process.' *Kesher* 5 (Summer 1997): 23–34.

——. 'The Sabbath Day and How to Keep It.' *Mishkan* 22 (1995): 23–28.

Shulam, Joseph, with Hilary Le Cornu. *A Commentary on the Jewish Roots of Romans*. Baltimore: Lederer Books, 1997.

Sizer, Stephen R. 'Dispensational Approaches to the Land.' In *The Land of Promise: Biblical, Contemporary and Theological Approaches*, edited by Philip Johnston and Peter Walker, 142–171. Leicester: Apollos, 2000.

Sim, David C. *The Gospel of Matthew and Christian Judaism: The History and Social Setting of the Matthew Community*. Studies of the New Testament and Its World. Edinburgh, Continuum/T.&T. Clark, 1998.

Skarsaune, Oscar. 'The Christological Dogma of Nicaea – Greek or Jewish?' *Mishkan* 1 (1984).

Skjøtt, Bodil. 'Messianic Believers and the Land of Israel – a Survey.' *Mishkan* 26, no. 1 (1997): 72–81.

——. 'Sabbath and Worship in Messianic Congregations in Israel – A Brief Survey.' *Mishkan* 22, no. 1 (1995): 29–33.

Sobel, B. Zvi. *Hebrew Christianity: The Thirteenth Tribe*. New York: John Wiley and Sons, 1974.

Soulen, R. Kendall. *The God of Israel and Christian Theology*. Minneapolis: Fortress Press, 1996.

Sperling, Harry, Maurice Simon and Paul Levertoff, trans. *The Zohar*. Vol. 3. London: Soncino Press, 1934, reprinted 1978.

Stark, Rodney and William Sims Bainbridge. 'Of Churches, Sects, and Cults: Preliminary Concepts for a Theory of Religious Movements.' *Journal for the Scientific Study of Religion* 18, no. 2 (June 1979): 117–33.

Stern, David H. *The Complete Jewish Bible*. Jerusalem: Jewish New Testament Publications, 1998.

——. 'Israel's Messianic Jews and the Deity of Yeshua: An Update.' *Israel Today* (July 2002). http://mayimhayim.org/Academic%20Stuff/David%20Stern/Article.htm (accessed 24th May 2007).

——. *The Jewish New Testament*. Jerusalem: Jewish New Testament Publications, 1989.

——. *The Jewish New Testament Commentary*. Jerusalem: Jewish New Testament Publications, 1992.

——. 'Making the Issues Clear: The Land from a Messianic Jewish Perspective.' In *The Bible and the Land: An Encounter*, edited by Lisa Loden, Peter Walker, and Michael Wood, 37–54. Jerusalem: Musalaha, 2000.

——. *Messianic Jewish Manifesto.* Jerusalem: Jewish New Testament Publications, 1988.

——. 'Messianic Jews Should Make *Aliyah.*' In *Voices of Messianic Judaism: Confronting Critical Issues Facing a Maturing Movement*, edited by Dan Cohn-Sherbok, 193–201. Baltimore: Lederer, 2001.

——. *Restoring the Jewishness of the Gospel.* Jerusalem: Jewish New Testament Publications, 1990.

——. 'The Significance of Jerusalem for Messianic Jews.' In *The Enduring Paradox: Exploratory Essays in Messianic Judaism*, edited by John Fischer, 95–104. Baltimore MA: Lederer, 2000.

——. 'Summary Essay: The Future of Messianic Judaism.' In *How Jewish is Christianity? Two Views on the Messianic Movement.* Edited by Stanley N. Gundry and L. Goldberg, 175–92. Grand Rapids: Zondervan, 2003.

Stokes, Bruce H. 'Messianic Judaism: Ethnicity in Revitalization.' PhD diss., University of California, Riverside, 1994.

Tabaksblatt, S. 'The Doctrine of Hypostases in the Synagogue and the Trinity in the Church.' Translated by H. L. Ellison. *The Hebrew Christian* 52, no. 1 (Spring 1979): 16–22.

Tanner, Katherine. *Theories of Culture: A New Agenda for Theology.* Minneapolis: Augsburg Press, 1997.

Telchin, Stan. *Messianic Judaism is not Christianity: A Loving Call to Unity.* Grand Rapids: Baker/Chosen Books, 2004.

Thompson, John B. *Ideology and Modern Culture.* Oxford: Blackwell, 1990.

Torrance, Thomas Forsyth. *The Mediation of Christ.* Colorado Springs: Helmers and Howard, 1992.

Tucker, Ruth *Not Ashamed: The Story of Jews for Jesus.* Colorado Springs: Multnomah, 2000.

Turner, Denys. 'Doing Theology in the University.' In *Fields of Faith: Theology and Religious Studies for the Twenty-First Century*, edited by David Ford, Ben Quash and Janet Soskice, 25–38. Cambridge: Cambridge Univeristy Press, 2005.

Union of Messianic Jewish Congregatations. 'The Tri-Unity of G-d from a Messianic Perspective.' UMJC position paper. http://www.umjc.org/aboutumjc/ theology/triunity.htm (accessed March 12, 2003).

——. 'UMJC Doctrinal Statement, Article 2.' http://www.umjc.org/main/documents/DoctrinalBasis.pdf (accessed August 8, 2005).

——. *Kesher: A Journal of Messianic Judaism.* 1979–2007. http://www.kesherjournal.com (accessed June 2007).

Unterman, Alan. 'Shekinah.' In *Encyclopedia Judaica*, vol. 14:1350–51.

Urbach, Chaim. 'The Land of Israel in Scripture.' *Mishkan* 26, no. 1 (1997): 22–31.

Varner, William. 'The Christian Use of Jewish Numerology.' *The Masters Seminary Journal* 8, no. 1 (Spring 1997): 47–59.

Vermes, Geza. *Jesus the Jew*. London: SCM Press, 1979.

Wallace, Anthony F.C. 'Revitalization Movements.' *American Anthropologist* 58 (1956): 264–81.

Warshawsky, Keri Zelson. *Returning To Their Own Borders: A Social Anthropological Study of Contemporary Messianic Jewish Identity in Israel*. PhD Dissertation, Hebrew University of Jerusalem, 2008.

Wasserman, Jeffrey S. 'Messianic Jewish Congregations in North America.' *Mishkan* 27 (1997): 26–35.

——. *Messianic Jewish Congregations: Who Sold This Business to the Gentiles?* Lanham, Maryland: University Press of America, 2000.

Webster, John. 'Theological Theology.' In *Confessing God: Essays in Christian Dogmatics II*, 11–32. Edinburgh: Continuum International Publishing Group/T.&T. Clark, 2005.

Weisbard, Talya. 'The Music of Messianic Jews: Strategies for Outreach.' Harvard Judaica Collection Student Research Papers No.7. *Studies in Jewish Musical Traditions: Insights from the Harvard Collection of Judaica Sound Recordings* (2001): 205–21.

Weiss-Rosmarin, Trude. *Judaism and Christianity: The Differences*. New York: Jonathan David, 1943.

Wertheim, Janie-Sue, ed. *Messianic Family Haggadah*. San Francisco: Purple Pomegranate Productions, 2007.

Winer, Robert I. *The Calling: The History of the Messianic Alliance of America 1915–1990*. Philadelphia: MJAA, 1990.

Wolfson, Elliott R. 'Judaism and Incarnation: The Imaginal Body of God.' In *Christianity in Jewish Terms*, edited by Tikva Frymer-Kensky, David Novack, Peter Ochs, David Fox Sandmel and Michael A Signer, 239–54. Boulder, CO: Westview Press, 2000.

——. 'Messianism in the Christian Kabbalah of Johann Kemper.' In *Millenarianism and Messianism in Early Modern European Culture: Jewish Messianism in the Early Modern World*, edited by Matthew D. Goldish and Richard H. Popkin, 139–87. The Netherlands: Kluwer Academic Publishers, 2001.

Wright, N.T. *The Climax of the Covenant*. Minneapolis: Fortress, 1992.

——. *The New Testament and the People of God*. Minneapolis: Fortress, 1992.

——. *What Saint Paul Really Said*. Grand Rapids: Eerdmans, 1997.

Wurmbrand, Richard. *Christ on the Jewish Road*. London: Hodder and Stoughton, 1970.

Wyschogrod, Michael. *Abraham's Promise: Judaism and Jewish-Christian Relations*. Edited by R. Kendall Soulen. Grand Rapids: Eerdmans, 2004.

——. *The Body of Faith: God and the People Israel*. 2nd ed. Northvale: Jason Aronson, 1996.

Yangarber-Hicks, Natalia. 'Messianic believers: reflections on identity of a largely misunderstood group.' *Journal of Psychology and Theology* 33, no. 2 (2005): 127–39.

Yellin, Burt, *Messiah: A Rabbinic and Scriptural Viewpoint*. Denver: Congregation Roeh Yisrael, 1984.

Yellin, Burt, Rachmiel Frydland and Marvin Rosenthal. 'Studies Supporting The Triune Nature of G-d.' http://www.messianic-literary.com/trinity. htm (accessed June 2007).

Yuval, Israel Jacob. *Two Nations in Your Womb: Perceptions of Jews and Christians in Late Antiquity and the Middle Ages*. Berkeley: University of California Press, 2006.

Zakaria, Jéridi. 'Les judéo-chrétiens deux mille ans après. Une anthropologie urbaine. [A propos du livre de J. Gutwirth: Les judéo-chrétiens d'aujourd'hui. Republication de Les Cahiers Internationaux de Sociologie 1991].' In *Textes d'anthropologie urbaine offerts à Jacques Gutwirth*, edited by Colette Pétonnet and Yves Delaporte, 189–197. Paris: L'Harmattan (Connaissance des hommes), 1993. http://halshs.ccsd.cnrs.fr/halshs– 00003996 (accessed March 17, 2003).

Zaretsky, Tuvya, ed. *Jewish Evangelism: A Call to the Church*. Lausanne Occasional Paper No. 60, Thailand: Lausanne Committee for World Evangelisation, 2005.

Glossary

Spellings and transliterations have been standardised except where in direct quotation. English equivalents are given for Hebrew and Yiddish terms.

afikoman. The hidden and restored piece of matzah in the Passover meal.

aishet khayeel / ayshet hayil. A woman of worth, the opening words of Proverbs 31, traditionally recited to the woman of the house at the beginning of the Sabbath.

aliyah. Immigration to Israel. The honour of reading the Torah portion.

am ha'aretz. Lit. 'people of the land' – common people.

Ashkenazi. Jews from Northern and Eastern Europe.

bar mitzvah. Coming of age ceremony for boys.

bat mitzvah. Coming of age ceremony for girls.

berachah. Blessing.

bet din. Religious court.

bet Hillel. Lenient 1st century Rabbinical school.

bet Shammai. Strict 1st century Rabbinical school.

Beth Yeshua. 'House of Jesus', Messianic Congregation in Philadelphia.

biblical kashrut. Application of foodlaws as found in the Bible but without later Jewish developments (e.g., the mixing of milk and meat is permitted).

birkat hamazon. Grace before and after meals.

brit chadashah / hadasha. New Testament.

brit milah. Circumcision of males.

challah. Sabbath bread.

cohen. Priest.

ekklesia. Congregation, Church (the Greek term is preferred because of the negative associations of the word 'church').

erev shabbat. Eve of Sabbath service.

G-d. God (Orthodox Jews and some Messianic Jews do not write every letter, out of respect).

gefilte fish. Minced, stuffed fish. An Ashkenazi delicacy.

gemara. 'Completion' – the larger portion of the Talmud.

gentile. Non-Jew.

goy kadosh. Holy people.

had gadya. 'Only one kid' – a Passover song.

haftarah. Reading from the Prophets in the synagogue service.

haggadah. Liturgy for the Passover meal and celebration.

halachah / halakah. Commandment – specific practical legislation.

HaShem. 'The name' – periphrasis for 'God'.

Hashivenu. 'Cause us to return' – Torah-observant group within the UMJC.

havdalah. Short service in the home at the close of the Sabbath.

kabbalah. Jewish mystical tradition.

karaite. Small Jewish group that does not accept Rabbinic tradition.

kashrut / kosher. Permitted foods.

Kedushah / kiddush. Holiness/service of sanctification.

kippah / yarmulka. Male head-covering (plural *kippot*).

Maimonides / Rambam. Medieval Rabbi (12th c.) who combined Judaism with Aristotelian philosophy.

matzah. Unleavened bread used at Passover.

matzah tash. Bag for matzah with three compartments.

Messianic Rabbi. Someone ordained by a Messianic Jewish organisation (UMJC, MJAA,etc) as congregational leader.

mezuzah. Small box placed on doorposts, containing scripture portions.

middoth of R. Ishmael. Thirteen principles of rabbinic exegesis of Scripture.

midrash. Jewish exegesis, interpretation of scripture, commentary, or compilation of interpretations.

Mishnah Brura. Standard Orthodox Jewish version of Jewish Law by the Chofetz Haim.

mikveh. Ritual bath, immersion for purification.

minhag. Custom.

mishnah. 2nd century CE commentary on biblical law.

mitzvah. Specific commandment of the Torah.

mitzvah berachah. Blessing for performing the Mizvah (of candle-lighting).

Moshe Rabbenu. Moses our teacher.

niddah. Ritual purity laws concerned with menstruation.

nomos. Law (in NT Greek).

Olam HaBa. The age and world to come.

Oneg Shabbat. 'Joy of Sabbath'. Informal Sabbath gathering and celebration.

Pirke Avot. 'Sayings of the Fathers' – a tractate of the Mishnah.

posek. A Rabbi who gives rulings on Halacha.

Rosh Hashanah. The Jewish New Year.

Ruach. The Holy Spirit (shortened form of **Ruach Hakodesh**).

seder. The Passover service.

Sephardi. Jews from Spain, North Africa and the Middle East.

shechitah. Jewish ritual slaughter of animals for food.

shaliach. Apostle, also referred to as 'emissary'.

shalom. Peace, wholeness, well-being.

shema. 'Hear' – the first word of Deut 6:4, Israel's declaration of the unity of God.

shevirat hakelim. Shattering of vessels. Allowing the divine sparks to emerge from the evil in creation.

shofet. Judge with executive authority.

Shulchan Aruch. Codification of Jewish law by Joseph Caro (16th C.).

siddur. Prayer book.

tallit. Prayer-shawl worn in morning service.

Talmud. 'Teaching' – The 4th and 5th century Babylonian and Palestinian compilations of the Mishnah and Gemara.

Tanakh / Tenach. The Hebrew scriptures.

tareyfah / tereyfah / treif. Food that is not kosher.

Taryag Mitzvot. Traditional list of the 613 Commandments revealed given to Moses.

Tefillin. Phylacteries – small boxes containing portions of scripture worn during Morning Prayer.

tikkun. Restoration.

Torah. Lit. 'Instruction', often translated as 'Law'. Can refer to the Pentateuch, the Hebrew Scriptures, or the whole of Jewish tradition. Can also refer to the scroll of the Pentateuch used in Synagogue worship.

Torah she b'al peh. The Oral Torah, Law of Rabbinic tradition, includes Mishnah and the Talmud.

Torah shebiktav. The Written Law, the Pentateuch.

Tzedakah. Charity.

Tzitzit/Tsitsit/Tzitziyot. Ritual garment fringes.

Yeshua/Y'shua. Jesus.

Yiddishkeit. Cultural Jewishness reflecting the Ashkenazi Diaspora experience.

Yigdal. 'Exalted' – a traditional sysnagogue prayer, hymn paraphrasing Maimonides' 13 articles of Faith.

Yom Kippur. The Day of Atonement.

Yoma. Tractate of the Talmud dealing with Yom Kippur.

zemirot. Traditional Sabbath songs

Zohar. 'Splendour' –medieval mystical text.

Index

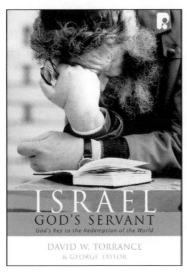

Israel God's Servant

God's Key to the Redemption of the World

David W. Torrance and George Taylor

What is the place of the nation of Israel within God's ongoing purpose to redeem all creation? How should we understand the theological relationship between Israel, humanity, Christ and the Church? What are the reasons for Anti-Semitism? How can we make sense of the political turmoil that has centered round the State of Israel since its foundation in 1948? This book seeks to present an informed and Reformed, Christ-centered answer to these questions. It seeks to acknowledge Israel's faults whilst at the same time affirming her essential place in God's eternal covenant of grace.

> 'This book is grounded in careful reflection on Scripture, deep theological sensitivity, an informed awareness of history and current affairs as well as a Christian love for Israel. I strongly commend it to you!' – **R.T. Kendall**, author and speaker, RT Kendall Ministries, Florida, USA

> 'The authors have done an excellent job spelling out Israel's struggle to exist as a Jewish State in the mostly Muslim Middle East, with excellent historical as well as contemporary information. This is a book well worth reading.' – **David Dolan**, author, journalist and speaker based in Jerusalem, Israel

> 'An extraordinary gift to Gentile Christians and Jews alike. The authors point the way toward a more adequate account of the relations between Israel and the Church for the sake of the redemption of all people. This is one of the most significant contributions on these topics to appear in quite some time.' – **Elmer Colyer**, Professor of Historical Theology and Stanley Professor of Wesley Studies, University of Dubuque Theological Seminary, USA

David W. Torrance is a retired Church of Scotland pastor. He is a longtime participant in joint Christian/Jewish dialogue, and an author and speaker on questions relating to the Jewish people. **George Taylor** is a pseudonym. The author works at a College in Europe.

978-1-84227-554-2

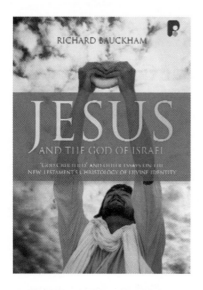

Jesus and the God of Israel

'God Crucified' and Other Studies on the New Testament Christology of Divine Identify

Richard Bauckham

Is the Christian belief that Jesus is divine incompatible with the strong Jewish monotheism of the earliest believers in Messiah? The basic thesis of the heart of this important book on New Testament Christology is that the worship of Jesus as God was seen by the early Christ-believers as fully compatible with their Jewish monotheism. These Jewish believers in Jesus, argues Bauckham, believed that their Lord participated in the divine identity of the one God of Israel. So in the earliest churches we see that worshipping Jesus was not thought to be in any way idolatrous. Readers will find in this volume not only the full text of Bauckham's classic book God Crucified but also seven other groundbreaking essays written subsequently. These essays provide more detailed support for, and an expansion of, the claim that a high Christology in Christian thought is both very early and very Jewish.

> 'This fine collection gathers together fifteen years' extraordinarily fruitful labour on the early church's worship of Jesus.' – **Markus Bockmuehl**, Professor of Biblical and Early Christian Studies, University of Oxford

> 'With its painstaking collection of evidence and its careful exegesis and collation of the texts the resulting discussion is quite indispensable for all students of New Testament and early church Christology. It is a major contribution to its subject and yet another proof of its author's quite extraordinary command of the world of New Testament scholarship and his capacity for fresh, helpful insights.' – **I. Howard Marshall**, Emeritus Professor of New Testament Exegesis, University of Aberdeen

Richard J. Bauckham is Emeritus Professor of New Testament Studies at the University of St Andrews in Scotland and Senior Scholar at Ridley Hall in Cambridge.

978-1-84227-538-2

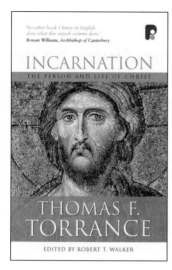

Incarnation

The Person and Life of Christ

Thomas F. Torrence
(edited by Robert T. Walker)

Thomas F. Torrance's new book on Christology combines heart and head in a deeply biblical, unified, Christ-centred and Trinitarian theology. It presents a full account of the meaning and significance of the life and person of Jesus Christ, arguing that his work of revelation and reconciliation can only be understood in the light of who he is (real God and real man united in one person). Torrance argues that the whole life of Jesus Christ – from his birth, through his ministry, cross, resurrection, and ascension to his second coming – is of saving significance.

'No other book I know in English does what this superb volume does in presenting with absolute clarity the full classical doctrine of the universal church on the person and work of Christ. It is a wonderful legacy from one of the very greatest English-language systematic theologians.' – **Rowan Williams**, Archbishop of Canterbury

'No theologian in the latter half of the 20th century devoted more attention to the mystery of the Incarnation than T.F. Torrance. These magnificent posthumously published lectures give us the most sustained and rounded account of his views that we will ever have. In depth of learning, profundity of insight and purity of faith, nothing comparable has appeared from the pen of an English-speaking theologian since John Henry Newman.' – **George Hunsinger**, Hazel Thompson McCord Professor of Systematic Theology, Princeton Theological Seminary, USA

Thomas F. Torrance MBE (1913-2007) served for 27 years as Professor of Christian Dogmatics at New College, Edinburgh and was the author of many academic books and articles. **Robert T. Walker,** nephew of T.F. Torrance, studied theology (with his uncle) and philosophy. He now divides his time between teaching theology at Edinburgh University and teaching outdoor pursuits.

978-1-84227-607-5

For Zion's Sake

Christian Zionism and the Role of John Nelson Darby

Paul Richard Wilkinson

Wilkinson locates Christian Zionism firmly within the evangelical tradition and takes issue with those who have portrayed it as a 'totally unbiblical menace' and as the 'road map to Armageddon'. Charting in detail its origins and historical development, he argues that Christian Zionism lays the biblical foundations for Israel's restoration and the return of Christ. No one has contributed more to this cause than its leading architect and patron, John Nelson Darby. This groundbreaking book challenges decades of misrepresentation exploding the myth that Darby stole the doctrine of the pre-tribulation Rapture from his contemporaries. By revealing the man and his message, Wilkinson vindicates Darby and spotlights the immanent return of Jesus as the centerpiece of his theology.

'A valuable contribution to prophetic studies.' – **Tim LaHaye**, Minister, educator and author

'A major step forward in the study of the origins and impact of Christian Zionism.' – **Crawford Gribben**, Trinity College, Dublin

'A breath of theological and historical fresh air.' – **Mark Hitchcock**, Dallas Theological Seminary

'This book is essential reading.' – **Randall Price**, Liberty University, Virginia

Paul Wilkinson is Assistant Minister at Hazel Grove Full Gospel Church in Stockport, Cheshire, UK.

978-1-84227-569-6